Religion and Law in Finland

Religion and Law in Finland

Third Edition

Matti Kotiranta

This book was originally published as a monograph in the International Encyclopaedia of Laws/Religion Law.

Founding Editor: Roger Blanpain
General Editor: Frank Hendrickx
Volume Editor: Wouter Druwé

Wolters Kluwer

Published by:
Kluwer Law International B.V.
PO Box 316
2400 AH Alphen aan den Rijn
The Netherlands
E-mail: lrs-sales@wolterskluwer.com
Website: www.wolterskluwer.com/en/solutions/kluwerlawinternational

Sold and distributed by:
Wolters Kluwer Legal & Regulatory U.S.
920 Links Avenue
Landisville, PA 17538
United States of America
E-mail: customer.service@wolterskluwer.com

ISBN 978-94-035-1959-3

e-Book: ISBN 978-94-035-1969-2
web-PDF: ISBN 978-94-035-1979-1

The Author

Matti Kotiranta is a Professor of Church History at the University of Eastern Finland, Joensuu, and a former Head of the School of Theology (2010–2017).

Born in Kuusjärvi, Finland, in 1958, he studied religious philosophy and ethics and received his Doctoral degree in Theology in 1995 at the University of Helsinki. In 2001, he obtained his habilitation in Dogmatics (Docent).

In 2010–2011, Prof. Kotiranta was president of the European Consortium for Church and State Research, of which he is a member.

He is the author of many books and numerous articles in journals and edited volumes on various aspects of Church and State relations. His writings have been published in English, Italian, French, Russian, and Finnish. His research is characterized by a predominant interest in issues of comparative and international law relating to the treatment of freedom of religion and belief in relation to the evolution of Finnish church–state relations and issues of religious freedom.

A selection of the author's publications includes: *Kirche, Staat und Religionsfreiheit in Finnland.* In: Zeitschrift für evangelisches Kirchenrecht 45 (2000): 1, pp. 233–256; *Tserkov, gosudarstva i religioznaja svoboda v stranah Baltii* (2003); *The Legal Position of Religion and the Media in Finland.* In: The Portrayal of Religion in Europe: The Media and the Arts (2004), pp. 41–56; *The Teaching and Study of Church–State Relations in the Nordic Countries in the United Kingdom and in Ireland.* In: The Teaching and Study of Church–State Relations in EU (2005), pp. 110–138; *La Finlandia tra tassa ecclesiastica e sostegno statale delle confessioni.* In: Quaderni di diritto e politica ecclesiastica (2006), pp. 27–49; *Religious Entities as Legal Persons in Finland.* In: Religious entities as legal persons (2008), pp. 51–72; *Status of Religious Communities.* In: Legal Aspects of Religious Freedom (2008), pp. 63–81; *Financing Churches and Religious Associations in Finland.* In: The Funding of Churches in the EU (2009), pp. 145–153; *FINLANDE Fondements contemporains des relations Églises-État en Finlande.* In: Dictionnaire Droit des Religions (2010), pp. 348–355; *The Application of Freedom of Religion Principles of the European Convention on Human Rights in Finland.* In: Religious Freedom in the European Union: The Application of the European Convention on Human

Rights in the European Union (2011), pp. 129–152; *Religious Education in Finland.* In: The Routledge International Handbook of Religious Education (2012), pp. 104–112; Religion and Criminal Law (with Norman Doe) (2013), *Religion and the Secular State in Finland.* In: Donlu D. Thayer (ed.) Religion and the Secular State: National Reports. Reports issued for the occasion of the XVIIIth Congress of the International Academy of Comparative Law, Washington 2010 (2015), pp. 262–291; *'Finland'.* In: Encyclopedia of Law and Religion 4 (2016), pp. 108–119. Also available in Brill's online edition (2016); *Law and Religion in the Workplace (Finland).* In: Law and Religion in the Workplace (2016), pp. 155–175; *Religious Assistance in Public institutions: Finland.* In: Religious Assistance in Public institutions (2018), pp. 105–117; *Finnland, Staat und Religion – Staatlich.* In: Lexikon für Kirchen und Religionsrecht (2019), pp. 54–57; *State and Church in Finland.* In: State and Church in the European Union (3rd ed. 2019), pp. 613–640; *Securitization of Religious Freedom: Religion and the Limits of State Control in Finland,* In: Securitization of Religion and the Limits of State Control in Europe (2020), pp. 199–218; *Das Verhältnis von Staat und Kirche in Finnland,* In: Staatkirchenrechtliche Abhandlungen, Band 56/II (2020), pp. 269–289; *Religionsfreiheit im postkommunistischen Europa – Ein historischer Rückblick.* In: Staat – Religion – Recht. Festschrift für Gerhard Robbers zum 70. Geburtstag (2020), pp. 369–392. *The Specific Role and Equal Rights of Religious Minorities in Finland.* In: The Legal Status of Old and New Religious Minorities in the European Union (2021), pp. 275–291; *Islam, Human Rights, and State Policy in Finland,* In: Islam and Human Rights in the European Union (2022), pp. 161–202. *FINLAND.* In: Atlas of Religious or Belief Minority Rights, https://atlasminorityrights.eu/countries/Finland.php (2022); *FINLANDE. Fondements contemporains des relations Églises-État en Finlande.* In: Dictionnaire Droit des Religions (2nd. ed. 2023), pp. 357–365. *Uskonnollisten vähemmistöjen oikeusasema Suomessa. Uskonnonvapauslaki 100 vuotta (The Legal Status of Religious Minorities in Finland. 100 years of the Freedom of Religion Act).* In: Kirkko yhteiskunnassa: suhteet ja rajapinnat. Uskonnonvapauslaki 100 vuotta (2023), pp. 41–86; *Philosophical and Non-Religious Beliefs in Finland: Legal and Social profiles.* In: The Complex World of Philosophical and Non-Religious Beliefs. Legal and Social Aspects (2024), pp. 275–301; *The Impact of Covid-19 on Migration and Migratory Flows in Finland.* In: The Impact of Covid-19 on Migration and Migratory Flows: New Challenges in Tackling Cultural and Religious Diversity (2025).

Table of Contents

List of Abbreviations

Abbreviation Finnish	**English**
Hallintovaliokunta	Administration Committee
Hallintotuomioistuin	Administrative Court
HAO (*Hallinto-oikeus*)	Administrative Court of First Instance
Hallintolainkäyttöasia	Administrative Judicial Matter
Hallintoasiain oikeudenkäyntimenettely	Administrative Judicial Procedure
Muutoksenhakutuomioistuin	Appellate Court
AFSJ (*Vapauden, turvallisuuden ja oikeuden ala*)	Area of Freedom, Security and Justice
§ *Artikla*	Article
Oikeusjuttu	Case
Kihlakunnanoikeus	Circuit Court
Raastuvanoikeus	City Court
Riita-asia	Civil Matter
Riita-asiain oikeudenkäyntimenettely	Civil Procedure
Oikeudenkäymiskaari	Code of Judicial Procedure
Syyteharkinta	Consideration of Charges
PL (*Perustuslaki*)	Constitution
Perustuslakivaliokunta	Constitutional Law Committee
Euroopan neuvosto	Council of Europe
Euroopan unionin neuvosto	Council of the European Union
Tuomioistuin	Court
Tuomioistuimen päätös	Court Decision
HO (*Hovioikeus*)	Court of Appeal
Ylin oikeus	Court of Final Appeal
Alioikeus	Court of First Instance

List of Abbreviations

Ylioikeus	Court of Second Instance
Rikosasia	Criminal Matter
Rikosasian oikeudenkäyntimenettely	Criminal Procedure
Esteellisyys	Disqualification
Diss. (*Väitöskirja*)	Dissertation
Käräjäoikeus	District Court
AsK *Asiakirja*	Document
Euroopan unioinin perusoikeuskirja	EU Charter of Fundamental Rights
Euroopan komissio	European Commission
ECHR (in Finnish EIS) (*Euroopan ihmisoikeussopimus*)	European Convention on Human Rights
ECtHR (in Finnish EIT) (*Euroopan ihmisoikeustuomioistuin*)	European Court of Human Rights
ECJ	European Court of Justice
Euroopan unioinin tuomioistuin	European Court of Justice, officially the Court of Justice
Euroopan parlamentti	European Parliament
ELCF (*Suomen Evankelis-luterilainen kirkko*)	Evangelical Lutheran Church of Finland
Seurakuntayhtymä	Federation of Parishes
FDF	Finnish Defence Forces
§ (S) *Pykälä*	Finnish Equivalent of 'Section'
OPH (*Opetushallitus*)	Finnish National Agency for Education
Yleinen tuomioistuin	General Court/General Court of Law
HE (*Hallituksen esitys*)	Government Bill
Valtakunnanoikeus	High Court of Impeachment
Vankeusrangaistus/vankeus	Imprisonment
Vakuutusoikeus	Insurance Court
ICCPR (in Finnish KP-sopimus) (Kansalaisoikeuksia ja poliittisia oikeuksia koskeva kansainvälinen yleissopimus)	International Covenant on Civil and Political Rights
Tuomari	Judge/Justice (member of the *court*)
Tuomio	Judgment
Oikeudenkäyntimenettely	Judicial Procedure

Oikeuslaitos	Judiciary/Judicial System
Tuomiopiiri	Jurisdiction/Juridical District
Työtuomioistuin	Labour Court
LRF (*Uskonnonvapauslaki*)	Law on Religious Freedom
Asia	Matter
OKM (*Opetus- ja kulttuuriministeriö*)	Ministry of Education and Culture
Tiedoksianto	Notification
PeVL (*Perustuslakivaliokunnan lausunto*)	Opinion of the Constitutional Law Committee
OSCE	Organization for Security and Co-operation in Europe
OCF (*Suomen ortodoksinen kirkko*)	Orthodox Church of Finland
P (*Kappale*)	Paragraph
Vp (*Valtiopäivät*)	Parliament
Ennakkopäätös	Precedent
RFA (*Uskonnonvapauslaki*)	Religious Freedom Act
HaVM (*Hallintovaliokunnan mietintö*)	Report of the Administration Committee
PeVM (*Perustuslakivaliokunnan mietintö*)	Report of the Constitutional Law Committee
SDP	Social Democrats
Erityistuomioistuin	Special Court of Law
KHO (*Korkein hallinto-oikeus*)	Supreme Administrative Court
KKO (*Korkein oikeus*)	Supreme Court
SopS (*Suomen säädöskokoelma*)	The Finnish Legislative Collection (is the official source of legislation in Finland)
TEU (*Sopimus Euroopan unionista*)	Treaty on European Union
TFEU (*Euroopan unioinin toiminnasta tehty sopimus*)	Treaty on the Functioning of the European Union
UN	United Nation
US	United States
UEF (*Itä-Suomen yliopisto*)	University of Eastern Finland

List of Abbreviations

Preface

In 2023, Finland celebrated the 100th anniversary of the adoption of the Religious Freedom Act (RFA). Freedom of religion is a fundamental right for all citizens. For many, it also means the freedom to live without religion. Freedom of religion is the oldest fundamental right internationally, although its history, both in Europe and in Finland, is short.

The means to integrate religion and belief under the protection of freedom of religion is based on international human rights treaties, in particular the United Nations (UN) Universal Declaration of Human Rights and, in Europe, the European Union jurisprudence, where Member States have attempted to interpret their Constitutions on the basis of religious freedom, tolerance, state neutrality, and the equal treatment of religions. However, the laws of individual states have not usually attempted to define the religion or belief content of their provisions more precisely. On the other hand, the content related to religious freedom itself has been open to almost unlimited interpretation in terms of national laws. Clear examples of this are the United States (US), French, Italian, and German constitutions and religious laws, which interpret the equality of religious communities from very different positions.

Despite its personal character, religion is not a private matter, since it also has a public, institutional, social, and cultural dimension. In the Finnish legal tradition, partly as a result of the radicalism of the 1960s and Finland's proximity to the former Soviet Union, there has been a tendency to approach religion and freedom of religion from the point of negative religious freedom. Prior to the start of further integration within the European Union – including the period between Finnish independence in 1917 and its joining the EU at the start of 1995 – there was no perceived need to open up the legal framework to outsiders in any significant way.

The increasing integration of the European Union, which has included increased intergovernmental cooperation and the development of legislation, has obliged Finland to completely re-think the concept of freedom of religion and, concomitantly, the position of the churches and religious bodies. Since Finland's joining the European Union in 1995, church–state relationships and human rights issues have developed into a matter of renewed interest.

It can in fact be argued that the greatest change in the history of state-church relations since Finnish independence in 1917 is that the human rights documents of the 1990s issued by the Council of Europe and the Organization for Security and Co-operation in Europe and European integration have genuinely forced the State – and the major Lutheran and Orthodox churches as public entities – to evaluate church–state relations on the basis of the principle of freedom of religion. Today, freedom of religion is regarded positively as a right that can be enjoyed by both the individual and the religious community. For the individual, this means the innate right of everyone to practice religion, publicly and privately, according to their conscience, their understanding, and their choice. It still encompasses the right not to practise a religion, the freedom to live without religion, and the right to remain outside any religious community.

The Republic of Finland has signed numerous international treaties protecting freedom of religion or belief. Some of these agreements – for example, the International Covenant on Civil and Political Rights, the Convention on the Rights of the Child, and the Convention on the Elimination of All Forms of Discrimination against Women (CEDAW) – have had a substantial influence on the development of the country's internal legislation and have in fact been incorporated into Finnish Law through Acts of Parliament. In church policy, this means that major churches and registered religious communities are required to be actively responsible for the implementation of fundamental civil rights within their own communities.

In addition, a great change has taken place in the general atmosphere of the debate, which can be seen in terms of an openness to the development of a new approach to church–state relations: Traditional considerations, the realization of religious freedom (positive religious freedom), and the religious neutrality of the state are to be interpreted in a manner appropriate to the civil society of a modern democratic state, assuming a belief in the necessity for the state, the church, and religious communities to work together, since ultimately it all concerns the same citizens.

A positive interpretation of freedom of religion that has gained a high profile since the Second World War in international documents dealing with freedom of religion has been reflected particularly in the revised Finnish Constitution of 2000 and the Finnish RFA of 2003. The latter, in particular, has already exerted a very important influence on the development of relations between state and church and will continue to do so.

In describing the Finnish law related to religion, an attempt has been made here to adhere to the basic structure developed by the editor of the present series. This will enable the reader to compare the Finnish system with those presented in the other national volumes. It has to be kept in mind, however, that this approach does not always fit the usual Finnish legal doctrine and its structures, since it occasionally gives rise to unavoidable structural repetition (especially in the case of the RFA). Some general information in addition to the basic law on religion has also been provided in order to enhance understanding of this specific field of law.

I am greatly indebted to the editor of this series, Professor Wouter Druwé, and to those who have provided invaluable assistance in the completion of this study: Tuomas Ojanen, Professor of Constitutional Law, Kimmo Nuotio, Professor of Criminal Law at the University of Helsinki, and Matti Halttunen, emeritus Church Counsellor of the Evangelical Lutheran Church of Finland (ELCF). I would also like to express my gratitude to Dr John A Stotesbury FEA for helping to work on the language of my text.

General Introduction

§1. GENERAL BACKGROUND OF THE COUNTRY

I. Basic Structures

1. The Republic of Finland, or simply Finland, is a Nordic country located in Northern Europe and surrounded on two sides by the Baltic Sea. It is a country that during the past 150 years has undergone a transformation from a principally agrarian and traditional society to a post-industrial service industry society. With globalization and during the relatively short period since the Second World War, Finland has become part of an ever-mobile world and changed from being a country of net emigration to one of net immigration.[1]

2. Nevertheless, Finland is one of the least populated countries in Europe; population density is relatively low, with approximately 18 people per km^2. Geographically, the population is very unevenly distributed. A majority of Finns live on the coast, in the south and southwest of the country, and more than one million people live in the metropolitan area. The population density is highest in the province of Uusimaa: 178 people/km^2, while the lowest stands at only 2 people/km^2 in the province of Lapland, at the northern edge of the Arctic Circle.

1. The number of immigration to Finland has quadrupled since 2000. In 2023, the number arriving in Finland was 57,914 (net migration), which is more than at any time since Finland's independence in 1917. *See*, https://stat.fi/en/publication/cln4jbq3b6u210avtv0wphb8k. Accessed 26 Aug. 2024.

Map 1

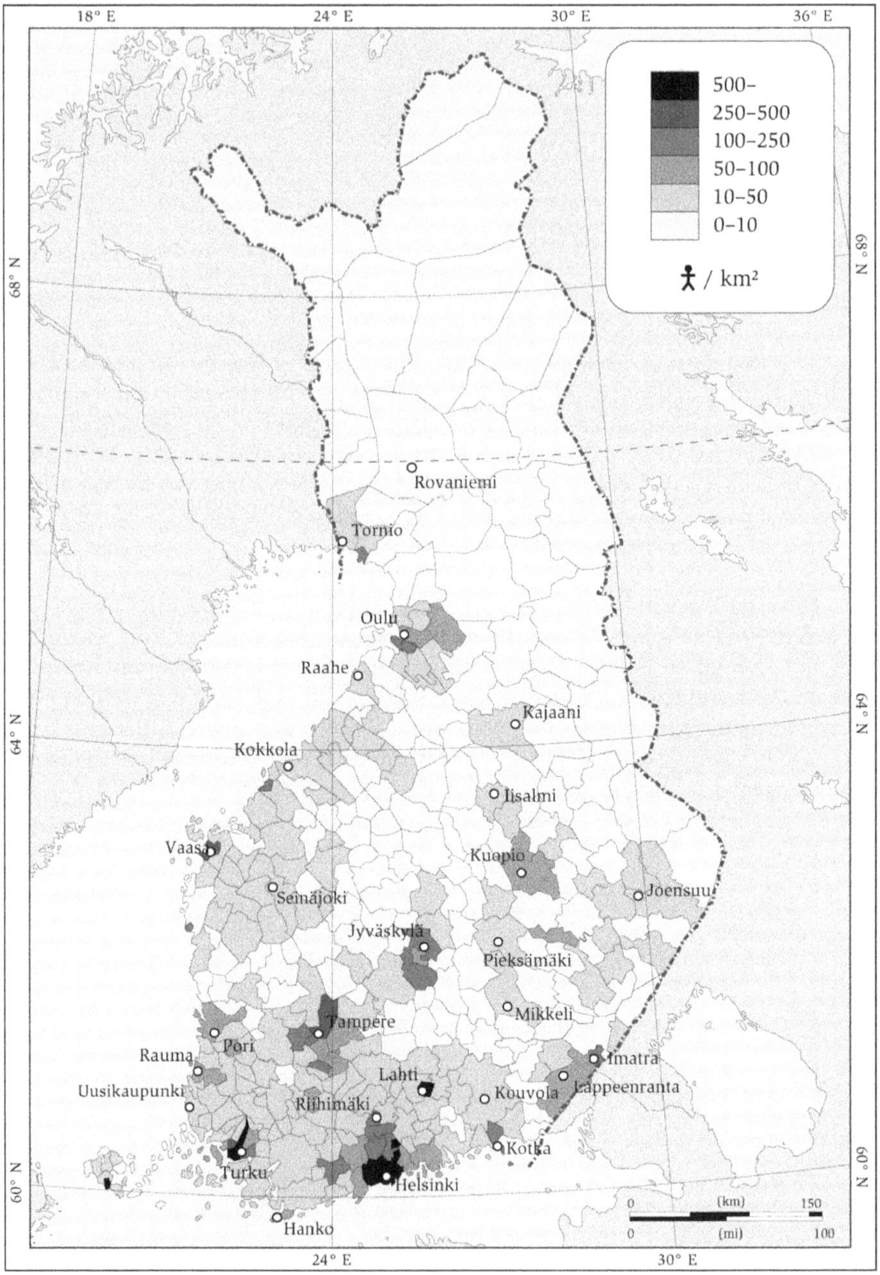

Source: Wikimedia Commons.

3. The Finnish population in 2023 was 5,603,851.[2] Some 6% of them are non-Finnish, with a wide range of national backgrounds. In 2023, there were 372,973 people living in Finland whose nationality was other than Finnish. Over a fifth of them were Estonian and 10.3% were Russian. In addition, over five thousand citizens stemmed from Sweden, Afghanistan, China, India, Iraq, Somalia, Syria, Thailand, and Vietnam.

4. The religious and socio-political map in Finland has long remained fairly stable. For centuries, the majority of the Finnish population (5,603,851 by 31 December 2023) has belonged to the ELCF (63.6%, with 3.6 million members in 2023).[3] The second largest religious group in Finland is the Finnish Orthodox Church (1.0%, with 55,957 members in 2023).[4] These Christian national churches have played a major role in Finnish society and have had great political influence in the development of religious freedom in Finland. The emergence of multiculturalism in recent decades has also been somewhat reflected in the growing membership of non-Christian religious communities. As a percentage, however, they still play only a limited role, constituting 1.8% of the total population.

5. Human rights form the basis of the entire legal and political system, which is particularly evident in the revised Constitution of the year 2000 (HE 731/1999). Human rights are widely respected, and an independent judiciary[5] is a stronghold when individual cases of violations of human rights occur. In addition, *Finland is largely a consensus society* whose national ideology emphasizes the unity of the people, social equality, and cultural unity in a single Law (the Finnish Constitution), including the legal guarantees of minority rights.

6. This stronghold approach to fundamental rights is a dominant feature of Finnish law.[6] Limits to any fundamental right, such as limitations imposed on religious freedom, must always be interpreted in the light of the importance of the right that is to be restricted. All legitimate interests, the interests of religious freedom as well

---

2. At https://stat.fi/en/statistics/vaerak#tables. *See also* https://stat.fi/tup/suoluk/suoluk_vaesto_en.html#Population%20structure%20on%2031%20December. Accessed 26 Aug. 2024.
3. *See* Statistical Yearbook of Finland 2023, Statistics Finland 31 Dec 2023. For details, *see* https://stat.fi/tup/suoluk/suoluk_vaesto_en.html#Population%20structure%20on%2031%20December. Accessed 26 Aug. 2024.
4. *See*, https://stat.fi/tup/suoluk/suoluk_vaesto_en.html#Population%20structure%20on%2031%20December. Accessed 26 Aug. 2024; https://aamunkoitto.fi/ajassa/jasenkato-haaste-mutta-suomen-ortodoksisella-kirkolla-voi-silti-olla-assa-hihassaan. Accessed 26 Aug. 2024.
5. The principle of parliamentarism and of the independence of the judiciary is expressed in Ch. 1 of the Constitution on the Basics of the Constitution. The Constitution also provides for the rule of law and its two essential components. Chapter 2 declares that the use of public authority must be based on law and all public activities must be strictly governed by law.
6. *See* Tuomas Ojanen & Martin Scheinin. 'Suomen valtiosäännön perusperiaatteet, PL 1 §' (Basic principles of the Finnish constitution, §1)'. In *Pekka Hallberg, Heikki Karapuu, Tuomas Ojanen, Martin Scheinin, Kaarlo Tuori, Veli-Pekka Viljanen, Perusoikeudet* (Fundamental rights). (2nd revised edn. WSOYpro, 2011), 217–226. (Ojanen & Scheinin 2011 c). *See also* Tuomas Ojanen, *Johdatus perus- ja ihmisoikeusjuridiikkaan* (Introduction to Fundamental and Human Rights Law). (Helsinki: Oikeustieteellinen tiedekunta (Helsingin yliopisto), Forum Iuris, 2009), 223–229.

as the interests limiting religious freedom, must be given adequate space. Fundamental rights may be restricted only if the Constitution allows the provision of a statutory exception. Section 6, paragraph 2, of the Constitution requires an 'acceptable ground'. The requirements for such a justification are very high for the criteria listed in the provision.

II. General Legal System

7. The reformed Finnish constitution (HE 731/1999) that came into force on 1 March 2000[7] and the new law concerned with Religious Freedom (453/2003) together contain the most important provisions in Finnish law affecting religion.

8. The main manifestations of freedom of religion and of conscience in the Constitution 11 §§1–2 subsection refer to the right to profess and practice religion, the right to express one's convictions, and the right to be a member of a religious community, in addition to the so-called negative freedom of religion, i.e., the right to decline to be a member of any religious community.[8]

9. Article 11 states:

> Article 11 [Freedom of religion and conscience]
>
> (1) Everyone has freedom of religion and conscience.
> (2) Freedom of religion and conscience entails the right to profess and practise a religion, the right to express one's convictions, and the right to be a member of or decline to be a member of a religious community. No one is under the obligation, against his or her conscience, to participate in the practice of a religion.

10. In the Constitution of 2000, there is an emphasis on the freedom of the individual. It was clear that the Law on Religious Freedom (LRF) had to be updated from the previous Freedom of Religion Act passed in 1922. A revised RFA came into force on 1 August 2003. In its report, the committee responsible for preparing the law related to the freedom of religion discussed the question of freedom of religion *as a fundamental civil right* and the freedom of religion and conscience as laid down in section 11 of the Finnish Constitution. The committee concluded that this latter provision should form the basis for all legislation in Finland concerned with freedom of religion and conscience.

---

7. It repealed four previous constitutions and unified and modernized the constitutional regulation in Finland.
   The Constitution has subsequently been amended by the Act amending Arts 35 and 90 of the Finnish Constitution (596/2007), the Act amending Arts 9 and 38 of the Finnish Constitution (802/2007) and the Finnish Constitution (1112/2011).
8. *See* closer HE 309/1993 vp, 55, PeVM 10/2002 vp, 2.

11. The purpose of the Constitution is to establish a stable constitutional basis for the functioning of the political system and a framework for all other legal orders.[9] Because of this aspect of the Constitution, it is more permanent than other laws. Within the framework of the Finnish law, the hierarchy of norms begins at its top with the Constitution. The Constitution establishes a framework for both the content and the regulatory level of other legislation.[10] The starting point for drafting new laws is that the draft laws are prepared in accordance with the Constitution (Basic Law).

12. The Constitution also confirms Finland's positive attitude towards international cooperation. The principles laid down in the Constitution and established practices arising from those oblige the Finnish Parliament both to approve international agreements that are binding upon Finland and to grant them force of law to the extent that they contain provisions that 'are legislative in nature'.[11]

13. The provisions of most treaties and other international obligations are brought into law in Finland in the form of 'blanket laws' which state that they 'shall come into force in the manner agreed upon'. The approval of such blanket or hybrid law (and/or statute) implies 'incorporation' of agreement into the internal legislation of Finland, but in addition to this it is possible and quite common for specific alterations to be made to existing legislation in the same sphere, i.e., this 'incorporation' is supplemented with 'transformation'. Once an agreement is brought into force in the manner described above, it becomes a part of Finnish law and applicable in principle in the same manner as any other part of the legislative code.[12]

---

9. In the regulation of the division of state tasks, the starting point is the traditional division of power with legislative, governmental and judicial powers. Legislative power is exercised by Parliament, which also decides on government finances. The government is exercised by the President of the Republic and the Government, whose members must enjoy the confidence of Parliament. The judiciary is exercised by independent courts, the Supreme Courts being the Supreme Court and the Supreme Administrative Court.
10. The legislative hierarchy shown here is based on *Lainkirjoittajan opas*. Oikeusministeriö, lainvalmisteluosasto (Guide to the Law Writer. Ministry of Justice, Law Enforcement Division.). *See* http://urn.fi/URN:ISBN:978-952-259-318-4. (The guide describes the constitutional significance of the Constitution and other general legislation, and provides guidance on regulations). *See also* Kimmo Nuotio, Sakari Melander & Merita Huomo-Kettunen (eds), *Introduction to Finnish Law and Legal Culture*. Helsinki: Helsingin yliopiston oikeustieteellinen tiedekunta, Forum Iuris, 2012.
11. The relevant principles were contained in §33 of the original Constitution and §69 of the Parliament Act. The corresponding paragraphs of the new Constitution are §94 and §95. In common with the other Nordic countries, Finland has principally adopted a dualistic model with regard to the relationship between international agreements and the country's internal legislation. *See* more detailed Part IV, Ch. 1. *International Law Effects on Religious Communities*.
12. PeV 2/1990 vp, Matti Pellonpää, *Euroopan ihmisoikeussopimus* (ECHR, Helsinki, 4th edn 2005), 54. About Finland's ability to influence EU legislation in its preparation, *see* Laura Hämynen, *Suomen vaikuttaminen Euroopan unionin lainvalmisteluun ja direktiivien kansallinen täytäntöönpano* (Finland's influence on European Union lawmaking and the national implementation of directives). (Helsinki: Oikeuspoliittisen tutkimuslaitoksen tutkimustiedonantoja 108), 2011 and Anna Hyvärinen, *Suomen mahdollisuudet vaikuttaa valmisteilla olevaan EU-lainsäädäntöön* (Finland's ability to influence EU legislation in its preparation). (Helsinki: Oikeuspoliittisen tutkimuslaitoksen tutkimuksia 241), 2009.

14. The next level is formed by ordinary laws (*yleislait*) passed by the legislature, and which must be drafted in accordance with the Constitution. This level also encompasses international law that is not qualified in terms of the 'general rules' of international law: mostly, international treaties and international customary law.

15. Below this level, there are statutory instruments, by-laws, and regulations (*eräät yleiset sääntelyt*), which may limit fundamental rights only if an ordinary law entitles them to do so. Any limitation of any fundamental right must be based in ordinary law.

16. The Constitution establishes the value base of the Finnish constitution.[13] The rule of law guarantees the inviolability of human dignity and individual freedoms and rights and promotes justice in society. The requirement of inviolability of human dignity expresses the universal basis of fundamental rights and refers to the principle of the equality of all human beings.

17. The reference to the protection of individual rights and freedoms emphasizes the dominant role played by fundamental rights in the Finnish constitution and refers to the basic principle of the individual's right to self-determination as the basis for the exercise of many other rights.[14] Every individual is, in principle, free to determine himself or herself and his or her actions. The requirement of justice refers to equality and to economic, social and cultural rights.[15]

§2. Social Facts about Religion

I. Religious Affiliation

18. At the beginning of the twenty-first century, Finland was still a country that was relatively homogenous in terms of religion, although the change brought by multiculturalism has also been reflected, to some degree, in the development of membership of denominations and religious communities. In this, Finland has followed similar trends to those in the other Nordic Countries, albeit at a slower pace.

---

13. For more detail about the value base of the Finnish Constitution and the interpretation of Constitutional Law, *see* Antero Jyränki & Jaakko Husa, *Valtiosääntöoikeus* (Constitutional Law, 2nd edn). (Vantaa 2015); Veli-Pekka Hautamäki, *Perustuslain auktoritatiivinen tulkinta – Oikeusvertaileva tutkimus perustuslain tulkinnan auktoritatiivisista instituutioista ja niiden käyttämästä argumentaatiosta Suomessa ja Norjassa* (Authoritative Interpretation of the Constitution – A Comparative Study of the Institutional Interpretation of the Constitution and its Argumentation in Finland and Norway). (Helsinki: Suomalaisen lakimiesyhdityksen julkaisuja, A, No. 232, 2002). *Diss.*
14. *See* Heikki Karapuu, 'Perusoikeuksien käsite ja luokittelu' (Concept and classification of fundamental rights). In *Pekka Hallberg, Heikki Karapuu, Tuomas Ojanen, Martin Scheinin, Kaarlo Tuori, Veli-Pekka Viljanen, Perusoikeudet* (Fundamental rights). (2nd, revised edn WSOYpro, 2011), 63–87. *See also* Juha Lavapuro, 'Perusoikeusargumentaation kontrolloitavuudesta' (On the controllability of the fundamental rights argument), 143–177. In Tuuli Heinonen & Juha Lavapuro (eds), *Oikeuskulttuurin eurooppalaistuminen. Ihmisoikeuksien murroksesta kansainväliseen vuorovaikutukseen.* (Vantaa, 2012); and Lavapuro, *Uusi perustuslakikontrolli* (New constitutional control). (Helsinki, 2010).
15. HE 309/1993 vp, 42.

19. It is a characteristic of the Finnish religious landscape that despite the dominance of two major churches – the Lutheran and Orthodox churches – most of the world religions that have found their way to continental Europe also have followers in Finland, but only in very small numbers. In recent years, the rising numbers of refugees and asylum seekers have resulted in an increasing religious diversity.[16]

20. Finnish membership of registered religious denominations in 1990, 2000, and 2022 was as follows:[17]

Table 1 Religion in Finland: Numbers of Members

	1990	*%*	*2000*	*%*	*2022*	*%*
Total population	4,998,478	100	5,181,115	100	5,563,970	100
Evangelical Lutheran Church of Finland	4,389,230	87.8	4,409,576	85.1	3,625,007	65.1
Other Lutheran Churches	2,588	0.1	2,228	0.1	827	0.0
Greek Orthodox Church of Finland	52,627	1.1	56,807	1.1	58,472	1.1
Other Orthodox Churches	800	0.0	1,088	0.0	4,225	0.1
Jehovah's Witnesses	12,157	0.2	18,492	0.4	16,193	0.3
Free Church in Finland	12,189	0.2	13,474	0.3	14,635	0.3
Roman Catholic Church	4,247	0.1	7,227	0.1	15,016	0.3
Islamic congregations	810	0.0	1,199	0.0	22,261	0.4

16. For more detail, *see* Matti Kotiranta, 'Securitization of Religious Freedom: Religion and the Limits of State Control in Finland'. In *Merlin Kiviorg (ed.), Securitization of Religious Freedom: Religion and the Limits of State Control in Europe.* (Granada: Comares, 2020), 199–218.
17. Cf. Statistics Finland 2022. For more detail, *see* https://pxdata.stat.fi/PxWeb/pxweb/en/StatFin/StatFin__vaerak/statfin_vaerak_pxt_11rx.px/table/tableViewLayout1/. Accessed 23 Nov. 2023.

	1990	*%*	*2000*	*%*	*2022*	*%*
Adventist Churches	4,805	0.1	4,316	0.1	3,137	0.1
Pentecostal Church in Finland	–	–	–	–	13,242	0.2
Church of Jesus Christ of Latter Day Saints	2,883	0.1	3,307	0.1	3,125	0.1
Baptist congregations	2,565	0.1	2,395	0.0	2,362	0.0
Methodist Churches	1,251	0.0	1,260	0.0	1,282	0.0
Jewish congregations	1,006	0.0	1,157	0.0	1,073	0.0
Other registered communities	712	0.0	720	0.0	20,843	0.4
No religious affiliation	510,608	10.2	659,979	12.7	1,781,751	32.0

21. Looking at the statistics from 2010 to 2022 regarding the members of religious communities, Finland remains a country with a predominantly Christian tradition. In 2022 the majority of the Finnish population (5,565,519) still belonged to the ELCF (65.1% in 2022). The second largest religious denomination in Finland was the Finnish Orthodox Church (at just over 1% and 58,472 members).

22. The Orthodox Church of Finland (OCF) has repeatedly highlighted that it is a religious minority, although the legal status of the Orthodox Church (Orthodox Church Law 985/2006) is fully comparable to the special status of the Lutheran Church in the Constitution (§76). The Church Acts of both churches *include provisions with a clear denominational character as regulated through Acts of Parliament.* Between 2000 and 2022, the membership of the Lutheran Church decreased considerably; specific societal events over the years have been reflected more clearly than before in departures from the church, and also in the numbers of new members joining it.

23. The proportion of those belonging to the old minority religious communities has to some extent increased during the opening years of the twenty-first century, but within this group, there are some very different trends. The Jehovah's Witnesses and the Free Church of Finland are among those whose membership has decreased slightly. They were the largest of the old registered communities. A rising trend has been observed in the Catholic Church in Finland, whose membership has more than tripled (1990: 4,247 and 2022: 15,016), although it is still a relatively small community. In contrast, the membership of the Seventh Day Adventists has been declining, while the membership of the Mormon Church (Church of Jesus Christ of Latter-day Saints) has remained much as before.

24. The membership of the Pentecostal congregations is at approximately the same level as the Orthodox Church; it is currently estimated at around 50,000 baptized members, and if children are included, it has a total membership of approximately 60,000. However, not all Pentecostals are registered as a religious community but as ideological associations, for example. At present, the Pentecostal movement has been increasingly organized as a religious body. Since the beginning of 2002 the movement's organizational structure has been supplemented with the establishment of a registered religious community, the Finnish Pentecostal Church (*Suomen Helluntaikirkko*), to enhance inter-parish cooperation and to promote the Pentecostal movement within Finnish society and internationally. The number of registered Pentecostals in 2022 was 13,242 members.

25. Within the Finnish Evangelical Lutheran Church there still exist a number of *old, minor revival movements that are religious movements within the 'official' Church.* Hence, in practice, they are not in fact classified as old minorities. These popular, spontaneous revival movements began to spring up among the rural population in the mid-eighteenth century as a reaction to the Finnish Enlightenment, functioning in their essence as expressions of a reserved attitude towards the idea of progress and other related cultural trends among the intelligentsia. These revival movements – *Supplicationism* (rukoilevaisuus), the *Awakened* (herännäisyys), and the Evangelical revival (evankelisuus) – originated in the western parts of Finland, from where they then spread elsewhere. The northern Lappish revival, known as *Laestadianism* (lestadiolaisuus), was a protest against secularization and against the differing values and ways of life of the towns and countryside. In addition to the domestic revival movements, Anglo-American revivalism reached Finland at the turn of the twentieth century: 'To simplify slightly, one might say that the Anglo-American movements had largely a similar emphasis to that of the Finnish revival movements, but whereas the latter represented a domestic revival within the Lutheran Church, the former represented foreign movements which eventually became separate denominations. These were the Seventh Day Adventists, the Pentecostal movements, the Methodist Church, the Salvation Army, the Baptist Union and the Free Church', as *Religion in Finland* puts it.[18]

---

18. *See* 'Religion and early modernization'. In Kimmo Kääriäinen, Kati Niemelä & Kimmo Ketola, *Religion in Finland. – Decline, Change and Transformation of Finnish Religiosity*. (Publications of the Church Research Institute 54, Jyväskylä 2005), 53–53. *See also*, Hanna Salomäki, 'Herätysliikkeet suomalaisessa yhteiskunnassa' (Revival Movements in Finnish Society). In Ruth Illman, Kimmo Ketola, Riitta Latvio & Jussi Sohlberg (eds), *Monien uskomusten ja katsomusten Suomi (Finland – A Country of Many Religions and Beliefs),* 65–75. (Kirkon tutkimuskeskuksen verkkojulkaisuja 48), https://evl.fi/documents/1327140/45386794/Ktk+-+Monien+uskontojen+ja+katsomu sten+Suomi/c8c8d8be-e49b-5998-3539-6b2a29a4903d.

26. Followers of Islam are the largest non-Christian movement in Finland. *Islam is both an old and a new minority in Finland.* The roots of Islam in Finland stretch back at least two centuries, to the nineteenth century. Invariably, the first Muslims were soldiers serving in the Imperial Russian Army in Finland when it was still an autonomous Grand Duchy of Russia. The more permanent Muslim community started to settle in as early as the 1870s when the Tartars began to move from Nizhni Novgorod to Finland. The Muslims living in the country were granted Finnish citizenship shortly after independence, and in 1923 they were granted the right to register as a religious community. The first registered Islamic community, the Finnish Islamic congregation, was established two years later, in 1925 – it was initially known as the Mohammedan Parish of Finland. Tartars are often seen as a positive example of Islamic integration into Finnish society and are less preoccupied with their own status than in the case of other Muslims. Traditionally, the Tartars have also been relatively well-educated and wealthy. They have also actively participated in inter-religious dialogue and have established good relations with Judaism. However, in relation to other Muslims, the Tartars maintain a certain distance and do not accept them as members of their community. In the early 1990s, only about a thousand Muslims mainly of Tartar origin were living in Finland.[19]

27. In recent decades, however, the situation has been changing rapidly, with the number of Muslims in Finland increasing considerably. The principal reason for this has been that, since the beginning of the 1990s, immigration from the Muslim world has increased. *Initially, Islam was regarded in particular as a new religious minority.* The first major group of arrivals were the Somalis who started to arrive in Finland as refugees in the early 1990s. The number of Muslims increased tenfold in Finland in 1990–2011, and it is currently estimated that they now number some 120,000–130,000. However, deciding on a precise number is difficult, because few of the Muslims have organized themselves into registered religious groups. Despite this, registrations have clearly increased in the first part of the twenty-first century (1990, 810; 2000, 1,199; and 2022, 22,261).

28. As mentioned previously, since the large-scale entry of Muslims into Finland occurred later than in many other European countries, developments have been slower than elsewhere. However, there are signs now of a difference between generations with regard to religious practice. In recent years, for example, a number of young Finnish Muslims have come up with their own associations and communities whose motive is to respond specifically to the religious needs of young people.

29. The Islamic Council of Finland, SINE, was established in November 2006 and coordinated at that time by the Office of the Ombudsman for Minorities. The aim of the authorities was to establish an umbrella organization for Islamic communities and associations, which would act as a liaison body with the authorities.

19. For closer information, *see* Teemu Pauha, Suaad Onniselkä & Abbas Bahmanpour (2017), 'Kaksi vuosisataa suomalaista Islamia' (Two hundred years of Finnish Islam). In Ruth Illman, Kimmo Ketola, Riitta Latvio & Jussi Sohlberg (eds), *Monien uskomusten ja katsomusten Suomi (Finland – A Country of Many Religions and Beliefs),* 104–115.

This goal was also shared by the wider Muslim community, although the communities and organizations that were not aligned with SINE founded an alternative Islamic umbrella organization that decided to use the old name of the Islamic Federation of Finland.

30. With respect to other recently established religious minorities, in 2022, there were six registered Buddhist communities, with 1854 members, and two registered Hindu communities with 379 members.[20]

31. In this context, it is interesting to note that the *Scientology movement* has not achieved the status of a registered religious community in Finland. The Ministry of Education denied its access to the register of religious communities at the end of 1998. The Ministry justified the rejection of the application on the grounds that 'in the activities of the scientologists fundraising was seen to be more important than the practice of religion'.[21]

32. According to a recent study, there are also 1,781,751 (in 2022) individuals in Finland who belong to no religious community. This number has more than tripled – in 1990 there were 510,608.

II. Religious Practice

33. In the large established churches, service attendance is not strong. For a considerable number of Finns religion is characterized by a high degree of privacy and low religious participation. Less than half (24.8%) of Finns consider themselves religious, and the public practising of their faith is minimal. According to the latest survey, *Gallup Ecclesiastica* (2022), 5.6% of Finns attend divine service at least once a month, while 20.5% of Finns attend church less frequently than this, but at least once a year. Every fourth Finn (24.2%) attends divine service less than once a year, while every second (47.5%) reports not having gone to church at all in recent years. Furthermore, one-third of Finns 26.5% attend a church concert or other performance of sacred music at least once a year.[22]

34. Among the established churches the membership of the Lutheran Church decreased considerably between 2000 and 2022; specific societal events over the years have been reflected more clearly than previously in departures from the church. Secularism, atheism, agnosticism, and probably even more a simple lack of interest in religion, have become widespread.

---

20. For more detail, *see* Kimmo Ketola, *Uskonnot Suomessa 2008. Käsikirja uskontoihin ja uskonnollisiin liikkeisiin* (Religions in Finland 2008. Handbook for Religions and Religious Movements). (Tampere: Kirkon tutkimuskeskuksen julkaisuja 102), 2008.
21. Decision on the non-inclusion of a religious community named 'Church of Scientology of Finland' in the Register of Religious Communities. No. 85/901/94, dated 2 Oct. 1998.
22. Church Institute for Research and Advanced Training: *Gallup Ecclesiastica* 2022. The version is not publicly available. I am grateful to Veli-Matti Salminen, DSocSc, of the Church Institute for Research and Advanced Training for providing the latest data.

35. Even though secularism is significant, it has not been as straightforward and obvious in Finland – and the same applies more widely in the Western world – as it was previously thought to be. There are also other trends in addition to those involving resignations from church membership. Religion not only diminishes but also acquires new forms. A slight growth of interest in religious questions has become apparent in the last few years. Immigration and many other social and cultural factors have increasingly transformed, revitalized, and diversified the religious landscape in Finland. This has not only led to the growth of new, smaller or esoteric religions but has also given birth to new forms of religiosity.[23]

36. According to the most recent Finnish studies, changes in religion suggest that one cannot speak of a single rise of an alternative religious culture. Instead, it is obvious that spiritual and religious exploration is being directed along many paths. Different religious and cultural phenomena and currents are increasingly intertwined. People can, for example, practice yoga, meditation, and mindfulness, participate in retreats and seek help in energy management. Innovatory views, which may be seen as manifestations of present-day folk religion, often overlap with Christian tradition. More important than, for example, doctrinal questions are whether a religious or spiritual practice provides resources and tools for everyday life. Thus, in many areas of life, the transformed religion is influenced by new forms of action, often not even considered religious. Their historical roots are, however, often rooted in religion or religious traditions.

37. According to the *Gallup Ecclesiastica 2022* survey, 56.9% of the Finnish people consider themselves to be Christians, 21.7% to be definitely not religious (atheists), and 30.9% agnostics. Those considering themselves Lutherans amount to 50.2%. However, compared with Europeans, Finns are not passive in their private religious practices. Every fifth Finn (16%) prays every day, 7.1% pray at least once a week, and every third (32.2%) less frequently. Every third person (39.9%) reports not praying at all in recent years. In addition, 7.9% read the Bible at least once a year, while 8.5% of Finns read the Bible at least once a month. Regardless of whether they believe in the main tenets of Christianity, (in 2015) most Finns (66.3%) consider the teachings of Christ and instructions for life to be appropriate tenets for living in our time. Only 11.5% of Finns considered such tenets to be not at all applicable to the present time, while 9% had no opinion. Those not belonging to any religious movement generally also consider the teachings of Christ to be relevant for people in the present time.[24]

38. There is no up-to-date information about Finns' beliefs concerning life after death. According to the *Gallup Ecclesiastica* 2015 survey, this has been variable: 71% were of the view that no one can know what happens after death, while

23. For more details, *see* Ruth Illman, Kimmo Ketola, Riitta Latvio & Jussi Sohlberg (ed.), *Monien uskontojen ja katsomusten Suomi* (Finland – a country of many religions and beliefs) (Kuopio: Kirkon tutkimuskeskuksen verkkojulkaisuja 48, 2017), 7–11.

24. The statistics concerning the question of whether 'the teachings of Christ are relevant for people in present times' were no longer in Gallup Ecclesiastica 2022. The percentages shown here are from Gallup Ecclesiastica 2015.

approximately half of the Finnish population believed there was something after death but they were not sure what (49%). On the one hand, 33% believed that the living can feel a connection with the deceased, in some way or other. On the other hand, 18% believed that there is some kind of intermediate state after death, where we await a final destination. In 2015, 13% believed in the possibility of rebirth, while 39% expected that all life would cease after death. Thus, it can be seen that the notion of all life ceasing after death is gradually becoming more widespread.[25]

§3. Historical Background: Religion in the History of Finland

I. Christianity's Arrival in Finland

39. The earliest Christian influences came to Finland both from the west and from the east. In the early twelfth century, Scandinavia, including the region of Finland (Finland Proper), belonged to the Catholic Hamburg-Bremen Church Province. Its leadership sought to make Bremen the ecclesiastical centre of the European north. Hence, from the 1120s, the western parts of Finland began to grow into Catholic Christendom and its culture.[26]

25. *See*, Figure 2.7. Finnish perceptions of death, percentage of respondents. *Gallup Ecclesiastica* 2015, N=4,275. https://julkaisut.evl.fi/catalog/Tutkimukset%20ja%20julkaisut/r/1529/viewmode=infoview/fc=37%3A13.
26. For a more detailed description, *see* Kaarlo Arffman, 'Katolisesta lähetysalueesta Ruotsin luterilaisen kirkon osaksi' (From Catholic Mission area to the Swedish Lutheran Church). In Anssi Mäkinen, Veikko Kallio & Rakel Kallio (eds), *Kristinuskon historia 2000. Kristinusko Suomessa.* (Porvoo: Weiling & Göös, 2000), 8–52.

Map 2

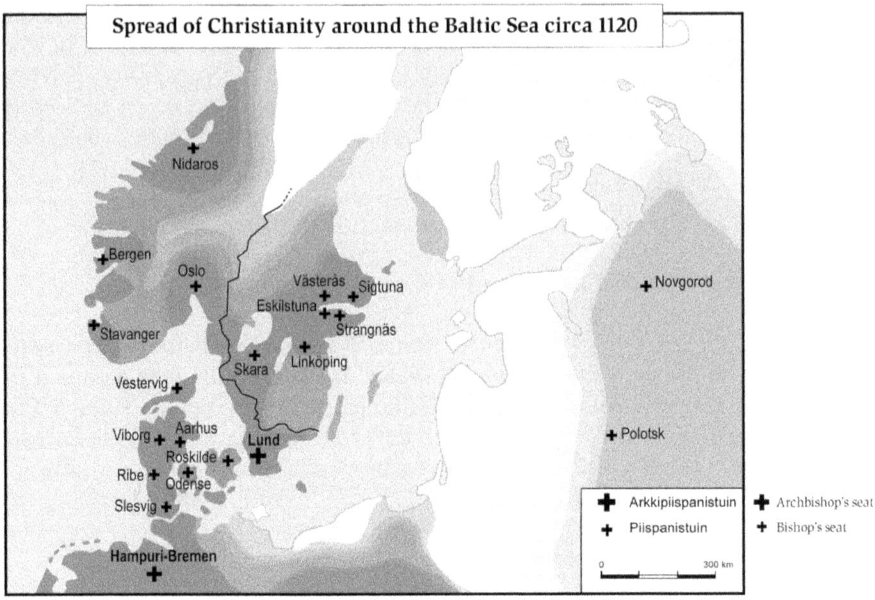

Source: Christianity in Finland, Weiling & Göös, Kaarlo Arffman, p. 12.

40. According to current research, Finland was incorporated into Christendom gradually and not by force or 'conquest' as was previously supposed. An earlier study suggested that Finland was incorporated by force into the Catholic Church and under Swedish rule in three phases: in the 1150s,[27] 1248, and 1293. The first of these phases was the crusade of Saint Eric, King of Sweden, to southwest Finland, while the second phase came with the commander and warlord Earl Birger's conquest of Häme (Tavastia), and the third with the Swedish Marshal Torkel (Tyrgils) Knutsson's military expedition into Karelia, where he built Vyborg Castle (Viipurin linna) to keep the Karelians and Russians at bay. Tyrgil's success meant that the Karelians, subjected to Swedish rule, became western Christians.[28]

27. Kauko Pirinen, Simo Heininen & Tuomas M.S. Lehtonen consider 1157 to be the correct timing. According to Mauno Jokipii's exhaustive exploration of the subject, the first crusade was undertaken in 1155 or 1158. For more details, *see* Eino Jutikkala & Kauko Pirinen, *Suomen historia* (History of Finland) (Helsinki 1966), 28; Tuomas M.S. Lehtonen, Suomi, Ruotsi ja läntinen kirkko (Finland, Sweden, and the Western Church) (Helsinki, 2002, 84) and Mauno Jokipii, '*Ensimmäinen ristiretki Suomeen ja sen lähin jälkimaine*'. In *Muinainen Kalanti ja sen naapurit.* ('The first crusade to Finland and its immediate impact'. Ancient Kalanti and its neighbours). (Helsinki, 2003), 306.

28. For further detail, *see* Markku Heikkilä & Simo Heininen, *A History of the Finnish Church*. (Helsinki: SKS, 2016), 11–26.

41. Later research, however, has refuted the conquest theory, concluding, as noted above, that Finland was incorporated into Christendom peacefully. The first symbols of Christian belief have been found in burial sites that can be dated to as early as the sixth century. Changes in burial practices – a transition from cremation to burial, with the body's head laid to rest facing the east and the rising sun, as a symbol of the returning Christ – can be seen as signalling the adoption of the new religion during the period of 1000–1200.[29]

42. Part of the background of the adoption of Christianity in Finland coincided with the efforts of missionaries sent to the northern lands from the British Isles and continental Europe. As elsewhere in the missionary areas, the process of Christian conversion in Scandinavia and Sweden spread downwards from local noblemen and the upper strata of society. The missionary period was then followed by the church's formation as an organizational structure: *a network of parishes and diocese structures was created, churches were constructed, and a taxation system was established.* It was during this phase that the crusades of King Eric and Henry, Bishop of Uppsala, took place in the 1150s.[30]

43. The first Mission diocese was established in Nousiainen, where Bishop Henry is said to have been buried.[31] From there, it was transferred at the time of Bishop Thomas (1220–1245) to Maaria's Koroinen, the central region of southwest Finland. The next three bishops were former Chancellors of the King of Sweden and were appointed by him. The Pope's letter of 1259 for the first time mentions the Bishop of Turku (the former capital of Finland), and the same title appears a little later in the seal of the bishop himself. According to Bishop Paulus Juusten's[32] chronicle, the 'first cathedral chapter was established at the church of Koroinen in 1276'.

44. The first priests were foreigners, mainly Benedictine monks. However, the first religious order to become domiciled in Finland was Dominican, setting up convents in Turku in 1249 and Vyborg in 1329. The monasteries at Rauma and Kökar (in Åland) were founded in the mid-fifteenth century. The priests of the missionary period were trained abroad, but by the end of the thirteenth century, the Finns had their own (Dominican) cathedral school in Turku.[33]

---

29. Markus Hiekkanen, *Suomen keskiajan kivikirkot* (Finnish Medieval Stone Churches). (Helsinki: SKS (87), 2014), 12–14; Heikkilä & Heininen 2016, 13.
30. *Ibid.*, 14.
31. For more detail about Bishop Henrik and his legend, *see* Tuomas Heikkilä, *Pyhän Henrikin legenda*. (Helsinki: SKST 1039, 2005), 90–98.
32. *Paulus Petri Juusten* was Bishop of Vyborg (1554) and Turku (1563), Rector of Turku Cathedral School and Ambassador of the Swedish King Juhana III. He wrote the bishopric chronicle, known as Paulus Juusten's Chronicle, and was knighted in 1572.
33. Many of the friars belonging to the convent in Turku were sent to study in different parts of Europe. For further detail, *see* Jussi Nuorteva, *Suomalaisten ulkomainen opinkäynti ennen Turun akatemian perustamista 1640* (Finnish Study Abroad before the Foundation of the Royal Academy of Turku [Academia Aboensis] in 1640). (Helsinki: Bibliotheca Historica 27, and Helsinki: SKST 177, 1997).

45. The first churches were private institutions, wooden structures built by local magnates. The establishment of local district parishes (approximately forty in number) occurred in the time of Bishop Thomas in the first half of the thirteenth century. By the end of the Middle Ages, there were one hundred parishes in Finland, twenty-two in the Åland and Åbo archipelagos, twenty-six parishes in the province of Finland, fifteen in Satakunta, fourteen each in Nyland and Tavastia, twelve in Ostrabotnia, eight in Karelia, and three in Savo.[34]

Map 3

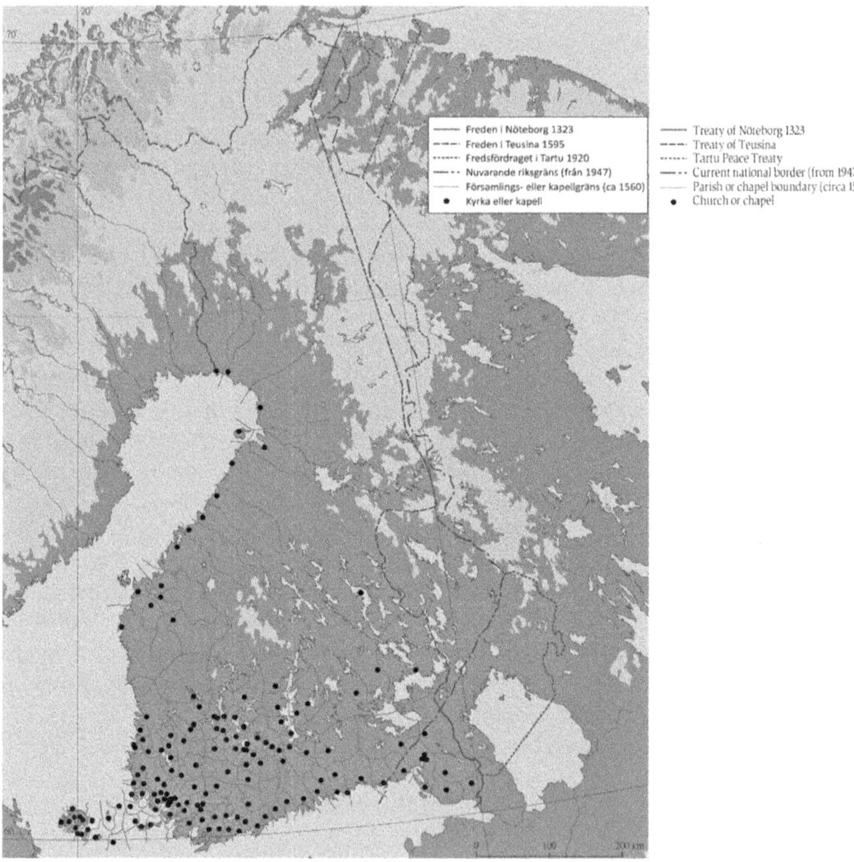

Locations of the parish churches and chapels, cathedrals, monastic churches, and estate churches constructed in Finland up to c. 1560.

34. Markus Hiekkanen, *Suomen keskiajan kivikirkot* (Finnish Medieval Stone Churches). (Helsinki: SKS (87), 2014).

Source: Markus Hiekkanen, Finlands medeltida stenkyrkor. Översätning av Camilla Ahlström-Taavitsainen (Stockholm: Kungl. Vitterhets Historie och Antikvitetsakademien, 2020), 28. Copyright Markus Hiekkanen.

46. In the Middle Ages, the administrative structure of the church in Finland was focused by canon law on the bishop himself. In consequence, the bishop first had the supreme authority in matters of consecration and the highest authority as far as confessions were concerned. Second, he was also the supreme doctrinal authority, while, third, the bishop was the highest authority in administrative and judicial matters. The cathedral chapter elected its bishop, generally from among its own members, and the election had to be endorsed by the Pope.[35]

47. The Church was the first Finnish tax collector, and the Bishop of Turku was the wealthiest man in Finland. A third of all church tax proceeds were allocated to the bishop, mainly in the form of rye, butter, and furs. In the dioceses, the revenue received from tithes was divided and allocated to the local bishop, the priest, and the parish church, respectively.[36]

48. Christianity in the eastern part of Finland, Karelia, dates back to the first half of the twelfth century. According to the taxation records, the Archbishop of Novgorod was already receiving payments in 1137 from Aunus, Syväri, and some of the eastern areas of Ääninen. Burial findings indicate that Christianity has been gradually adopted in Karelia over a long period of time.[37]

49. With the expansion of the western Church eastwards, in 1227 the Novgorodians decided to ensure the practice of the common faith in Karelia, orthodoxy, in their area of Eastern Finland. In 1227, Prince Vladimir the Great of Novgorod sent priests to baptize large numbers of Karelians, when the faith of the Eastern Church began to establish itself in the Karelia of Käkisalmi.[38]

50. The ongoing battle between Sweden and Novgorod was interrupted by the Treaty of Nöteborg (Pähkinäsaari) in 1323. On 12 August 1323, the border between the churches of the East and the West stabilized. The Treaty of Nöteborg – after thirty years of fighting between Sweden and Novgorod – established the cultural border between the churches of the West and the East and the eastern border of the then Diocese of Turku.[39]

---

35. Heikkilä & Heininen 2016, 27–28.
36. *Ibid.*, 13.
37. Arffman 2000, 17.
38. *Ibid.*, 17.
39. For further information about the subsequent wars between Sweden and Novgorod on the Finnish border in the seventeenth century and the Treaty of Stolbova in 1617, *see* Pentti Laasonen, *Novgorodin imu. Miksi ortodoksit muuttivat Venäjälle Käkisalmen läänistä 1600-luvulla* (The Pull of Novgorod. The reasons for the Orthodox migration from the Käkisalmi province to Russia in the seventeenth century). (Helsinki: SKS, 2005).

51. Parishes of the Lutheran Diocese of Turku, and The Orthodox Karelia parishes of Käkisalmi in 1400:

Map 4

- - - Probable frontier of the Treaty of Nöteborg (Pähkinäsaari).
—— The western border of the Turku diocese.

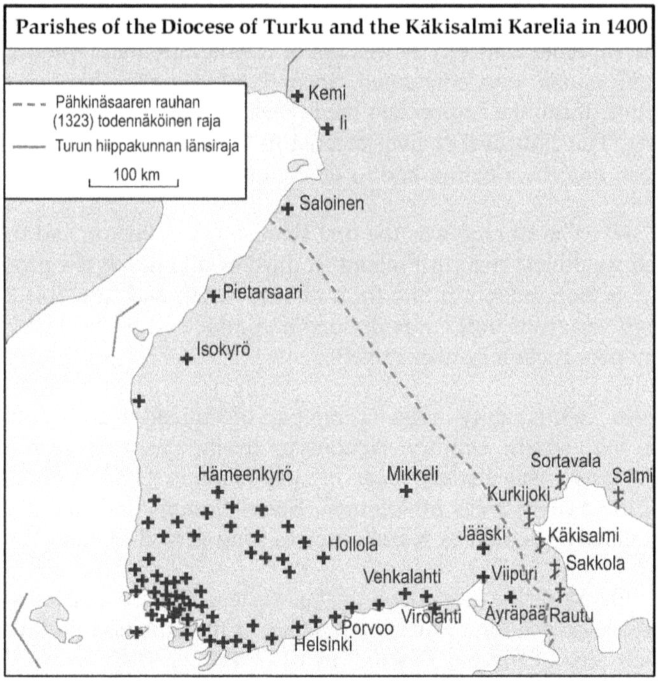

Source: Christianity in Finland, Weiling & Göös, Kaarlo Arffman, p. 23. Copyright K. Arffman.

II. The Reformation of Sweden in the 1520s and Its Impact on (Its Province) Finland

52. During the period of Swedish rule the state and the church were essentially the same entity, bound together by a particular form of religion: first influenced by Catholic Christianity and later led by the Lutheran Reformation.

53. The historical roots of church–state relations in Finland rest in the great social, religious, and ecclesiastical changes brought about in the 1520s by the Reformation in 'Sweden-Finland'. With the coronation of Gustav Vasa in 1523 and the Diet of Västerås in 1527, Sweden broke with Rome. The connection with the supranational papacy, with its independence from the state and its separate legal system, was now severed, and in its place, a national church arose. Its position was regulated by new ecclesiastical regulations and social legislation. While the medieval

Catholic Church in Sweden was affected by both internal canon law and the external ecclesiastical code contained in contemporary provincial laws, canon law did not entirely disappear with the Reformation, but its sphere was considerably reduced. In practice, the Reformation was introduced as a result of decisions made by the state. At the Synod of Uppsala in 1536 the Church of Sweden became a national evangelical church, and at the Diet of Västerås in 1544 Sweden declared itself an evangelical kingdom. The important church constitution of *Laurentius Petri* (1561) was published with the approval of the king in 1571. Thus, with the Reformation in 'Sweden-Finland', as in other Lutheran countries, the Church became an integral part of the State. From a legal point of view, the change was considerable.

54. The development of church–state relations initiated by Gustav Vasa was properly formalized during the reign of King Charles XI by the Church Law of 1686. The Law obliged all citizens of the realm to adhere to the Lutheran Confession (the so-called 'compulsory confession'). In this period of ecclesiastical discipline and order, population registers started to be kept. Lutheranism had become the state religion at the Synod of Uppsala in 1593, and this principle was also written into the Constitution of 1634. In that constitution, the Lutheran Church and its doctrine (*Confessio fidei*) were given secure status. Although freedom of religion in the full sense of the word was not recognized, after the Peace of Stolbova in 1617 a number of religious minorities – Orthodox, Reformed, and Anglican – were granted concessions and given the right to private religious observance. This change affected particularly the Orthodox population of Käkisalmi and Ingria. At first, attempts were made to convert the Orthodox to Lutheranism, but the pressure exerted on the Orthodox population did not lead to the desired result. In 1658 they were granted the right to their own clergy and services according to the Orthodox rite. The general policy was, however, that concessions in the seventeenth and eighteenth centuries should solely concern foreigners residing in the country. In the 1780s freedom of religion was extended to members of all Christian denominations, and Jews were also given permission to practice their religion. The importance of religious uniformity with its cohesive influence on the State was clearly stated in the Constitution of 1634, in the words 'Unanimity in faith and right worship are the strongest foundation of worthy, harmonious and enduring government.' These words were later repeated in all constitutions up until Finnish independence in 1917.[40]

III. Finland's Incorporation into the Russian Empire as an Autonomous Grand Duchy (1809–1917)

55. Finland's centuries-long state connections with Sweden were severed in 1809 when Finland was incorporated into the Russian Empire as an autonomous Grand Duchy. However, the 1686 Church Law of Sweden remained in force and

40. A solid general presentation on this subject may be found in Pentti Laasonen's, *Suomen kirkon historia. Vuodet 1593–1808* (History of the Church of Finland, 1593–1808). (Helsinki: WSOY, 1991).

thus became part of the legislation of the Grand Duchy of Finland. Curiously, the Orthodox Czar of Russia became head of the Lutheran Church of Finland, although there was no change in the legal status of the Church. The ELCF retained its doctrine and organization in accordance with a decree issued by Czar Alexander I at the Diet of Porvoo.

56. In the Finnish Lutheran Church, however, fears were expressed concerning the religious policies of the sovereign of another faith. After Old Finland (territories, which were handed over to Russia in compliance with peace treaties in 1721 and 1743) was annexed to the rest of Finland in 1811, the Orthodox population increased tenfold to approximately 30,000 members. In 1827 an imperial edict opened up military and civil posts in Finland to members of the Orthodox Church. Because the Orthodox professed the 'Czar's faith', they enjoyed his special protection. All attempts to convert the Orthodox to Lutheranism were forbidden. The confessional Lutheran thaw instantaneously became an Orthodox cold spell in the spring. In this altered religio-political situation it was felt that the Finnish Lutheran Church should be given a more independent position. After the Czar granted his approval in the 1860s, the Finnish Senate set up a committee to reform Church law. Frans Ludvig Schauman (1810–1877), a professor of theology, became a member of the committee and his proposals formed the basis of the new ecclesiastical legislation.

57. The Church Law of 1869 (drawn up by F.L. Schauman) meant that once again the Church became a community under public law, separate from the State. The new Church Law was also a significant step towards freedom of religion. Compulsory confession was abandoned, and the state's commitment to the Lutheran confession was relaxed. Although the law was enacted solely for members of the Lutheran Church, it recognized that there were members of other faiths than the Lutheran Church living in Finland. Special mention was introduced into the law to the effect that citizens could not be tied to membership of the Lutheran Church contrary to their convictions, nor could they be prevented from leaving the Lutheran Church and joining another denomination. The law did not, however, by any means recognize full freedom of conscience and religion. According to the Church Law of 1869, freedom of religion primarily meant freedom of religious observance. In the 1869 Church Law, a religiously neutral state remained an unknown concept.

58. To sum up, Finland's connection with Russia during the Period of Autonomy created, paradoxically enough, the basis for independence for the Church. When the Lutheran Church emphasized the Western ecclesiastical tradition in its Nordic form alongside the different Church of the Czar, maintaining that it was the representative of Western Christianity in Finland, it was successful in ensuring for itself a new, legally guaranteed status of non-interference. Before the increasing integration of the European Union, there was no perceived need to open the special preserve enjoyed by the ELCF and the OCF, with their associated cooperation with the state, to outsiders in any significant way.

IV. The Twentieth and Early Twenty-First Centuries

A. *From the Foundation of the Finnish Republic in 1917 to the Times of War (1919–1938)*

59. The new constitution of the Republic of Finland introduced in 1919 was based on the denominational neutrality of the state. This guaranteed citizens freedom of religious practice and made their rights and obligations independent of the religious community to which they belonged. Freedom was now part of the fundamental rights of all Finnish citizens:

> Finnish citizens have the right to practice their religion in public and in private, unless this is contrary to the law and good conduct, and also, according to separate provisions, the freedom to leave the religious community to which they belong and to join another community.[41]
>
> The rights and obligations of Finnish citizens are independent of whatever religious community they belong to, or whether they belong to any such community. The specific restrictions laid down with regard to public offices shall however remain in force until such time as otherwise stipulated by law.[42]

60. However, the 1919 constitution retained the legal and administrative links between the Evangelical Lutheran Church and the state. The strict system of a 'state church' had been promulgated in the new constitution, but many of its denominational rights and administrative features remained. The constitution defined the Lutheran Church as a public law entity and retained the right of the President of the Republic to appoint bishops. The state paid the salaries of the Lutheran and Orthodox bishops and for the maintenance of the cathedral diocese. In addition, many administrative decisions of Lutheran and Orthodox Church matters, such as the definition of parish boundaries and the construction of new churches, were subject to Cabinet approval. The state also paid the costs of military and prison chaplains. Certain features of the state church were also involved in legislation concerned with taxation, school education,[43] and marriage.

61. The state also recognized the swearing of religious oaths. The feast days and public holidays of secular society were run within the framework of the ecclesiastical calendar and were laid down in the Church law. The President of the Republic was the person to make the announcement of Lutheran Church prayer days. A continuation of this same tradition could furthermore be seen in the church services

41. Article 8 of the Finnish Constitution (AsK94/1919).
42. Article 9 of the Finnish Constitution (AsK94/1919).
43. In 1921 the Education Board prepared a proposal on the structure of the primary school system. The proposal did not remove religious instruction from the curriculum. Instead, along with religious instruction, it proposed the teaching of ethics on a non-religious basis, to be compulsory for all pupils, and in addition to religious instruction. Under strong pressure from the church community, however, *religious instruction according to the denomination of a pupil's parents was retained*. History of religion and ethics were taught thought only to pupils exempted from religious instruction.

held at the start and end of the parliamentary session and also at the opening of sessions of the ordinary courts and courts of appeal.

62. In the Constitution of 1919 and the Freedom of Religion law passed in 1922 (267/1922), the special legal and administrative status of the Orthodox Church in parallel with the Lutheran Church was also confirmed. The Professor of Finnish language and literature, E.N. Setälä[44] (1864–1935), who was Head of the Department of Ecclesiastical Affairs in the Senate, played a highly important role in this respect. He set up a working group consisting of Finnish nationalist Orthodox believers, on the basis of whose deliberations Prime Minister Paasikivi's cabinet issued the decree of 26 November 1918 concerned with the Finnish Orthodox Church, even earlier than the denominational neutrality of the state was enshrined in the Constitution.

63. Setälä's impact on the national status of the Finnish Orthodox Church continued after he became the first Minister of Education in the independent Finland. Very much with his support, the Orthodox Church Assembly recognized in 1919 that its dependence on Russia in matters of canon law was no longer supportable in the new political landscape. Setälä was also a delegate of the Finnish state when negotiations were conducted in 1923 in Constantinople with the Ecumenical Patriarch Meletios (Metaxakis, 1871–1935) *on bringing the Church under the authority of Constantinople.*[45] His Eminence did not grant the autocephaly sought by the Church, but the Finnish Orthodox Church gained autonomous status – 'Autonomous Orthodox Archdiocese of Finland' – under his authority. The basis of the canon-law arrangements of the Finnish Orthodox Church became 'tomos' issued by the Synod of the Ecumenical Patriarchate in July 1923.[46]

64. According to the decree of 26 November (1918), the administration of the Finnish Orthodox Church was to be largely the same as that of the Lutheran Church. *As government legislation, the decree did not assume any position with regard to Orthodox canon law issues.* It declared the Finnish Orthodox Church as a minority state church alongside the Lutheran majority church. In the legislation, Orthodox parishes were given the right to collect church taxes from their members and they

44. Professor E.N. Setälä, a Senator and later a Member of Parliament, made a long and influential career as a politician and statesman in Finland. He was among the founding figures of the National Coalition Party, the leading right-wing coalition in the Finnish politics.
45. 'The Orthodox Archdiocese of Finland' was earlier established within Russian Orthodox Church in 1892, and it was administered by the Russian bishops.
46. However, only two decades later, in 1945–1957, there was a canonical controversy between the Finnish Orthodox Church and the Moscow Patriarchate. *See* closer chapter '*The change in the Finnish politics after the war years – Paasikivi–Kekkonen-Line and real politics vis-à-vis the former Soviet Union*'.

also had the right to celebrate marriages. Setälä, as Minister of Education, was planning the same kind of administrative decree for the Roman Catholic Church in Finland. However, the historical division between Protestantism and Catholicism 'proved stronger, and the idea did not gain approval in the political circles supporting the state church system'.[47]

65. As in the Lutheran Church, the supreme administrative authority of the Orthodox Church was vested in the State, which had the role of appointing bishops, funding diocese administration, and maintaining theological training. *As far as the structure of the church and parish administrations was concerned, the decree followed the models of the Lutheran Church and municipal administrations.*

66. The special legal status of the Lutheran and Orthodox state churches and certain features of ecclesiastical legislation, as described above, lasted as such until 1995, when Finland joined the European Union.

67. With respect to the various religious communities, the old Freedom of Religion Act from 1923 defined a completely new type of legal person in addition to the Evangelical Lutheran Church and the Orthodox Church, i.e., the 'religious community', currently the registered religious community. These religious communities were approved by Cabinet decision for entries in the Population/Civil register (Väestörekisteri, Siviilirekisteri). In the period 1928–1945, these communities were as follows:

> Finnish Baptist community (1928), Finnish Episcopalian Methodist Church (1924), Finnish Free Church (1923), Finnish Mohammedan Community (1925), Finnish Free Evangelical Lutheran Parish Federation (1928), Finnish Free Evangelical Lutheran Church (1929), Catholic Church in Finland (1929), Finnish Anglican Church (1936), Finnish Adventist Church (1943), and Jehovah's Witnesses (1945).

68. In addition, the establishment of religious communities was no longer limited to Christian doctrine, but the Freedom of Religion Act of 1923 gave the government the ability to oversee the communities that practised religion publicly. There was also the possibility of remaining outside any religious community. Registration was important in cases where a community was obliged to keep the population register of its members if it required state subsidies for some purpose, or if it wished to celebrate marriages.

69. The Methodists and Baptists caused some apprehensiveness since they had already been organized under the Nonconformists Law (1889). Within both movements there had been those who would not have wanted to be organized in the form of a registered community or would rather have practised their religious activities in the form of an ideological association.

---

47. Markku Heikkilä & Simo Heininen. *A History of the Finnish Church.* (Helsinki: SKS, 2016), 187–188.

B. *The End of the War Years 1939–1944 and Its Immediate Effects on the Church–State Relations, and on Denominational Religious Instruction and Taxation*

70. In the autumn of 1939 war broke out between Finland and the Soviet Union. The Winter War was fought for 'home, religion and fatherland', as Commander-in-Chief, Marshall Mannerheim, described it in his Order of the Day. Finland fought in the Christian patriotic spirit: 'We have God and Mannerheim, the Russians have nothing' was a well-known slogan of that time. The Winter War united the people and relieved the wounds of the 1918 civil war between the Reds and the Whites; furthermore, the union of the church and the people became an ideal that was cherished in ecclesiastical circles for decades afterwards.

71. In wartime, the church and parish life of the Lutheran and Orthodox churches and religious communities was disrupted in many different ways. Services had to be organized in uncertain conditions, and attendance numbers were low.[48] In addition, the signing of the Moscow Peace Treaty (on 12 March 1940) after the 105-day Winter War forced the churches to engage in social work to a greater extent than ever before. They also had to play a part in caring for refugees and organizing the necessary arrangements for relocated Lutheran and Orthodox parishes. Of the pre-war Orthodox parishes, only eleven remained on the Finnish side of the border. A total of around 430,000 inhabitants were evacuated during the war years, including more than 50,000 Orthodox believers who had previously lived in the Ladoga region of Karelia.

---

48. It is worth mentioning, that during the war years of 1939–1944 more people joined the Lutheran Church than left it. Large numbers of members started to leave at the end of the 1940s and in the 1950s. The reasons were generally financial.

Moscow Peace Treaty.

Map 5

Source: Wikimedia Commons

72. The Continuation War (1941–1944) ended on 19 September 1944, when the Moscow Armistice was signed between Finland on the one side and the Soviet Union and the United Kingdom on the other. After the War, the Allied Control Commission (Liittoutuneiden valvontakomissio), appointed by the Soviet Union, settled the implementation of the conditions for peace. This was headed by Andrei Ždanov. The Peace Treaty of 1944 included the terms of payment of war reparations, the leasing of Porkkala, the return of soldiers to civilian life, the expelling of the German troops from Northern Finland (known as the Lapland War of 1944–1945), the abolition of 'fascist' organizations, and the trying and sentencing of war criminals. These contributed to the fear that Finland would experience the same fate as the countries of Eastern Europe, which, as a result of the Soviet Union, became socialist democracies. The Porkkala base, which was located only twenty kilometres from Helsinki, was also an additional deterrent and in principle would have permitted the capital of Finland to be swiftly taken over.

Moscow Armistice.

Map 6

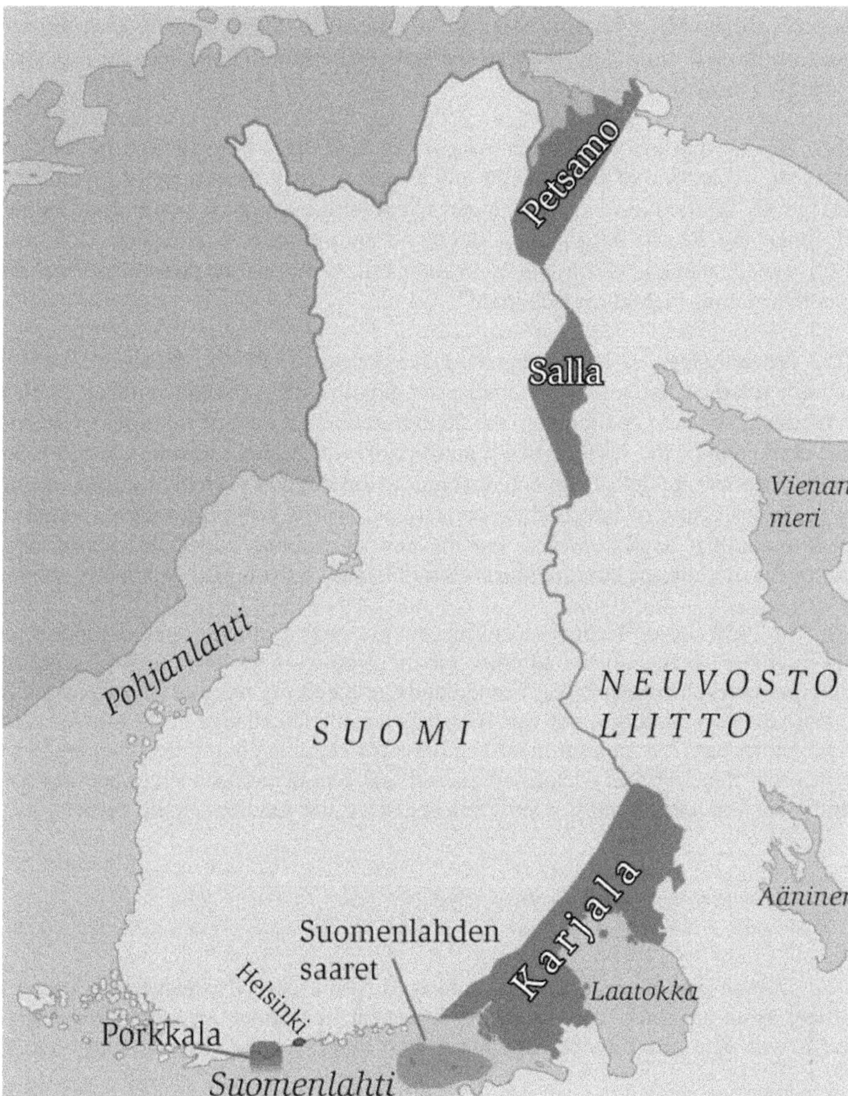

The areas ceded by Finland to the Soviet Union after the Continuation War. Porkkala was returned to Finland in 1956.

Source: Wikimedia Commons

73. The Communist Party of Finland was also liberated in the peace treaty. This meant that a significant change took place in the Finnish political situation. The banned Communist Party was legalized and under its leadership the far left grouped as the Finnish People's Democratic League (SKDL). The SKDL immediately became part of Prime Minister J. K. Paasikivi's government, and one of its representatives, Johan Helo, became Minister of Education. Many free thinkers and politicians on the left wing believed that the time had come to complete the separation of church and state.

74. Helo's approach to church issues was moderate, even though he was promoting the separation of state and church as part of the government's agenda. However, the SKDL soon discovered that its radical religious policy was widely disliked, and hence the SKDL began to moderate its ambitions. Some Social Democrats (SDP) joined with the Communists in their efforts to restrict denominational religious instruction in primary schools.[49]

75. Nevertheless, in the new curriculum introduced in 1952, the teaching of religion still retained its denominational basis, albeit with a smaller number of classroom hours. The next challenge to the denominational nature of religious instruction came at the end of the 1960s when a number of educational reformers hoped to follow the Swedish model of 'objective religious instruction', which reduced the subject to the provision of information on religion. Again, however, religion taught on a denominational basis survived, but the new curriculum added instruction about other faiths, both in the comprehensive schools and in the higher secondary schools.

76. In 1959 the collection of church tax for both Lutheran and Orthodox parishes was integrated into the advance payment taxation system used for gathering municipal taxes, a measure that immediately reduced the number of people resigning from the two churches, nor was there any significant change in the total amounts of church tax paid by communities. The basis for keeping church tax unchanged was the fact that the churches performed certain tasks on behalf of society and the community, such as maintaining population registers and tending public cemeteries.

C. The Change in Finnish Politics after the Years of War – The Paasikivi–Kekkonen Line and Realpolitik vis-à-vis the Former Soviet Union

77. In post-war Europe, Finland managed to preserve its independence and its political system, which was based on European parliamentary democracy. However, it was also much more dependent than before on its eastern neighbour, the

---

49. For more detail, *see* Matti Helin, *Uskonto Skdl:n politiikassa 1944–1961* (Religion in Skdl Politics 1944–1961). (Turku: Annales Universitatis Turkuensis, Ser C, 121), 63–67, 75–91. *See also* Jussi Pikkusaari, *Vaikea vapaus: Sosialidemokratian häviö kirkolle 1850-luvulta 1920-luvulle käydyssä Suomen kulttuuritaistelussa* (Hard freedom: The loss of social democracy for the church in the cultural battle 1850–1920 in Finland). (University of Oulu. Bibliotheca historica 32. Helsinki: Suomen historiallinen seura, 1998), 58–59, 233–137 (Religious education). *Diss.*

Soviet Union. J.K. Paasikivi, and after him, President Urho Kekkonen, were the key figures setting the new political course – the Paasikivi–Kekkonen Line – used by Finland to build good cultural relations with the Soviet Union. The 'dangerous years' (Vaaran vuodet) of the 1940s, when Finland feared that it would become a communist state either through occupation by the Soviet Union or by a communist coup, were now succeeded by Finland's experience of the Cold War, which was marked by greater stability in its social and ideological relations. Nevertheless, for Finland, the period also included a process of being obliged, for economic reasons, to favour, or at least not oppose, the interests of the Soviet Union despite not being politically allied with it. This balancing attitude, understood in Finland as 'Realpolitik', was not always understood in positive terms in Western Europe, and in 1975 the German magazine *Der Spiegel* named it 'Finlandization',[50] which, abroad, became a popular way of describing Finnish politics in the 1970s and 1980s.

78. Maintaining good cultural relations with the Soviet Union also became a challenging task in the area of church politics in relation to the Moscow Patriarchate. And not always in a positive sense. This can be seen especially in what became known as the canonical controversy between the Finnish Orthodox Church and the Moscow Patriarchate, which shook the position of the Finnish Orthodox Church in 1945–1957. Within the Finnish Government itself, it was principally the Ministers of Education, Foreign Affairs, and the Interior who were engaged in the re-affiliation process; it was their ambition to return the Finnish Orthodox Church to the Moscow Patriarchate. Their actions carried heavy political overtones, which in turn undermined their credibility and aroused opposition in Finland to the notion of re-affiliation. The pressure brought upon the Finnish Orthodox Church by the Moscow Patriarchate was simply too obvious. Most of the Finnish Church leadership and lay members were opposed to the idea.

79. The initiative came from the Soviet side in May 1945, when Metropolitan Grigori of Leningrad and Novgorod arrived in Finland carrying a strongly worded message from the Moscow Patriarchate and Patriarch Alexei (Simansky): put baldly, the Autonomous Orthodox Archdiocese of Finland must revert to the Moscow Patriarchate. The church's political motive behind this 'offer' was, that in the 1940s the Moscow patriarchate tried to become the leading patriarchate in the Orthodox World by undermining the authority of the Ecumenical Patriarchate. On the one hand, Moscow exerted this policy by incorporating local churches that were under Constantinople into its own jurisdiction. On the other hand, the Moscow Patriarchate made itself subservient to the political interests of the Soviet Union in the Cold War world in order to gain the bridgehead of becoming the 'Fifth Column' in Finland.

---

50. The term 'Finlandization' means literally 'to become like Finland'. It meant uncritical and humble attitude towards the Soviet Union and setting the agenda of the Soviet Union ahead of the national interest of Finland. Jukka Seppinen, *Suomettumisen syövereissä* (In the abyss of Finlandization). (Jyväskylä: WSOYpro Oy, 2011), 10–13; Timo Vihavainen, *Kansakunta rähmällään. Suomettumisen lyhyt historia.* (The nation bow to the east. A brief history of Finlandization.). (Helsinki: Otava, 1991), 9–17.

80. The ultimate conclusion of this canonical controversy was, that the Moscow Patriarchate failed to gain supremacy over Orthodoxy in Finland. The year 1948 was also a wider turning point in Finnish politics. The communists suffered a crushing defeat in that year's parliamentary election and went into opposition. The political climate changed, and the atmosphere in the Finnish Orthodox Church relaxed. Re-affiliation with the Moscow Patriarchate was no longer a topic! Even though Finland and the Soviet Union concluded the YYA Treaty (Treaty of Friendship, Co-operation, and Mutual Assistance) in 1948, Finland's connections with the Western world grew so firm that Finland – and the OCF – was no longer expected to become a satellite 'people's democracy' subjected to eastern neighbour.[51] Relations between the churches within Finland were strained for some years, but the issue was resolved in 1955 when the Finnish Orthodox Church Assembly declared its own position, and that of the Constantinople Patriarchate, to the effect that there was no longer any need for any changes to be made to its canon-law position.

81. Another area where the Soviet Union tried to exert its political influence in church relations during the period of the Cold War was the subject of Peace in the Theological Discussions between the Finnish Evangelical Lutheran Church and the Russian Orthodox Church (1970–1989).[52] The Soviet Union had already in 1920s put forward a programme prompting general and complete military disarmament, and it repeated this in 1959 at the UN's General Assembly. The purpose of this programme was to demonstrate that as a state the Soviet Union was strongly in support of peace. The two Churches formulated their Finnish-Soviet communiqués[53] in a form that was similar to the communiqués issued between Finland and the Soviet Union. In the church communiqués of the years 1974, 1977, 1980, 1983, and 1986 the term 'disarmament' was regularly employed. The dialogue between the Churches undoubtedly had its own special (theological) character in interstate relations and it can even be said that the dialogue took place separately from the ideological regulations of the Eastern Block. Even though the major opinion, especially that voiced by the delegates, was that the negotiations were purely theological, it can undoubtedly be argued that there was a greater amount of secular politics

51. *See* closer Juha Riikonen, *Church in the Embrace of politics. The Canonical Controversy between the Finnish Orthodox Church and the Moscow Patriarchate, 1945–1977* (University of Joensuu, Publications in Theology, JYTJ 2007, 2007). *Diss. See* especially the background and interests on the Canonical Controversy, 302–303 and 348–349.
52. The theological discussions between Evangelical Lutheran Church of Finland and the Russian Orthodox Church were initiated by Archbishop Simojoki in 1970 and it was strongly supported by academic theologians. These discussions continued until 2014, when Archbishop Kari Mäkinen, together with Patriarch Kirill and Metropolitan Hilarion, agreed to suspend them. The decision did not interrupt other cooperation between the churches and did not rule out the possible continuation of discussions at a later date.
53. The Finnish-Soviet communiqués between the States, as well as between the Churches, contained mutually agreed statements. The aim was to create a text which could be accepted by both parties. The first mutual communiqué was released in 1954 in connection with the visit of the Minister for Foreign Affairs Urho Kekkonen in Moscow. The last one was released in 1989 when the Chairman of Presidium of the Supreme Soviet Mikhail Gorbachev visited Finland.

involved in the discussions than has been previously admitted.[54] 'Finlandization' had become so deeply rooted in Finnish society that in later times it became a sensitive spot for the participants who later had to acknowledge the extent to which were actually part of Finlandization itself.

D. Towards an Increasingly Pluralistic Society: The Watershed Decade of the 1960s

82. At the beginning of the 1960s, the situation of the Finnish churches began to change. The industrialization process continued, and an increasing number of the rural population moved to the growing urban centres. In their bid to find work, some migrated to neighbouring countries and further overseas, particularly to Sweden and Canada. Thus, from the 1960s onwards, what had once been a homogeneous and relatively immobile society became increasingly differentiated. Finnish society was growing ever more individualized in ways that had not been possible during the war years. At the same time, the culture became increasingly pluralistic and a range of different lifestyles began to emerge.

83. Concomitantly, public opinion also became increasingly polarized and an active media sector – TV, radio, newspapers, and magazines – provided space for the expression of both the new liberalism and also left-wing ideologies. Traditional institutions such as the schools, the defence forces, and the church had difficulty adjusting to the rapid changes that were taking place. The Church was viewed as undemocratic and overly engaged in defending outmoded concepts of morality. The Christian student movement,[55] in particular, was ready to acknowledge that the church was out of date, and called for it to change course.

84. As a result of external pressures, the General Synod of the Lutheran Church set up several working groups to prepare proposals for such reforms. Moderate changes were required in order to adapt the structure of the church to the changes taking place in society. This touched especially on church reforms such as the ordination of women and a new translation of the Bible. The Finnish debate over female ordination was long and intense, and to some extent, it has continued to the present day. In 1973, however, the Synod agreed by seventy votes to thirty-three that female

54. For closer information, *see* Marita Tuomi, 'The Subject of Peace in the Theological Discussions between the Finnish Evangelical Lutheran Church and the Russian Orthodox Church during the Cold War'. In *Matti Kotiranta (ed.), The Finnish and Estonian Churches during the Cold War.* (Joensuu: Publications of the University of Eastern Finland. Reports and Studies in Education, Humanities, and Theology 15, 2016), 74–84. *See also* Marita Tuomi, *Rauhaa ja politiikka. Suomen evankelis-luterilaisen kirkon ja Venäjän ortodoksisen kirkon käsitykset rauhasta kirkkojen oppineuvotteluissa 1970–1986 ja 1995.* (Peace and Politics. The Understanding of Peace in the Bilateral Negotiations between the Evangelical Lutheran Church of Finland and the Russian Orthodox Church in 1980–1986 and 1995). Joensuu: Dissertations in Education, Humanities, and Theology 191, 2022. *Diss.*

55. *See* Risto Lehtonen, *Story of a Storm. The Ecumenical Student Movement in the Turmoil of Revolution, 1968–1973.* (Grand Rapids: MI: Wm. B. Eerdmans, 1998 and Helsinki: the Finnish Society of Church History), 1998.

ordination was indeed compatible with the church's beliefs and doctrine. But the actual reform did not proceed immediately, since a change to the Church Law required a 75% majority. The vote fell a few votes short of a majority in 1984, but in 1986 the Synod finally approved female ordination by eighty-seven votes to twenty-one. The first female pastors were ordinated in March 1988 and the first female bishop, Irja Askola, on 12 September 2010.

85. The demands of the new liberalism and industrial society also impacted the traditional Christian feasts. After the Second World War, there were still a large number of public holidays on the Finnish calendar, such as Christmas, New Year's Day, Epiphany, the second day of Easter, Ascension Day, and Independence Day. Celebrating Christmas, New Year and Independence Day on weekdays was taken for granted, but the other holidays were regarded as threatening a breakdown in production in an industrial society. The General Synod of the Lutheran Church, which under Church Law was responsible for stipulating the feast days and holidays to be observed, agreed to the demand of employers' organizations that Epiphany and Ascension Thursday should be moved to Saturdays. The Synod also renamed Ascension Thursday as 'Christ's Ascension Day', and Whit Monday was replaced with the 'Saturday before Whitsun'. These feast days existed nowhere else in the Christian world, nor did they survive for long in Finland. A decade later, Epiphany and Ascension Thursday were moved back to their former places. It is of interest that this return to the old calendar was made not by the Church but by the initiative of a secular society.

E. Finland's Accession to the European Union and Its Impact on Church–State Relations (1995–)

86. Since Finland joined the European Union (in 1995) the issue of church–state relations has become a matter of interest in Finland in a novel way. The deepening integration of the European Union, the associated intergovernmental cooperation, and the development of EU-centred legislation have raised the question of the importance of freedom of religion and of the position of the churches and religious bodies in the Finland of the future.

87. In the religiously uniform Scandinavia and Finland of the past, there was no urgent need to re-evaluate church–state relations. In the Nordic countries, political and social development has taken place without abrupt crises in the position of the churches. Nevertheless, a fixed state church system has gradually disintegrated in most Nordic countries. In comparison with Norway and Sweden, Finland can be regarded as a good example of a country where traditional church–state relations have been dismantled in stages but without a complete separation between church and state.

88. There has been constant debate in Finland as to whether and in what sense the Lutheran Church is a 'state church'. The Lutheran Church has certain links with the state, and in Finland has retained certain features of a state church. The special position of a state church is clearly shown by certain features of ecclesiastical legislation, such as the legal status of the church; until 1995, the state's obligation to maintain the diocesan chapters; until 2000, the President's right to nominate bishops; many economic ties to the government, the right to levy church tax, the employment of chaplains (army, prison, and for the blind and deaf), etc. In the truest sense of the word, however, the ELCF has not been a state church since the Church Law of 1869 and the Constitution of 1919. The Finnish State is neutral in matters of religion, and the Evangelical Lutheran Church is legally and administratively independent in relation to the state.

89. Actually, only as recently as the 1990s did the human rights documents of the Council of Europe (CE) and the Organization for Security and Co-operation in Europe (CSCE, now OSCE) and European integration genuinely force the Nordic churches to evaluate the organization of church–state relations on the basis of the principle of freedom of religion, albeit from a quite new perspective.

90. On the one hand, in the 1990s church–state relations were evaluated in human rights documents primarily from the point of view of the religious freedom of the individual. Does the close relationship between the Lutheran Church and the state infringe on the religious freedom of the individual – or to what extent does the privileged position of one or two churches in a country encroach upon the rights and freedom of other religious bodies? In this connection, it needs to be emphasized that, for example, one of the eccentricities of the Finnish system is that to this day two churches, the Lutheran and Orthodox, occupy a legal and economic position that differs from that of the other churches and religious communities. While other religious bodies are required to register on the basis of the law on freedom of religion, the status of the Lutheran and Orthodox churches is based on specific regulations. The formulation of church policy, as presented in the new Finnish Constitution 2000 (maintaining the *status quo* and thus supporting the relevant section 76 concerning the Lutheran Church), does not, however, suggest that the state has adopted a more favourable attitude towards the Lutheran Church in particular. The judicial position of the church does not reveal the profound nature of the relationship between the state and the church, not to mention the overall value attached to religious values in Finnish society.

91. On the other hand, the whole discussion of church–state relations has changed in nature. The old-fashioned idea of 'freedom from religion' and an ideological antithesis between church and state is losing ground. Similarly, the antithesis between Christian values and the values of society is also losing ground. They have been replaced by a positive interpretation of freedom of religion that has been given a high profile in international documents on the subject of freedom of religion since the Second World War. Citizens have the right to a religion and its communal practice and not only the right to be unattached to anything connected with religion.

92. In the new Constitution of Finland (HE 731/1999), which came into force on 1 March 2000, the freedom of the individual has been emphasized. As a result, the RFA (1922) has been updated: a new RFA was passed in 2003. This Act deals with various issues relating to state and church. The Law will make all Christian churches and other religious communities more equal in society. In addition, the dominant status of the ELCF has decreased. A sign of this is that the family of pupils who are not members of the ELCF is no longer required for exemption from Lutheran religious education in schools. Instead, they are automatically exempt unless the family wishes to sign up for education in the Lutheran religion. In addition, teachers belonging to other religions are now permitted to teach Lutheran religious education, as long as they have a university-certified qualification (Class teacher qualification, Decree 986/1998, §4).[56] Another sign of the equality of all Christian churches and other religious communities is that seceding from a church or religious community has been made easier.

93. An amended **Orthodox Church Law** came into force in 2007 (985/2006). Parallel to the Lutheran Church, the Orthodox Church's legal status within the state has remained as before: the church retains the right to submit proposals for amendments to its Law and other legislation affecting it.

94. In conclusion, it is noteworthy that the new Constitution no longer prescribes that the President of the Republic should appoint the bishops of the Lutheran Church. Under the amendments to the Orthodox Church Law, the function of the appointment of bishops has also been transferred to the Orthodox Church itself, as in the case of the Lutheran Church. In addition, the Holy Synod of the Ecumenical Patriarchate and the Ecumenical Patriarch also endorse the election of the archbishop under canon law, while the (Finnish) Synod of Bishops endorses the election of other bishops. These nuances reflect the general atmosphere of change in state-church relations in a more neutral direction.

95. Relations between the state and the ELCF went through a certain amount of change during the period from 1993 to 2000. In the field of politics as well as in the Church there now exists a greater independence from the Church, on the one hand, and the State, on the other. For this reason, in 1993 Lutheran Church law was divided into two parts: a Church Code passed by the State regulates the relations between Church and State, while a Church Order passed by the Church regulates the Church itself – its doctrines as well as its life.[57]

F. The Church Act Codification Work in 2005–2023

96. The latest stage in the Finnish Church Code work represents the active committee work of the ELCF in 2005–2018. The work started in 2005 as an initiative

56. A class teacher is required to have a master's degree in education, multi-disciplinary studies in the subjects and subject areas taught in primary school, and pedagogical studies as a teacher.
57. For further detail, *see* Matti Halttunen & Pirjo Pihlaja & Risto Voipio. *Kirkkolainsäädäntö 2008 – Kirkkolain, kirkkojärjestyksen ja kirkon vaalijärjestyksen kommentaari* (Church Law 2008 – Commentary on Church Law, Church Order and Church Election Order). (Helsinki: Kirjapaja), 2010.

that aimed at a comprehensive reform of the Church Act. This was followed in 2009 by the Codification Committee's report, resulting in an extensive round of consultation. The work was, however, temporarily interrupted as a result of several large-scale legislative projects. A new Working Group Report was established in 2014, and in 2016 the draft for a Bill was sent for a further period of consultation. This was then followed by the Church Council's proposal to the General Synod (5/2017, Reform of the Church Act and the Church Order), and the drafted law was referred to the Committee on Legal Affairs (Legal Affairs Committee Report 1/2018). The process ended on 16 May 2018, when the General Synod of the ELCF voted for a new Church Act (Proposal of General Synod; Explanatory Memorandum, Bill).

97. The proposal for a new Church Act was passed on to the Government. This, in turn, led to a Government proposal to Parliament on the Church Act (19/2019), and the Government proposal was presented to Parliament on 19 September 2019. The Church Act was due to enter into force in 2020 following the parliamentary review.

98. In the following, there is an outline of the main steps in the Committee's work:

a) The Church Act 2010 Committee

99. On 25 October 2005, the Church Council of the ELCF appointed a committee whose task to be fulfilled by 31 December 2006 was: (a) to inspect the basic principles of Church Law paying particular attention to the part of the material field of the Church Act that would also, in the future, be enacted according to the same order prescribed for the enactment of the present Church Act, and (b) to outline an elemental solution to the regulatory level and the order of enactment to be used for the rest of the norms concerning the Church.

100. The committee named itself the Church Act 2010 Committee[58] and submitted its report, *Kirkkolaki 2010, Kirkkolainsäädännön perusteita ja kirkkolain alaa tutkineen toimikunnan mietintö* (Church Act 2010, the report of the committee investigating the basic principles of Church Law and the legal field of the Church Act), on 20 December 2006.[59]

---

58. The committee's president was the Church counsellor Matti Halttunen, a large body of experts in the field of church law (eleven people), and the church lawyer Matti Mäkinen, who served as secretary.
59. Suomen ev.lut. kirkon keskushallinto. (Sarja C 2006:9) (The Central Administration of the Evangelical Lutheran Church of Finland. Series C 2006:9). In its summary of the scope of the Church Act, the committee took the view that the Church Act should contain regulations related to seven thematic fields. In this context, it is worth pointing out that, of the first four of these, three (numbers 1-3) are closely related to the Constitution of Finland (2000):

    1. The basic principles concerning the constitution and administration of the Church as stated in subsection 76 § of the Constitution. This meant that minor regulations and details supplementing the Church Act could follow the order of enactment of the Church Order and the Order of Church Elections. In addition, the autonomy of a religious community included in subsection 11 § of the Constitution provides authority for the introduction of a wider range of norms for the Church.

101. According to the committee's proposal, in its work on the codification of the Church Act attention needed to be paid not only to the regulatory level but also to the systematic development of the regulations, primarily with the aim of achieving reach as harmonious a system of regulations as possible. The Church Act, the Church Order, and the Order of Church Elections needed to be structured so that there would be a better chance of deploying a harmonized set of norms related to the Church administration at all levels. Such norms were concerned especially the principles and procedures of administration and the various church elections. In this way, it would also be possible to bring in new laws that had been enacted subsequent to the Church Act, such as the general laws and regulations concerning administration, the Municipal Law, and the Election Law. Furthermore, the regulations should be written in as general a form as possible in order to avoid overly casuistic regulation.

102. In its final report, the committee emphasized the fact that the codification work could be carried out in accordance with the order of enactment prescribed for the present Church Act.

b) The Codification of the Church Act Committee

103. In its plenary meeting held on 27 February 2007, the Church Council appointed a committee charged with the task of drawing up a proposal on the codification of the Church Act that would adhere to the guidelines set out by the Church Act 2010 Committee.[60] This committee needed to submit its proposal by 31 December 2008.

104. The report proposed that a new Church Act be enacted related to the ELCF to replace the then-current Church Act that had been passed in 1993. The proposal suggested a total codification of Church Law with the aim of achieving a Church Act that would be structurally more logical than the law currently in force and one that would be clearer from the perspective of those who exercised it. It would take into consideration the amendments required by the Constitution and other legislation, and, in particular, the regulatory level of the Church Act and the Church Order, as prescribed by the Constitution. Because of the nature of the codification of the proposal, no changes in church–state relations were included in the report, and the proposal was primarily related to the technical legislative procedure.

105. It was proposed that the Church Order be renewed in a similar fashion. The Church Order should be passed in a similar way to that currently used by the General Synod within the scope of the authority given to it by the Church Act. The

---

2. The regulations in the field of the Church Act that require the same level of law as that prescribed in section 2 of the Constitution concerning civil liberties.
3. The regulations concerning the basic principles of the rights and responsibilities of individuals as prescribed in subsection 80 § 1 of the Constitution.
4. The basic issues concerning Church–State relations that are not regulated by a separate law.

60. The committee's president was Church Counsellor Matti Halttunen, a large body of experts (fourteen people) in the field of church law, and church lawyer Matti Mäkinen served as a secretary.

Church Order needed to include regulations concerning the constitution, administration, and function of the Church that were in operation at a level below that of the general law. The Church Order should as far as possible follow the same structure and division as the Church Act. There would be no need to enact a separate Order of Church Elections, but the regulations concerning church elections that would exist below the level of law would be included in section 3 of the Church Order.

106. The proposal also contained suggestions about the content of the law. The Church administration should be streamlined by dissolving certain subordinations. The subordination obligation of the parishes when alienating real property should be restricted in planned zones. In addition, the submission obligation should be abandoned with respect to the cemetery plan, the cemetery land-use plan, and the changes in the starting times of church services. The regulations concerning church elections were also to take into consideration the development of a general Election Law and the decisions of the General Synod.

107. The archive services of the Church needed to be developed by incorporating new and more extensive regulations about church archives in the Church Act and the Church Order. The Church was required to follow, to an appropriate extent, the general legislation concerning archives.

108. The proposal contained a technical reform of the regulations concerning the liability of an individual parish member to pay parish taxes. This was to be done by repealing the law concerning the official buildings and funds of the Evangelical Lutheran parishes and by enacting a new law concerning the liability of the members of Evangelical Lutheran parishes to pay taxes to their parish. At the same time, the law concerning the legal basis of certain payments to the parishes should be abrogated. It was also proposed that the law that had been passed concerning the Church Central Fund should be repealed, and the regulations that were required concerning the Church Central Fund should be included in the Church Act and the Church Order. The proposal also contained technical readjustments to the law concerning the Collective Bargaining Contract of the Workers of the Evangelical Lutheran Church and the Evangelical Lutheran Church Pensions Act.

109. The committee completed its work on 20 April 2009 with the submission of its report. The proposal was intended for the Spring 2010 General Synod, which would then be able to accept it in the course of its term. In this way – as it was then thought – the new Church Act and the rest of church legislation could take effect no later than at the beginning of 2013.

110. As already noted, the committee work was interrupted for a while because of a number of large-scale legislative projects. On 20 September 2011, the Church

Council made a decision to set up a new codification committee,[61] which continued the work of the Church Act 2010 Committee. A new Working Group Report was established in 2014, and in 2016 the draft of a Bill[62] was sent for the usual round of consultation to the various administrative parties of the Church and also to the Ministries of Education and Culture, Justice, and Finance.

c) The Government Proposal to Parliament Concerning the Church Act (HE 19/2019)

111. When finalizing and accepting the new Church Act, the General Synod also accepted the new Church Order (decision of the General Synod on Church Order), which was to take effect at the same time as the new Church Act. The Church Act, the Church Order, and the Church Election Order that were then currently in force were duly repealed.

112. The new proposal for the Church Act (HE 19/2019 vp) *codified the existing church legislation so that its content was largely retained.* The aim was to create a structurally coherent set of instruments that would be clear for its users. The reform took into account the necessary changes required by the Constitution and other legislation. *Because of its nature as a codification, the suggested reform did not include changes in the relationship between church and state.* In other respects, the suggested reform was mainly legislative in nature, with the exception of some changes that were made in response to the need for the ecclesiastical administration to develop. At the same time, in the proposal the Church Act, the Church Order, and the Church Election Order in force were supposed to be repealed.[63]

113. The proposal of a new Church Act gained prominence in the spring of 2019. Although the General Synod had approved the proposal in May 2018 and sent it to Parliament for approval, the Constitutional Law Committee[64] nevertheless found

---

61. The president of the Church Act 2011 codification committee was Church Counsellor Pirjo Pihlaja, whose task it was to lead a body of experts in the field of church law (six people), and Katri Kuuskoski (General Secretary of General Synod), Liisa Aarnio-Jääskeläinen (Administrative Secretary), and Juha Hämäläinen (church lawyer), who served as secretaries.
62. The Church Act 2011 committee acknowledged that its work remained unfinished and hence it continued to work under the direction of the Administration Department of Church Council. The third version of the Church Act was completed by the Church Counsellor Pirjo Pihlaja, the lawyer Outi Perkiönmäki, and the Administrative Manager Asta Virtaniemi.
63. For more detail, *see* Government Proposal (HE 19/2019), General explanation/Ch. 1. *Introduction*, Chs 3 and 4. *Objectives and Main Proposals*, 13–16.
64. There is no constitutional court in Finland. Therefore, the Constitutional Law Committee of the Parliament in practice interprets the Constitution in terms of the legislative stage. Its function is to issue statements on bills sent to it for consideration and on the constitutionality of other matters and their bearing on international human rights instruments.

    The Constitutional Law Committee – as the Parliament's official website says – 'drafts the Constitution as well as legislation closely connected to it, such as the legislation pertaining to autonomy of Åland, election, citizenship, language and defence. The Constitutional Law Committee also deals with matters having to do with the alleged malfeasance of a minister, the reports of the Chancellor of Justice and the Parliamentary Ombudsman and the Government Annual Report. Furthermore, the Committee conducts an assessment of those who have registered an interest in the position of Parliamentary Ombudsman and Deputy Parliamentary Ombudsman for purposes of the election of these

problems with it and considered that the proposal could not be dealt with using the ordinary legislative procedure. According to the Administration Committee (hallintovaliokunta), the bill was too detailed and contained confessional points that were not appropriate for Parliament to decide on.[65] The Committee considered it appropriate to redraft the proposal as a whole so that it would meet the Constitutional Law Committee's recommendations on the procedure for enactment and hence returned the bill to the church.

114. A key constitutional problem for the Constitutional Law Committee and the Administration Committee of the Parliament was the so-called confession clause in the proposal:

> **2 §**
>
> The Church confesses the Christian faith based on the Bible as expressed in the three creeds of the early Church and in the Lutheran confessional documents. In accordance with its confession, the Church proclaims the Word of God, administers the sacraments, and otherwise works to spread the Christian message and to fulfil its task of neighbourly love.

115. According to the interpretation of the Constitutional Law Committee, it would be better to have a confessional article in the Church Order decided on by the General Synod itself, rather than in the Church Act adopted by Parliament. If it is provided for in the Church Act, the confession may become dependent on the political will of the legislature, for example in a situation where the church might want to change the content of the confession, but the legislature did not make such a change.

d) The New Church Act (HE 652/2023 vp)

116. The General Synod of the Evangelical Lutheran Church did not, however, follow the interpretation of the parliamentary Administrative Committee but considered that the freedom of religion guaranteed by the Constitution should include a certain degree of autonomy for the religious community, including the right to decide on the content of its own confession in the Church Act, which is included in

---

officials that is held in a plenary session'. *See*, https://www.eduskunta.fi/EN/valiokunnat/perustuslakivaliokunta/Pages/default.aspx.

From the Constitutional Law Committee, the proposals move forward to the Administrative Committee, which 'deals with matters concerning internal security, accident investigation and national capacities for civil crisis management, as well as matters related to foreigners, integration and citizenship. *The Committee's responsibilities also include* municipal legislation, municipal division and municipal economy, general legislation of wellbeing services counties, regional division, general legislation of the financial system and funding of rescue operations, as well as general regional and structural policy and *church affairs*'. [Italics mine] *See*, https://www.eduskunta.fi/EN/valiokunnat/hallintovaliokunta/Pages/default.aspx.

65. After the Constitutional Law Committee's statement PeVL 4/2020, the Administrative Committee HaV, which discussed the matter, decided on 1 April 2020, to send a letter to the Church Board and the Ministry of Education and Culture. In its letter, HaV suggested correcting the motion and explained why it could not be accepted in parliament in the proposed form. *See* https://www.eduskunta.fi/FI/vaski/KokousPoytakirja/Documents/HaVP_18+2020.pdf.

the exclusive right of initiative of the Church Synod guaranteed by Article 76 of the Constitution (the sole right of initiative of the General Synod as well as the non-interference of the legislative bodies of the state in the content of the church legislative requests of the synod).

117. On 20 October 2020, the Church Government made a new proposal[66] to the General Synod, which replaced the previous government's proposal for the Church Act (HE 19/2019 vp) and the supplementary government proposal (HE 93/2019 vp).

118. On 11 November 2021, the General Synod adopted a proposal for a new Church Act.[67] In the course of the debate, the representatives of the General Synod gave 150 speeches, most of which concerned precisely the place of the article on confession. The discussion was based on report 1/2021 of the Law Committee of the General Synod, in which it was proposed that there should be the further inclusion of a confession clause in the second article of the Church Code. The General Synod adopted the report by 57-49 votes, and thus the inclusion of a confession clause in the law, thus also opposing the proposal of the Church Government and the position of the Parliamentary Administrative Committee and the Constitutional Committee.

119. The Government Bill (HE 108/2022 vp[68]) on the Church Act and related laws, prepared by the Ministry of Education and Culture on the basis of the proposal of the General Synod, was submitted to Parliament on 30 June 2022. The proposed laws were intended to enter into force on 1 January 2023.

120. In addition, on 30 June 2022, the Government withdrew the previously submitted government bill HE 19/2019 vp and its supplementary bill HE 93/2019 vp.

121. On 2 March 2023, Parliament passed the Church Act (652/2023)[69] and other related laws[70]. The President formally approved the laws on 14 April 2023, and they came into force on 1 July 2023.

122. The key highlights of the new Church Act include the following:

> The new Church Act contains some substantive amendments. The provisions concerning changes in the parish divisions were revised so that the Church Act would now provide the requisite conditions for changes in the parish divisions

66. https://evl.fi/documents/1327140/43471940/Kirkkohallituksen+esitys+10-2020+kirkkolaiksi+ja+liittyviksi+laeiksi.pdf.
67. https://evl.fi/documents/1327140/43471940/HALLITUKSEN+ESITYS_20.12.2021_FINAL.pdf/e765267c-c5f8-7a8b-2ae4-84c861b53cfd?t=1641208055033.
68. https://www.eduskunta.fi/FI/vaski/HallituksenEsitys/Documents/HE_108+2022.pdf.
69. https://finlex.fi/fi/laki/alkup/2023/20230652.
70. Other issued laws: 653/2023 (https://www.finlex.fi/fi/laki/alkup/2023/20230653), 654/2023(https://www.finlex.fi/fi/laki/alkup/2023/20230654), 655/2023. (https://www.finlex.fi/fi/laki/alkup/2023/20230655), 656/2023; (https://www.finlex.fi/fi/laki/alkup/2023/20230656).

and for the organization of the administration of the parish section. A provision concerning opportunities for the participation and influence of parishioners was added to the Church Act, supported by regulations on communications and the obligation to provide openly available information.

123. The new Church Act completely abolished the procedures of subordination in church administration. The aim has been to simplify the administration of the church and to clarify the roles and limits of the competence of the various authorities. The law emphasizes the independence and freedom of action of congregations. Decisions made at parish level will in future become the responsibility of the parishes themselves.

124. The decision-making process of the church authorities has undergone development so that the provisions would permit both electronic meetings and also electronic decision-making. Ecclesiastical archival activities have been expanded further by including more comprehensive provisions on ecclesiastical archival activities in the Church Act and the Church Order. The Church itself follows, where applicable, the general archival legislation. At the same time, the Act governing General Administrative Information concerning Public Administration Information Management partially applies to the church authorities.

125. In addition, the new Church Act introduces changes in the keeping of church registers so that the general central registers will in future be maintained by the parishes, which would act as the registrars of the church registers. The central registries would take care of official duties related to the ecclesiastical population registers, as provided by law. With regard to the common register of members of the Church, the Church Board would act more clearly than before as a joint registrar, in accordance with the EU's general data protection regulation, alongside the central registers.

126. The separately prepared Church Order has been reformed in a similar way. The organization of the church is to be approved by the General Synod on the basis of the authorization contained in the Church Act. The organization of the church contains more detailed provisions concerning the recognition and mission of the church, and also concerning the form, administration, and operation of the church, including provisions falling within the internal legislative authority of the church.

127. The new legislation also introduces a new law on the office of the Evangelical Lutheran Church. The current provisions of the Church Act concerning a church official's legal status have been transferred into this new law. Some of the provisions also apply to other employees of the Church.

128. Other key highlights of the new Church Act include the following:

The new Church Act also differs from the provisions of the previous Church Act (1054/1993) concerning the Commission for Church Employers (Kirkon työmarkkinalaitos) of the Evangelical Lutheran Church and differentiates them from the Church Act, by being a new law related to the labour market institution of the Evangelical Lutheran Church. In connection with the Church Board, the Commission for Church Employers acts as guardian of the interests of parishes, parish associations, court chapters and the Church Board in matters related to the labour market. It is supposed to independently perform the functions assigned to it by the Law on Collective Agreements of the Evangelical Lutheran Church and the Law on Collective Agreements of the Evangelical Lutheran Church in the manner provided for in those laws.

129. In addition, the new law changes the situation with regard to the Church Pension Fund. The new law incorporates the provisions for the Church Pension Fund contained previously in the old Church Act (1993), the Church Order and the Act on the Financing of the Evangelical Lutheran Church's Pension Fund. The new regulation includes provisions related to the principles of corporate governance, the obligation to maintain a list of positions of trust, the policy on conflicts of interest and the transactions concerned with management and its related parties. Provisions were added to the law regarding the trustees of the Church Pension Fund and the public register of the securities holdings of trustees.

130. As already stated above (in connection with the previous Church Act proposal, HE 19/2019 vp), the new Church Act is a comprehensive codification of the legislation governing the Church, although the Church Act does not include changes in the relationship between church and state. The aim of the Church Act is the provision of a structurally more consistent and user-friendly church law which considers the necessary changes required by the Finnish Constitution, other legislation, and the church administration's own development needs.

131. The difference between the *proposal for the Church Act* (HE 19/2019) and the new Church Act (HE 652/2023) from the point of view of relations between the church and the state lies in the fact that in the latter, the regulation of church officials, the Commission for the Church Employers and the pension fund have been separated out from the Church Act, which is subject to the exclusive right of initiative on the part of the church and moved into the area of so-called ordinary legislation. This means that the state will henceforth be responsible for the development of such legislation. Previously, the amendment or repeal of such legislation was also the exclusive competence of the Church.

Part I. Legal Framework and Sources

Chapter 1. Constitutional Position of Religion

§1. Basic Law

I. Fundamental Provisions of the Constitution

132. The new Finnish constitution (HE 731/1999) came into force on 1 March 2000. It repealed the four previous constitutions: the Finnish Form of Government (from 1919), the Parliamentary Order (from 1928), the Act on National Law (273/1922) and the so-called Ministerial Responsibility Act (on the right of the Parliament to examine members of the Government and the Chancellor of Justice and the Parliamentary Ombudsman. Law on Legitimacy of Crews, 274/1922). The reform unified and modernized the system of constitutional regulation in Finland.

133. The new constitution provides a general understanding of the central criteria of the Finnish state system, the use of public power and the legal status of the individual.

134. The Finnish constitution starts with the following three paragraphs, stating in Chapter 1 – Fundamental provisions, *Section 1 – The Constitution*:

(1) Finland is a sovereign republic.
(2) The constitution of Finland is established in this constitutional act. The constitution shall guarantee the inviolability of human dignity and the freedom and rights of the individual and promote justice in society.
(3) Finland participates in international cooperation for the protection of peace and human rights and for the development of society. Finland is a Member State of the European Union (1112/2011, entry into force 1 March 2012).

135. In the Finnish constitution, there is no reference to God and no mention that would in some way link the constitution with the will of God, as is the case in some European countries' constitutions, such as those of Ireland and Greece.

136. The fundamental provisions of the Constitution – Articles 1–5 – do not refer to any specific notion referring to the teaching of God, whether Christian, Jewish, Muslim or any other specific concept of God. Instead, the provisions underline the following principles: Section 2 – *Democracy and the rule of law*, section 3 –

Parliamentarism and the separation of powers, section 4 – *The Territory of Finland*, and section 5 – *Finnish citizenship*.[71]

137. Any reference to God is a reference to religion as such, as stated in the main manifestations of the freedom of religion and conscience in the Constitution 6 §2 subsection and 11 §§1–2 subsections. The first of these talks about equality: no one shall, without an acceptable reason, be treated differently from any other person on the grounds of religion or conviction. The latter implies the right to profess and practise religion, the right to express one's convictions, the right to be a member of a religious community, and also the right to decline to be a member of any religious community.

II. Freedom of Religion and Belief

138. The Finnish Constitution guarantees freedom of religion in its Article 11, thus in a rather prominent position. Article 11 states:

Article 11 [Freedom of religion and conscience]

(1) Everyone has the freedom of religion and conscience.
(2) Freedom of religion and conscience entails the right to profess and practice a religion, the right to express one's convictions and the right to be a member of or decline to be a member of a religious community. No one is under the obligation, against his or her conscience, to participate in the practice of a religion.

III. Institutional Guarantees

139. The relationship between the state and religious communities has been defined for the Lutheran Church in the Constitution (§76) and for other churches and religious communities in the new RFA (453/2003). These two create a general structure for the institutional guarantees of religious communities.

140. The central feature of the public law status of the Finnish Evangelical Lutheran Church is the special mention of the Church law in the constitution (§76):

Article 76 – The Church Act:

(1) Provisions for the organization and administration of the Evangelical Lutheran Church are laid down in the Church Act.

71. For further detail, *see* Tuomas Ojanen & Martin Scheinin. 'Suomen valtiosäännön perusperiaatteet, PL 1 §' (Basic principles of the Finnish constitution, §1)'. In *Pekka Hallberg, Heikki Karapuu, Tuomas Ojanen, Martin Scheinin, Kaarlo Tuori, Veli-Pekka Viljanen, Perusoikeudet* (Fundamental rights). (2nd revised edn WSOYpro, 2011), 217–226. (Ojanen & Scheinin 2011 c).

(2) The legislative procedure for enactment of the Church Act and the right to submit legislative proposals relating to the Church Act are governed by the specific provisions in that Code.

141. For the position of the Evangelical Lutheran Church, the method of the legislation of the Church law (652/2023) is essential (Church Act 1, section 5 paragraphs 1–3), which contains the sole right of initiative of the General Synod as well as the non-interference of the legislative bodies of the state in the content of the church legislative requests of the synod. In practice, this means that the Church's own organ, the Synod, has the power to take initiative on the enactment of the Church's Law and on changes in the text of the law. *The final parliamentary vote has only the right to accept or reject a proposal for a church law.*[72]

142. **The new RFA**, on the other hand, contains provisions that concern membership of religious associations, the procedure when joining or leaving a religious association, the oath and affirmation, and the application of the law of assembly in relation to the public practice of religion. To put it more precisely, the Law enacts in detail and exhaustively the legal status and foundation, and the rights and obligations of churches and registered religious associations.

143. In the Finnish context, three different types of legal persons can be distinguished in religious associations:

(1) *The Evangelical Lutheran Church.* Its status under public law is guaranteed in the constitution (§76).
(2) *The Finnish Orthodox Church.* In the new constitution, there is no direct provision for the Finnish Orthodox Church to regulate its position in society. In this respect, the legislative status of the Orthodox Church differs from that of the Lutheran Church. The Orthodox Church is the subject of a new law concerning the Orthodox Church, 2007 (985/2006).
(3) *The registered religious communities.*

144. The Evangelical Lutheran Church, the Orthodox Church, and their parishes are public entities whose status is based on the Church Act of the ELCF and the Orthodox Church Act (985/2006). On the other hand, in Finland, a registered religious association is a special type of community. Its foundation and legal status are enacted in subsection 2 of the Freedom of Religion Act. Such a religious body gains the status of a legal person, that is, it can acquire property, enter into commitments, and be a litigant in court and with other authorities once it is entered into the register of religious associations. In this respect, the regulation observes the principle otherwise observed in Finnish community law, whereby the community achieves

72. The new Church Act (625/2023) for the ELCF has replaced the previous Church Act of 1993 (1054/1993). The Government Bill HE 625/2023vp for a new Church Act was presented to Parliament on 2 March 2023. The Church Act came into force on 1 July 2023. The new legislation codifies former church legislation so that its content is largely retained. *Because of its nature as a codification, the reform does not include changes in the relationship between church and state.*

legal capacity once it is entered into the register of associations kept by the authorities, in this case, the National Patent and Register Board.

IV. Religious Instruction in State Schools

145. The Constitution does not specifically provide for religious education in the state schools. This is regulated separately in the RFA (453/2003) and in the School Laws – Act on Early Childhood Education and Care (Varhaiskasvatuslaki) (540/2018) §3, P 6, on The Basic Education Act (Perusopetuslaki) (629/1998) §11 and §13, and Act on General Upper Secondary Schools Education (Lukiolaki) (629/1998), §7 and §9.

146. The constitution, however, guarantees educational rights in its Article 16. Article 16 of the Constitution reads:

(1) Everyone has the right to basic education free of charge. Provisions pertinent to the duty to receive education are laid down by an Act.
(2) The public authorities shall, as provided in more detail by an Act, guarantee for everyone an equal opportunity to receive other educational services in accordance with their ability and special needs, as well as the opportunity to develop themselves without being prevented by economic hardship.
(3) The freedom of science, the arts and higher education is guaranteed.

147. Because the majority of Finns are members of the ELCF, in practice the instruction in religious education is given mostly according to the Lutheran majority.

148. However, the new law of religious freedom (2003) links religious education to membership of a denomination. As required by the new law, the term 'education according to individual religious affiliation' in the law on comprehensive and upper secondary education was replaced with 'teaching the pupil's own religion'[73] According to current legislation, all pupils in Finland have the right to receive education according to their own religion, providing that the minimum criteria on the number of pupils are met.[74] If religious education in relation to one's own religion or denomination is available, the pupil has no right to opt out of it. Students who do not belong to a church or religious community participate in global ethics (Ethics,

73. *See* https://www.finlex.fi/en/laki/kaannokset/1999/en19990731.pdf The Constitution 13§ (6.6.2003/454) and Lukiolaki (General Upper Secondary Schools Education Act) 9§ (6.6.2003/455).
74. The religious education of other religious denominations will be organized if three conditions hold. First, the denomination must be a registered religious community in Finland. Second, the denomination must have a curriculum (one of the National Framework Curricula) approved by the National Board of Education. The approval is not automatic and some Christian minority groups do in fact participate the Lutheran religious education lessons. Third, instruction is implemented if there is a minimum of three pupils in one municipality who belong to the community and who will participate in this instruction.

id est Life stance education, Elämänkatsomustieto, ET).[75] The status of Orthodox instruction differs from that provided for other religious minorities. If there is a minimum of three Orthodox children in a municipal school, instruction is automatically provided and the parents' request is not needed.

149. In recent years, teaching and education in the field of religion in schools has become a relatively common topic in public debate, including the concerns of the legal practitioners regarding Christian hymns (especially the 'Summer Psalm'),[76] and Christmas plays and customs, asking whether they are supportable in the public space as a part of the Finnish cultural heritage, or whether they in fact violate the beliefs of a non-religious person.[77]

V. Equal Treatment

150. The Constitution also provides explicit rules on equal treatment in relation to religions in Article 6 subsection 2 and the aforementioned Article 11 subsection 2.

151. Article 6 section 2 of the Constitution reads:

> (2) No one shall, without an acceptable reason, be treated differently from other persons on the ground of sex, age, origin, language, *religion*, conviction, opinion, health, disability or other reason that concerns his or her person.[78]

152. Section 1 of the same Article – what has become known as the general equality clause in §6.1 of the Constitution – supplements the rule of non-discrimination in §6.2:

> (1) Everyone is equal before the law.

153. Article 11 section 2 of the Constitution reads:

---

75. The city or other organizer of education is required to offer Life Stance Education (ET) to any such student who does not belong to a religious organization; the minimum is that there are at least three students who do not belong to any religious denomination.
    Members of minority religions can take Life Stance Education instead on their parents' or guardian's request. If the student is a member of the Finnish Lutheran Church, they cannot take Life Stance Education, but according to current legislation, they need to take part in Lutheran religious studies without exception.
    For more detail about the Life Stance Education in Finnish legislation, *see* Basic Education Act (628/1998), 13§. *See also* https://et-opetus.fi/wp-content/uploads/2017/05/et-esite-2011-en-fi.pdf. Accessed 23 Nov. 2023.
76. At https://lyricstranslate.com/en/suvivirsi-summer-psalm.html.
77. For greater detail, *see* Part XI. *Religion and Culture*, Ch. 4. *Religion and Public Debate.*
78. Italics mine.

> (2) Freedom of religion and conscience entails *the right to profess and practice a religion, the right to express one's convictions* and the right to be a member of or decline to be a member of a religious community. *No one is under the obligation, against his or her conscience, to participate in the practice of a religion.*[79]

154. Furthermore, Article 22 of the Constitution protects equal basic rights and liberties:

> The public authorities shall guarantee the observance of basic rights and liberties and human rights.[80]

VI. Oath of Office

155. Finland's history has known several different oaths. Oaths have been used in many areas of life and in many occupations. The extensive use of oath-swearing in various parts of society has led to a faith in the viability. The best-known oaths, which are still in use, are the oath of office, the soldier's oath, and the Hippocratic Oath. Most of the oaths have long been completely abandoned. Historical and traditional oaths, such as those required by a judge, have also been replaced by a sworn affirmation.

156. In Finland, the President of the Republic no longer swears a religious oath but makes a solemn declaration before Parliament when taking up his/her duties. Similarly, the President of Parliament and the Vice Presidents will make a solemn declaration before taking up their occupation.

157. Article 5 of the RFA provides for the oath and for a declaration based on honour and conscience. A member of a registered religious community may, on the basis of his or her own choice, either swear an oath or make the declaration. In contrast, any person who is not a member of any religious conviction will be required to make a declaration based on honour and conscience. Any oath or declaration required for employment with the Evangelical Lutheran Church and the Orthodox Church or other religious community is, however, governed by and shall be subject to special provisions.

158. The oath is religious in nature, while a declaration based on honour and conscience is neutral in relation to a person's religious belief. The oath and declaration are intended to strengthen the individual's duty to remain true and to emphasize his or her responsibility in performing the tasks entrusted to him or her. When

79. *Ibid.*
80. For further detail about fundamental and human rights in Finnish jurisprudence, *see* Tuomas Ojanen, *Johdatus perus- ja ihmisoikeusjuridiikkaan* (Introduction to Fundamental and Human Rights Law). (Helsinki, 2009).

an oath or declaration is made, the formulas for both the oath and the insurance are governed by different legal acts and not the RFA.

159. The formulas for the oath of office and declaration in Finland were (until 2016) the following:

Oath of office

I, N.N., promise and swear to the Almighty and the All-Knowing God (or: I promise with my honour and conscience) that in my office I will abide by the constitutions and other laws, and act fairly and impartially for the benefit of citizens and society.

Judicial Oath (Judge's oath)

The formula for the judicial oath has remained unchanged since 1734:
'I, N.N, promise and swear by God and His Holy Scripture to the best of my understanding and conscience that, in all judgments I will endeavour to make and provide justice for both the poor and the rich and to serve God and [Sweden] according to the law and legal rules: I swear never to dishonour the law, and I will commit no injustice, either for fear or favour, or for any other cause, or as a result of guilt or because of those guilty of wrongdoing, for all those who work for justice behind closed doors. For the sake of all this I shall fulfil the law faithfully, honestly, and truthfully, without covetousness or conspiracy, so God will help me in the body and the spirit.'

Judicial Declaration (Judge's declaration)

I, N.N., promise with my honour and conscience that I, to the best of my understanding and conscience, will act fairly in all judicial matters in accordance with the law.

Written declaration

'I, N.N., promise and declare on my word of honour that I will strive to follow the constitution and other laws and act fairly and impartially, and I will implement my official duty both conscientiously and to the best of my ability. I will also not disclose to third parties any such thing that has come to my attention through my office but will keep it in secrecy.

160. In the course of 2006–2016, the Oath of Office (or Declaration) was sworn by:

(1) State Chancellor of Justice and Deputy Chancellor of Justice.
(2) Permanent Secretary of the Office of the President of the Republic, Permanent Secretary of the Prime Minister's Office and Ministry, State Secretary, Under-Secretary of State and Head of Department, and Permanent Secretary and Deputy Head of the Legal Chancellery.
(3) Director General of the Central Office.
(4) Governors.

(5) A foreign affairs officer assigned to the post of head of diplomatic mission or consular post referred to in section 3 of the Foreign Affairs Act (1129/77).
(6) Officers serving in the military service of the armed forces and border guard.
(7) Prison Directors.

161. Members of the Courts and those who, alone or in a collegial procedure, decide on matters of administrative jurisdiction swear a judicial oath or make a judicial declaration. The District Court Chancellor will swear the judge's oath or provide a written declaration before commencing in law enforcement in the District Court.

162. The general provisions for swearing an oath or declaration are contained in the RFA (453/2003). Article 5 stipulates that, under the law or regulation, it is obligatory to swear or give a declaration based on honour and conscience, whether or not to belong to a religious community, either to swear an oath or to provide a declaration. The declaration is always provided if it is prescribed as the only form of commitment.

163. The explanatory memorandum appended to the proposal of the Government of the Freedom of Religion (HE 170/2002 vp) states that a declaration is neutral in relation to a person's religious beliefs. Oath and declaration based on honour and conscience seek to strengthen the individual's duty to remain truthful and to emphasize his or her responsibilities in the performance of the tasks entrusted to him or her. According to the article, a religious community which, according to law or regulation, is obliged to swear or provide a declaration based on honour and conscience may choose to swear an oath or provide a declaration. However, if the declaration is specifically required as the only form of commitment, a member of a religious community may only provide a declaration.

164. In the case of witnesses, the religious oath disappeared at the beginning of 2016. They now provide a declaration 'based on honour and conscience'. In addition, the police force and the medical oath have been made religiously neutral.

165. At the end of June 2016, Parliament decided to remove the current judge's oath, which was sworn using the formula of 1734, 'through God and His Holy Gospel'. Since 2017 all new judges have provided a similar non-religious judicial declaration.

166. Until 2016 the new ministers were required to swear either a ministerial oath of office or a declaration and a judge's declaration. The religious oath was sworn by appealing to the Bible to God, while the declaration was based on honour and conscience.

167. The practice has been confusing: For example, at the beginning of 2017, when the judge's oath had already been abolished, Antti Häkkänen (Coalition

Party), Jari Leppä (Centre), and Sampo Terho (Blue Reform), who were appointed as ministers in May of that year, swore the religious oath and thus did not adhere to the law.[81]

168. In matters of this kind, 'confusion' is no longer possible, as the Ministry of Justice has, since the beginning of 2018, made the necessary amendments to the 'old oath regulation' related to judges and other similar legislative professions.

169. The Minister of Justice has considered it justified to adopt a model for the formulation of policies governing declarations made by the President of the Republic and the President of Parliament. The plan was that in the future, ministers will be required only to provide a judge's declaration. The government proposal (HE 70/2018 vp) stated:

> Any new member of the Government will swear a solemn oath or make a declaration before taking up his or her duties. The swearing of a solemn oath or affirmation will replace the previously required official oath of loyalty and judge's declaration.

170. This bill, however, expired during the parliamentary term 2019.

81. Helsingin Sanomat (HS) 25.7.2017. Following this case, the Deputy Chancellor stated that the ministers should have followed the law of the court and sworn the judge's declaration rather than the oath. However, the Deputy Chancellor did not consider the incident to be directly unlawful since there was some ambiguity in the regulations. At that time, for example, a whaling regulation of 1988 still existed which allowed ministers to use either formula.

Chapter 2. Other Legislation Related to Religion

§1. Scope of Legislation

171. There is no specific law on the relationship between the state and religious communities in Finland in the sense of a comprehensive act relating to these issues.

172. Investigating the relationship between the state and religion in Finland requires looking at the legal order in its entirety. Many provisions also relate to religion without reference to any specific religious community.

173. The provisions clearly regulating issues of religion and religious communities at levels below the Constitution are: the RFA (453/2003), the Church Act (652/2023) of the Evangelical Lutheran Church (mentioned in Article 76 of the Constitution), the Orthodox Church Law (985/2006), and the School Laws mentioned previously.

174. In addition, the detailed arrangements of the constitutional foundation for a church–state system are further elaborated and specified in numerous regulations in the legal provisions ranked below the level of the Constitution. The status of religious communities is regulated within the various contexts at stake.

175. This means that the general laws on taxation also contain provisions on taxation related to religious communities, the school laws[82] contain provisions on religious communities and schools, and the secular law recognizes the legal impact of actions performed according to religious law. Worth mentioning in this context are matrimonial law and family law.

§2. Treaty Law

176. The Republic of Finland has not concluded treaties (concordats) with religious communities as has been the case in some European countries such as France, Germany and Poland.

177. There are no concordats (treaties with the Holy See) or treaties with religious communities, including the Jewish faith communities and also non-religious, philosophical or ideological communities (in German *Weltanschauungsgemeinschaften*).

178. The simple fact is that the RFA (453/2003) and School Laws regulate cooperation between the state and the religious communities, and also the guarantees and

82. The 'School Laws' are: The Act on Early Childhood Education and Care (540/2018) 3§, P 6, The Basic Education Act (629/1998) 11§ and 13§, and The Act on General Upper Secondary Schools Education (629/1998) 7§ and 9§.

arrangements affecting religious instruction in public schools, and the position of the religious community in the public sphere.

§3. Basic Structures of Legislation

179. With the exception of the Act on Religious Freedom and the Church Laws of the Lutheran and Orthodox churches, Finnish law has not been profoundly influenced by concepts pertaining to religion. Concepts that have been developed in the RFA (2003) describe the specific status of religious communities or specific beliefs held by individuals that are primarily Christian or non-Christian or have developed in Jewish or Muslim contexts.

180. The predominantly Christian influence on the law can be seen throughout the legal structures in concepts such as freedom and equality, subsidiarity, rule of law, democracy, and solidarity.[83] It is also quite obvious in the notion of human dignity and human rights, as well as in that of a distinction between the state and religious communities (the Lutheran 'Two Kingdoms' doctrine), although these ideas can also be justified by general humanistic considerations.

83. Robert Louis Wilken, an American professor of the Early Church history, argues in his recent study, *Liberty in the Things of God: The Christian Origins of Religious Freedom* (Yale University Press, 2019), that the idea of religious freedom extends to ancient Christian thinkers. According to Wilken, the Church father Tertullian was the first to use the term 'freedom of religion' (Lat. *Libertas religionis*) and further developed the concepts and arguments of religious freedom.

Chapter 3. Typology of the System

§1. The Denominational Character of the Finnish System and the Basic Principles of a Church–State Relationship

181. Among the church–state systems prevalent in Europe, Finland differs from most of the other EU countries. There is no strict separation of the secular state and the churches and religious communities in the sense that the state and the religious communities would respect the positionality and independence of their opposite number.[84] The Finnish State is neither nondenominational nor denominational. However, there are still constitutional and legislative links between the State and the Lutheran and Orthodox Churches. The Church Acts of the Finnish Lutheran and Orthodox Churches include provisions that bear a clear denominational character *as regulated through Acts of Parliament*. In this special situation, it is easy to agree with Professor Martin Scheinin's opinion, and that of most other scholars, that 'there still are two State Churches in Finland despite a gradual process towards fewer constitutional or other official links between the State and the two Churches'.[85]

182. Freedom of religion or belief is the very basis of the legal system of cooperation between secular and religious institutions in Finland. The legal basis of the Finnish system of church–state relationship is structured by several basic principles, among which neutrality, tolerance, parity, and pluralism may be regarded from a legal point of view as the most prevalent. Openness to religion on the basis of fundamental rights is a dominant feature of the system.

§2. State Neutrality

183. The first constitution of the Republic of Finland (1919) was based on the denominational neutrality of the state. This guaranteed citizens freedom of religious

---

84. It should be noted that this common feature of the church–state systems existing in Europe does not automatically imply a hostile attitude towards religion, nor does it exclude any interaction at all between the state and religion.

85. *See* Martin Scheinin, 'State and Church in Finland'. In *State and Church in the European Union* (2nd edn). Edited by Gerhard Robbers. (Baden-Baden: Nomos, 2005), 527. Gerhard Robbers (2019, 679) has pointed out that it is possible in the European Union to differentiate between three basic types of law and religion systems. Robbers states: 'The first basic type is characterised by the existence of a State Church or predominant religion. In this system there are close links between State power and existence of the Church. The systems of England, Denmark and, to some extent, Greece, Malta and Finland belong to this basic category. On the other hand there are systems founded on the idea of a strict separation of State and religion, for instance in France, with the exception of the eastern *départements* and a number of overseas territories, and also in the Netherlands. There is to a great extent a legal separation in Ireland also. The third type features the basic separation of the State and religion while simultaneously recognising a multitude of common tasks, in the fulfilment of which State and religions activity are linked: Belgium, Poland, Spain and Italy, Hungary, Austria, the Baltic States and Portugal belong this group'. Gerhard Robbers, 'State and Church in the European Union'. In *State and Church in the European Union* (3rd edn). Edited by Gerhard Robbers. (Baden-Baden: Nomos, 2019).

practice and rendered their rights and obligations independent of the religious community to which they belonged. Thus, freedom was a part of the fundamental rights of all Finnish citizens.

184. However, the 1919 constitution retained the legal and administrative links between the Evangelical Lutheran Church and the state. The strict system of a 'state church' had been reduced in the constitution, but many of its denominational rights and administrative features remained, which is still the case in the constitution of the twenty-first century.

185. Neutrality means non-intervention, that is, the state is not allowed to take decisive action in the affairs of religious communities. In the Finnish Constitution, there is no comprehensive act related to this issue that would explicitly state that 'Every religious community regulates and administers its own affairs independently within the framework of the general law that applies to all', as is the case, for example, in the German *Grundgesetz* or Constitution.[86]

186. Article 11 section 2 of the Finnish Constitution states only that 'Freedom of religion and conscience entails the right to profess and practice a religion, the right to express one's convictions and the right to be a member of or decline to be a member of a religious community'.

187. However, the RFA, Article 3 section 1 states more profoundly that:

> Everyone has the right to decide on his or her religious status by joining or resigning from a religious community that accepts him or her.

188. This right of self-determination is valid, regardless of the legal status of the religious congregation.

189. And section 5 of the same Article continues:

> The law of the Evangelical Lutheran Church and the Orthodox Church can provide and establish the conditions for membership in the community order of the registered religious community. In such a case, membership may be made subject to the condition that the person is not at the same time a member of another religious community.

190. Neutrality also includes positive neutrality. This concept obligates the state to actively support religion (to give purpose) and to provide for the space that religion needs in order to flourish. It makes it possible and requires, for example, for the state to include religious needs in planning law. This is clearly observable in the RFA (2003), which reads:

86. Gerhard Robbers, *Germany.* In *International Encyclopaedia of Laws: Religion*, edited by Rik Torfs. Alphen aan den Rijn, NL (Kluwer Law International, 2013), 61.

The purpose of the registered religious community is to organize and support the individual, communal, and public activities of the recognition and practice of religion, based on the creed, the scriptures, or other well-established foundations of action.

The community must fulfil its purpose with respect for fundamental and human rights.

The purpose of the community is not to seek economic profit or otherwise to organize economic activities. The community cannot organize activities for which an association under the Association Act (503/1989) cannot be established or for which the association can only be founded subject to authorization.

191. This kind of positive neutrality prevails throughout the official discourses of the state authorities and not solely in the law. It is actively supported – with respect for both fundamental and human rights – and implemented by the courts and state authorities.

192. A new challenge has, however, become visible with respect to the integration of the Muslim population, with their specific needs, and at the same time to support those Islamic communities and associations that function as a liaison body with the authorities.

§3. Tolerance

193. The principle of tolerance obliges all state authorities to respect the various religious and non-religious confessions and beliefs and at the same time to create an atmosphere of positive tolerance in society, at both State and individual levels.

194. As Article 2 of UNESCO's Declaration of Principles on Tolerance – which the Member States of the UN have adopted – reads, tolerance *at the State level* requires:

(1) just and impartial legislation, law enforcement, and judicial and administrative process. It also requires that economic and social opportunities be made available to each person without any discrimination. Exclusion and marginalization can lead to frustration, hostility, and fanaticism;
(2) in order to achieve a more tolerant society, states should ratify existing international human rights conventions and, where necessary, draft new legislation to ensure equality of treatment and opportunity for all groups and individuals in society;

At the level of the individual, Article 1 section 4 of the Declaration emphasizes that:

(3) consistent with respect for human rights, the practice of tolerance does not mean toleration of social injustice or the abandonment or weakening of one's convictions. It means that one is free to adhere to one's own convictions and accepts that others adhere to theirs. It means accepting the fact that human

beings, naturally diverse in their appearance, situation, speech, behaviour and values, have the right to live in peace and to be as they are. It also means that one's views are not to be imposed on others.

195. As indicated above, while the neutrality of states refers predominantly to the organization of religion and belief, tolerance focuses more on the individual. In terms of religious principles, individually focused tolerance plays a very prominent role. In Finland this has affected two items in particular: on the one hand, religious education in the comprehensive and upper secondary schools, which has become one of the most contested issues regarding religion and culture in Finland today; and on the other hand, religiously motivated behaviour in state schools, more specifically the use of religious symbols and religious garments.

196. With regard to the resolution of problems that have arisen in recent years, religious education in the state schools has been described as 'weakly confessional'. Pupils study religious education according to their 'individual religious affiliation'. Thus, religious education includes content that is based on the respective traditions of the students but does not include elements of their religious practice.[87] This has been found to be more appropriate in generating an atmosphere of reciprocal tolerance between diverging world-views. If, however, religious education related to one's own religion or denomination is not available, the pupil has the right to opt out of any instruction. This particular principle has understandably gained importance in view of Muslim pupils and their religious needs.

197. Concomitantly, there is in Finland no law or regulation that forbids the wearing of religious symbols (e.g., crucifixes or scarves), although the question of religious garments worn by either teachers or students has not yet been discussed by the Finnish National Board of Education.[88]

198. In total, only a few cases regarding religious headdress and clothing have been brought to court nationally. For example, the uniforms of security guards and police officers are regulated by-laws and decrees, and religious headdress is not a part of the uniform. This neutral uniform easily limits the access of those who use a headdress, such as Sikhs and female Muslims, as far as certain types of positions are concerned.

199. The Finnish Chancellor of Justice and the Finnish Ombudsman monitor the activities of the authorities, and hence they are able to take a position on whether a particular dress code is constitutional. Before a complaint can reach them, it must first be made, and ultimately, the court will decide on the appropriateness of a complaint. Another way in which a given situation can be changed is to have a Member of Parliament introduce a bill on the matter.

---

87. Students of different Christian denominational backgrounds are separated for the classes on religion.
88. For more detail, *see* §7. Protected Manifestations, II. Specific Issues, B./1 Dress Requirements.

200. In addition, the National Non-discrimination and Equality Tribunal and the employment protection authorities, which monitor compliance with the Equality Act in all public and private arenas, may also resolve cases related to the use or restriction of the use of religious symbols.[89]

201. However, only one of the regional state administrative offices in the whole of Finland – that of Southern Finland – has handled four cases (in 2018) concerned with religious headdress and clothing. Of these, three concerned the use of the Muslim veil and one with the use of a turban.

§4. Parity

202. Parity means the obligation to treat all religious communities equally. In the Finnish Constitution, there is no explicit differentiation in the ways in which the state should treat the various religious communities.

203. Equal treatment is, nevertheless, a key feature in the RFA (453/2003) and it is closely linked to the prohibition of discrimination based on religion or belief contained in Article 6 (paragraphs 1 and 2) of the Constitution:

(1) Everyone is equal before the law.
The word 'everyone' in paragraph 1 indicates that freedom of religion is the right of every individual within the Finnish legal system, regardless of nationality.

(2) No one shall, without an acceptable reason, be treated differently from other persons on the ground of sex, age, origin, language, *religion*, conviction, opinion, health, disability or other reason that concerns his or her person.[90]

204. This prohibition, among other matters, is accompanied by an obligation on the part of the public authorities to treat all religious communities and world-views in a balanced manner.

205. Equal treatment does not require identical treatment but means treating equally what is equal and treating unequally what is not equal, according to the extent of the differences.

206. In the Finnish system, it follows, equal treatment finds its critical point in the case of the two national – Lutheran and Orthodox – churches that have, in the course of the country's history, gained a special position and different status *under public law* in comparison with the other religious communities. This status is also

89. These cases are discussed in more detail in Part II, Ch. 1, §7. Protected Manifestations, D., 2. *Religious Food Requirements in Public Institutions* and in Part VI. The Labour Law Within the Religious Communities, Ch. 1, II., *A. Refusal to Carry Out Work Duties Because of Religious Convictions* and II., *B. Religiously Dictated Dress Codes.*

90. Italics mine.

guaranteed through a constitutional differentiation in their legal status, i.e., by Article 76, which maintains the *status quo* concerning the Evangelical Lutheran Church. In parallel with the Lutheran Church, the legal status of the Orthodox Church in relation to the state has remained as it was previously in the Orthodox Church Law (985/2006).

207. However, the RFA, passed in 2003, deals with various issues related to state and church and aims to make all Christian churches and other religious communities more equal in society. In addition, the dominant status of the ELCF has been reduced by this law, which has created a parity that has to provide an adequate basis for dealing with the social phenomena affecting the whole range of religious communities.

§5. Pluralism

208. As already indicated, the legal basis of the Finnish system concerned with the state-church relationship consists of a number of basic principles, with neutrality, tolerance, and parity being the most central.

209. In addition, mention should be made of the concept of pluralism, which from a legal point of view can be considered the most prevalent.

210. Although there are two privileged national churches in the Finnish system, the state and state authorities have no set preferences in favour of particular religions. It is more a question of their different statuses under public law. Belonging to a particular religion may not, and in general is not, a reason to favour or discriminate against state actions. Every human being in Finland has – despite the multitude of religions, confessions, and non-confessional concepts of life – the full constitutional freedom of religion or belief.

211. Thus, in general, there is no reason for any favouring or disfavouring state action, since adherence to a particular religion cannot, by law, exist as such.

§6. Institutionalism

212. Religious institutions enjoy a freedom of faith, which exists as a corporative right.

213. As mentioned previously, the relationship between the state and religious communities has been defined for the Lutheran Church in the Constitution (§76) and for other churches and religious communities in the RFA (453/2003). These two create a general structure for the institutional guarantees of the religious communities.

214. The RFA enacts in detail and exhaustively the legal status and foundation, and the rights and obligations of all churches and registered religious associations.

215. In the Finnish context, three different types of legal persons can be distinguished in religious associations: those representing the Evangelical Lutheran Church, the Orthodox Church, and registered religious associations. These religious bodies gain the status of a legal person, that is, they can acquire property, enter into commitments, and become litigants in a court of law and with other authorities once they have been entered into the register of religious associations.

216. Some bodies engaging in religious activities have not, however, organized as registered religious associations but as ideological associations, for example.

217. If the religious association (or any other body) is not registered, it cannot receive competent legal person status nor gain rights and obligations. Persons acting on behalf of such an unregistered body are responsible personally for all of their commitments.

218. There are no regional differences in the legal status of religious bodies as far as registration is concerned because Finland does not have a federal system.

§7. Openness Towards Religion

219. Since the introduction of the Constitution of 2000, a fundamental feature of the system has been its simultaneous neutrality to and openness to religion. It is noteworthy that religion is nowadays regarded as something more positive and a phenomenon that also forms part of the public sphere.

220. The old-fashioned idea of 'freedom from religion' and an ideological antithesis between church and state has, to some degree, lost ground. Similarly, the antithesis between Christian values and the values of society in general is also losing ground. They have been replaced by a more positive interpretation of freedom of religion that, since the Second World War, has achieved an increasingly higher profile in international documents on the subject of freedom of religion. Citizens have the right to a religion and its communal practice and not only the right to be unattached to anything to do with religion.

221. It can be argued that Finnish law does not use 'laicism' and 'secularism' as legal concepts. In the international legal debate, 'laicism' (and the French-derived term 'laicity', from 'laïcité'[91]) is widely regarded as a term that represents a basically hostile stance or at least a fundamentally negative attitude on the part of the state towards religion and religious communities. When these words are used in Finnish discussion, they are used by those who would prefer a fundamental change of the system. A constant and intense debate has been led mainly by freethinkers who have questioned the relationship between the state and religion, and religion

91. For further detail about 'laïcité', *see* Jean-Marie Woehrling. In: Francis Messner (ed.), *Dictionnaire du droit des religions*. (Paris: CNRS Éditions 2022), 443–446.

and culture, as well as the foundations of the Finnish legal and political system and its links with its Christian heritage and with other religions.

§8. Freedom of Religion or Belief

222. The basic principles of the law on religion are also to be seen in the setting of the Freedom of religion or conscience according to Article 11 of the Constitution. It is in section 2 that one finds the requirement of *a positive stance towards religion.* Freedom of faith is guaranteed in order to give every individual the right to believe what he or she wishes:

> (2) Freedom of religion and conscience entails the right to profess and practice a religion, the right to express one's convictions and the right to be a member of or decline to be a member of a religious community. No one is under the obligation, against his or her conscience, to participate in the practice of a religion.

223. Also included is the freedom of faith *in a negative aspect*, this is the right not to have a creed and/or the right not to belong to any particular religious faith. Religious freedom also guarantees the right to act according to one's beliefs.

224. As a result, conscientious beliefs present a problem in certain criminal cases. A good example is the exemption of Jehovah's Witnesses from military service, which has been the subject of a variety of debates. The end result is that the exemption law for Jehovah's Witnesses was repealed because such an advantage could not, in the name of equality, be reserved solely for adherents to that particular faith. The precedent was set by the ruling of the Helsinki Court of Appeal, which even applied the uncommon provision of Article 106 of the Constitution[92] and left a total objector who, despite not being a Jehovah's Witness, was unable to be sentenced to imprisonment. This issue will be discussed in greater depth in Chapter 7, Protected Manifestations, 6. *Conscientious Objection and Military Service.*

225. According to current legislation, freedom of faith in the sense of positive tolerance also allows for the possibility of the state offering the opportunity for all pupils in state schools to have the right to receive education according to their own religion. The state is required to provide for the religious needs of all pupils in upper secondary schools or vocational upper secondary education and training. This applies equally to the National Defence Force and the penal institutions.

---

92. Section 106 – Primacy of the Constitution reads: 'If, in a matter being tried by a court of law, the application of an Act would be in evident conflict with the Constitution, the court of law shall give primacy to the provision in the Constitution.'

Part II. Religious Freedom in General

Chapter 1. Individual Religious Freedom

§1. Normative Structures

226. Individual freedom of religion or belief in Finland is guaranteed in Article 11 of the Constitution. Article 11 guarantees freedom of religion and conscience (paragraph 1) and specifies its dimensions (paragraph 2). Freedom of faith and of conscience, and the freedom to profess a religious or philosophical creed, shall be inviolable; and no one is under the obligation, against his or her conscience, to participate in the practice of a religion.

227. The article does not contain a specific (qualified) restriction clause. Thus, any restrictions on freedom of religion and conscience are subject to general conditions of restriction of fundamental rights.

228. The close connection in Article 11 of the Constitution between freedom of religion or belief, on the one hand, and freedom of conscience, on the other is to show the importance that the Constitution attributes to deeply held individual convictions. It also shows the respect that the legal order pays to those personal convictions. In court practice, conscience or belief may well be based on non-religious and also on non-philosophical convictions.

229. The freedom of religion and conscience is closely linked to the prohibition of discrimination based on religion or belief contained in Article 6(2) of the Constitution.[93] This prohibition is, among other things, accompanied by an obligation on the part of public authorities to treat all religious communities and worldwide trends equally.

230. The security of freedom of religion and conscience is broad-based. Freedom of conscience within the meaning of this provision covers both religious and other world and life views.[94]

93. HE 309/1993 vp, 55. PeVL 7/2005 vp, 4, PeVL 28/2004 vp, 2.
94. HE 309/1993 vp, 55.

§2. FUNCTIONS

231. Article 11 of the Constitution is **regarded as an individual guarantee**. It protects freedom of religion or conscience for individuals and for legal entities.

232. All fundamental rights, including freedom of religion or conscience, are at the heart of Finnish legislation. Fundamental rights are primarily seen to be defensive rights. This means that the state may not interfere with the legal position of the individual unless there is a special reason to do so.[95]

233. The fundamental rights – such as freedom of assembly, freedom of the press and of opinion, and the right to vote – traditionally give citizens the right to participate in the democratic political process. This also applies to religiously based activities and views. Religious or belief convictions as fundamental rights cannot be a reason to allow or prohibit a person's or organization's participation in the public democratic process.

234. Among the most important manifestations of freedom of religion and conscience, Article 6(2) of the Constitution mentions the right to confess and practice religion, the right to express conviction, religious freedom of association, and **negative religious freedom**, i.e., the right not to belong to a religious community.[96]

235. Negative religious freedom also implies that no one can be forced to attend religious services or other religious practices in violation of his or her conscience. However, this does not block other people's positive freedom of religion.[97]

236. The recognition and practice of religion also include the teaching of religion 'according to one's own religion'. Religious freedom requires the individual to have access to religious or philosophical teaching. Teaching and upbringing must respect the individual's conviction, the rights of the child, and the right of the guardian to respond to the child's development.[98]

237. Based on the concepts of freedom of religion and conscience, actions that violate human dignity or other fundamental rights or are contrary to the principles of the legal order cannot be pursued. For example, the rule of fundamental rights cannot, under any circumstances, justify the mutilation of human beings, such as the

95. For further detail about the importance of fundamental rights in legislative work, *see* Veli-Pekka Viljanen, 'Perusoikeuksien merkitys lainsäädäntötyössä'. (The importance of fundamental rights in legislative work). In *Pekka Hallberg, Heikki Karapuu, Tuomas Ojanen, Martin Scheinin, Kaarlo Tuori, Veli-Pekka Viljanen, Perusoikeudet* (Fundamental rights). (2nd revised edn WSOYpro, 2011), 833–873. (Viljanen 2011a). *See also* Viljanen, 'Perusoikeuksien soveltamisala' (Scope of fundamental rights). In *Pekka Hallberg, Heikki Karapuu, Tuomas Ojanen, Martin Scheinin, Kaarlo Tuori, Veli-Pekka Viljanen, Perusoikeudet* (Fundamental rights). (2nd revised edn WSOYpro, 2011), 89–137. (Viljanen 2011c).
96. HE 309/1993 vp, 55. PeVM 10/2002 vp, 2.
97. HE 309/1993 vp, 55. PeVM 10/2002 vp, 3–4.
98. HE 309/1993 vp, 55–56. PeVM 10/2002 vp, 3–4.

circumcision of women, despite the possible link between such a measure and a religious trend. The same applies, for example, to polygamy, which is incompatible with the Finnish legal system.

238. Nor does the constitutional security of freedom of religion or conscience preclude the adoption by law of ordinances of a moral and ethical value generally accepted in society, which must be taken into account, either in religious or similar ways, of different religious practices.

239. In particular, other fundamental human rights considerations must be taken into account when interpreting how far the provision of fundamental rights, such as the right to practice religion, extends. For example, the fundamental rights of a child, such as the right to life and personal integrity, must not be violated by invoking the freedom of other religions and consciences.[99]

240. **The right to freedom of religion or conscience also has an institutional meaning.** It guarantees the institution of the neutrality of the state in matters of religion or belief. As such it forms part of an 'objective level' of constitutional guarantee strengthening the 'subjective rights' of individuals.

241. Fundamental rights are also a guarantee of organization and procedure. The state must provide appropriate organizational and procedural structures to ensure the prompt and effective protection of fundamental rights.

242. In addition, religious freedom includes the possibility that each religious community decides its own religious practices. Among religious practices, worship can be regarded as one of the core areas of the right to exercise religion in a state of religious freedom. Marriage is also part of the right to practice religion in a religious community.

243. Religious freedom of assembly also includes a degree of internal autonomy on the part of the religious community and its right to determine its own affairs, such as the recognition of faith and matters relating to the practice and teaching of religion and the other spiritual activities of the community, as well as the choice of religious leaders, priests, and teachers.[100]

§3. Scope of Individual Guarantee

I. Nationality

244. Freedom of religion or belief ('conscience' in Finnish jurisprudence) is a human right. It does not depend on the nationality of individual persons.

---

99. HE 309/1993 vp, 56.
100. PeVL 28/2006 vp, 2, PeVL 20/2003 vp, 2, PeVL 57/2001 vp, 2.

II. Religious Maturity

A. The Role of Parents and Legal Guardians

245. Children also enjoy freedom of religion or belief. In the Finnish context, legal and religious maturity is reached only at the age of 18. Until minors have reached religious maturity, it is up to their parents to act on behalf of their children in matters of religion and belief, thus also exercising their own individual right to raise and educate their children *according to their religious tradition* in conjunction with Article 3 of the RFA.

246. Once a child has reached the age of 15, with written parental consent he or she can decide on his or her personal religious confession. From the age of 12 years onwards, the religious confession of the child cannot be changed against his or her will.

247. On the other hand, the Constitution contains specific provisions concerning the fundamental rights of children. According to Article 6(3) of the Constitution, as individuals, children should be treated equally, and they should be able to influence their own affairs accordingly.[101] This constitutional provision must be properly taken into account when regulating the right of the child to be heard in matters concerning him- or herself.[102]

248. Under Article 19(3) of the Constitution, public authority must support the possibilities of the family and other persons responsible for the care of the child in order to secure the child's well-being and individual growth. The special need for protection of children has also been taken into account in Article 12(1) of the Constitution. According to the law, pictorial programmes that are necessary for the protection of children may be limited by the restrictions necessary for the protection of children.[103]

B. Practical Implications of Religious Maturity

249. Until minors have reached religious maturity, it is up to their parents or legal guardians to act on behalf of their children in matters of religion and belief, to have their children baptized, to decide on their children's participation in religious ceremonies and worship or prayers; and to send them to a kindergarten of a religious or belief character or to a school run by a religious or belief community. Article 3(2) of RFA provides the right for parents to have their children educated in accordance with their religious and other views.

101. HE 309/1993 vp, 23–24.
102. PeVL 30/2010 vp, 3, PeVL 24/2010 vp, 3–4, PeVL 58/2006 vp, 6–7.
103. HE 309/1993 vp, 23–24.

250. The same Article continues:

> However, if the division of duties between the child custodians is agreed by the Social Welfare Board under a law on child custody and access rights (361/1983) or otherwise decided by a court decision, the agreement approved by the Social Welfare Board or the court decision will be followed. (08.02.2019/199)

251. In matters of medical treatment influenced by religious or belief convictions – such as blood transfusion and circumcision – the same age limits apply. In Finland, an adult always has the right to refuse all or part of a medical treatment. The cause may be religious, but there is no need to report any particular reason.

252. Finnish law does not allow **circumcision** with separate rules nor does it prohibit it. Regarding the religious female circumcision of minors, the articles of the Penal Code apply to abuse or gross misconduct. For boys, circumcision is in practice allowed, although the male circumcision of minors has occasionally triggered intense public debate. In 2008, the Supreme Court (KKO) ruled that freedom of religion does not justify the circumcision of boys, but circumcision is nevertheless allowed in support of 'identity development' and 'attachment to the community'. In 2016, in the case KKO:2016:25, the Supreme Court permitted circumcision if permitted by both parents.

253. The Supreme Court refers here to its earlier resolution, (KKO 2008:93), where the circumcision of a 4.5-year-old boy was considered permissible. The circumcision was permitted not as a result of religious freedom but because of the boy's identity and attachment to the community. In its decision (KKO 2008:93), the Supreme Court held that the mother, who was the sole custodian of a 4.5-year-old boy when her son underwent circumcision on religious grounds, did not commit punishable abuse of the child, since the circumcision was related to her child's religion and was carried out using all medical care and without causing unnecessary pain to the child. The Supreme Court decided that, in this case, circumcision had been in the best interest of the child. However, as the mother who consented to the circumcision was the sole custodian of the child, there was no need to comment on the possible impact of the fact that the child's other legal guardians might disagree over the circumcision (paragraph 6).

254. In the other case (KKO 2016:25), a dispute had arisen over a young baby (C) whose mother (D) was a Finn and whose father (A) was Nigerian. The child was circumcised on 7 November 2009, and at the time of the circumcision the child's parents were married and the child was in their joint care, with the family permanently resident in Finland. The procedure was performed by a licensed doctor (B) at the father's family home. The mother did not support the circumcision. The Supreme Court specified that not only religious but also cultural reasons could be sufficient. But in an unclear situation such as this, the child should be left uncircumcised. The position of the father was spelt out in some detail.

255. The Supreme Court found that C's circumcision had been motivated by cultural factors related to his own background and family that were relevant to assessing the admissibility of the measure in terms of criminal liability:

> … cultural circumcision could have similar positive effects on the boy's own identity and social inclusion as if the action were to be taken for religious reasons.

256. However, in this case, A had eventually opted deliberately out of the circumcision of his son in terms of the joint care provided by parents, contrary to the will of the other parent. In doing so, A has acted in breach of the duty of cooperation in Article 5 of the Child Care and Right of Access Act. The Supreme Court concluded that A had committed assault in the manner described in the prosecution:

> The action would be directed at a particularly intimate area of the individual and would be irreversible in nature. Such interference with the physical integrity of a child may only be justified for non-medical reasons if it is clearly and unambiguously in the best interest of the child.
>
> ... Although the circumcision of the child has been closely linked to the cultural background of A, under the circumstances described there have been understandable reasons for the measure, and A must have realized that circumcision could not be clearly considered the best interests of the child. Hence, A cannot be considered exempt from a punishable offence under the differences of opinion set out in Chapter 4, Section 1 of the Penal Code.

257. A decision of the Supreme Court also stated case (KKO 2016:25) that it was irrelevant that offender (B) had also been a doctor: 'decisive from the point of view of criminal liability is not the physician who actually undertook the operation. The decisive factor is whether the measure had been undertaken on the basis of proper medical standards'.

258. In practice, the above-mentioned judgment can be understood as having been reached in relation to a child who has not been circumcised when the parents disagreed with each other.[104]

259. **In the case of transfusions**, Jehovah's Witnesses and some other Christian or Christian-based groups do not wish to receive blood transfusions at all.

260. The law on the status and rights of the patient (785/1992), Article 7(1), reads as follows:

> The opinion of a minor patient on a care or treatment measure should be investigated if it is possible, taking into account the patient's age or development.

104. *See* closer the complete solutions KKO 2016:25 and KKO 2016:24. Three Supreme Administrative Court decisions are now on record regarding the circumcision of boys. *See*, https://korkeinoikeus.fi/fi/index/ennakkopaatokset/precedent/1459333644350.html.

> The care of a minor patient must be done in agreement with the patient, if he can make decisions about the care taking into account age or development.

And Article 7 (2) continues:

> If a minor patient cannot make a decision on the care, he or she shall be cared for in consultation with his or her guardian or some other legal representative.

261. In practice, nowadays, a transfusion will be given in the case of an emergency despite the possible objections of the child's guardians. This is a preliminary precedent set by the Supreme Administrative Court.[105]

§4. *Forum Internum* and Manifestations of Religion or Belief

262. In modern international human rights theory, the absolute protection of freedom of thought, conscience, religion, and belief, as well as of freedom of expression and opinion, has been termed a *forum internum.*[106] In basic terms, this means that the individual is completely free and has the right to maintain his or her own thoughts, whatever they may be (the 'negative' liberty or right).[107] The fundamental right in Article 11(sections 1–2) of the Finnish Constitution provides first for the *inner freedom* to believe, whatever the belief. The second section of Article 11 also guarantees the *external freedom* to make one's belief known and to practise it – 'the right to profess and practise a religion, the right to express one's convictions … '. Implicitly, it also provides for the right of the individual to teach about his or her beliefs and to act according to his or her internal convictions and beliefs. In addition, the RFA, Article 3 section 1, states, that 'Everyone has the right to decide on his or her religious status by joining or resigning from a religious community that accepts him or her'.

§5. The Right Not to Believe

263. In its Article 11, the Finnish constitution also protects the right not to believe and not to confess any belief. The same Article (in its subsection 2) implies that no one is under the obligation, against his or her conscience, to participate in

---

105. KHO 2385/3/99.

106. Peter Petkoff (2012, 184–185) has made a noteworthy observation when he indicates that, with respect to the right to freedom of religion or belief, it has become almost inconceivable in modern international human rights law to conceptualize this right without the dichotomy between the *forum externum* and the *forum internum*. For further detail, *see* Peter Petkoff, 'Forum Internum and Forum Externum in Canon Law and Public International Law with a Particular Reference to the Jurisprudence of the European Court of Human Rights'. In *Jeroen Temperman (ed.), Religion and Human Rights: An international journal. Vol. 7 (3). (Nijhoff: Brill, 2012).*

107. For *Defining freedom in the forum internum in terms of negative liberty, authenticity, and capability, see* Mari Stenlund & Pamela Slotte. 'Forum Internum Revisited: Considering the Absolute Core of Freedom of Belief and Opinion in Terms of Negative Liberty, Authenticity, and Capability'. *Human Rights Review* (19 (4) (2018): 425–446), 430–435.

the practice of a religion. Moreover, everyone also has the right to decline to be a member of any religious community. This right not to believe is usually called a 'negative freedom' without any derogatory intention. The 'negative' right to freedom of religion or belief also protects against having to participate in religious activities or ceremonies of whatever kind. An example of this is the right of pupils not belonging to any religious community to opt out of confessional religious instruction at state public schools. Within the school system, itself this means separate education in the field of ethics, or total exemption.[108]

264. The 'negative' right to freedom of religion also implies that only members of the qualified registered religious community and no one else can be obliged to pay church tax.

§6. Definitions of Religion and Belief

265. The conventional practice of associating both religion and belief under the protection of religious freedom is based on international human rights treaties. In general, as in the laws of individual states, no attempt has been made to further define the content of religion and belief. For example, in the UN's Universal Declaration of Human Rights, the words 'religion' and 'belief' are used as such without any attempt to propose their content. Subsequent international human rights treaties and declarations have also sought to avoid defining religion and its parallel expressions. With regard to the concept of religion, it has been difficult to find a definition that is sufficiently comprehensive but not so broad that it would lose its meaning.[109]

266. National laws, on the other hand, have made it possible to interpret the concept of religion and religion in an almost limitless way. In addition to the practice of religion, it has been possible to incorporate the freedom of expression of all views of life, including agnosticism and atheism. In such an interpretation, the word 'faith' includes both its religious and its non-religious dimensions. However, it is more common – as is the case in Finland – to use the notion of 'religion' and 'belief' in parallel when the protection of religious freedom is to be extended not only to religions but also to different ways of life and different worldviews.[110] Since religion and philosophical creed (belief) are protected in the same way under the Finnish constitution, it is not important for the legislator to find a clear-cut distinction between these two.

---

108. The formulation used in the relevant laws is neutral. Based on the law of religious freedom (453/2003) and the current school laws, every student in comprehensive and upper comprehensive schools has a right to religious teaching according to his or her own confession. The communal school system is responsible for its organization and funding. Students who do not belong to a church or religious community participate in world-view studies (ethics). In the matriculation examination, it is possible to take either a test related to one's own religion or to world-view studies.

109. Juha Seppo, *Uskonnonvapaus 2000-luvun Suomessa* (*Freedom of Religion in 21st Century Finland*) (Helsinki: Edita, 2003), 12.

110. *Ibid.*

267. However, religion is not, in terms of content, comparable to belief, although it is often referred to as 'religious belief'. Religion differs most from belief in the way that religion and its practice are often associated in one way or another with worship. The practice of religion is not only private but also communal and public, with an institutional, social, and cultural dimension.

268. Belief (conviction) is a much more private phenomenon than religion. Nonetheless, belief and its expression rarely have communal dimensions, not to mention that the belief of the individual would always be public. In Finnish tradition, the concept of belief or conviction is often associated with the political sphere rather than with a general philosophy of life. In the context of religious freedom, belief refers to life or to worldview. The content of the belief may vary from religious to completely non-religious and anti-religious beliefs. The question always concerns the individual's worldview, his or her fundamental values of life, and the solutions related to them.[111]

269. In Finnish law, the distinction between practising religion and expressing one's belief is noticeably evident, for example, in the Criminal Code (536/1998). It criminalizes not only blasphemy but also violation of the peace of faith (uskonrauhan rikkominen) and the obstruction of religious practice (CC 17: 10, 11). Blasphemy and insults against any religious community operating in Finland is punishable act. Expression of conviction or belief has no equivalent criminal law protection.[112]

270. In criminal law, the protection of religion is based on the idea of the public nature of the communal practice of religion. Hence, no private view or conviction (belief) – whether religious or non-religious – falls within the scope of criminal law protection. This does not naturally mean that, for example, criticism of an atheist worldview could be anchored in defamation, slander or shame.

271. Professor Kimmo Nuotio[113] draws attention to the fact that the case law on religious offences is rather limited, making it difficult to reach definite conclusions. 'As regards blasphemy, it is likely that all of the cases that have arisen so far have dealt with protection of a traditional core area of such provisions, namely blasphemy against God.'[114]

111. *Ibid.*, 10.
112. Kimmo Nuotio, 'Religion in the Criminal Law of Finland'. In Matti Kotiranta & Norman Doe (eds), *Religion and Criminal Law. Religion et Droit Pénal.* (Leuven: Peeters, 2013), 67–68.
113. Kimmo Nuotio is Professor of Criminal Law at the University of Helsinki.
114. Nuotio 2013, 67.

§7. PROTECTED MANIFESTATIONS

I. General Scope of Guarantee

272. Freedom of religion or conviction (belief) provides full freedom to practice religion undisturbed. Although Article 11 section 2 of the Finnish Constitution speaks only of religion and not explicitly of philosophical creed, it is clear that freedom of religion also equally protects the practice of philosophical creed. The right to profess and practice religion is conceived in a very broad sense and it includes also the right to change one's religion and the right to decide on one's religious status by joining or resigning from a religious community that has accepted the individual (RFA Article 3 paragraph 1).

273. The practice of religion covers cultic activities and the exercise of religious customs such as religious services, prayers, applying and receiving sacraments, processions, or bell-ringing on Sundays and festive times. It also covers the construction of churches and other religious buildings for the practice of religion. In addition, it includes religious education, religious events, and the education of free-religious or non-religious communities as well as other manifestations of religious or belief life. Religious freedom also provides for the right of the individual to the teaching of his or her belief and to act according to his or her internal convictions and beliefs.

II. Specific Issues

A. Proselytism

274. Proselytism is not prohibited, and it is both a legal and a legitimate religious practice as long as it does not disturb the public order.[115]

275. Advertising a religion in public is legal and it is quite common in Finland that some of the free churches and the Jehovah's Witnesses have stands on street corners. However, the legitimate needs and interests of other users of the street also have to be taken into account. Public order violations, such as a loud performance, shouting, or playing music excessively loudly for religious purposes may be illegal, like any other activity that violates the social space.

276. The distribution of religious magazines and flyers that are generally intended for households has recently become a problematic matter from the point of freedom of expression.

115. The provision on proselytizing was formally abolished as late as in 1971. Chapter 10 s. 5 in the penal code of 1889/1894, however, set relatively strict conditions for punishable proselytizing.

277. There exists a particularly interesting case concerning a violation of a church's freedom of expression in the 'Deputy Parliamentary Ombudsman's decision on the matter (3851/4/05)'. The Deputy Parliamentary Ombudsman determined that the Evangelical Lutheran Parish of Rekola in Vantaa had acted illegally when it distributed magazines intended for its members more widely, to households that were not members. In his discussion of the principles behind his decision, the Deputy Ombudsman referred to the freedom of religion provisions contained in section 11 of the Constitution and Article 9 of the European Convention on Human Rights (ECHR), which include the right not to belong to a given religious community.

278. The decision aroused criticism even in the Constitutional Law Committee (Perustuslakivaliokunta), which noted in its report (17/2006) with reference to Article 9 of the ECHR that both this document and the Constitution provide powerful protection for freedom of expression in matters of religious and philosophical communication. In its opinion, there was no justification for placing greater restrictions on the freedom of expression of church parishes or on the circulation of their publications than on the distribution of advertising leaflets or newspapers or the publications of political or other ideological bodies. In light of this opinion, the Council of the ELCF concluded that the statement issued by the Deputy Parliamentary Ombudsman was against the law.

B. Conscientious Objection

1. Dress Requirements

279. In Finland, individuals are free to wear religious symbols (e.g., crucifixes or scarves) in public places and in basic education or in upper secondary schools. There is no law or regulation, which forbids the wearing of religious garments, nor is there legislation that gives permission for an individual to use religious garments or scarves.

280. There are, however, two exceptions to this rule. The first is connected with safety regulations. The labour law obliges employers and employees to follow safety instructions. It is possible, for instance, that it is not permitted to wear a scarf if the individual is working with machinery, since this well may be injurious to health.

281. The second exception considers offending an individual's religious feelings. The current penal provisions no longer protect God's honour but, rather, the religious convictions and feelings of others, and religious peace in general. Religious peace means religious order, comparable with the general category of 'law and order'.[116] This means, in practice, that it is illegal to be dressed in an insulting manner that would openly affront another individual's religious convictions.

282. It is also noteworthy that the question of religious garments worn by teachers and students has yet to be discussed by the Finnish National Board of Education, and hence the Board has yet to issue official instructions for the guidance of schools.

283. A few cases regarding religious headdress and clothing have nevertheless been examined in courts nationally. For example, the uniforms of security guards and police officers are regulated by-laws and decrees, and religious headdress is not a part of such uniforms. For those who normally use a headdress, this neutral uniform can too easily limit the access of individuals who are Sikhs or female Muslims to posts and professions of certain kinds. The Finnish Chancellor of Justice and also the Ombudsman monitor the activities of the authorities hence they are frequently in a position on whether a particular dress code is constitutional. Until now, however, there has not yet been any case at either a local court or at the upper court level concerned with the wearing of a burqa (i.e., a black, full-cover garment with a headscarf).

2. Co-educative Physical Education

284. Objection on the basis of religious convictions to participating in co-educational Physical Education classes is not permitted. Elementary school students in Finland participate in the basic education laid down by the Basic Education Act and Decree. Section 11 of the Act contains a list of the subjects provided in primary education.

285. The law does not recognize the possibility of not participating in basic education because of religious or ethical beliefs. In the case of disagreement, the content of a given subject has to be agreed upon with the child's guardian, and the school will provide the guardian with a range of solutions that may be feasible according to the day-to-day organization of the school. In other words, the school has the final say.

286. Primary school student teachers receive the undergraduate education provided by the Basic Education Act and the Decree, where section 11 of the Act contains a list of the subjects to be followed in primary education.

287. The Finnish National Agency for Education (Opetushallitus) and the Education Division of the City of Helsinki recommend that 'the school is permitted to

116. For further detail, *see* Kimmo Nuotio, 'Religion in the Criminal Law of Finland'. In Matti Kotiranta & Norman Doe (eds), *Religion and Criminal Law. Religion et Droit Pénal* (Leuven: Peeters, 2013), 65 and Part VII, Ch. 8. *Penal Law and Religion.*

follow flexible teaching arrangements and to vary its teaching within the stated limits'. Thus, the City of Helsinki has the following guidelines for Muslim exercise:

> When using the shower, Muslim students can be treated flexibly so that they may be permitted to take their shower a little earlier than the other students. In some schools, Muslim students may also be permitted to use a separate shower cubicle, subject to availability at the school.
>
> The physical exercise itself must be undertaken in appropriate clothing. The clothing should not prevent the student from moving freely, and within the framework of the Muslim dress code, it is possible to find appropriate footwear and other accessories that can be used for physical exercise classes.

288. Some Muslim parents have agreed that girls may swim while wearing a long T-shirt. This must, however, always be agreed in advance with the swimming bath, since not all swimming baths permit long T-shirts for swimming.

3. Work on Religious Holidays

289. Objection to working on religious days of rest is part of freedom of religion. Work on Sundays or religious holidays can be ordered only with the consent of the employee if the extra pay is also regularly performed on Sundays or by agreement in the employment contract. Many employers are ready to consider their employees' religious needs.

290. Church holidays for which Sunday instruction is applied are New Year's Day, Epiphany, Good Friday, Easter Monday, Ascension Day, Midsummer Day, Independence Day, Christmas Eve, and the First and Second days of Christmas.

291. Compensation for work done on religious (public) holidays is also determined by collective agreements in the field. Sunday work must pay a salary that is increased by 100%. The work done as Sunday work cannot be exchanged for free time, and the work done on Sundays must also be paid to the employee for any additional overtime compensation if they are entitled to such pay.

292. The Competitiveness Agreement (kilpailukykysopimus, kiky-agreement) concluded by the labour market organizations in the Spring of 2016 agreed on an extension of actual working time and also amended the provisions related to public holidays in some collective agreements.

4. Conscientious Objection to Medical Treatment

293. An adult always has the right to refuse all or part of the medical treatment offered. The grounds for such refusal may be religious, but there is no obligation on the part of the patient to provide any particular reason. In matters of medical treatment influenced by religious or belief convictions – such as blood transfusion and circumcision – the age of legal maturity is reached at 18. For closer information, *see* Part II, Chapter 1, §3, II B. *Practical Implications of Religious Maturity.*

5. Conscientious Objection to Taking an Oath

294. The right to object to taking an oath on religious grounds is protected. No one can be obliged to take an oath that includes a religious formula; an alternative form of affirmation is provided. For further details, *see* Part I, Chapter 1, VI. *Oath of Office.*

6. Conscientious Objection and Military Service

295. Objection to military service is a fundamental right made explicit in Article 127 subsection 2 of the Finnish Constitution: 'Provisions on the right to exemption, on grounds of conscience, from participation in military national defence are laid down by an Act.' The details are regulated by the Conscription Act (1438/2007). (15.3.2019/331), where Article 3, subsection 2, states:

> Provisions on exemption from participation in military defence due to conviction are contained in the Civil Service Act (1446/2007).

296. More precisely stated, religion and belief constitute reasons based on conviction that permit objection to compulsory military service. The Civil Service Act (1446/2007) reads:

> A conscript who for reasons based on conviction is prevented from fulfilling his or her duties under the Conscription Act (1438/2007) is exempt from duty and is ordered to perform civil service in accordance with the provisions of this Act.
>
> This law also applies to women who apply for civilian service after the expiry specified in section 4, subsection 1, in the Act on Voluntary Military Service for Women (194/1995).

297. It is a criminal offence in Finland not to perform the compulsory military or civil service. This has led to problems in cases where people have objected to both the military and the alternative civilian service. This has occurred especially in cases involving Jehovah's Witnesses, who were previously referred to as total objectors. Jehovah's Witnesses were released from both military and civilian service in the mid-1980s by statutory exception.

298. The disqualification arose in the debate in 2018 after the Helsinki Court of Appeal released a 23-year-old total objector and repealed the sentence that had been previously imposed on him. The man said that 'he considered it discriminatory to exempt Jehovah's Witnesses from national defence forces on the basis of conviction, whereas the same argument does not apply to other convictions'. The Court of

Appeal ruled that the man's reasoning was correct. Shortly thereafter, the Ministry of Defence working group proposed abandoning the exemption entirely.

299. Thus, Jehovah's Witnesses will no longer be released from military service. Exemptions based on religious beliefs passed into history on 20 February 2019. The bill was amended during the parliamentary process so that the law on exemption was repealed without a transitional period. Jehovah's Witnesses can now no longer apply for an exemption from military service on the basis of their religion.[117]

C. Parental Care

300. A family's inner religious teaching is conducted in Finland either by a child's guardians, by one of his or her guardians, or by a particular religious community. Belonging to a small religious community or sect is not a legitimate reason to suspend the right of custody nor does it justify the refusal of custody of a child in the event of divorce.

301. 'Religious education' – that is, the transmission of a religious tradition from one generation to another – can be practised by both individuals and communities. In this case, the educator's goal is to socialize the child in order to promote the standards, values, and practices of a particular religious community. The guardians of religious families often regard religion as so important in their lives that they desire to pass on religious doctrines and values to their forthcoming generations.

302. A religious upbringing can be considered successful when it serves the needs of a child's mental health and well-being in general. When, however, the religion of the child's guardians is too restrictive, both religion and religious home education may also have adverse effects on the child's life.

D. Ritual Slaughter and Other Religious Food Requirements

1. Ritual Slaughter

303. Ritual slaughter is permitted in accordance with freedom of religion. In general, for the sake of animal protection, the Finnish Animal Protection Act prohibits slaughtering without previous stunning of the animal. The minimum standards for killing and slaughtering are laid down in the Animal Protection Act, the Animal Welfare Regulation, the Ministry of Agriculture and Forestry's decision on animal protection requirements for the killing of farm animals of mammalian and

117. About 'Disobedient Subjects', *see* closer Kati Nieminen, 'Disobedient Subjects – Constructing the Subject, the State and Religion in the European Court of Human Rights'. Social Identities (2015) 21 (4): 312–327. *See also*, Kati Nieminen, https://helda.helsinki.fi/bitstream/handle/10138/195911/THELAWTH.pdf?sequence=1&isAllowed=y. *Diss.*

bird species and its amendment, and the decision and its amendment produced by the Ministry of Agriculture and Forestry regarding the animal welfare requirements applicable to animal slaughter.

304. Legislation makes it compulsory to treat animals well and to prohibit them from undergoing unnecessary suffering. The killing of an animal must be carried out as quickly as possible so that the animal is spared any avoidable pain, suffering, injury, and fear. The killing of an animal may be carried out only by a person who has sufficient knowledge of the techniques of slaughter, including the particular techniques to be applied in the process of slaughtering a particular animal species, including the competence to perform the actual procedure.

305. At the beginning of 2013, Council Regulation (EC) No. 1099/2009 concerning the protection of animals at the time of slaughter, i.e., the application of the termination regulation, came into force in Finland. The Closure Regulation 'lays down rules for the slaughter of animals reared or kept for the production of food'.

306. The Council Regulation also obliges animals to be protected against avoidable pain and suffering during their slaughter and related activities. The preamble to the regulation states, among other things, that: 'The slaughter of animals may cause pain, distress, fear, or other forms of suffering to the animals even under the best available technical conditions. --- any person involved in the slaughter of animals should take the necessary measures to avoid pain and minimise the distress and suffering of animals during the slaughtering or killing process, taking into account the best practices in the field and the methods permitted under this Regulation' (paragraph 2).

307. In order to prevent avoidable pain, distress, and suffering, and thus a prerequisite for a successful cessation event, emphasis is placed on the importance of advance planning and the appropriate training of personnel.

308. Shehita (Hebrew שחיטה) is a ritual slaughter method practised by Jews. According to the Finnish Animal Protection Act, the animal must be stunned before bleeding. If the animal is not stunned before bleeding, slaughter will cause pain. The main problem is that Jews are not permitted to stun their slaughter animals before or even at the same time as opening the throat, because the animal must be in good condition and completely undamaged at the time of slaughter. For this reason, the righteous shechita slaughter is forbidden in Finland, and kosher meat is brought into Finland from abroad.

309. In contrast, Muslim Halal meat is slaughtered by cutting the animal's throat swiftly with a knife. This permits a special type of slaughter for religious reasons where bleeding is initiated simultaneously with the stunning of the animal. In practice, in accordance with Finnish legislation, halal meat is slaughtered in Finland only by stunning the animal first before bleeding. Many Islamic communities accept this practice. According to animal protection legislation, a veterinarian inspector must always be present when slaughter is carried out in accordance with a specific method of slaughter for religious reasons.

310. The Animal Welfare Act contains a provision on religious slaughter and the Animal Welfare Regulation contains a whole chapter on how such slaughter is to be conducted. There is also a penalty provision contained in the law.

311. Animal Protection Act, section 14 (585/2013) reads:

> **Animal welfare crime**
>
> Anyone who, intentionally or through gross negligence by means of assault, excessive strain, neglect of the necessary care or nourishment, or otherwise provisions by
>
> 1) the Animal Welfare Act (247/1996) or any provision made under it,
> 2) the Animal Transport Act (1429/2006) or any provision made under it,
> 3) Annex I to Council Regulation (EC) No 1/2005 on the protection of animals during the transport and related operations and amending Directives 64/432 / EEC and 93/119 / EC and Regulation (EC) No 1255/97;
> 4) Council Regulation (EC) No 1099/2009 on the protection of animals at the time of killing
>   (b) treat an animal cruelly or with unnecessary suffering, pain or distress, be punishable by a fine or imprisonment for up to two years.

312. Section 14a (14/1/2011) reads:

> **Aggravated animal welfare offences**
>
> An animal welfare crime has been committed if:
>
> 1) the offense is committed in a particularly cruel or cruel manner;
> 2) the crime involves a significant number of animals; or
> 3) by seeking significant economic benefits
>
> and the crime as a whole is also gross, the offender must be sentenced to a minimum of four months and a maximum of four years for a serious animal welfare offence.

313. Section 15 (14/1/2011) reads:

> **Minor animal welfare offences**
>
> If the animal welfare offence, taking into account the extent of the suffering, pain or discomfort of any kind caused or any other circumstances related to an offence involved in the slaughter, the offender must be fined for a minor animal welfare offence.

In light of the evidence found, it does not appear that there are any precedents governing religious slaughter in Finland.

2. Religious Food Requirements in Schools and Public Institutions

State Schools

314. In the Finnish legal system, the school authorities must do what is possible to answer the dietary needs of religious students. Meals are implemented in accordance with the curriculum (National Board of Education): 'School meals take into account the health, social and cultural significance of meals.'

315. Diets deviating from the basic diet at school:

> The pupil is in a safe learning environment at school and is offered school meals as part of pupil care. Sometimes, for example, health reasons require eating that is different from the actual menu. The special needs of a child with allergies, ethics, or religion are taken into account when planning his or her schoolwork and meals. The planning and implementation is based on the operating principles of the municipality or school.[118]

316. How the special needs of religion are taken into account depends on the guidelines of the various municipalities. In large cities such as Helsinki, religiously related school meals are organized in connection with special diets. A Muslim halal meal or a Jewish kosher meal will not be delivered separately.

317. Parents of each student must complete a card for the school nurse stating allergies and special diets. Muslim parents *do not necessarily tell directly about the special needs of religion, but report food restrictions:* 'no pork, no cutting of skin, and no food made of blood'.

318. Regarding the observance of Ramadan, the instructions of imams in Finland are that students do not have to observe fasting in schools during Ramadan. Problems usually arise, however, from the fact that older students want to follow Ramadan.

319. In large cities, teachers are provided with guidelines outlining what teachers should consider for religious minorities (Muslims, Jews, etc.). The instructions of the City of Helsinki Education Department[119] put it in the following way:

> SCHOOL MEALS
>
> According to the Qur'an, a Muslim cannot eat pork or its derivatives (ham, cold cuts, etc.) or any blood dishes. Beef, mutton, chicken and turkey, which are commonly used in Finland, are allowed. For some families, the way meat is slaughtered can become a problem. Some Muslims eat nothing but the so-called halal meat slaughtered by draining blood from a carcass and reciting

---

118. At https://www.oph.fi/fi/koulutus-ja-tutkinnot/kouluruokailu-kuuluu-kaikille.
119. *See* http://achiaro.mbnet.fi/docs/muslimioppilaat_hki.pdf.

a Muslim prayer during the procedure. 'There is a passage in the Qur'an that eating meat slaughtered by Jews and/or Christians is allowed, and many Muslim families use ordinary Finnish beef, mutton, chicken and turkey.

Additives that may contain porcine substances (e.g., gelatin) are sometimes a problem. The fat in the additive can be checked with the manufacturer if the Muslim family is accurate in this matter. There are no resources or obligations for staff or service providers to review school food additives. The guardian or student can verify the matter with the manufacturer. Some products have already been reviewed, such as ice creams from Valio that contain only herbal additives. Many Muslim families follow the interpretation that in the process of making the additive, substances derived from pigs have decomposed and combined with other substances so that they are no longer a prohibited substance within the meaning of the Qur'an.

Schools offer a varied, full-fledged and guided school meal that covers part of a young person's daily nutritional needs. School meals complement home-based meals. Meals are arranged in the school restaurant as a self-service, allowing the student to prepare their own meal. School lunch is served daily from 10 a.m. to noon. The meal includes hot food, salad, grated or fresh piece, crispbread and Lei fat. Milk, buttermilk and water are available as food drinks. The menus (basic and vegetarian menus) are revolving and last for six weeks.

Approximately 70%–80% of the main dishes on the basic menu are suitable for Muslims as such. The suitability of dishes for Muslims is clearly and illustratively marked on school menus. If the main course at school is pork-based, there is an alternative hot meal available to Muslim students, compiled based on basic and vegetarian options. If for some reason the available option does not satisfy the student, the meal can be supplemented with bread, milk, salad and grated.

The need for a Muslim diet is indicated by the guardian on a special diet form. The form is returned to the school nurse or class teacher. Participation in fasting is one of the five basic pillars of the Islamic religion. A holy month of fasting, Ramadan takes place at a slightly different time each year. Usually, children under adolescence do not fast, but this varies depending on the family. Some children may fast as early as primary school, some practise fasting one or two days a week. In many families, internship days are on the weekends so that schoolwork does not suffer. It has been found to be a good practice for the guardian or student himself to inform the kitchen in advance whether he intends to fast and whether there are any interruptions in the fast. Students in the upper grades should be reminded to report.[120]

Public institutions

320. Religious food requirements are respected in public institutions. As stated in the Order of Criminal Sanctions Authority (Food Service and Diets, Dnro 8/004/

---

120. *Ibid.*, 8–9.

2015), prison authorities must ensure that prisoners are able to follow their religious communities' nutritional rules. Departures from the basic prison diet on the grounds of religious or other legitimate beliefs will be decided by a supervising prison officer or security officer.

321. Article 6.2.1. of the Order of Criminal Sanctions Authority, Dnro 8/004/2015, subsection 1, states:

> The prisoner's own declaration of his religion constitutes a justification for a special diet based on religion. The demands of religion regarding diet are taken into account on the basis of what is commonly known about them within a given religion.

322. However, the prisoner's special wishes cannot be considered as religious claims. Subsection 2 states:

> It should be possible to provide a given religious diet by means of the normal prison food procurement procedures and contracts. No special products will be available at the expense of the prison that cannot be obtained from the usual places of purchase used by the prison.

323. Subsection 3 emphasizes that the basic diet of the prison should be followed as much as possible. In the prison kitchen, meals that differ from the basic diet offered to prisoners of different religions must be recorded. As far as possible, a diet that is based on religious grounds will follow the nutritional recommendations of the Finnish Nutrition Advisory Board.

324. Hospitals must also respect religious food requirements. Special diets based on enhanced diet, altered diet, illness, allergy, or religious reasons will be followed as required. However, there is no specific legislation in this field, although some large hospital districts have provided guidance on how religious needs can be taken into account when meals are being designed.

325. With regard to the Finnish Defence Forces (FDF), the General Service Regulations 2017 include a brief annex on 'specific issues of religious practice'. It explicitly mentions Judaism and Islam, but the principles also apply to other religions. Here, religious diets 'also seek to take ethical diets into account'. During Ramadan, Muslims must be given the opportunity to dine between sunset and sunrise. Muslims are also given the opportunity to pray during the breaks in their military service.

§8. Horizontal Application

326. Freedom of religion or conviction (belief) is today understood as the right of both the individual and the religious entities (communities). In relation to the individual, this implies the innate right of every person to practice religion publicly and privately according to their conscience, understanding and choice. Everyone is free to recognize his/her faith and practice it with others. This presupposes that general law has to be interpreted and applied in a way that is compatible with the values expressed in the fundamental rights[121] guaranteed by the Constitution.

327. The horizontal application of fundamental rights and thus freedom of religion is realized in Finland primarily through the positive obligations of the state to act and, in practice, through legislation, which then also applies to the interpersonal relationship between individuals. Here, one particularly central law is the Equality Act (1325/2014) and its section 8, which deals with the prohibition of discrimination and its enforcement.[122]

328. In light of Finnish court cases,[123] it seems that the conflicts occurring between the freedom of religion or conscience and tasks required in an office have been resolved on a case-by-case basis. However, it would be ideal that the conflicting interests of private individuals could be weighed up so that both parties in the conflict could exercise as many of their rights as possible. This is of considerable importance in the field of labour law but also includes many other areas of life. In Finland, one can refuse employment completely or can refuse to do any part of a job on the basis of one's own religious beliefs.[124] One can also refuse to do work for a specific time period, or an employee could request permission to use the veil

---

121. Fundamental rights protect all persons within the jurisdiction of Finland. As a matter of fundamental rights – as the subject of the fundamental right – the owner is usually *everyone*. Everyone is a natural person. Instead, *legal persons* are indirectly protected by fundamental rights because the lack of legal personality may constitute a violation of the rights of the individual behind the legal entity. HE 309/1993 vp, 21–25.

122. Section 8 of the Equality Act (1325/2014) on the Prohibition of discrimination reads:

   (1) No one may be discriminated against on the basis of age, origin, nationality, language, religion, belief, opinion, political activity, trade union activity, family relationships, state of health, disability, sexual orientation or other personal characteristics. Discrimination is prohibited, regardless of whether it is based on a fact an assumption concerning the person him/herself or another.
   (2) In addition to direct and indirect discrimination, harassment, denial of reasonable accommodation as well as an instruction or order to discriminate constitute discrimination as referred to in this Act.

123. *See*, for example, the following cases: A Muslim wanted to use the veil at work and was not offered employment. Unemployment benefits could not be withheld. The vote was 4 to 1 (*see* Insurance Law 1713:96); A non-Lutheran refused to clean a Lutheran Church. According to Insurance Law, unemployment benefits could not be withheld. The vote was 4 to 1 (*see* Insurance Law 05142/96/955); A Jehovah's Witness refused clerical work with the Finnish Armed Forces, and unemployment benefits could not be withheld. The vote was 4–1 (*see* Insurance Law 12569:95); A 'can advocate' interpretation, according to which a person can refuse to work on a Saturday without losing unemployment benefits (*see* Attorney General 420/1/99) and a pacifist who had completed service as a conscientious objector refused work as a warehouse worker in an Armed Forces Unit, and unemployment benefits were not withheld. The vote was 3 to 2 (*see* Insurance Law 4286:99).

124. The Act on Employment Insurance 30.12.2002/1290 states briefly: *The job seeker has a valid reason to refuse employment if the employment is against his or her religion or consciousness.* In comparison, other approved non-physical reasons for refusing employment are included in the act as 'obscene or improper' work.

or make a similar type of request. This raises questions of when an employer has the right to dismiss an employee, when the unemployed person loses, for example, his or her unemployment benefits if they refuse a job offered to them. However, in general, a reasonable solution can be found, and many companies have, for example, organized prayer rooms for Muslim employees, while working processes have been scheduled in a way that believers can follow their religious rules.

§9. Limitations to Freedom of Religion or Belief

I. General Principles of Limitation

A. *Special Importance of Freedom and Religion or Belief*

329. The Finnish constitution guarantees the freedom of religion or conviction (belief) in its Article 11 without providing for any specific, explicit limitations. More precisely, the article does not contain a specific (qualified) restriction clause. This does not mean that no limitations exist. Freedom of religion or conviction holds a foremost place in human rights and is considered by the Constitution to be of the utmost importance. Any restrictions on the freedom of religion and conscience are therefore subject to restrictions on fundamental rights. Religious freedom is closely linked to the prohibition of discrimination based on religion or belief contained in Article 6 §2 of the Constitution. In addition to this denial, there is an obligation on the part of the public authorities to treat all religious communities and world views equally.[125]

B. *The Variety of Limitations*

330. There is no general law in Finland on limitations of fundamental rights. This concerns both freedom of religion and *all fundamental rights, which share the same constitutional validity*. Nor does the Constitution provide for a general rule on limitations.[126]

331. Since the Finnish Constitution does not contain a general rule on the restriction of fundamental rights, the permissibility of restrictions on fundamental rights is determined by the fulfilment of the general conditions of the restriction of fundamental rights developed in Finnish legislation and law.

125. HE 309/1993 vp, 55; *See also* PeVM 10/2002 vp, 2.

126. Nevertheless, regarding with Ch. 10 of the Constitution – **Supervision of legality** – there need to be two important clarifications. First, according to Art. 106, the court of law shall give primacy to the provision in the Constitution ' … if, in a matter being tried by a court of law, the application of an Act would be in evident conflict with the Constitution'. Second, according to Art. 107, ' … a provision in a Decree or another statute of a lower level than an Act shall not be applied by a court of law or by any other public authority'.

332. Fundamental rights are primarily binding and obligatory for public power. Traditionally, the rule of fundamental rights has been to protect the individual's freedom from interference from the state. However, not all public activities can be restored to state actions. Similarly, the activities of the municipality, the Association of Finnish Local and Regional Authorities, *the Evangelical Lutheran Church*, the Province of Åland, and the activities of a public law body, as well as activities similar to those of public authorities, are public activities in terms of fundamental rights.[127]

333. In relationships between private individuals, fundamental rights are generally influenced by ordinary law.[128] However, some fundamental rights provisions have been formulated as precise and unconditional bans.[129] Therefore, they cannot be exempted from ordinary law.

334. Before it is possible to talk about the restriction of a fundamental right – such as freedom of religion – it is necessary to decide whether it is a matter of the fundamental rule of law, that is to say, whether a provision of fundamental rights is relevant to the regulation of a person's behavioural limitations (e.g., prisoners, soldiers)[130] or absence of an individual's legal status (e.g., fundamental rights of children *v.* religious maturity, which is reached only at the age of 18).

335. In cases of doubt, the interpretation approach can be broadly interpreted in relation to the scope of the fundamental right. For example, the circle of freedom of expression *as such* covers all kinds of expressions, whatever their purpose may be. Thus, for example, religious advertising – distribution of religious magazines and leaflets – cannot be excluded from the protection of freedom of expression, but the regulation imposed on them must be seen as a restriction whose assessment of admissibility may be relevant to the fact that religious advertising, which is not restricted solely to members of a certain religious community, is not considered to be a core area of freedom of expression. Thus, the Deputy Parliamentary Ombudsman's decision on the matter (3851/4/05), in which he determined that the Evangelical Lutheran Parish had acted illegally when it distributed magazines intended for its members to households that were not members. The Deputy Ombudsman's

---

127. HE 309/1993, 25–29. Italics mine.
128. HE 309/1993, 25–29.
129. Such unconditional prohibitions of the Constitution are: Non-discrimination (s. 6(2)), Prohibition of treatment death penalty, torture and dignity (s. 7(2)), Prohibition of arbitrary interference with one's personal integrity and arbitrary detention (s. 7(3)), Prohibition of retrospective Penal Code (s. 8), Prohibition preventing Finnish citizens from entering the country and prohibiting them from leaving the country (s. 9(2)), Restriction on the deportation of foreign nationals (s. 9(4)), and Prohibition of undeclared work (s. 18(3)).
130. The national defence obligation provided for in Art. 127(1) of the Constitution states, in itself, an acceptable justification for limiting the fundamental rights of conscripts: 'Every Finnish citizen is obligated to participate or assist in national defence, as provided by an Act.'

decision referred to the freedom of religion provisions contained in section 11 of the Constitution and Article 9 of the ECHR, which include the right not to belong to any religious community.[131]

336. The basic constitutional provisions of the Constitution of Finland are absolute in the sense that they are not to be restricted in any way. Certain fundamental and human rights (such as discrimination on grounds of skin colour, religion and ethnicity, prohibition of torture, death penalty, slavery, and forced labour) are inviolable under all circumstances, including in exceptional circumstances such as war. Likewise, the prohibition of retrospective punishment and, in general, the principle of legality in criminal law.[132] Since the human rights treaties set a minimum level of domestic fundamental rights protection, the ECHR and the International Covenant on Civil and Political Rights (ICCPR) treaties also apply to the Finnish constitution.

337. The need for limitation is often based on a collision of different fundamental rights. It is important to notice that limiting one fundamental right is a prerequisite for the implementation of another fundamental right. In the case of a collision of fundamental rights, a solution must be sought which would as much as possible ensure the simultaneous realization of all competing fundamental rights. The aim is thus to achieve the best possible balance between the fundamental rights to be reconciled. The conflicts between fundamental rights have to be resolved both in general terms when legislating and in a concrete legislative situation.

338. From the point of Finnish jurisprudence, a more general theoretical framework[133] that highlights the differences between US and European (especially German) fundamental rights thinking is the two-fold theory – external constraints *v.* internal borders – first presented by Dr Mikko Hoikka[134] and further developed by Elina Finska in terms of the application of fundamental rights is very useful here:

> The fundamental interest in the application of fundamental rights is the assessment of the legitimacy of the limitation of rights. The justification for objectively securing the applicability of a particular fundamental right in the particular case is not so significant. In his study, Mikko Hoikka states that the scope of the relationship between discretion and restriction doctrine is based on the so-called theory of external constraints in such a framework. The theory

131. For closer information, *see* I. Specific Issues, A. *Proselytism.*
132. For more detail, *see* Art. 15 of the ECHR and Art. 4 of UN's ICCPR agreement, and Art. 23 of the Finnish Constitution.
133. **The most important conditions for restrictions, i.e., how they actually work in the formulation of Finland's fundamental rights,** is described in more detail in the following section: *III. Limitations of Limitations (Restrictions of Restrictions), 1–7.*
134. Originally, the area of freedom of speech according to the theory of external constraints. *See* Mikko Hoikka. *Sananvapaus Euroopan unionin oikeudessa* (Freedom of Expression in European Union Law). (Helsinki: Suomalainen lakimiesyhdistys, A 289, 2009), 63. *Diss.*

implies that while the scope of the individual rights is defined broadly, their content must be determined through permissible and prohibited restrictions of rights.

339. In *the theory of external constraints* (Figure 1), the fundamental scope of the fundamental right is defined as all measures regardless of their content and form (I). Instead of the inherent limits of fundamental rights, the review focuses on restrictive measures and their legitimacy, and on prohibited and permitted restrictions on fundamental rights (II and III). Since the appropriateness of many fundamental rights, and often the existence of a restriction, is not a problem in the interpretation practice, the fundamental rights argument is generally directed at the criteria according to which restrictions may be interpreted as constitutional or contrary to the so-called restrictions on fundamental rights or restrictions on restrictions (limitations on limitations).[135] Examples of the practice, which follows the theory of external constraints, are the decisions of the German Constitutional Court and the European Court of Human Rights (ECtHR).[136]

Figure 1

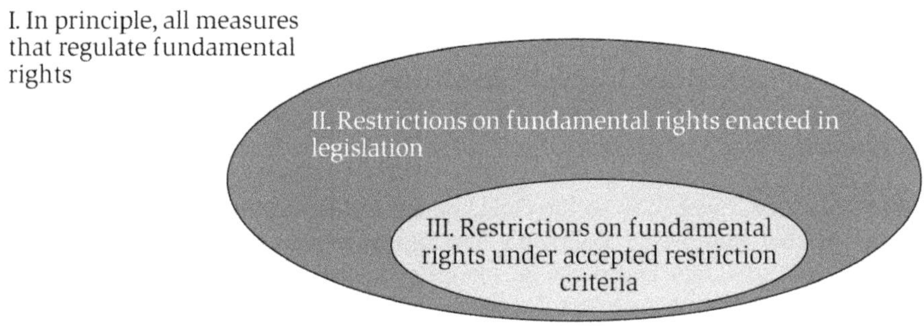

340. According to *the theory of internal borders* (Figure 2), fundamental rights have their own internal boundaries, which define the measures that fall within and outside the scope of fundamental rights. Acts whose interpretation falls within the scope of the protection of fundamental rights cannot be prohibited or restricted by law (I). Measures that are not interpreted as enjoying the protection of fundamental rights can, from a constitutional point of view, be either allowed or prohibited freely (II and III). In other words, the fact that the content of a measure is not prohibited by the legal system does not necessarily mean that it is a constitutional exercise of fundamental rights. The theory of internal borders has also been incorporated not only in the US and France but also, in the praxis of the European Union Court.[137]

135. *See also* Gerhard Robbers, *Germany*. In *International Encyclopaedia of Laws: Religion*, edited by Rik Torfs. Alphen aan den Rijn, NL (Kluwer Law International, 2013), 87–88.
136. Hoikka 2009, 63 and Finska 2014, 37. (*See* the following note).
137. Hoikka 2009, 62 and Elina Finska, *Perusoikeuksien rajoittamistestien vertailu Euroopan unionin tuomioistuimen ja Euroopan ihmisoikeustuomioistuimen ratkaisukäytännöissä* (Comparison of fundamental rights restriction tests in the case law of the European Court of Justice and the European

Figure 2 III Measures Prohibited by Legislation

C. System of Limitation Clauses

341. In addition to the above-mentioned multiple restrictions, it is possible to find something like a system of limitation clauses.

342. Professor Veli-Pekka Viljanen[138] has stated that the Finnish legal doctrine basically distinguishes three levels of limitations to fundamental rights: (1) limitations according to the balance between the two fundamental rights, (2) reservations by law: a collision of fundamental rights may occur as a collision between the different fundamental rights of the same person, and (3) limitations inherent in the Constitution.[139]

343. So, first, there may be the fundamental rights of two people. For example, the unrestricted exercise of a person's freedom of movement may threaten another person's right to safety and personal integrity. In the weighing situation, coherent criteria should be used to assess the balance between the two fundamental rights. The fundamental prioritization of the various fundamental rights easily leads to practical interpretations that are not based on reasonable judgment.[140]

344. Second, a fundamental right collision may occur as a collision between different fundamental rights of the same person. For instance, the protection of a person who is lost in the wilderness may require that his or her other fundamental

---

Court of Human Rights). (Tampere: University of Tampere, 2014). About praxis of the European Union Court, *see* Allan Rosas & Lorna Armati, *EU Constitutional Law – An Introduction* 2nd edn Bloomsbury: Hart Publishing, 2012.

138. Veli-Pekka Viljanen is Professor of Constitutional Law at the University of Turku.

139. Veli-Pekka Viljanen in https://verkkokirjahylly-almatalent-fi.ezproxy.uef.fi:2443/teos/GABBIXCTDG#/kohta:12/piste:b74; kohta 211/piste:b47; kohta 214–216/piste: b74; kohta 218–221/piste:b74. Accessed 15 May 2021. (Updated 9 Jan. 2024) *See also Viljanen, Perusoikeuksien rajoitusedellytykset* (Conditions for limitation of fundamental rights). (Vantaa, 2011).

140. *Ibid.*, kohta 130–131/piste: b47; kohta 225/piste: b74.

rights, such as the protection of privacy, be restricted, for example, in order to determine the location of a mobile phone. In practice, the collision of the different fundamental rights of the same person becomes actual only when he or she has not, for one reason or another, actively expressed his or her choice.[141]

345. Third, fundamental rights can be restricted on the basis of heavy societal interests. Such a restriction of fundamental rights requires very strong arguments to support such a restriction, precisely because of the constitutional nature of fundamental rights. No social interest can be a reason for limiting the fundamental rights of an individual.[142]

II. Specific Limitations to Freedom of Religion and Belief

A. *Scope of Limitations*

346. Since freedom of religion or conviction (belief) is guaranteed by Article 11 of the Constitution without providing for any specific, explicit limitations, only those limitations apply that are inherent to the Constitution. Thus, Muslims serving in FDF can make use of the fundamental right to pray during the breaks of military service or during Ramadan to follow the order to dine between sunset and ascent. However, this right can be restricted by the General Service Regulations (2017), which include a brief annex on 'specific issues of religious practice'. The same applies to prisoners in state jails. Authorities have to ensure that prisoners are able to comply with their religious communities' nourishment rules as stated in the Order of Criminal Sanctions Authority (Food Service and Diets, Dnro 8/004/2015). Here, too, there can be a restriction: prisoner's special wishes cannot be considered to be religious claims. A religious diet should be able to prepare normal prison food procurement procedures and contracts.

347. The fundamental rights of other persons and the principles of general constitutional law are the foremost limitations to freedom of religion. On the basis of freedom of religion and conscience, actions that violate human dignity or other fundamental rights or are contrary to the rule of law cannot be pursued. Thus, the rule of fundamental rights cannot, under any circumstances, justify the mutilation of human beings, such as the circumcision of women, despite the possible link between such a measure and a religious practice. The same applies, for example, to polygamy, which is incompatible with the Finnish legal system.

348. Moreover, the constitutional certainty of religious freedom and conscience does not prevent the law from providing moral and ethical standards that are generally recognized in society, which must be taken into account in religious and non-religious practices. In particular, the fundamental rights aspects of other people must be taken into account when interpreting how far the provision of fundamental rights,

141. *Ibid.*, kohta 215/piste: b74.
142. *Ibid.*, kohta 231/piste: b74.

such as the right to practice religion, extends. For example, the fundamental rights of the child, such as the right to life and personal integrity, must not be undermined by other freedom of religion and conscience.[143]

B. Structural Limitations

349. Structural restrictions on religion or conviction are such limitations that do not specifically limit the freedom of religion, but they follow from the structures of the legal system. They are not inevitably identified as such within the Finnish legal system. However, such a structural limitation can be seen in the protection of days of rest that have their historical, cultural, and traditional basis in Christian convictions. Thus, it is the Sunday (and a large number of public holidays on the Finnish calendar, such as Christmas, New Year's Day, Epiphany, the Second day of Easter, Ascension Day and Independence Day) that are protected by the law as days of rest.

350. In Finland, Christian holidays prevail and enjoy more intense protection than the holidays of other religions and creeds. The latter are not protected by law in any specific way.

351. Furthermore, objection to work on religious days of rest is part of freedom of religion. Work on Sundays or religious holidays can be ordered only with the consent of the employee if the work is also regularly performed on Sundays or by agreement in the employment contract.

352. Another structural limitation can be seen in the way that certain rights are attributed to religious groups. These groups or religious communities can enjoy rights only when they are organized in the structures provided for by the legal system. This requires specific legal structures. On this particular issue, there is a very basic document on religious freedom, the Freedom of Religion Act (2003), whose provisions and restrictions touch on the legal personality of what are termed 'registered religious communities'. In Finland, a registered religious association's foundation and legal status are enacted in subsection 2 of the Freedom of Religion Act. Such a religious body gains the status of a legal person, that is, it can acquire property, enter into commitments, and be a litigant in court and with other authorities once it is entered into the register of religious associations. Without registration, religious communities have no state-guaranteed fundamental rights.

143. HE 309/1993, 56.

C. *State of Defence or Emergency: No Valid Reason for Limitation of Religious Freedom*

353. A state of defence or emergency as such would not be grounds for restricting religious freedom. Article 23 of the Constitution on *Basic rights and liberties in situations of emergency* (1112/2011, entry into force 1 March 2012) reads:

(1) Such provisional exceptions to basic rights and liberties that are compatible with Finland's international human rights obligations and that are deemed necessary in the case of an armed attack against Finland or in the event of other situations of emergency, as provided by an Act, which poses a serious threat to the nation may be provided by an Act or by a Government Decree to be issued on the basis of authorization given in an Act for a special reason and subject to a precisely circumscribed scope of application. The grounds for provisional exceptions shall be laid down by an Act, however.

(2) Government Decrees concerning provisional exceptions shall without delay be submitted to Parliament for consideration. Parliament may decide on the validity of the Decrees.

354. As quoted verbatim, it can be seen implicitly that no specific limitations to any fundamental right, including religious freedom or belief will be permitted in a state of emergency.[144] The state of defence as such would not be considered just grounds. The idea that the state of defence as such would be an appropriate reason to restrict religious freedom is a somewhat hypothetical assumption.

355. In connection with Article 23, Finnish legislation must also take into account the obligations of the UN ICCPR and the ECHR.

356. In this context, it should be mentioned that the State of Emergency has developed into a completely new situation with regard to the COVID-19 pandemic. The Finnish authorities have also been forced to deal with religious freedom in the context of the coronavirus.

357. On 16 March 2020, the Government, in cooperation with the President of the Republic, stated that Finland was existing under exceptional circumstances due to the coronavirus situation. In consequence, on that date, the Emergency Powers Act (1552/2011)[145] was introduced for only the second time since Finland's independence in 1917. The possibility of implementing the emergency law provoked a lively debate, especially among constitutional lawyers, who widely criticized the

144. For further discussion of the emergency laws, *see* Veli-Pekka Viljanen, 'Poikkeuslakien välttämisen periaate' (The principle of avoiding emergency laws). *Lakimies* 6–7 (1999): 961–972.

145. The current Emergency Powers Act and its predecessor of the same name (1080/1991) were designed to replace the exceptional legislation previously distributed in several different laws. For more detail about the Emergency Powers Act 2011, *see* https://www.finlex.fi/en/laki/kaannokset/2011/20111552.

introduction of the law.[146] The exercise of powers under the Emergency Preparedness Act was eventually waived and the exceptions expired on Tuesday, 16 June 2020.

358. Since the second coronavirus wave commenced in Finland in January 2021 and as a result of the spread of mutant varieties of the virus, the government has again tightened the restrictions on movement, especially in southern and south-western Finland, but thus far the emergency law has not been re-introduced (16 March 2021).

359. On 27 February 2020, the Ministry of Social Affairs and Health set up a coordination group to plan, lead and coordinate control measures for the new coronavirus in the areas of social and health care. Municipalities, associations of municipalities, hospital districts and regional government agencies have received instructions on how to prepare for the coronavirus situation and prevent the spread of infections.[147]

360. Numerous recommendations and instructions have been given to the elderly and other at-risk groups, including restrictions governing gatherings, public events, youth and club facilities, hobbies, sports competitions and series, borrowing from libraries, access to leisure facilities and hospitals, and time spent in travelling at home and abroad.

361. Contrary to what might be expected, the bans imposed by the Regional State Administrative Agency under the Communicable Diseases Act (1227/2016) do not apply to religious communities since in Finland religious communities themselves decide on the necessary restrictions related to COVID-19. Decisions taken by the public authorities do not oblige them to restrict their normal activities, which come under a different law, the Assembly Act. Under the Assembly Act (530/1999), religious communities in principle lie outside the restrictions related to assembly.[148]

362. Ultimately, the proclamation of any restriction is about religious freedom. The application of the Communicable Diseases Act (1227/2016) is linked to the Assembly Act. The Gathering Act does not apply to public religious ceremonies held on the premises of religious communities or on similar premises, which are governed by the principles of the freedom to practise religion.

---

146. *See*, for example, the Constitution Blog (Perustuslakiblogi) by Pauli Rautiainen: 'What is the Emergency Powers Act?', https://perustuslakiblogi.wordpress.com/2020/03/13/martin-scheinin-valmiusl aki-koronavirus-perustuslaki-ja-ihmisoikeussopimukset/; Constitution Blog (Perustuslakiblogi) by Martin Scheinin: 'Emergency Powers Act, coronavirus, constitution and human rights treaties', htt ps://perstitutional law blog.wordpress.com/2020/03/13/martin-scheinin-preparability law-korona virus-constitution-and-humanrights/.

147. For more detail, *see* https://stm.fi/varautuminen-koronavirukseen.

148. Assembly Act (530/1999; Amendments up to 824/2002 included). For more detail, *see* https://ww w.finlex.fi/en/laki/kaannokset/1999/en19990530_20020824.pdf. The objectives of 'This Act (Ch. 1, s. 2, subs. 4) does not apply to official events arranged by public corporations, nor to the characteristic events of religious communities where these are arranged for the purpose of public worship in the community's own premises or in a comparable place.

363. Nevertheless, with a few exceptions, religious communities have complied with very general restrictions and recommendations in Finland. Within the framework of the Finnish Evangelical Lutheran Church and the Finnish Orthodox Church, the restrictions have been strictly observed. In an interview, Soile Lahti, Director of the Regional State Administrative Agency of Eastern Finland, stated: 'They have been very responsible and have voluntarily applied the same restrictions in their operations, even if they are not obliged to do so. For example, the Diocese of Kuopio follows these instructions and recommendations precisely.'[149]

364. In practice, church worship services and other ecclesiastical ordinances are limited, and some events can only be attended online. All other events that bring people together have thus far been cancelled.

365. Of the cities in southern Finland, the city of Vantaa has wished to restrict the number of people attending churches and mosques to a maximum of twenty. Here, too, immigrant organizations have joined forces. The Vantaa Russian Club, the Hakunila International Association, the East Vantaa Somali Cultural Association and the Sahan Society together handle the given information under a joint project. COVID-19 newsletters, translated into Russian, Somali and Arabic, reach thousands of city dwellers via Facebook, WhatsApp and email lists.[150]

366. As a result of the COVID-19 pandemic, there has been a requirement that religious communities should be covered by the Communicable Diseases Act since restrictions on gatherings have not applied to events such as religious worship.

367. The Minister of Science and Culture, Annika Saarikko (Centre Party), stated in an e-mail on 16 October 2020 that she intended to invite representatives of the religious communities to discuss the reform of the law and its possible application to the practice of religion.[151] The discussions have not led to any change in the legislation.

III. Limitations of Limitations (Restrictions of Restrictions)

368. All laws providing for limitations imposed on fundamental rights must themselves meet further constitutional requirements; they themselves are limited and must follow the Constitution.

369. Perceptions of the criteria supporting the admissibility of restrictions on fundamental rights have been clarified in the fundamental rights reform in 1995 and in the practice of interpretation of the Constitutional Law Committee following the reform. The list of restrictions on fundamental rights, as recorded in its report on

149. *See*, https://yle.fi/uutiset/3-11677505.
150. *See*, https://yle.fi/uutiset/3-11662193.
151. For further detail, *see* https://yle.fi/uutiset/3-11598864.

the fundamental rights reform of the Parliamentary Constitutional Law Committee,[152] has been received in the evaluation of the permissibility of the key role played by restrictions. This can now be considered a general measure used to assess the permissibility of restrictions imposed on fundamental rights. According to the committee, some of the general restriction requirements can be derived from the system of fundamental rights and from the nature of the rights as fundamental rights guaranteed by the Constitution. These are the following:

(1) Legal requirement: Restrictions must be based on the Parliamentary Act.[153]
(2) Punctuality and precision requirement: Restrictions must be strict and well-defined.[154]
(3) Requirement of admissibility: The grounds for restriction must be acceptable for the fundamental rights system, demanded by a heavy social need.[155]
(4) The requirement for the integrity of the core area: Normal law cannot impose a restriction on the core of the fundamental right.[156]
(5) Proportionality requirement: Restrictions must be necessary to achieve the objective and proportionate to the legal well-being protected by fundamental rights and to the importance of the social interest underlying the restriction.[157]
(6) Legal requirement: In order to limit the fundamental right, adequate legal safeguards must be provided.[158]
(7) Compliance with human rights obligations: Restrictions must not conflict with Finland's international human rights obligations.[159]

370. It should be emphasized here that the conditions for restraint are cumulative. Failure to comply with one means that the restriction is unconstitutional. In practice, for example, when a draft (a bill) is corrected, the wording of the article is clarified in order to achieve consistency. It is also important to note that, since the reform of fundamental rights in 1995, there has been a strong tendency in Finnish jurisprudence to avoid emergency laws in general. If a bill that potentially restricts fundamental rights is not brought into line with the conditions for the restriction of fundamental rights, it will be dropped from the current discussion (i.e., it will be regarded as having lapsed), but this is very rare.

152. In this context, it should be mentioned that there is no Constitutional Court in Finland, but a Constitutional Law Committee of Parliament. There has been some discussion as to whether a constitutional court is needed in Finland as well. *See* Liisa Nieminen, 'Tarvitaanko Suomessakin valtiosääntötuomioistuin?' (Do we need a constitutional court in Finland as well?). *Lakimies* 1 (2007), 3–24. For more about the work of the Constitutional Law Committee, *see* Anssi Keinänen & Matti Wiberg, 'Perustuslakivaliokunta lausuntovaliokuntana ja asiantuntijoiden kuulijana' (The Constitutional Law Committee as an opinion and expert hearing committee). *Oikeus* 1 (2012): 86–106. *See also* Anssi Keinänen, Maija Pitkänen & Outi Saarinen. 'Kokonaisvaltaista perustuslainmukaisuuden valvontaa' (Comprehensive constitutional review). *Oikeus* 1 (2013): 28–48.
153. PeVM 25/1994 vp, 4–5.
154. *Ibid.*
155. *Ibid. See also* HE 309/1993 vp, 24 and 49, PeVL 12/1998 vp.
156. PeVM 25/1995 vp, 95.
157. PeVM 25/1994 vp, 5.
158. *Ibid.*
159. *Ibid.*

§10. Examples of Case Law on Limitations to Freedom of Religion and Belief

I. Criteria of Selection

371. The longer and more comprehensive the list of fundamental rights is, the more friction between the fundamental rights there will be.

372. Many of the situations in which an individual may experience the fundamental rights of others as violating their own fundamental rights (e.g., freedom of religion) are not subject to conflicts over fundamental rights. According to Professor Martin Scheinin,[160] potential conflicts between fundamental rights can be divided into three types of situations:

(1) A situation in which different fundamental rights of the same person appear to conflict with each other.[161]
(2) A situation where the same fundamental rights of different persons are in conflict.[162]
(3) A situation where different fundamental rights of different persons conflict.[163]

---

160. Martin Scheinin has been a Professor of State Law and International Law at Åbo Akademi and is now working as a Professor of International Law and Human Rights at the European University Institute in Florence.

161. In the first situation described by Scheinin an example is the situation where a religious conviction afforded by a person's freedom of religion leads to a violation of the protection of the person's equality. However, the situation as such is not a conflict of fundamental rights, but its problem is the interpretation of the field of fundamental rights and its content. The protection of the individual in the name of fundamental rights based on his or her own choices is patronizing, but the fundamental rule must be the status of fundamental rights as a safeguard of individual freedom. Martin Scheinin, 'Perusoikeuskonfliktit' (Conflicts between Fundamental Rights). In *Tuuli Heinonen & Juha Lavapuro (eds), Oikeuskulttuurin eurooppalaistuminen. Ihmisoikeuksien murroksesta kansainväliseen vuorovaikutukseen.* (Vantaa, 2012), 125–132. *See also* Martin Scheinin, 'Characteristics of Human Rights Norms', In Catarina Krause & Martin Scheinin (eds), *International Protection of Human Rights: A Textbook.* (Turku: Åbo Akademi University Institute for Human Rights, 2012), 19–37.

162. In the second type of situation the same fundamental rights of different individuals, which cannot be exercised simultaneously, are the opposite. In this case, for example, the person invokes the protection of property as the basis for obtaining a certain property in his name. Even in this situation it is not a conflict of fundamental rights but a conflict of law based on fundamental rights which can be resolved by the interpretation of the court concerned. Scheinin 2012, 127.

163. The third scenario described by Scheinin is the only one that can be called a real fundamental conflict of rights. This is not just a process between the individual and the State, but also a set of horizontal relationships in which the various parties invoke their own fundamental rights. In the case of one example, freedom of speech and the privacy of a politician are opposed to the freedom of an editor-in-chief. From the structural process of the European Court of Human Rights it follows – even if it is initially question of a collision between the different fundamental rights of individuals – that the court is required to assess the conflict between one party and the Contracting State. *Ibid.* 2012, 131. In the case of *Karhuvaara and Iltalehti v. Finland*, App. No. 53678/00 (16 Nov. 2004) (Art. 10 of the ECHR), the ECtHR determined a violation of freedom of expression when the editor-in-chief of a tabloid newspaper was sentenced to a penalty for violating the privacy of a member of parliament. The ECtHR considered that there had been disproportionate condemnation of the case by Finland against the opposing fundamental rights.

373. The restrictions on freedom of religion or conviction have been elaborated in a substantial number of case laws concerning freedom of religion or belief. The cases discussed in the following will only be examples of the multitude of cases concerning freedom of religion or belief. Nevertheless, they reflect general Finnish legal practice.

II. Cases

A. *Cases Where §9 of the ECHR Has Been Applied*

374. It is possible to find important precedents that reflect the basic structure of limitations on freedom of religion or belief from among the rulings in which §9 of the ECHR has been applied,[164] although only one of these concerns Finland: the *Case of Konttinen v. Finland (1994).*

1. The Case of *Konttinen v. Finland*: Man (Seventh-Day Adventist) Rejected Working Hours for Religious Reasons (Sabbath)

375. (§9 [Freedom of thought, conscience and religion] *Konttinen v. Finland* [Ruling of the Commission on Human Rights in the case of Appeal no. 24949/94]).

376. In response to this appeal concerning the interpretation of the ECHR, the European Commission on Human Rights ruled that §9 of the ECHR had restricted the rights of the public authorities to dismiss employees for refusal to discharge certain duties on the grounds of conscience. §9 was not, however, regarded as permitting the plaintiff, a member of the Adventist Church who had been dismissed by the Finnish State Railways, to absent himself from his place of work without permission on religious grounds. In the commission's opinion, the ultimate guarantee of religious freedom was *the right of resignation from employment.*[165]

377. The judgment reached by the European Commission on Human Rights in the case of *Konttinen v. Finland* was in conformity with the line on religious freedom adopted in the earlier case of *X v. Denmark.*[166] In the present case, however, the plaintiff was not an employee of the Adventist Church but merely represented

---

164. For example, The cases of *X v. Denmark* (1976), *Karlsson v. Sweden* (1988), *Kokkinakis v. Greece* (1993), *Otto-Preminger-Institut v. Austria* (1994), *Kalac v. Turkey* (1997), *Bessarabian Metropolitan Church et al. v. Moldavia* (2001).

165. Martin Scheinin, 'Uskonnon ja omantunnon vapaus, PL 11§' (Freedom of religion and conscience). In Pekka Hallberg, Heikki Karapuu, Tuomas Ojanen, Martin Scheinin, Kaarlo Tuori & Veli-Pekka Viljanen, *Perusoikeudet* (Fundamental rights) 413–458 (WSOYpro 2nd revised ed. 2011), (Scheinin 2011b). For closer details, *see* Pekka Leino, *Kirkko ja perusoikeudet* (Church and Fundamental Rights), 203–220. (Helsinki, 2003).

166. Case 7374/76 of the European Commission on Human Rights (*X v. Denmark*), decision of 8.3.1976, DR 5. This was the case of a minister who had insisted that the parent of a child brought to be baptized should first receive religious instruction. It is noted in the explanation appended to the

the doctrinal opinions of that church. His convictions were not, however, in conformity with the policies of his employer, the Finnish State Railways, which would not agree to his observance of holy days in accordance with the calendar of that church.[167]

B. Important Precedents Which Have Proceeded to the Supreme Court and the Administrative Courts

378. When evaluating the dividing line laid down by the European Human Rights Commission in the case *Konttinen v. Finland* (1994), it should be noted that it is impossible to reach any direct conclusions regarding the situation in Finland merely by comparing the individual case of a minister who had lost his appeal against the state church of Denmark, partly on formal grounds, in that §6 does not apply to dismissal from a public office (*X v. Denmark*), with the case of a person whose convictions did not conform to the policies of a state-owned company (i.e., a public body).[168]

---

judgment that this was specifically a question of a minister of the state Church of Denmark performing the duties required of him in a parish belonging to that church who insisted that the parents should attend a course of five lectures concerning 'baptismal instruction'. The Ministry of Church Affairs (Kirkeministeriet) supported the finding that the minister could not attach such conditions to the conducting of a baptism and ordered him to choose between abandoning that practice or resigning. When the plaintiff, known simply as the Rev. X, refused to comply, the ministry set up a consistory court of an advisory character to adjudicate on the matter. The plaintiff's demand for a public discussion of his case was not accepted as the public prosecutor regarded the case as a disciplinary rather than a criminal matter. The consistory court nevertheless postponed discussion of the matter pending a decision from the European Commission on Human Rights.

The plaintiff had appealed to the Commission on the grounds of freedom of thought, conscience, and religion, as permitted in §9 of the European Convention on Human Rights, which included the freedom to practise religion.

In the Commission's view, the church as a religious body was to be understood as a community of persons who were of like mind, so that the protection afforded by §9 could be regarded as applying to the church itself and its practice of religion. In the state church system, the personnel are employed precisely to teach the doctrines of the church concerned. Thus *the individual freedoms of thought, conscience, and religion of a minister of such a church may be regarded as being exercised in the acts of entering employment with it, terminating that employment, or resigning from membership of the church.* The commission went as far in its ruling as to indicate that a church does not have to ensure the freedom of religion of its employees and members in the same way as the state is obliged under its own legislation to ensure the religious freedom of its citizens.

In other words, the commission did not regard a minister (in the state church system) as having the right under §9(1) of the European Convention on Human Rights to impose conditions for the baptism of a child that were contrary to the regulations of the highest administrative authority, the Ministry of Church Affairs. The commission also ruled, contrary to the plaintiff's demands, that a matter that was internal to a particular religion or belief did not fall within its jurisdiction or within the provisions of §6(1) of the European Convention on Human Rights. *See*, Peter Garde, 'Ret og tro'. Indlaeg ved Kirkeretlig Konference 2. Oktober 1999 på Logum-kloster Hojskok. In *Om norm & rätt i trosamfunden,* 76. (Uppsala: Nordisk Ekumenisk Rådet, 2001); Pekka Leino, *Kirkko ja perusoikeudet* (Church and Fundamental Rights), 205–206. (Helsinki, 2003).

167. For more detail, *see* the decision of the ECtHR in the case of Appeal no. 24949/94: https://hudoc.echr.coe.int/fre#{%22itemid%22:[%22001-3379%22]}.

168. Matti Pellonpää, *Euroopan ihmisoikeussopimus* (ECHR, Helsinki: Talentum, 4th edn 2005), 399; Pekka Leino, *Kirkko ja perusoikeudet,* 207.

379. On the one hand, it should be noted that the approach adopted, at least so far, by the Supreme Administrative Court in Finland, in which freedom of religion has been interpreted as freedom of withdrawal (i.e., freedom of religion is exercised by resigning from a religious or public community whose principles the individual is unable to accept), can be regarded as consistent with the decisions of the ECtHR, as expressed in its judgment in the case *X v. Denmark*.[169]

380. Thus, it may be said that in Finnish high court praxis, a person who is employed by a church or other religious community and finds himself or herself in conflict with that church or community on an issue of belief or conviction is deemed to have exercised his or her individual religious freedom in the act of taking up such employment. Once s/he has done so, s/he cannot thereafter appeal to the freedom of religion in order to depart from the tenets of that religious community.[170]

381. Nevertheless, as also in the state churches of Denmark and Sweden (previously), instances of an office-holder (including a minister) refusing to carry out certain obligations have also been interpreted in Finland purely on grounds of administrative law as neglect of duty. These decisions of the Finnish Supreme Court have mostly concerned one of two groups of cases: those in which a minister has placed conditions of his or her own on the baptism of a child,[171] and those in which a bishop has refused to ordain women as priests. This was the approach adopted by

---

169. Martin Scheinin, 'Uskonnon ja omantunnonvapaus, PL 11§' (Freedom of religion and conscience). In *Pekka Hallberg, Heikki Karapuu, Tuomas Ojanen, Martin Scheinin, Kaarlo Tuori, Veli-Pekka Viljanen, Perusoikeudet* (Fundamental rights), (2nd, revised edition. WSOYpro, 2011), 413–458. Pekka Leino, *Kirkko ja perusoikeudet*, 208.

170. This is also suggested in the statement made by the Parliamentary Constitutional Law Committee (PeVL 22/1997) on the bill for alterations to §16c of the law on the Orthodox Church in Finland:

    – Every person enjoys the fundamental right of the freedom of speech, although more precise regulations regarding this are given in law. It is in the nature of the offices mentioned in the bill that their holders should teach in accordance with the precepts of the Orthodox Church and that they should be aware of this fact when taking up such an office.

    It is similarly noted in the statement on disciplinary proceedings that:

    – […] matters concerned with the right to remain in public office have been demonstrated in the practices of the Human Rights Commission to lie beyond the scope of Article 6 of the European Convention on Human Rights.

    Admittedly, no instances of problems or conflicts, or even of differences in interpretation, have arisen with regard to the doctrines of the Orthodox Church of Finland.

171. One example that could be mentioned is a case in which a minister of the church at Sulkava in the Diocese of Mikkeli refused to accept an unmarried couple as godparents for a child. The Supreme Court, having first granted on 7 Oct. 1988 an injunction on the execution of the relevant decision of the Eastern Finland Court of Appeal (no. 1347, 30.8.1988), overturned the Appeal Court decision in its ruling no. 2792 of 13 Oct. 1989 (KKO 1989:122). As a result, the charge of intentional neglect of duty and the accompanying punishment upheld by the Appeal Court was commuted to a charge of indiscretion in the performance of one's duties, leading to an official caution. The

the Chancellor of Justice in resolution 561/24.5.1989, for example, regarding a bishop as an official of the state, and considering his right to refuse to ordain women as priests in light of this.

382. It should be mentioned in the latter connection that the law allowing the ordination of women is perhaps the most far-reaching change that has been enacted in the ELCF in the past four decades. It has been an exemplary piece of legislation, in spite of being the subject of protracted deliberations. However, its implementation continues to present problems,[172] and there are still many people employed by the church for whom this majority decision runs against their convictions. One confounding factor is an additional resolution regarding the definition of the place of residence for persons opposed to women in the priesthood, which has been recently revived, even though a part of the early phase in the process was already in effect and should no longer be of any significance. This resolution has thrown the spotlight onto a number of young priests who have not adapted to the ordination of women,[173] as they are inclined to regard it as having the force of law.

383. The leadership of the Lutheran Church has taken a firm stand against this resolution and decreed that the clergy no longer have any right to refuse to officiate alongside women priests. This may be regarded as making it more difficult than ever for a minister who objects to the ordination of women to be vicar of a parish which already employs women priests.

384. The decisions of the Supreme Court in Finland have also consistently emphasized that following the enacting of the law of equality of opportunities, the Evangelical Lutheran Church has opened the ministry to women. In accordance with this, the court has ruled that, since it is a matter of the practice of religion, the church's freedom to choose its ministers is governed by the provisions of the Constitution and the requirement to respect the equality of the sexes. In that respect, the Supreme Court and the Supreme Administrative Court have established four interesting precedents with regard to the law on equality: The Supreme Court decision of 19.1.2001 (no. 88/DNo. S 99/1215), Supreme Administrative Court decisions of 13.3.2001 (deposit no. 469) and 23.9.2002 (T 2260) and the decision of the Turku Administrative Court reached on 13 June 2007 (00362/07/2302). It is worth considering the first of these and the last two in more detail, as these are instances in which the church administration has been forced by the courts of law to recognize that the regulations governing fundamental freedoms also apply to the church.

Supreme Court ruled that it was part of the duties of a minister to ascertain that the people proposed as godparents fulfilled the requirements laid down in §36 of the Ecclesiastical Law of 1964. Thus the minister had not exceeded his powers as the Diocesan Chapter and the Court of Appeal had maintained.

172. Matti Halttunen, Church Counsellor of the Evangelical Lutheran Church of Finland, 2007, 6 (Interview in the weekly newspaper Kotimaa 38/20 Sep. 2007).

173. Those opposed to the ordination of women in Finland include a revivalist movement, the Finnish Lutheran Evangelical Society (SLEY), the Luther Foundation, and some of the missionary organizations within the Evangelical Lutheran Church of Finland.

1. Case: Supreme Court 19.1.2001; Selection of a Curate (The ELCF)

385. The relation between the system of Ecclesiastical Law and the two fundamental freedoms, equality and freedom of religion, was defined in the Supreme Court verdict of 19.1.2001 (no. 88/DNo. S 99/1215). The verdict was in favour of the law on equality, when pitted against the church's right to decide on questions which it regards as its own internal matters. The Supreme Court based its judgment on the view adopted in a government proposal (57/1985) that equality of the sexes is a principle which is also accepted by the church.

2. Case: Supreme Court 23.9.2001: Election of a Vicar (The ELCF)

386. The Supreme Administrative Court (Deposit no. 2260) considered that a diocesan chapter was justified in ruling as ineligible for election to the office of vicar an applicant who, in view of his negative attitude towards the ordination of women and his actions consistent with that, could be regarded as incapable of discharging the duties of vicar in a parish, where three of the eight ministers were women.[174]

3. Case: Turku Administrative Court 13.6.2007: Election of a Vicar (The ELCF)

387. In this case (00362/07/2302) the Turku Administrative Court came to a similar decision as the aforementioned. The plaintiff was not prepared to undertake to conduct divine services with a woman minister, leading the diocesan chapter to conclude that he would evidently not be able to discharge the duties and obligations belonging to the office of vicar, so that arrangements would have to be made, contravening the law on equality. The court therefore ruled that there was a serious and demonstrable reason for regarding the plaintiff as incapable of acting as vicar of the parish of Kalanti.[175]

388. Also consistent with this line of reasoning was the decision by the Diocese of Oulu (3 October 2007) to suspend a minister from office for two months for refusing to conduct services together with a woman. The minister in question has publicly announced that he intends to take his case to the Oulu Provincial Court of Appeal and then to higher instances, if necessary.

174. For the legal principles applied, *see* PL 6,2 and §21.
175. For the legal principles applied, *see* PL 6,2, KL 5, §1, 1st mom. and §8, 1, KJ 5, §1, 1st mom., KJ 6, §18, §22 and §24, 1st mom., §3 and 34, and the law on equality between men and women §2, 1st mom. clause 1, §4, §6 and §7.

389. It has not yet been necessary in Finland, however, to decide directly on the right of a minister who is opposed to the ordination of women to become vicar of a parish where there are women ministers, as has happened in Sweden (the case *Karlsson v. Sweden* 12356/86).[176]

C. Important Precedents Which Have Not Proceeded to the Supreme Court

390. Three further cases have been recognized in Finland that are comparable to the *Konttinen v. Finland* case and constitute important precedents with respect to the ECHR but have not proceeded to the Supreme Court.

1. Case: Muslim Woman's Right to Keep Her Head Covered During Office Hours

391. This was the first case involving a Muslim woman's right to keep her head covered during office hours. The woman had been offered a full-time job as an office worker in a travel agency and had said that she was willing to accept the job but had informed the employer at the interview that she wished to wear a *hijab* for religious reasons. The employer did not accept this and refused to employ the woman. The authorities then denied the woman her right to unemployment benefits on the grounds that she had herself refused employment which had been offered her. The woman did not accept the decision, appealing to the Insurance Court, which concluded by a vote of four against one that the woman was entitled to unemployment benefits. The court's reasoning for the decision was that the woman had the right to practise her religion and as a Muslim woman she would customarily keep her head covered, without being held responsible for the cancellation of the employment contract.

2. Case: Woman (Jehovah's Witness) Who, for Religious Reasons, Rejected a Job That Had Been Offered

392. The second case concerned a woman belonging to the Jehovah's Witnesses who had been offered a temporary job as a cleaning lady in an Evangelical Lutheran Church. The woman rejected the job offered for religious reasons, referring, for instance, to a line in the Epistle to the Corinthians, which forbids one 'to be partners with demons'. The Unemployment Benefit Society, however, concluded that the woman had rejected a job offered to her without an acceptable reason and refused to pay her daily unemployment benefit. The Appeal Board confirmed this

176. For the sake of accuracy, the following indications of the European Commission on Human Rights in its judgment need to be pointed out: the Swedish government had specifically established that the refusal to accept Karlsson as a candidate had not been connected with his views on the ordination of women. In the commission's view, protection should also be given to the 'official' approved doctrines of the state church.

decision on the grounds that labour policy did not consider religious beliefs an acceptable reason for rejecting a job offer. The Insurance Court overturned the decisions made by the Unemployment Benefit Society and the Unemployment Appeal Board. As in the case of the Muslim woman, it concluded by a vote of four against one that the woman's religious beliefs were an acceptable reason for refusing to clean a Lutheran Church. The Insurance Court thus ordered that the woman should be paid her daily unemployment allowance for the three weeks during which it had been denied to her.

393. The Insurance Court based its decisions concerning both the Muslim woman and the Jehovah's Witness on the Freedom of Religion Act in the European Convention for the Protection of Human Rights and Fundamental Freedoms, its reasoning being that under the act, freedom of religion could be restricted by rule of law only in cases in which the restrictions served a justified purpose, such as the maintenance of general order or the protection of health or morality.

3. Case: Woman Belonging to the Jehovah's Witnesses Thought Her Religious Beliefs Justified Her Refusal to Participate in the Work of the Army

394. The third case supporting this view concerned a decision by the Insurance Court according to which a woman belonging to the Jehovah's Witnesses had the right to reject a job as an office employee offered by the Ministry of Defence without losing her unemployment benefit. The woman thought her religious beliefs justified her refusal to work for the army in the same way as a male Jehovah's Witness may refuse military service. The Insurance Court decided in favour of the woman, referring to the fact that men belonging to the Jehovah's Witnesses are exempt from both military and non-military service during peacetime.[177]

395. In light of the above cases, one may ask, as the late Professor Juha Seppo remarks, whether or not the interpretation of the Finnish Insurance Court concerning the limits of freedom of religion follows the views adopted by the European Human Rights Commission.[178]

177. Nowadays Jehovah's Witnesses can no longer be exempted from military service. Exemptions based on religious beliefs passed into history on 20 Feb. 2019. This issue was discussed in greater depth in Ch. 7, Protected Manifestations, *6. Conscientious objection and Military Service.*

178. Juha Seppo, 'Church and State in Finland 1997'. *European Journal for Church and State Research. Revue eurpéenne des relations Églises – État* 5 (1988): 121–130.

D. Cases Affecting Freedom of Speech and Religion

1. Case: ECtHR Decision on the Case of *Jehovah's Witnesses v. Finland* (Application no. 31172/19) 9 May 2023: The Jehovah's Witnesses' Religious Activities in Finland and Their Compatibility with the Data Protection Regulations

396. On 9 May 2023, the European Court of Human Rights (ECtHR) reached a decision concerning the case involving Jehovah's Witnesses and their religious activities in Finland, addressing particularly the compatibility of those activities with the data protection regulations.

397. The ruling asserted that Finland did not violate the right to a fair trial or the freedom of thought, conscience, and religion, as safeguarded by the European Convention on Human Rights (ECHR).

Background to the complaint:[179]

> In 2013, the Data Protection Board prohibited Jehovah's Witnesses from compiling lists of names or taking notes during their door-to-door preaching without meeting the conditions stipulated by the Personal Data Act. This prohibition was contingent upon the explicit consent of the individuals concerned with the compilation and utilisation of lists and notes.

398. The Jehovah's Witnesses appealed to the Administrative Court, which annulled the decision of the Board. The Data Protection Ombudsman appealed to the Supreme Administrative Court (KHO). Subsequently, the Supreme Administrative Court requested a preliminary ruling from the Court of Justice of the European Union. The CJEU determined that the Jehovah's Witnesses were obligated to adhere to EU regulations regarding the protection of personal data concerning their note-taking practices during door-to-door preaching. The court deliberated on whether such notes qualified as personal data forming a 'personal data file' within the meaning of the Personal Data Act (henkilötietolaki, personuppgiftslagen, Act no. 523/1999, paragraphs 30–35).

399. In December 2018, the Supreme Administrative Court (KHO) overturned the Administrative Court's decision, affirming that Jehovah's Witnesses must comply with the Data Protection Board's ruling. It emphasized that the compilation and use of lists of names and notes necessitated the explicit consent of the individuals concerned.

400. Subsequently, Jehovah's Witnesses appealed the Supreme Administrative Court's decision to the European Court of Human Rights. In their appeal they argued that the ruling had violated several rights guaranteed by the ECHR, including the right to a fair trial (Article 6 ECHR) and freedom of thought, conscience,

179. For more detail, *see* Press Release – Chamber Judgments | Published On 09/05/20, https://hudoc.echr.coe.int/eng-press?i=003-7642144-10526463.

and religion (Article 9 ECHR). The Jehovah's Witnesses contended that the case should have undergone a hearing and that they should not have been barred from taking notes for personal use during door-to-door preaching without the express consent of the individuals involved.

401. The ECtHR concluded that since there was no disagreement on the merits of the case, then no oral hearing was required. Nor did the legal issue in the case require an oral hearing. The failure to hold an oral hearing was justified and did not violate the right to a fair trial.

402. The ECtHR considered that the case concerned a balance between freedom of thought, conscience and religion and respect for private and family life. The ECtHR considered it appropriate and necessary for the protection of privacy that individuals be asked to consent to the drawing up and use of lists of names and notes.

403. The ECtHR did not see how asking for consent would undermine the religious freedom of Jehovah's Witnesses. The ECtHR found that the reasoning of the national courts was relevant and sufficient to show that the interference was necessary. The authorities had acted within the state's margin of appreciation to strike a fair balance between different interests. The ECtHR did not find a violation of any of the articles.[180]

2. Case: Decision of the District Court of Helsinki (14.11.2023, R22/1094[181]) to Acquit a Christian Democrat Politician and MP, Päivi Räsänen on 30 March 2022 of Charges of Incitement (Hate Speech) Against a Population Group

404. In recent years Finland has seen several cases that ignited debates about the boundaries of freedom of expression. These cases involved instances of offensive speech, often termed 'hate speech', both against and in the name of religion.[182] One particularly noteworthy case revolved around the Helsinki District Court's decision

---

180. For the judgment on the ECtHR website, *see* https://hudoc.echr.coe.int/eng?i=001-224559. Accessed 20 Aug. 2023.

181. https://oikeus.fi/hovioikeudet/helsinginhovioikeus/fi/index/tiedotteet/2023/hovioikeushylkasisyytteenkansanedustajapaivirasasenrikosasiassa160.html.

182. J. Hannonen and T. Hyttinen, 'Kiihottaminen kansanryhmää vastaan alioikeuskäytännössä' (Incitement against a population group in the case law of the lower courts), (2023) 2 *Defensor Legis*, 308. *See also* Kimmo Nuotio, 'Sananvapausrikosten sääntelyn ja soveltamisen kehitystrendejä ja kehittämiskohtia eräiden kotimaisten oikeustapausten valossa' (Trends and development details in the regulation and application of freedom of expression offences in the light of several domestic cases), in *Viestin viemää: Viestintäoikeuden vuosikirja 2021*. Korpisaari, P. (toim.). Forum iuris: Helsingin yliopiston oikeustieteellisen tiedekunnan julkaisuja (Forum iuris: Publications of the Faculty of Law of the University of Helsinki), 2022 Helsinki, 47–63.

Korpisaari, P. (ed.). Forum iuris: Publications of the Faculty of Law of the University of Helsinki (2022 Helsinki, 47–63).

to acquit Päivi Räsänen, a Christian Democrat politician and Member of Parliament, of charges related to incitement against a national group (homosexuals) on 30 March 2022. While the District Court acknowledged that some of Räsänen's statements were offensive to homosexuals, they deemed that these statements did not qualify as hate speech falling outside the protections of freedom of expression.

405. Following the District Court's ruling, Prosecutor General Raija Toiviainen and State Prosecutor Anu Mantila expressed their dissatisfaction, leading to the case being forwarded to the Helsinki Court of Appeal. According to the prosecutors, the district court erred in its assessment of fundamental rights and set the threshold for incitement too high. 'The statements conveyed a demeaning view of homosexuals,' the prosecutors asserted in their appeal. When discussing homosexuality as a disorder or deviation, unhealthy or unnatural, the prosecutors highlighted the inherently negative connotations.[183]

406. 'According to Räsänen, if homosexuality is a genetic trait, then it is genetic degeneration and genetic inheritance that causes disease and disorder. The claim is untrue and degrading to homosexuals. Nothing factual exists to support this claim. In addition, this includes Räsänen's religious view that homosexuals are not created by God as heterosexuals, hence rendering them inferior to heterosexuals,' the indictment said.

407. Kerttu Tarjamo, Secretary General of the human rights organization SETA, also emphasized in an interview that Räsänen's speeches deeply offended sexual minority representatives. Tarjamo stressed the importance of addressing hate speech against LGBTQ+ individuals (rainbow people) in a legal context, even if it is presented within a religious framework.[184]

408. The accusations against Päivi Räsänen encompassed several incidents:

> The oldest allegation pertained to Räsänen's publication, 'Man and Woman Created He Them,' released by the Luther Foundation in 2004. In this pamphlet, Räsänen characterized homosexuality, for example, as a disorder in psychosexual development.[185]

409. Another charge against Räsänen stemmed from a social media post in 2019, in which she questioned the compatibility of the [Evangelical Lutheran] church's doctrinal principles, as outlined in the Bible, 'The church has announced that it is SETA's Pride 2019 official partner. How does the Church's doctrinal foundation, the Bible, fit in with the fact that shame and sin are a matter of pride?'[186]

---

183. District Court of Helsinki 30.3.2022 no 22/113590 (R 21/3567), 1–3.
184. Lasse Kerkelä, 'Professori: Päivi Räsäsen vapauttava tuomio ei oikeuta vihapuheeseen uskonnon varjolla' (Professor: Päivi Räsänen's acquittal does not justify hate speech under the guise of religion. Helsingin Sanomat. https://www.hs.fi/kotimaa/art-2000008718049.html?ref=menokone. Accessed 20 Aug. 2023.
185. District Court of Helsinki 30.3.2022 no 22/113590 (R 21/3567), 1–3.
186. District Court of Helsinki 30.3.2022 no 22/113590 (R 21/3567), 5.

410. The third charge revolved around Räsänen's statements made during a radio programme hosted by journalist Ruben Stiller on the Yle Puhe channel. Prosecutors argued that Räsänen's remarks were offensive to homosexuals.[187]

411. The prosecutors sought a fine to be imposed on Räsänen on three charges of incitement against an ethnic group, and one on Juhana Pohjola, the Bishop of the Luther Foundation. Like Räsänen, Pohjola also refuted the charges, citing grounds based on freedom of expression and freedom of religion.

412. In its ruling on 14 November 2023, the Helsinki Court of Appeal dismissed the charges against Päivi Räsänen, the Christian Democrat MP and Juhana Pohjola, the Bishop of the Luther Foundation. The Court of Appeal upheld the District Court's judgment without alteration. Like the lower court, the Court of Appeal shared the opinion that Räsänen's written expressions were not intended to demean or offend homosexuals. The Court of Appeal supported the District Court's assertion that Räsänen's aim was not to insult or offend homosexuals but rather to advocate for the traditional concepts of family and of marriage between a man and a woman, in accordance with her religious beliefs. Consequently, the Court found that the statements, as alleged in the indictment, did not constitute hate speech violating the equality and dignity of homosexuals or fostering intolerance of them.

413. The rulings from both the Helsinki District Court and the Helsinki Court of Appeal align with the general interpretation of the ECtHR. Permitting even offensive expressions is the ECtHR's foundational principle.[188] The District Court and also the Court of Appeal have taken into consideration the practice of the European Court of Human Rights regarding Article 10, on freedom of speech, and Article 11, on freedom of religion. These demonstrate that speech that is offensive and may even contain extreme opinions in a discussion programme may not necessarily constitute an acceptable basis for punishment. The fundamental domain of freedom of expression enjoys specific protection. Political discourse, exemplified by Räsänen's statements, falls squarely within this fundamental area. As the Court and the academia have noted, the speech of an MP has a political character (a political right), which should rather broaden – rather than restrict – their freedom of speech. It should also be noted that 'In a western constitutional state, speech cannot be ascribed a meaning beyond its literal words, as the presumption of innocence must also extend to offences related to freedom of expression. The challenge in the

187. District Court of Helsinki 30.3.2022 no 22/113590 (R 21/3567), 5–6.

188. One of the most notable cases is the ECtHR's ruling in *Handyside v. United Kingdom* (5493/72, judgment on 7 December 1976, passages 48–50.) In this case, the ECtHR affirmed that freedom of speech doesn't solely protect positive, harmless, or indifferent ideas but also includes thoughts that may offend, shock, or disturb the state or a section of the population. This consistent line of interpretation has been evident also in several other cases that restricting the use of religious freedom of speech has not been acceptable. *See* cases of *Kokkonakis v. Greece* (14307/88, judgment on 25 May 1993), *Manoussakis and Others v. Greece* (18748/91, judgment on 26 September 1996), *Nasirov and Others v. Azerbaijan* (58717/10, judgment on 20 February 2020), and the *Religious Community of Jehovah's Witnesses v. Azerbaijan* (58717/10, judgment on 20 February 2020).

Räsänen case lies in the fact that the indictment seems largely based on assumptions about Räsänen's thoughts rather than on her stated opinions',[189] as the researcher Antti Korpi has emphasised.

414. In an interview with Helsingin Sanomat dated 14 November 2023, the State Prosecutor Anu Mantila expressed her inclination to file an appeal with the Supreme Court. She contends that the Court of Appeal dealt with the case inadequately and the demarcation between what is forbidden and what is permissible should be more precisely defined.[190] The decision regarding the appeal rested with the Prosecutor General Ari-Pekka Koivisto. The appeal was granted. On 19 April 2024, the Supreme Court gave the State Prosecutor leave to appeal in the case of the MP Päivi Räsänen (Christian Democrats), and the case proceeded to the Supreme Court for consideration. The handling of the case is continuing in the Supreme Court with respect not only to Päivi Räsänen but also to Juhana Pohjola. The State Prosecutor is demanding a fine in the case of Räsänen in relation to three counts and of Pohjola in relation to one count of incitement against an ethnic group. However, it is improbable that the decision would be changed if the cases were heard in a higher court or in the European Court of Human Rights.[191]

---

189. Antti Korpi, 'Räsäsen vapauttava tuomio lopputulokseltaan EIT:n linjan mukainen. – Uskonnollisen puheen erityisasema Suomessa vielä tunnistamatta' (Räsänen's acquittal is ultimately in line with the ECtHR's stance. – The special status of religious speech in Finland still unrecognized), (2022) 4 *Defensor Legis*, 103, 1117–1125. For more detail, *see* https://www.edilex.fi/defensor_legis/1000850014.pdf. *See also*, Riitta Ollila, 'Päivi Räsäsen syytteet hylättiin – tuomion keskeiset tulkintakysymykset'(The Dismissal of Charges Against Päivi Räsänen – Key Interpretation Questions in the Verdict), https://www.sananjauskonnonvapaus.fi/ajankohtaista/ott-riitta-ollila-pivi-rssen-syytteet-hylttiin-tuomion-keskeiset-tulkintakysymykset.

190. In an article published in 2020 the prosecutor Anu Mantila has suggested that since the constitution ensures the inviolability of human dignity and then messages that violate human dignity are not permissible even within the core area of freedom of speech. She argues that the conflict seems to have been resolved to the detriment of freedom of speech. Mantila notes that if a broad content is attributed to human dignity the resulting criminal liability for incitement would become wider than could be accepted in a democratic society. For more detail, *see* Anu Mantila, 'Saako myös tämän sanoa? Milloin puhe muuttuu rangaistavaksi vihapuheeksi?' (Can one say this too? When does speech become punishable hate speech?) Oikeus 2/2020, 154–171, 158–159, 162–163.

191. Compare *Féret v. Belgia*, 15615/07, the judgment delivered on 16 July 2009, passages 72–80 and *Perinçek v. Switzerland*, 27510/08, and the judgment delivered on 15 October 2015, 120–124, passages 4–14. In the case of *Féret v. Belgium*, the ECtHR addressed the restriction imposed on freedom of expression concerning a Belgian politician. The case revolved around political activity and, more specifically, the criticism of certain groups and religions. The court assessed whether limiting expression was necessary in a democratic society and whether it was proportionate within the context of political debate.

In contrast, the case of *Perinçek v. Switzerland* related to a dispute concerning the nature of the Armenian genocide. The ECtHR examined the boundary between freedom of speech and hate speech when a Swiss politician denied the reality of the Armenian genocide and accused Switzerland of violating freedom of expression by expressing this view publicly.

These cases are important because they have helped delineate how freedom of speech and expression are balanced against other human rights, such as respect for human dignity and non-discrimination. The courts have attempted to impose limits on the extent to which states can restrict their freedom of expression, by referring, for example, to public order or the protection of other individuals' rights.

415. Hate speech is discussed in more detail in Part VII, Chapter 8, Penal Law and Religion, *§9. Crimes against International Law.*

Chapter 2. Collective Religious Freedom

§1. Basic Principles

416. For the individual, although the practice of religion, or religious freedom, implies the innate right to practise religion, publicly and privately, in accordance with one's conscience, understanding, and choice, religious freedom also generally requires communities and institutions to be taken into account. Religious freedom is never exercised in a vacuum. Each individual and every religious community is in its own way linked to its own socio-cultural environment. The same applies, naturally, to an individual who does not profess any religion or community of religion.

417. Collective religious freedom in Finnish legal doctrine means that everybody has the right to exercise his or her freedoms in community with others (or express non-religious or anti-religious convictions). Central to collective religious freedom is the freedom of worship, the right to worship, and religious activities related to it. Religious freedom of the religious community and the association also essentially involves the right of the community to decide on its own matters, such as the community's doctrine and recognition, the community's membership and its terms and conditions, the forms of organization and the selection of religious leaders, priests, and teachers, and also the establishment of educational institutions.

418. Collective religious freedom also gives a religious community greater social influence than individual religious freedom. Churches and other religious communities have the opportunity – at least as opinion-makers – to intervene in much more effective ways in political, social, economic, and cultural solutions which they question, for example, with regard to human dignity and fundamental rights. However, this approach does not have much significance in Finnish legal practice. In the case of churches and religious communities, it is actually more a question of public influence or opinion-forming. Significant, however, is the notion of a 'collective fundamental right' by which an organization as such can have rights.

Chapter 3. Organizational Religious Freedom

§1. Basic Principles

I. Collective Religious Freedom

419. Organizational religious freedom in Finnish legal doctrine and practice is known as 'collective freedom of religion or conviction (belief)'. Churches and registered religious associations enjoy freedom of religion or belief in their own right. Organizations not only represent the rights of their members but *also have their own proper rights*. This means that they have the status of a legal person, which allows them to decide their own affairs – and this status by the RFA (453/2003) – enacts in detail and exhaustively the rights and obligations of churches and registered religious associations. In Finnish jurisprudence, fundamental rights also apply to religious communities as legal persons to the extent permitted by the nature of such rights.

420. When the new RFA (2003) was drafted, one of the main tasks of the Religious Freedom Committee was, in addition to individual freedom, to investigate how the establishment and status of registered religious communities should be regulated by the new law. Such communities in Finland previously included all other religious communities in addition to the Evangelical Lutheran Church and the Orthodox Church.

421. According to the Committee's basic solution, religious communities registered under the RFA were also provided for as a separate legal entity. The Committee emphasized that *the religious community has specific regulatory needs that are significantly different from normal associations*. In principle, this policy can also be considered important because, when interpreted in this way, membership-based religious practice was also considered an independent phenomenon and mode of action, separate from other community activities.

422. As a concrete outcome of the legislation process, the new RFA distinguished three different types of legal persons in religious associations, the Evangelical Lutheran Church, the Orthodox Church, and other registered religious associations. These religious bodies assume the status of a legal person, that is, they can acquire property, enter into commitments, and be a litigant in court and with other authorities once the group or organization is entered into the register of religious associations.

423. In accordance with the Constitution, the new law (453/2003) also recognizes that some bodies engaging in religious activities have organized not as registered religious associations but as ideological associations.

424. This is linked to Article 13(2) of the Constitution (*Freedom of assembly and freedom of association*), which guarantees everyone the right to freedom of association. This provision guarantees the right, without separate permission, to form an association, to belong or not to belong to an association, and to participate in an association's activities. Freedom of association, guaranteed by the Constitution, *refers primarily to the right of association as an ideological association.* On the other hand, the constitutional provision does not exclude the legislation of what are known as public law associations for their public service.[192]

II. Freedom to Form Religious Communities

425. Everyone has the right to freely associate in order to form a religious organization. Churches and other religious communities determine for themselves the preconditions for the formation of their associations and how they accept their members. For example, the path to membership of the Evangelical Lutheran Church, as well as membership of the Orthodox and Catholic Churches, is achieved through baptism and not automatically by the child's parents belonging to the church or declaring him or her a member of that Church.

426. When the RFA (2003) was being drafted, many religious minority communities would in fact have hoped for a change in the Act, in the sense that it would have increased equality between all churches and other religious communities with respect to the state.

427. However, the new RFA (453/2003) did not change the prevailing religio-political and ecclesiastical situation of the major churches. Thus, the Evangelical Lutheran Church and the Orthodox Church still have their own statutes (§76 of the Constitution and the Orthodox Church Law [985/2006]), while other religious communities must be registered in accordance with Chapter 2 of the Act in order to obtain the status of a religious community.

428. Membership of a religious community is guaranteed in Article 3 of the RFA, which contains a provision for the application of the Law of Assembly (530/1999) to the exercise of public religion. Sections 1 and 2 of the Act contain two provisions related to membership of a religious community. First, it lays down all of the conditions for religious membership:

> Everyone has the right to determine his or her religious status by joining or withdrawing from a religious community that has accepted them.

429. Second, it lays down the criteria for determining the religious status of minors:

> The child's religious status is decided jointly by his or her guardians. However, if, after the birth of the child, the parents do not agree on the child's religious status, the mother, as child's custodian, may decide within one year of

192. HE 309/1993 vp, 60.

the child's birth whether or not to have the child formally linked with a particular religious community. However, if the court, in accordance with Article 9(3) of the Child Custody and Access Act (361/1983), decides differently on the division of duties between the parents, the court's decision shall prevail.

430. And section 3 of the same Article specifies the religious status of minors:

> A child over the age of fifteen, with the written consent of his or her guardians, may join or leave a religious community. A person over the age of twelve may be affiliated with or denounced by a religious community only with his or her written consent. The law governing the Evangelical Lutheran Church and the Orthodox Church, as well as the statutes of a registered religious community, may and shall determine the conditions for membership in the community. In this case, the conditions for membership may be determined so that the person is not simultaneously a member of another religious community.

431. The final sentence of section 3 is important in terms of the regulation of membership of a religious community. The right of a religious community to determine the terms of its membership is consistent with the community's freedom and autonomy. In doing so, it may make it a condition for a member not to be a member of another religious community at the same time. However, when the new RFA no longer prohibits the simultaneous membership of one or more religious communities, it will, on the other hand, provide flexible membership practices for communities whose membership is not violated by such a procedure.

III. Fundamental Rights of Legal Persons

A. *Scope of Legal Persons*

432. Finnish law defines 'Legal person' as a 'legally viable independent legal person (entity) with full rights and obligations'.[193]

433. In Finland, legal persons are divided into two categories: legal persons governed by public law and legal persons governed by private law.[194]

Legal Persons Governed by Public Law

434. In Finland, the organization of public administration is divided into three main areas: state administration, municipal administration and indirect public administration. In addition, the public administration organization includes the Provincial Government of Åland, the administration of the Evangelical Lutheran Church, and the administration of the Orthodox Church. In addition, European

193. HE 95/1993: Yksityiskohtaiset perustelut, luku 1 (Detailed explanation, Ch. 1), 27 (para. 5).
194. For more on the legal basis of Finnish public law, *see* Jaakko Husa & Teuvo Pohjolainen, *Julkisen vallan oikeudelliset perusteet – johdatus julkisoikeuteen*. (Legal Basis of Public Power – Introduction to Public Law., 4th, revised edn). (Helsinki, 2014).

administrative units that influence the Finnish jurisdiction by their administrative functions can be integrated into the organization of public administration. In addition to the state and municipalities, the Evangelical Lutheran Church and the Orthodox Church and their parishes have legal personality under public law.[195]

435. The ELCF and the Orthodox Church have legal personality and control over their internal affairs. Internal issues within the Church are part of the Church Order and are settled by the General Synod.

Legal Persons Governed by Private Law

436. The most prominent of the legal persons governed by private law are limited liability companies, partnerships (avoimet yhtiöt), limited partnerships (kommandiittiyhtiöt), and thousands of general associations and registered religious associations.[196] Registered associations can be either non-profit or financial associations. Foundations are independent legal entities, consisting of a mass of assets earmarked for a specific purpose and registered in a register of foundations. Other legal persons in the private sector are the cooperatives (osuuskunnat) and the European economic interest grouping, which is essentially similar to a partnership.

437. It is worth mentioning here that communities always act through their representatives, i.e., they also function as 'natural persons'.

B. Domestic or Foreign Legal Persons? – No Differentiation in Finnish Legislation

438. Chapter 2 of the Constitution, which deals with fundamental rights ('Basic rights and liberties'), also, as a general rule, protects every human being within the jurisdiction of Finland. The fundamental rights provisions generally refer to everyone as the subject or holder of fundamental rights. *Everyone* means a natural person. The starting point is that fundamental rights protect the individual regardless of his or her age, gender, or nationality. Legal persons are indirectly protected by fundamental rights, as interference with the status of a legal person may constitute an interference with the rights of the individual underlying such status. Human rights belong to an individual throughout the course of his or her life.[197]

439. Unlike, for example, German law, Finnish law makes no distinction between domestic and foreign legal persons. In general, foreign legal persons enjoy the same fundamental rights within the jurisprudence of Finland. In civil law, this also applies to all legal persons with full legal capacity, such as foundations, registered associations, and companies. It also applies to associations with limited civil

195. Heikki Jaatinen, *Oikeushenkilön rangaistusvastuu* (Liability of legal persons). (Jyväskylä: Kauppakaari – Lakimiesliiton Kustannus, 2000), 68–69.
196. For further detail, *see* Part III. Legal Status of Religious Communities, Ch. 1. Formal Status of Religious Communities.
197. HE 309/1993 vp, 21–25.

legal capacity, such as non-registered associations. It means also that foreign religious communities can operate freely in Finland, even if the actual centre of their activity is located abroad (e.g., the Mormons, and the Salvation Army).

440. The main restriction comes from the Criminal Code when a legal person is being punished for crimes committed either within or outside Finland. The problem is more broadly linked to the question of which country should be considered as the 'domicile' (kotipaikka) of a legal person. First, domicile may mean the State under the law of which a legal person is established. Second, domicile may also be the State in which the legal person's business or other activities are conducted. The legal systems of different countries have dealt with this question differently.[198]

441. In Finland, according to Dr *Dan Helenius,* in light of Chapter 9 of the Criminal Code, it may at least be considered sufficient for a legal person to be established in Finland, i.e., registered in a trade or similar register. However, many instruments for convergence with EU criminal law also require that Member States should be involved when the offence is committed on behalf of a 'legal person established in the territory of the State' or 'in favour of a legal person whose head office is situated within the territory of that Member State'.[199] Consequently, the provisions do not appear to require the principal place of business in that particular State. Hence, legal persons subject to penalties under Chapter 9 of the Criminal Code must either be established in Finland or must have their principal place of business in Finland.[200]

C. Religious Communities as Ideological Associations under Private Law

442. Religious communities that have the status of non-profit ideological associations also fully enjoy fundamental rights within the scope of Chapter 2 (§6 and §11) of the Constitution and its Article 22. However, the status of ideological associations, even when they are religious associations, does not incorporate them into the state structures 'as registered religious communities'.

443. The position of religious communities when they are organized as ideological associations is governed by the Law on Associations (503/1989). Its main obligations are *also expressed* in Article 27 of the RFA.

198. Martin Böse, Frank Meyer & Anne Schneider (eds), *Conflicts of Jurisdiction in Criminal Matters in the European Union: Vol. I* (Baden-Baden: Nomos, 2013), 490–492.
199. HE 317/2010 vp, 36–37.
200. Dan Helenius, 'Oikeushenkilön rangaistusvastuu Suomen ulkopuolella tehdyistä rikoksista' (Liability of legal persons for crimes committed outside Finland). *Defensor Legis* 4 (2015): 775. For the interpretation of criminal law in the European context, *see* Kimmo Nuotio, 'Rikosoikeudellisesta laintulkinnasta eurooppaoikeudellisten oikeuslähteiden vaikutuspiirissä' (On interpretation of criminal law when sources of European law need to be taken into account). In Ville Hinkkanen & Leena Mäkipää (eds), *Suomalainen kriminaalipolitiikka: Näkökulmia teoriaan ja käytäntöön. Tapio Lappi-Seppälän juhlakirja.* (Helsinki: Helsingin yliopiston oikeustieteellinen tiedekunta, 2013).

444. The comprehensive legislation of the RFA brings together everything that regulates both registered religious communities and coincides with the regulatory needs of non-profit associations.

445. The Law on Associations (section 27 of the RFA) reads:

> In addition to the provisions of this Act, the following provisions of the Associations Act concerning registered associations shall apply *mutatis mutandis* to a registered religious association:
>
> 1) the provisions of section 5 on economic activities;
> 2) the provisions of Article 9 on bilingualism (Finnish/Swedish);
> 3) the provisions of Sections 14 and 15 concerning the expulsion from an association and the expulsion procedure;
> 4) the provisions of sections 32–34 on the voidability of resolutions, the voidness of resolutions, and the ban on enforcement;
> 5) the provisions of section 36 on the persons entitled to sign the name of the association;
> 6) the provisions of section 37 on disqualification;
> 7) the provisions of section 38 on auditing;
> 8) the provisions of section 39 on liability to pay damages;
> 9) the provisions of sections 40–42 of the dissolution of the association;
> 10) the provisions of section 45 on the termination of activities and the liquidators;
> 11) the provisions of section 46 on the competent court;
> 12) the provisions of section 58 on liability for obligations;
> 13) the provisions of section 60 on the court's obligation of notification;
> 14) the provisions of section 61 on the surrendering assets in bankruptcy.

446. Unregistered religious associations (unlike those associations that have the status of ideological associations under the Associations Act) do not have legal authority. Hence, they cannot assert any rights or obligations, enter into commitments, or act as litigants in a court. The obligations of an unregistered religious community shall be borne personally and jointly by those who have participated in the undesirable activities of such an association. Other members of the community are not responsible for such obligations.

D. Nature of Rights

447. As mentioned previously, Chapter 2 of the Finnish Constitution, which deals with fundamental rights and liberties, generally protects *every human being* within the jurisdiction of Finland.

448. The same reference to the value of the individual is already present in the very first Article of the Constitution, which declares that human dignity is inviolable: 'The constitution shall guarantee the inviolability of human dignity and the freedom and rights of the individual and promote justice in society'. Furthermore, the freedom of religion and conscience, as provided more specifically by Article 11 (sections 1 and 2) of the Constitution, presupposes an individual human being, since conscience is a purely individual phenomenon; no legal entity can have a conscience.

449. However, religious communities do enjoy freedom of religion or belief, as guaranteed in Article 3, section 1 of the Freedom of Religion Act. Religion and belief are matters that are experienced and lived in community with others. Legal persons rooted in a religious or philosophical ethos therefore enjoy those freedoms. Other legal entities, such as normal associations and business companies, do not enjoy freedom of religion or belief. The membership-based religious practice is considered to be an independent phenomenon and mode of action, separate from other community activities, as the Finnish Religious Freedom committee has emphasized.

E. The Notion of Religious Community

450. 'Religious community' in the sense of Article 2 of the RFA means 'the Evangelical Lutheran Church, the Orthodox Church, and the religious communities that have been registered in the manner described in Chapter 2' (Registered religious communities).

451. However, the meaning of the term 'religious community' is theologically and church sociologically very broad. In a Christian context, it primarily covers churches and religious communities as an organization of faith and everything that constitutes them as churches – dogma and synods, bishops and clerical hierarchy, liturgy and diaconia, etc.

452. The self-understanding of every religious community can be much wider than that understood by the traditional churches and religious communities, and hence the term 'religious community' encompasses all aspects of life where religion is practised from the cradle to the grave.

§2. Case Law

453. The cases concerning the nature of the rights of the registered religious communities are discussed in greater detail in Part VI, The Labour Law within the Religious Communities, *II. Religious Freedom and Employees' Rights in the Workplace.*

Chapter 4. Religious Freedom and Equality

§1. Constitutional Guarantees

454. Religious equality is made explicit in several provisions of the Finnish Constitution. Article 6(2) of the Constitution contains a list of certain prohibited grounds involving discrimination. It specifically mentions religion and belief.

455. Article 6 of the Constitution reads:

(1) Everyone is equal before the law.
(2) No one shall, without an acceptable reason, be treated differently from other persons on the ground of sex, age, origin, language, *religion, conviction*, opinion, health, disability or other reason that concerns his or her person.[201]
(3) Children shall be treated equally and as individuals and they shall be allowed to influence matters pertaining to themselves to a degree corresponding to their level of development.
(4) Equality of the sexes is promoted in societal activity and working life, especially in the determination of pay and the other terms of employment, as provided in more detail by an Act.

456. While the general equal treatment clause in Article 6 section 2 of the Constitution also covers matters that relate to religion, special equal treatment provisions are laid down in Article 11(1–2), which focus only on questions of religion. Article 11 of the Constitution reads:

(1) Everyone has the freedom of religion and conscience.
(2) Freedom of religion and conscience entails the right to profess and practice a religion, the right to express one's convictions and the right to be a member of or decline to be a member of a religious community. No one is under the obligation, against his or her conscience, to participate in the practice of a religion.

457. Although 'religion' and 'conviction' are specifically mentioned as prohibited grounds for differential treatment, the Constitution does not contain specific definitions of religion or belief. Neither preparatory work nor case law defines these concepts more specifically. Instead, the RFA (453/2003) defines a 'religious community' for the purposes of that act. As noted earlier, according to section 2 of the Freedom Religion Act, the term 'religious community' refers to the Evangelical Lutheran Church, the Orthodox Church and registered communities under the Act.

458. The relationship of Articles 6 and 11 can be expressed as follows. The first of these Articles is concerned with equality: no one shall, without an acceptable reason, be treated differently from other persons on the grounds of religion or conviction. The second concerns the right to profess and practice religion, the right to

201. Italics mine.

express one's convictions, and the right to be a member of a religious community, as well as the right to decline to be a member of any religious community.

459. In sum, it can be stated that the general equal treatment clauses (§6 and §11) of the Constitution form a part of the general principle of state neutrality in religious matters, in terms of both equality and also parity. It includes a prohibition on arbitrariness and the requirement that similar treatment be given in similar cases. The general equality clause also applies to the legislature. The law cannot arbitrarily place people or groups of people at an advantage or disadvantage. This touches also on religious faith or religious opinions, as well as on non-religious and anti-religious opinions and convictions.

§2. General Non-discrimination

460. Current anti-discrimination legislation in Finland can be characterized by a certain dualism and fragmentation, both of which have led to many amendments to this legislation over a long course of time. On the one hand, the older parts of the legislation, in particular the Constitution and Criminal Code (*Rikoslaki* [39/1889]), explicitly cover a large number of grounds for discrimination. On the other hand, the more recent parts of the legislation, in particular the Non-discrimination Act (Yhdenvertaisuuslaki [21/2004]) and the Act on Equality between Women and Men (*Laki naisten ja miesten tasa-arvosta* [609/1986]), contain more detailed provisions with regard to the definition of discrimination. In addition, religious and conscientious equality and the prohibition of religious discrimination are enshrined in sections 6 and 11 of the Constitution of 2000, respectively, as has been mentioned previously.

461. The latest stage in the evolution of the legislative work can be seen in the work of the committee appointed by the Ministry of Justice, the task of which was to renew Finnish legislation against discrimination and to improve it significantly by drawing on the equality and non-discrimination requirements laid down in the new Constitution. The committee delivered its report for a new Non-discrimination Act in December 2009, along with proposals for further revisions of the legislation.[202] The report proposed that the scope of the Act's application be expanded to make it applicable to all public and private activities and that all discriminatory grounds be made subject to the same legal remedies. Further, more specific provisions on exceptions to the scope of application were proposed for inclusion in the Act.[203] In 2010 various bodies, the Evangelical Lutheran Church among them, commented on the proposal.

---

202. Lausunto Yhdenvertaisuuslainsäädännön uudistamista koskevan toimikunnan mietinnöstä (Oikeusministeriön komiteamietintö 2009:4), Asiannumero 2008-00301, 15.4.2010 (Opinion on the Report of the Committee on the Reform of Equality Legislation [Ministry of Justice Committee Report 2009: 4], Case No. 2008-00301, 15.4.2010).

203. For further information about the committee work of 2007, *see* Heikkonen, Johannes & Pamela Slotte. 'Religion and Discrimination Law in the European Union: Finland'. In *Mark Hill QC (ed.),*

462. The proposal for the Equality Act (*Esitys yhdenvertaisuuslaiksi ja eräiksi siihen liittyviksi laeiksi*, HE 19/2014) and its amendment (111/2014) came into force in January 2015 as the Equality Act (1325/2014). The Act clarified the provisions on the definition of discrimination and any justifications for unequal treatment.

463. The new law (1325/2014) includes the following improvements, which were mentioned in the Preamble of the Government proposal of the Equality Act (19/2014):

- The legal protection of those discriminated against was improved by broadening the scope of the remedy provision. In some respects, the enforcement of the Equality Act [21/2004] was reformed.
- The current position of the Ombudsman for Minorities [vähemmistövaltuutettu] was replaced by that of the Non-discrimination Ombudsman [yhdenvertaisuusvaltuutettu]. The mandate of the Ombudsman was extended to cover all forms of discrimination within the meaning of the proposed Equality Act. However, as currently the case would be subject to enforcement by the labour protection authorities in individual cases concerning labour law. The role of the Non-discrimination Ombudsman would be to oversee compliance with the Equality Act and otherwise promote equality and prevent discrimination.
- The existing National Discrimination Tribunal [syrjintälautakunta] and the Equality Tribunal are to merge into National Non-discrimination and Equality Tribunal [yhdenvertaisuus ja tasa-arvolautakunta]. Its tasks would consist of those of the existing Equality Board and the National Discrimination Tribunal, and it is proposed to extend its remit to cover all grounds of discrimination.
- The promotion of gender equality and the prohibition of discrimination on grounds of sex would continue to be governed by the Law on Equality between Women and Men. The banning of discrimination on grounds of sex was extended to include discrimination based on gender identity or gender expression. The law was complemented by an obligation to prevent discrimination based on gender identity or gender expression.
- The equality provisions for educational institutions were clarified and extended to include primary education institutions. The workplace equality plan and the related payroll obligation were clarified. The implementation of gender equality would be further monitored and promoted by the Non-discrimination Ombudsman.
- The existing prohibitions on discrimination in the employment law were replaced by a reference to the Discrimination Act and the Equality Act.
- The legislation, like the existing legislation, implemented the so-called Discrimination and Employment Discrimination Directives.[204]

Religion and Discrimination Law in the European Union – La discrimination en matière religieuse dans l'Union Européenne. (Trier: European Consortium for Church and State Research, 2012), 130–139.

204. For further detail, *see* the Preamble of the Equality Act 1325/2014.

464. The new Equality Act (1325/2014) came into force on 1 January 2015. At the same time, changes were added to the Law on Equality between Women and Men, the Law on the Non-discrimination Ombudsman, and the Law on National Non-discrimination and Equality Tribunal. The purpose of the new law is to promote better equality and to prevent discrimination. The definition of discrimination is more precise and has been expanded to include reasonable accommodation for persons with disabilities.[205]

465. The Equality Act covers a wide range of grounds related to discrimination. In addition to direct and indirect discrimination, discrimination within the meaning of the new law includes harassment, denial of reasonable accommodation, and incitement to discriminate. Discrimination can occur even if it is not deemed in common opinion to be discriminatory. The enforcement of the Equality Act in the field of employment discrimination is a matter for the labour protection authorities.[206]

466. Obligations under the Equality Act apply to almost *all public and private activities.* In addition to the authorities, they apply to training providers, educational institutions, employers and now also service and goods providers. It therefore has a particular impact on companies and their responsibility to provide equal treatment.

467. Thus, the new law offers greater protection against discrimination. In addition to public activities, the law also applies to private activities, *with the exception of private life, family life, and religious practice.* As previously, the reformed legislation guarantees equal protection for all, regardless of whether they have been discriminated against on grounds such as age, origin, nationality, language, *religion, conviction*, opinion, state of health, disability, sexual orientation or any other personal reasons. Indeed, the protection of equality has been strengthened by extending it more uniformly to all areas of life and by subjecting discrimination on a variety of grounds to the most appropriate remedies and penalties.[207]

---

205. Reasonable accommodation means the necessary and appropriate changes and arrangements to be made on a case-by-case basis that do not impose an impossible or disproportionate burden, such as ensuring that persons with disabilities which enjoy all human rights and fundamental freedoms on an equal basis.

With the new law (1325/2014), the obligation to make reasonable adjustments was extended, as the obligation to adapt the old equality law (21/2004) was limited to employers and training providers. Now the obligation to adjust also extends to providers of services and goods (e.g., hotels, restaurants, shops). *See also*, Kevät Nousiainen, 'Tasa-arvon monet kasvot. Kansainvälisistä vaikutuksista Suomen tasa-arvo-oikeudessa (The many faces of equality. The international Impact on Equality Law in Finland). *Lakimies* 7–8 (2005): 1188–1209.

206. *See* the Equality Act (1325/2014), §20.

207. Italics in this paragraph mine.

§3. NON-DISCRIMINATION IN PUBLIC OFFICE

468. Finland has two guardian authorities that deal with discrimination: the Non-discrimination Ombudsman (*yhdenvertaisuusvaltuutettu*)[208] and the National Non-discrimination and Equality Tribunal (*yhdenvertaisuus- ja tasa-arvolautakunta*).[209] Their duty is to ensure that the public authorities and officials observe the law and fulfil their duties. They are also extremely important with respect to the prohibition of religious discrimination in the exercising of public powers.[210] Although previously their explicit area of study was discrimination based on ethnicity, nowadays their work can be considered as also encompassing religious discrimination, especially concerning religious minorities.[211] Finnish legality control – and therefore also non-discrimination – is also exercised by the Chancellor of Justice (*valtioneuvoston oikeuskansleri*).[212] In addition, the Parliamentary Ombudsman (*eduskunnan oikeusasiamies*) plays a very important role in the prohibition of religious discrimination.

469. The Ombudsman is appointed by the Council of State. The Office of the Ombudsman for non-discrimination works as an independent organ under the Ministry of the Interior and consists of several officials appointed by the Ombudsman. The Ombudsman for Non-discrimination has no actual judicial powers and therefore does more work in areas such as counselling and monitoring. The National Non-discrimination and Equality Tribunal of Finland, in turn, is an independent organ promoting legal protection in the area covered by the Non-discrimination Act. The tribunal is also appointed by the Council of State and, as with the Non-discrimination Ombudsman, works as an independent organ under the Ministry of the Interior. A decision reached by the National Non-discrimination and Equality Tribunal of Finland has the same legal effect as a judgment made by a general court of law. However, religions play no specific role in the work of either the National Non-discrimination and Equality Tribunal or the Non-discrimination Ombudsman.

470. In principle, the constitutional equality provision applies only to people. The principle of equality may also play a role in the assessment of the rules applicable to legal persons, in particular where the legal position of natural persons may be indirectly affected. The relationship between the principle of equality and legal personality was discussed in greater detail in Part II, Chapter 3.[213]

471. Equal treatment does not require identical treatment, but it is intended to treat equally what is equal and to treat unequally what is not equal, according to the

208. The predecessor of the Non-discrimination Ombudsman was the Ombudsman for Minorities (Vähemmistövaltuutettu).
209. The predecessor of the National Non-discrimination and Equality Tribunal was the National Discrimination Tribunal (Syrjintälautakunta).
210. For further detail, *see* Heikkonen & Slotte 2012, 132–133.
211. Heikkonen & Slotte 2012, 133.
212. The Chancellor of Justice supervises the lawfulness of the official acts of the Government, the ministries and the President of the Republic.
213. *See* further §1. Basic Principles, III. Fundamental Rights of Legal Persons.

extent of the differences. For example, normal state labour law applies (collective labour agreements) if there is a difference in treatment on grounds of the religion or beliefs of the employees of a religious community (regardless of their legal status). It is, however, modified in many circumstances on the basis of the new Freedom of Religion Act (2003). This will be discussed in greater detail in Part VI. (Labour Law within Religious Communities).

472. The provision in Finnish jurisprudence prohibiting discrimination does not prohibit all types of discrimination between persons, even if the discrimination is expressly mentioned in the provision. What matters is whether the distinction can be justified in a way that is acceptable to the fundamental rights system.[214] The requirements for justification are particularly high in the case of the prohibited discriminatory criteria listed in the provision. In addition to the acceptability of the distinction, the Constitutional Law Committee's practice has paid attention to the proportionality of the method chosen. In its opinions, the Constitutional Law Committee has assessed the acceptability of differential treatment based on, *inter alia*, sex,[215] age,[216] nationality,[217] religion or belief,[218] health and disability,[219] and other personal causes.[220]

473. The prohibition of discrimination from the point of public office also applies to: (a) pure discrimination (segregation); (b) indirect discrimination, that is to say, measures whose effects, albeit indirectly, would lead to discriminatory outcomes;[221] (c) affirmative actions, such as measures to improve the situation and conditions of women, children and minorities;[222] (d) and also provisions on the treatment of children, which ensure the equal status of children.[223] For example, the special treatment of children and young people is common in criminal law.[224]

---

214. *See* further Part II., Ch. 9., I. B. The Variety of Limitations and II. B. *Structural Limitations*.
215. PeVL 38/2006 vp, 2, PeVL 30/2005 vp, 5, PeVL 10/2003 vp, 3, PeVL 13/1995 vp, 3, PeVL 21/1994 vp, 1. 100
216. For a summary of age-based distinctions, *see* PeVL 44/2010 vp, 6.
217. PeVL 26/2010 vp, 2, PeVL 13/2009 vp, 2, PeVL 11/2009 vp, 7, PeVL 31/2008 vp, 2, PeVL 6/2008 vp, 2, PeVL 19/2005 vp, 3, PeVL 28/2004 vp, 3, PeVL 30/2002 vp, 2, PeVL 26/2001 vp, 2.
218. PeVL 9/2007 vp, 6, PeVL 28/2006 vp, 3, PeVL 19/2005 vp, 3–4, PeVL 28/2004 vp, 2, PeVL 57/2001 vp, 2. 103
219. PeVL 60/2010 vp, 3, PeVL 31/2006 vp, 3–4.
220. PeVL 23/2012 vp, 2–3, PeVL 14/2006 vp, 2, PeVL 59/2002 vp, 2, PeVL 18/2001 vp, 8, PeVL 36/2000 vp, 2, PeVL 23/2000 vp, 2, PeVL 9/2000 vp, 2–3, PeVL 37/1997 vp, 2. 105
221. HE 309/1993 vp, 44; *see also* PeVL 28/2009 vp, 2, PeVL 40/2004 vp, 2, PeVL 10/2003 vp, 2, PeVL 46/2002 vp, 6–7.
222. HE 309/1993 vp, 44; *see also* PeVL 56/2010 vp, 4, PeVL 38/2006 vp, 2, PeVL 34/2005 vp, 2, PeVL 40/2004 vp, 2, PeVL 10/2003 vp, 3, PeVL 20/1998 vp, PeVL 3/1997 vp.
223. HE 309/1993 vp, 45. The provision on the right of the child to influence his or her own affairs, in line with his or her level of development, demonstrates that each child should be treated as an individual and not merely as a passive subject. For closer information, *see* HE 309/1993 vp, 45, PeVM 25/1994 vp, 7.
224. For further information, *see* PeVL 21/2005 vp, 4, PeVL 59/2001 vp, 2.

§4. Institutional Equality

474. A special expression of the rule of equal treatment in religious matters is the principle of parity. It is generally accepted that the difference in status between (registered) religious communities and those religious communities that have the status of corporations (organized as ideological associations)[225] by civil law does not contradict the right to equal treatment. As such, they determine what is required of equal treatment according to the constitution. The difference in status draws its legitimacy first and foremost from the different status under public law, and second, from the historical relevance that various denominations and religions have had in the course of Finnish history. Each status also follows the provisions of the RFA (453/2003), where status – as a registered religious community – is defined when the individual religious community meets the minimum requirements.[226]

475. As indicated earlier (in Part I., Chapter 3 §4), parity means the obligation to treat all religious communities equally. In the Finnish system, however, equal treatment finds its critical point in the case of collective religious freedom: the two national churches, the Lutheran and the Orthodox, have through the course of history gained a special position and different status *under public law* compared to all other religious communities. This status is also guaranteed through a constitutional differentiation of their legal status, i.e., by Article 76, which maintains the *status quo* concerning the Evangelical Lutheran Church. In parallel with the Lutheran Church, the legal status of the Orthodox Church in relation to the state has remained as previously in the Orthodox Church Law (985/2006). From a minority perspective, however, this may be problematic. The preferential status of the major churches may negatively affect the status of other religious communities and also the lives of non-believers or free thinkers.[227] It may, therefore, happen that issues of presumed discrimination are often framed in terms of majority–minority issues.

§5. Equal Treatment of Non-religious, Philosophical Communities

476. The equal treatment of non-religious and philosophical communities from the perspective of the Constitution, the most important manifestations of freedom of religion and conscience, as already alluded to, is based on Article 11(2) of the Constitution, which declares the right to confess and practice religion, the right to express conviction, religious freedom of association, and what is termed *negative religious freedom,* i.e., the right not to belong to a religious community.[228]

225. These are governed by the Law on Associations (503/1989).
226. For greater detail, *see* Juha Seppo, *Uskonnonvapaus 2000-luvun Suomessa* (Freedom of Religion in 21st Century Finland), (Helsinki: Edita, 2003), 159–160, 169–175.
227. Martin Scheinin (*Ihmisoikeudet Suomen oikeudessa*, Suomalainen Lakimiesyhdistys) 1991, 157 has attracted attention that in the government bill on the ratification of the ICCPR, no specific attention was paid for instance to the implications which freedom of religion as prescribed in Art. 18 of the convention might have for the traditional Finnish church–state arrangement.
228. HE 309/1993 vp, 55. PeVM 10/2002 vp, 2.

477. Negative religious freedom also implies that no one can be forced to attend religious services or other religious practices in violation of his or her conscience. However, this does not prevent other people's positive freedom of religion.[229]

478. In this context, religious education in state and private schools should be mentioned separately. Compared with Western European practice, it is a peculiarity of the Finnish system that *the content of positive religious freedom belongs also the teaching of religion 'according to one's own religion*'. Religious freedom requires the individual to have access to religious or philosophical teaching. Teaching and upbringing must respect the individual's conviction, the rights of the child, and the right of the guardian to respond to the child's development.[230] The formulation used in the law of religious freedom (453/2003) and the current school laws, is neutral: every student in comprehensive and upper comprehensive schools also has a right to world-view studies (ethics).

479. In sum, it can be stated that non-religious communities and ideological associations that have the status of non-profit ideological associations also enjoy full fundamental rights and equal treatment within the scope of Chapter 2 of the Constitution (§6 and §11) and its Article 22. The status of ideological associations, even when they have religious functions, however, does not, according to Finnish jurisprudence, incorporate them into the category of 'registered religious communities'. As noted above, this may be problematic from a minority perspective, since the question of discrimination may be transposed into questions concerned with majority-minority rights.[231]

229. HE 309/1993 vp, 55. PeVM 10/2002 vp, 3–4.
230. HE 309/1993 vp, 55–56. PeVM 10/2002 vp, 3–4.
231. *See* Martin Scheinin, 'Secular Human Rights Perspectives: As a Challenge to Nordic Law & Religion Solutions', 125–141. In Lisbet Christoffersen et al. (eds), *Law & Religion in the 21st Century – Nordic Perspectives* (København: Djøf Publishing, 2010).

Part III. Legal Status of Religious Communities

Chapter 1. Formal Status of Religious Communities

480. There are two different forms of status that religious communities can acquire. Such statuses are organized according to either public law or civil law. In addition, given the legal status of religious freedom and conviction, every religious group is free to function even if it has no status as a legal entity, i.e., registration is not a required condition for a religious group to function as such.

481. Only the Evangelical Lutheran and Orthodox churches with their parishes and congregations are public law entities.

482. Private legal entities are registered religious associations within the meaning of Chapter 2 of the RFA. Similarly, non-profit organizations organized under the Law on Associations are governed by private law.

483. The administration of bodies governed by public law is governed by the principles of administrative law and the courts of administrative courts apply the line of Regional Administrative Court – the Supreme Administrative Court. Parish members have a general right of appeal. The churches are governed by the general laws of the administrative law, either as such or by means of Acquisitions, modified for the needs of the churches. Churches are also subject to legality control (the Chancellor of Justice and the Parliamentary Ombudsman).

484. When churches and parishes deal with matters of private law, such as construction work, they must comply with the rules of administrative jurisdiction and procedure which, in an appeal, are assessed by the administrative courts. If a dispute then arises about the content or performance of a private law contract, such as a works contract or purchase, the matter will be referred to the General Court by the District Court – Court of Appeal – Supreme Court.

485. Registered religious communities and ordinary associations operate in a manner similar to parishes under the Church Law and by-laws, under the Associations Act and their established rules. Registered religious communities are also subject to special provisions of the RFA, but the general rule is the Associations Act.

They are not subject to administrative legislation or general administrative and judicial review. Appeals concerning the decisions of these communities are made to the General Court, i.e., the District Court – Court of Appeal – Supreme Court. This is radically different from a public appeal, which is simple and cheap compared to litigation.

§1. Religious Communities as Public Law Corporations (Bodies)

I. General Principles

486. When study is undertaken of the legal status of churches and religious associations, since as long ago as 1922[232] it has been possible to distinguish between three types of religious communities whose different status under public law regulates their position in Finnish society, their sources of income, and also the financial support that they receive from the State. According to the Freedom of Religion Act (170/2002 vp), these religious communities are the Evangelical Lutheran Church, the Finnish Orthodox Church, and registered religious associations.

487. The status of the Evangelical Lutheran Church and its parishes under public law is secured in the Constitution (§76) and is based on the Church Act. Although Article 76 is placed in Chapter 6 of the Constitution, which provides for the relevant legislation, the article outlines an autonomous status for the Evangelical Lutheran Church in relation to its own legislation.[233]

488. In the new constitution, there is no direct provision for the Finnish Orthodox Church to regulate its position in society.[234] In this respect, therefore, the legislative status of the Orthodox Church differs from that of the Lutheran Church. The Orthodox Church is the subject of a new law concerning the Orthodox Church, 2007 (985/2006), where its status as a public entity is defined.[235]

489. In Finland, a registered religious association is, however, a special type of community. Its foundation and legal status are enacted in subsection 2 of the Freedom of Religion Act. Such a religious body gains the status of a legal person, that is, it can acquire property, enter into commitments, and be a litigant in court and with other authorities once it is entered into the register of religious associations. In this respect, the regulation observes the principle otherwise observed in Finnish

---

232. In the old Freedom of Religion Act from 1922 a completely new type of legal person was defined in addition to the Evangelical Lutheran Church and the Orthodox Church, i.e., the 'religious community', currently the registered religious community.
233. *See* above, Part I, §1. Constitution, III. Institutional Guarantees.
234. Earlier, the legal position of the Orthodox Church was based on the Orthodox Church Act (521/1969) and its supplementary statute (179/1970).
235. The Governmental proposal states that the Finnish Orthodox Church is 'at the same time a Finnish public body and part of a worldwide Orthodox Church' (HE 59/2006 vp, 6).

community law, whereby the community achieves legal capacity once it is entered into the register of associations kept by the authorities, in this case, the National Patent and Register Board.

490. Religious activities can also be practised in the form of an ideological association or, entirely without organizing, in the form of a legal person as laid down in civil law.

II. Special Rights and Duties of Religious Communities as Public Law Corporations

491. The most important public authorities are the state and the municipalities. Public authorities also include municipal federations and the Province of Åland. In addition, public bodies include the Evangelical Lutheran Church and the Orthodox Church, and statutory public law associations such as the Finnish Road Safety Council (*Liikenneturva*) and the Finnish gaming company, *Veikkaus Oy*[236] can also be counted as government entities. Other legal persons governed by public law are independent public law bodies (*julkisoikeudelliset laitokset*).

492. The State of Finland is a single legal entity with internal and external sovereignty. A key element of the State's internal sovereignty is the ability to regulate the powers of all public authorities and other bodies within the State. It also includes the power to decide on the content of the legal order, the functioning of state organs and the right to exercise public authority over people and objects within the territory of the State.[237]

493. The fact that the State is a single legal entity means that state administrative bodies do not have any such legal personality and they also do not have their own rights or obligations. For example, the Finnish tax administration (*Verohallinto*) does not have a legal personality even though it may exercise state authority in legal proceedings.[238]

494. Compliance with the rule of law requires that the public authorities always ultimately have their base in a recognition of their competence, as laid down by an Act of Parliament.[239] Thus, a public authority cannot have the power to use its public authority without explicit support for doing so in law. The starting point is that the competent authority in each case must be identified by law.[240] The conditions

236. Veikkaus Oy started operating on 1 Jan. 2017 when the Finnish gaming system was reformed and the previous three operators, Fintoto, Finland's Slot Machine Association (RAY), and Veikkaus merged into a single gaming company owned by the Finnish State.
237. HE 1/1998 vp, 71.
238. However, this division is not without exception, as the Bank of Finland and the Social Insurance Institution, for example, have their own rights and obligations.
239. HE 1/1998 vp, 74.
240. PeVL 67/2010 vp, 5.

provided for public administration duties other than for regulating the authorities are spelt out in §124 of the Constitution (*Delegation of administrative tasks to others than the authorities*). Article 124 reads:

> A public administrative task may be delegated to others than public authorities only by an Act or by virtue of an Act, if this is necessary for the appropriate performance of the task and if basic rights and liberties, legal remedies and other requirements of good governance are not endangered. However, a task involving significant exercise of public powers can only be delegated to public authorities.

495. A legal person governed by public law is a body which exercises public authority in the performance of its tasks.[241] A legal person governed by private law has no such public authority. Legal persons governed by public law also perform public functions when they perform legal acts under private law.

496. With regard to registered religious communities, the distinction between public and private legal entities (persons) is not absolute. For example, the Evangelical Lutheran Church and its parishes and the Finnish Orthodox Church are bodies governed by public law, and as public law entities, they enjoy a number of special rights that other registered religious communities (associations) do not have. Specific rights also correlate with specific duties.

497. The most important of these rights and duties are the following: the right to collect church taxes from their own members,[242] the right to have civil servants (ELCF),[243] the right to take disciplinary measures against their officials (ELCF & OCF),[244] the right to require oaths sworn by their officials (ELCF),[245] the right to keep public registration files,[246] the duty to maintain public cemeteries,[247] and the right to provide religious assistance to the armed forces, penal institutions, hospitals, and other public institutions.[248]

---

241. A legal person governed by public law is generally constituted by a special law which regulates its operation and functions. A legal person governed by public law thus has its own rights and obligations as well as the status of a legal person.
242. According to the Finnish Constitution, the right of taxation lies with the State (Art. 81), the municipalities (Art. 121) and sub-laws of these related to the Evangelical Lutheran and Orthodox Churches. For more detail, *see* Part VIII. Church Financing.
243. The term civil servant covers public sector employees. The employment relationship is a public service employment relationship. Officials are employed by the state, municipalities and federations *and the Evangelical Lutheran Church*. Parliament also employs civil servants and some public law institutions. Those employed by the municipalities and the Church are called 'officers'. Officials may be appointed for an indefinite period or may be of limited duration.
244. These sanctions can take various forms such as warnings, cuts in salary, transfer to another post as a matter of sanction, or administrative fines. *See* more detailed Part VI, Ch. 2. *Religious Ministers and Labour Law – Case-Law.*
245. In addition to the priestly oath, a priest of Evangelical Lutheran Church also swears an oath of office.
246. Act on the Openness of Government Activities (621/1999), §4, para. 8(2): 'Separate provisions apply to access to the documents of the Evangelical Lutheran Church.' For further details, *see* the

498. Membership in a registered religious community that is a corporation under public law is acquired by the act – the Church Act or Church Order – prescribed by the religious community. This means that, in the case of the major Christian churches, the membership criterion is baptism. The registered religious communities that are public law corporations – either legal persons such as the ELCF and the OCF or public law bodies such as registered religious associations – are integrated into the public registration system.[249] They inform the state-registration authorities about the data and changes of residence of their members.

499. With respect to the Evangelical Lutheran Church as a public entity, the processing of personal data within the meaning of the Church Act (652/2023) is subject to EU Regulation 2016/679 of the European Parliament and of the Council on the protection of natural persons with respect to the processing of personal data and the repeal of Directive 95/46/EC (the General Data Protection Regulation / 2018), the Act on the Openness of Government Activities and the Law on the Population Information System and the Certification Services of the Population Register Centre (661/2009). (29.3.2019/411).[250]

500. The right of the Church Council to use and disclose access and log-in information is governed by sections 54(1), 55, 57 and 58 of the Population Register Centre's right to use and disclose the user and log-in information provided by the Population Information System and the Population Register Centre Certification Services (17 December 2015/1498).[251]

501. The Criminal Code also protects religious communities (ELCF and OCF) as public entities against the unlawful assumption of public office when they perform public activities such as issuing certificates or making entries in the church books.[252]

502. Inheritances or bequests donated to domestic religious communities under public law (and to any non-profit organizations) are exempt from inheritance tax, as provided for Chapter 1, section 2 of the Inheritance and Gift Act. Section 2 of that Act reads:

Church Act (652/2023), Chapter 8, §1 (Relationship with other legislation), and Ch. 8, §3, §5 (Church Books and Parish Archives), and Church Order (657/2023), Chapter 3 (Church Books), §62, §63, §66, and Chapter 10, §§10–12.

247. Laki valtion rahoituksesta evankelis-luterilaiselle kirkolle eräisiin yhteiskunnallisiin tehtäviin (Government proposal HE 247/2016 to Parliament for Government funding of the Evangelical Lutheran Church for some social tasks) 430/2015, s. 1; *See also* Hautaustoimilaki (Law on burials) 457/2003, Ch. 1, s. 3.

248. *See* further Part XII. *Religious Assistance in Public Institutions.*

249. From more about the Law on the Register of Religious Communities (614/1998), *see* §4 and §5, and the information given in these sections.

250. *See* Church Act (652/2023), Ch. 8, §1.

251. *See* Church Act (652/2023), Ch. 8, §4 and §12.

252. Chapter 16 of the Criminal Code (39/1889), §7 and §8.

The tax provided for in this Act shall not apply to inheritance from the crown or to property which, under the rules of the Association, has been transferred to another or given by will or gift to the State or its body, province, municipality, municipal council, to a church or other religious community, and to a charity or educational institution.[253]

503. In addition, there are at least three other tax exemptions for religious communities that should be mentioned here: (a) registered religious communities are exempt from transfer tax; (b) desolate churches and monasteries are exempt from property tax; and (c) religious communities are exempt from any broadcasting tax. These questions are discussed in greater detail in Chapter VIII, Church Financing.

§2. Registered Religious Associations as Private Law Corporations (Bodies)

I. General Principles

504. Registered religious associations are private law corporations that are registered as private law bodies within the public registration system, which is maintained by the National Patent and Register Board under the Ministry of Education and Culture.[254] To be constituted as a religious private law body, the association has to be a religious rather than economic entity.

505. The purpose and forms of operation of a registered association are further specified in section 7 of the RFA (453/2003). Paragraph 1 of Article 7 defines the individual and public starting points for the recognition and practice of religion by a religious community. They may consist of a creed, sacred scriptures, or other identified, sacred, and established operating principles. On the other hand, the Paragraph does not make registration a precondition of religion, since the promotion of such a religion could be hindered by organized religion within the meaning of the Freedom of Religion Act.

506. Article 7(3) seeks to ensure that the registering association is essentially a religious entity and not an economic entity. The purpose of a registered religious association is neither to seek financial gain nor to bring profit to the founders and members.[255] Economic activities are not per se prohibited and are subject to the provisions of Article 5 of the Associations Act concerning registered religious communities. A community may engage in any economic activity prescribed by its community order. It is also permissible to carry on an economic activity or gainful activity of a minor nature or of economic value.

253. *See* the Inheritance and Gift Act, s. 2 (Perintö- ja lahjaverolaki 378/1940).
254. For the registration criteria, *see* above, Ch. 3, III. Fundamental Rights of Legal Persons, *C. Religious Communities as Ideological Associations under Civil Law.*
255. *See* Religious Freedom Act (453/2003), §7(3).

507. Establishing a registered religious association requires at least twenty adults. Thus, the formation of a religious association requires more members than the establishment of a non-profit association of more than three persons. Although the minimum number of twenty members required in Finland is internationally low or even very low, no attempt has been made to raise it because of the risk of restricting religious freedom.[256]

508. The establishment of a registered religious association has to be the subject of a constitutional charter signed by the founders of the community. This provision is in line with the practice of the Associations Act.

509. The community order must include basic information about the religious association to be registered. It includes the Finnish domicile of the association, the purpose and forms of activity of the religious association, the membership criteria, the membership fees of the community, the persons exercising decision-making power in the association, and the procedures for changing or dissolving the community order. Unlike in the case of non-profit associations, members can only be individuals. Community duties include the obligation under the law concerning the register of the membership of religions to keep a register of its members.[257]

510. Religious associations can define the relationship between the community and local communities according to their own criteria and needs. Local communities, formerly called parishes, may not be formed on a regional basis, but it is possible to use other types of structures for them to organize themselves. An example of this is the possibility for monastic communities to organize themselves into local communities.[258]

511. The founding documents must be submitted to the National Patent and Register Board.[259]

II. Registered Religious Associations in Finland

512. The religious associations registered in 2022 by the National Patent and Register Board were as follows.

513. At the end of 2022, there were a total of 142 communities in Finland. The following Table does not include the national churches, the ELCF and the OCF, nor any community that practises religion in the form of an ideological association or generally without the organization of a legal person.[260]

256. *Ibid.*, §8.
257. *Ibid.*, §§9–12.
258. *Ibid.*, §13.
259. *Ibid.*, §18.
260. For more about the religious affiliation of major churches, *see* General Introduction, above, §2. Social Facts about Religion, I. *Religious Affiliation.*

514. In addition, the Table below is not based on the official data contained in the Statistics Finland's (Tilastokeskus) 'Population by religious community in 2000 to 2022', but instead on Finnish unofficial data from compiled sources.[261]

261. *See*, https://fi.wikipedia.org/wiki/Luettelo_Suomen_rekisteröidyistä_uskonnollisista_yhdyskunnista. This data has been compiled from the following sources: (1) Sundström, Kimmo: Registered Religious Communities and their religions or local communities on 31 Dec. 2017 (2 Mar. 2018). Metropolitan area Atheists Association; (2) Religions in Finland: Community listing and classification criteria; (3) National Patent and Register Board of Finland: Association Internet; (4) Research Center of the Evangelical Lutheran Church of Finland: 'Religions in Finland'; (5) Registered religious communities on 31 Dec. 2007 (Population Register Centre). Accessed on 23 Jun. 2018. (Webarchive.org), and (6) Sundström, Kimmo: Registered Religious Communities of Certain Religions in Finland on 31 Dec. 2018. Metropolitan area Atheists Association, and https://uskonnot.fi/yhteiso/. The entire material has been updated on 23 Jan. 2024.

Registered Religious Associations in Finland

Name of Association	*Registered*	*Orientation*	*Members 2007*	*Members 2022*	*Note*
Jehovah's Witnesses	1945		18,071	16,495 (2021)	
Free Church of Finland	1923	Christian conviction	13,786	14,555 (2021)	
Catholic Church in Finland	1929	Christian conviction	9,117	14,795 (2021)	
Pentecostal Church of Finland	2003	Christian conviction	3,251	12,343 (2021)	
Orthodox Church of St. Nicholas	1984	Christian conviction	1,585	3,596 (2021)	
The Church of Jesus Christ of Latter-day Saints (LDS)	1948	Christian conviction	3,246	3,187 (2021)	Mormon Church
Adventist Church of Finland	1943	Christian conviction	3,813	2,982 (2021)	
Helsinki Islamic Center	1995	Islam	1,482	3,043	
Islamic Community of Finland	1987	Islam	769	3,998	
Islamic community of Tampere	1998	Islam	721	1,916	
Baptist Church of Finland (SBK)	1928	Christian conviction	1,498	1,584	
Islamic Community of Northern Finland	2000	Islam	206	1,210	
Jewish congregation in Helsinki	1918	Judaism	1,059	972	

Name of Association	*Registered*	*Orientation*	*Members 2007*	*Members 2022*	*Note*
The Islamic Rahma Center in Finland	1998	Islam	559	2,011	
Finlands svenska baptistsamfund	1980	Christian conviction	901	819	
Resalat Islamic Community –Ähl-e Beit of Finland	2001	Islam	247	1,078	Former Al-Risala Islamic Community. Represents Shia.
Methodist Church of Finland	1925	Christian conviction	676	714	
The Islamic Community of Turku	2008	Islam		1,191	
The Vietnamese Buddhist community of Finland	1998	Buddhism		27	
Finlands svenska metodistkyrka	1925	Christian conviction	595	605 (2021)	
Finnish-Thai Buddhist Community	2016	Buddhism		617	
Finnish Islamic Congregation	1925	Islam	574	455	Former Mohammedan parish of Finland
Evangelical Lutheran Congregation of Finland (Suomen evankelisluterilainen seurakuntaliitto)	1928	Christian conviction	522	458	Until 2012 Free Evangelical Lutheran Congregation of Finland
Islamic Parish of Helsinki	2006	Islam	308	475	

Islamic Diyanet Community of Finland – Finlandiya Diyanet Islam Cemaati	2016	Islam		651	
Orthodox Pokrova Parish	1926	Christian conviction	352	396	Until 2004 private Greek-Catholic ecclesiastical community in Vyborg
Islamic Center of Finland	1994	Islam	66	330	The group has a Pakistani background
The Bahá'í Community of Finland	1963	Baha'i	528	653	
Islamic Society of the Bosnjak Finns of Finland	1999	Islam		351	Until 2013, the Bosnian Islamic Community of Finland
Islamic Community of Espoo in Finland	1998	Islam		643	
The Community of Christ Finland (Suomen Kristiyhteisö)	1969	anthroposophy	207	286	
As-Salaam Islamic Center & Masjid As-Salaam	2014	Islam		648	
Confessional Lutheran Church of Finland (Suomen Tunnustuksellinen Luterilainen kirkko, STLK)	1929	Christian conviction	308	286 (2019)	

Name of Association	*Registered*	*Orientation*	*Members 2007*	*Members 2022*	*Note*
The Bosnjak Islamic Community of Turku	2013	Islam		317	
Islamic Multicultural Da'wah Centre	2005	Islam	91	263	The majority of members are immigrants
Islamic Community of Central Finland	1998	Islam	109	338	
Imam Sadeq Islamic Community	2013	Islam		256	Represents Shia
A community of Muslim homes (Muslimikodin yhdyskunta)	2008	Islam		209	
Missionskyrkan i Finland	2004	Christian conviction	168	256 (2021)	
Anjuman-e-Islahul-Muslimeen of Turku	1998	Islam	97	272	Until 2001 Islamic Dawa Community
Islamic community of Kainuu	2008	Islam		185	
New hope parishes (Uuden toivon seurakunnat)	2008	Christian conviction		229	Former Nokia Mission Church
Hindus in Finland	2013	Hinduism		238	
Islamic Community of the Vaasa Region	1998	Islam		201	The majority of its members are Somali
Anglican Church of Finland	1936	Christian conviction	90	192	
Finnish Port Churches	2009	Christian conviction		168	
Muslims of Helsinki	2012	Islam		142	

Lutheran Word Society (Luterilainen Sanan yhdyskunta)	1983	Christian conviction	161	149	
Ahmadiyya Muslim Jamaat Finland	2015	Islam		157	
Islamic Community of Savo	2000	Islam	137	170	
Islamic Community of East Vantaa	2016	Islam		357	
Islamic Community of Vantaa	2013	Islam		214	
Free Catholic Church	1929	Christian conviction	139	119	Roots in the theosophical movement
Finnish-Vietnamese Buddhadhamma Community	2015	Buddhism		144	
Finlands svenska pingstsamfund	2003	Christian conviction	143	107	
Word of Faith Church Finland	2014	Christian conviction		137	From Kokkola
NUUR Islamic Community (Nuur)	2017	Islam		125	
Krishna movement ISKCON in Finland	1984	Hinduism	74	114	
The Jewish congregation in Turku	1919	Judaism	120	97	
International Charismatic Bible Church	2014	Christian conviction		67	
Islamic Society of Salo	2007	Islam	20	90	
Imam Hossai Islamic Community	2018	Islam		71	

Name of Association	*Registered*	*Orientation*	*Members 2007*	*Members 2022*	*Note*
The Islamic Congregation of Tampere	1943	Islam	83	58	The members are mainly Tartars
Harvest Church Finland	2017	Christian conviction		97	
Soka Gakkai International Suomi	2009	Buddhism		75	Originating from Japan, a Mahayana Buddhist
Diamond Way (Timanttipolku)	2014	Buddhism		62 (2018)	
Vörå Frikyrkoförsamling	1995	Christian conviction	61	52	Born of the unification of the Baptist and Pentecostal churches
Bear people (Karhun kansa)	2013	Finland faith		63	
Islamic Community of North Karelia	2006	Islam	32	55	
A religious community of the Mandians	2014	mandaeanism		57 (2021)	
Vineyard Church of Finland	2014	Christian conviction		52 (2018)	*See* Helsinki Vineyard
Islamic Society of Rovaniemi	2014	Islam		48	
New Apostolic Church of Finland	1979	Christian conviction	33	47	Roots in Scotland

Danakosha Ling	2005	Buddhism	46	47	Formerly Nyingmapa Community and Danakosha Finland. Tibetan Buddhist.
Buddhist Dharma Center	1998	Buddhism	39	36	
The Word of Life in Finland (Livets Ord Finland)	2018	Christian conviction		57	New Charismatic
Armenian Apostolic Church Community	2016	Christian conviction		39	Orthodox
Deeper Life Bible Church	2014	Christian conviction		36	Pentecostal, headquarters in Nigeria
Al-Furqaan Center for the Advancement of Islamic Knowledge and Welfare	2015	Islam		37 (2018)	Former Al-Furqaan-Islamic and Arabic Education Center
Incorporated Church of Slavic – Aryan Kins (ICSAK)	2013			25	
Finnish Shia Muslims	2004	Islam	48	23	
The Islamic Community of Finnish Moroccans	2008	Islam		53	
The Vietnamese Buddhist Community of Finland	2013	Buddhism		27	

Name of Association	*Registered*	*Orientation*	*Members 2007*	*Members 2022*	*Note*
Jaferia Islamic Society	2012	Islam		27	
Tabernacle (Ilmestysmaja)	2016	Christian conviction		33	
The Gurdwara community of Finland	1998	Sikhism		30 (2018)	
The Church of Pentecost International-Finland (COP)	2007	Christian conviction	24	26	Pentecostal, centre in Ghana
Tariq Al-Hidaya Islamic Community (The Way of Leadership)	2009	Islam		83	
Gurudwara of the Sikhs of Finland	2018	Sikhism		31	
Imam Ali Islamic Community	2006	Islam	37	0	
Spaso-Preobrazenskaja (Church of the Transfiguration of Christ)	1994	Christian conviction	25	27 (2021)	
The Islamic Religion and Culture Community of Finland	2013	Islam		41	
Buddha Dhamma Ramsi	2009	Buddhism		25	Burmese members
The Islamic Community of the Caucasians in Finland	2014	Islam		26 (2018)	
Calvary Chapel	2018	Christian conviction		24	Religious movement from California
Lutheran Confession Church of Finland (SLT)	2004	Christian conviction	25	0 (2021)	

Lochen Jangchup Tsemo – Buddhist colony	2012	Buddhism		25	Tibetan Buddhist
Pentecostal Parish of Pori	2014	Christian conviction		332	Belongs to Pentecostal Church of Finland
The Torch Church (Soihtukirkko)	2018	Christian conviction		26 (2021)	New Charismatic
Islamic Community of Kokkola	2018	Islam		20	Name to 2004 Church of God. Belongs to Pentecostal movement
Church of God Prophecy (Linkkiseurakunta)	1983	Christian conviction	31	0 (2021)	Name until 2004
The Sikhs of Finland	2014	Sikhism		23	
Finnish Coptic Orthodox	2013	Christian conviction		0 (2021)	Coptic
Minhaj-ul-Quran International Finland (MQIF)	2014	Islam		26	
Islam and Love	1994	Islam	20	0	Sufism
Palpung Yeshe Gatshal Finland	2007	Buddhism	27	0	Tibetan Buddhist
Sri Caitanya Sangha	2006	Hinduism	18	0	Same religious tradition as the Krishna movement
Redeemed Christian Church of God (RCCG)	2004	Christian conviction	10	0	Originating from Nigeria

Name of Association	*Registered*	*Orientation*	*Members 2007*	*Members 2022*	*Note*
Church of Christian Deeds (Kristillisten Tekojen Kirkko)	1983	Christian conviction		0	
Communion of Kimbangu	1999	Christian conviction	below 20	0	Originating from Belgian Congo
Seventh Day Adventists Reformation Movement	1991	Christian conviction	below 20	0	
Islamic Al-Huda Community in Finland	1998	Islam	below 20	0	
Kairos Esxatos	2008	Christian conviction		dissolved 24.9.2020	Roman Catholic
Finland Pureland Learning Center	2013	Buddhism		0	Represents the Buddhism of a clean country
Islamic Calling Society	1998	Islam		0	
Friends of Truth	1958		below 20	0	
Brahma Kumaris Finland	2013	Hinduism		0	
Ikhlas	2014	Islam		0	
PAK-FIN Islamic Cultural Center	2016	Islam		35	
Al-Falah Islamic community	2016	Islam		22	
Jewish Religious Community Guul Gol	2017	Judaism		0	
Jangchup Choeling Buddhist Center	2017	Buddhism		0	

Lutheran Word's Church of Tampere &	1983	Christian conviction	149	Belongs to Lutheran Word's Community
Lutheran Word's Church of Luopioinen	1983	Christian conviction	–	Belongs to Lutheran Word's Community
Helsinki Debre Amin Abune Tekla Haymanot Church Under the Northwest European Diocese of Ethiopian Orthodox Tewahdo	2004	Christian conviction	-	
Home Churches of Finland	2008		0 (2021)	
Jesus Christ Assembly (JCA)	2014	Christian conviction	0 (2021)	
Helsinki – Medhanealem Ethiopian Orthodox Tewahedo Community	2014	Christian conviction	34 (2021)	
RCCG Jesus Centre Turku	2015	Christian conviction	0 (2021)	
Covenant Parish (Rccg)	2015	Christian conviction	0 (2021)	
Dominion Believers Assembly (DBA) ru	2015		0 (2021)	
Kingship International Ministry Finland	2017		0 (2021)	
Northwind Church	2017		92 (2021)	

Name of Association	*Registered*	*Orientation*	*Members 2007*	*Members 2022*	*Note*
The Temple of Zion International Ministry	2017			0 (2021)	
Houm kirkko (Houm kyrka)	2017			53 (2021)	
Kingdom Church	2018			94 (2020)	
Debre Selam Medhanialem Eritrean Orthodox Tewahdo Parish, Helsinki, Finland	2018	Christian conviction		233 (2021)	
Hanko Pentecostal Parish	2018	Christian conviction		25 (2019)	
River Church Finland	2018			296 (2021)	
Glory Realm Bible Church	2018	Christian conviction		21 (2021)	
The Church of God, the Mission of the World	2018			0 (2021)	
Grace Montagnard Alliance Church Finland	2018			103 (2021)	

III. Termination of Status of Public Law Corporations

515. The status of two national churches can be terminated only by constitutional amendment, because the status of the ELCF is guaranteed by the constitution itself (§76). The status of OCF as public entity, in turn, is defined in Orthodox Church Act (985/2006), given by the Parliament.

516. There are no specific provisions in Finnish law how such a termination of the status or the restriction of specific rights attached to that status could be accomplished.

IV. Specific Issues of Organization

517. Followers of Islam are the largest non-Christian movement in Finland. Islam is both an old (Tartars) and a new minority in Finland. The number of Muslims increased tenfold in Finland in 1990–2011, and there are currently estimated to be 120,000–130,000 in the country. However, finding a precise number is difficult, since few of them have organized themselves into registered religious communities. Their registrations have, however, clearly increased in the early twenty-first century (1990, 810; 2000, 1,199; and 2022, 22,261).[262]

518. Those Muslim organizations that have not enrolled in the register of associations kept by the National Patent and Register Board are mostly structured as registered associations following general association law. If the religious association (or any other body) is not registered, it cannot receive competent legal person status nor gain rights and obligations. Persons acting on behalf of such an unregistered body become personally responsible for all of their commitments.

519. The local mosque community is the smallest organizational unit that, in private law, would usually be structured as an association.

520. There are several independent Islamic religious communities that have been registered as registered religious communities. The oldest of these is the *Finnish Islamic Congregation* (Suomen Islam-seurakunta), which was founded in 1925.[263] Until 1963 it was called the *Mohammedan Parish of Finland.* In 2022 its official membership was 455,[264] all of whom were Tartars, with the peculiarity that other nationalities were not accepted since the use of their own language was – and remains – an important part of their identity. The congregation carries out no missionary work among other Finns. The community has a mosque in Järvenpää and prayer rooms in Helsinki, Kotka, and Turku and employs its own imam. The Tatar Mosque in Järvenpää is Finland's only custom-built mosque, while all of the other buildings are prayer rooms.

262. *See* above, General Introduction, §2. Social Facts about Religion, I. *Religious Affiliation.*
263. Registered as a religious community on 24 Apr. 1925.
264. *See* https://uskonnot.fi/yhteiso/suomen-islam-seurakunta/. Accessed 23 Nov. 2023.

521. The second registered community that should be mentioned here, is the *Islamic Community of Finland* (Suomen Islamilainen Yhdyskunta), founded in 1987.[265] It is also the largest immigrant Muslim community in Finland. Its official membership was 3,998 in 2022,[266] and its members are mainly Arabs but also include Finnish converts. The community has a mosque in Helsinki, maintains a Qur'anic school and teaches Arabic and Somali.

522. The third registered Muslim community is the *Islamic Diyanet Community of Finland*, (Suomen Diyanet Yhdyskunta – Finlandiya Diyanet Cemaati), which was registered as a Religious Community in 2016.[267] Its official membership in 2022 was 651.[268] The community includes several prayer and mosque buildings around Finland, the most significant of which are the mosques in Vantaa, Pori, Turku, and Lahti. In cooperation with the Embassy of the Republic of Turkey, the Islamic Diyanet Community has three official Imams in Finland who have previously held international positions in Islamic religion and development before coming to Finland. In addition to prayers, Islamic holidays, ordinations, and funerals, the community offers instruction in the Qur'an and religion, both in Turkish and in Arabic. The majority of the members of the community come from Turkey, Finland, and Iraq.

523. In total, there are forty to eighty actual mosque communities in Finland, at least ten of which are situated in the city of Helsinki (2008) and thirty in the Helsinki Metropolitan Area (2015). Most mosques operate multilingually, but English is the dominant language and also, increasingly, Finnish. In their religious publications the language used is Arabic.

524. Until now, most of the mosques have been established by members of the same national background, but the majority of mosque associations are now members of associations that have united within umbrella organizations. In the Helsinki area there now exist the Helsinki Islamic Center (founded in 1995), with 3,043 members (2022),[269] and the Islamic Center of Finland (founded in 1994), which in 2022 had 330 members, mainly of Pakistani origin.[270] In addition, there are at least five other Islamic communities in the metropolitan area, each with its own prayer room. The *Islamic Community of Finland*, mentioned above, is part of the Federation of Islamic Organizations in Europe and also has ties to the Muslim World League. The Federation of Islamic Organizations in Europe is considered to be the European organization representing the Muslim Brotherhood.[271]

---

265. Registered as a religious community on 20 Feb. 1987.
266. *See* https://uskonnot.fi/yhteiso/suomen-islamilainen-yhdyskunta/. Accessed 23 Nov. 2023.
267. FPRO (PRH), https://yhdistysrekisteri.prh.fi/advancedSearch, Registration no. 900.442, Registration date 26 Oct. 2016.
268. *See* https://uskonnot.fi/yhteiso/suomen-diyanet-yhdyskunta-finlandiya-diyanet-cemaati. Accessed 23 Nov. 2023.
269. *See* https://uskonnot.fi/yhteiso/helsinki-islam-keskus/. Accessed 23 Nov. 2023.
270. *See* https://uskonnot.fi/yhteiso/suomen-islam-keskus/. Accessed 23 Nov. 2023.
271. *See* https://www.globalmbwatch.com/federation-of-islamic-organizations-in-europe/. Accessed 23 Nov. 2023.

525. The *Islamic Council of Finland* (Suomen Islamilainen Neuvosto, SINE) was established in November 2006 and coordinated since then by the Office of the Ombudsman for Minorities. The aim of the authorities was to establish an umbrella organization for Islamic communities and associations that would act as a liaison body with the authorities.[272] This goal has also been shared by the Muslim community, although the communities and organizations outside SINE have founded an alternative Islamic umbrella organization that has decided to use the old name of the Islamic Federation of Finland.

526. With respect to other new religious minorities, in 2022 there were twelve registered Buddhist communities, with a total of 1010 members, and four registered Hindu communities with 352 members.

527. It is interesting to note in this context that the *Scientology movement* has not been granted the status of a registered religious community in Finland. The Ministry of Education denied it access to the register of religious communities at the end of 1998. The Ministry justified its rejection of the application 'because in the activities of the scientologists the fundraising was seen to be more important than the practice of religion'.[273]

528. According to the latest study, in 2022 there were also 1,781,751 individuals in Finland who did not belong to any religious community. This number has tripled in the past twenty-five years (1990: 510,608).[274]

§3. Other Communities with a Religious Purpose, Functioning as Civil Law Corporations

I. Non-profit Associations

529. As stated previously, religious activities can also be practised in the form of an ideological association or generally, without acquiring the organizational status of a legal person.[275]

530. The most common method of establishing a religious community as a legal entity is to make use of the civil law institution of a registered non-profit association. This is also referred to in Article 13(2) of the Constitution, which guarantees the right, with no separate permission, to form an association, to belong to it or not,

---

272. *See* https://uskonnot.fi/yhteiso/suomen-islamilainen-neuvosto-ry/. Accessed 23 Nov. 2023.
273. Decision on the non-inclusion of a religious community named 'Church of Scientology of Finland' in the Register of Religious Communities. no. 85/901/94 dated 2 Oct. 1998.
274. For more detail, *see* https://pxdata.stat.fi/PxWeb/pxweb/en/StatFin/StatFin__vaerak/statfin_vaerak_pxt_11rx.px/table/tableViewLayout1/. Accessed 23 Nov. 2023.
275. Article 13(2) of the Constitution also explicitly protects the negative freedom of association, that is, the right not to belong to an association and to withdraw from it.

and to participate in the activities of the association.[276] Freedom of association, guaranteed by the Constitution, refers primarily to the right to associate as what is known as a non-profit association. But the provision of the Constitution does not preclude the creation of public law associations for public purposes.[277]

531. Freedom of association also includes the right to be treated as a non-registered association.[278] For the legislator it is important that the general outlines of the association's activities can, within certain limits, be regulated by law. The dissolution or temporary suspension of an association may only be a method of last resort and a way of preventing the association from acting illegally.[279] For example, action to promote or support crime is not a question of exercising the freedom of association guaranteed by the Constitution.[280]

A. *Idealistic Aim*

532. Religious organizations that want to be registered as non-profit associations must have idealistic aims. A religious community cannot be primarily an economic entity. The community should only engage in economic activities as defined in the community order. Even then, only activities of little economic value should be considered. When the economic activity becomes the predominant goal, the non-profit association loses this status and has to register as a for-profit organization.

B. *Registration Requirements*

533. Religious entities, like any other entity wishing to be registered as a non-profit association, have to meet the formal requirements of the Finnish Associations Act (503/1989).[281] With regard to the administration of an association, Article 35 of the Act is central. It stipulates a minimum of three founding members and also that the chairperson may not be a person with no previous legal competence:

(1) An association shall have an executive committee which shall consist of no less than three members. The executive committee shall carefully attend to the affairs of the association in compliance with the law, the rules, and resolutions adopted by the association. The executive committee shall see to it that the

276. Article 13 (Freedom of assembly and freedom of association) of the Constitution, para. 2 reads: 'Everyone has freedom of association. Freedom of association entails the right to form an association without a permit, to be a member or not to be a member of an association, and to participate in the activities of an association. The freedom to form trade unions and to organize in order to look after other interests is likewise guaranteed'.
277. HE 309/1993 vp, 60.
278. *Ibid.*
279. HE 309/1993 vp, 60.
280. PeVL 7/2002 vp, 3.
281. An unofficial translation of the Finnish Associations Act (503/1989) can be found on the web pages of the Finnish Patent and Registration Office: https://www.prh.fi/en/yhdistysrekisteri/act.html.

association's bookkeeping conforms to the law and that its financial management has been organized in a reliable manner. The association shall be represented by the executive committee.

(2) The executive committee shall have a chairperson. The chairperson may not be a person lacking legal competence. Other members of the committee shall be 15 years of age or over. A person who is bankrupt may not function as a member of the executive committee.

In addition, the chairperson's domicile is an item of central importance in the Finnish Associations Act.

(3) The chairperson of the executive committee shall be resident in Finland, unless the Finnish Patent and Registration Office grants an exception to this provision.

534. Along with Article 35, the most important of the formal requirements are *also identical to the registered religious associations* mentioned in Article 27 of the RFA.[282]

535. The comprehensive legislation of the RFA brings together everything that regulates registered religious communities and also coincides with the regulatory needs of non-profit associations.

C. Special Treatment of Religious Communities

536. It is noteworthy that the religious freedom of registered religious communities requires the civil law on associations to adapt to the special needs of religious associations. This is based on Article 27 of the Freedom of Religion Act (453/2003) and especially on the right to self-determination of religious communities as guaranteed by Article 13(2, 3) of Constitution. The civil law has to be interpreted so that it brings together the specific religious needs of these entities.

D. Termination of Non-profit Associations

537. When the common good is clearly endangered, an association can lose its legal entity status at the discretion of the authorities. The Court of First Instance of the municipality in which the association is based (the domicile) may, on the basis of an action brought by a prosecutor, the Finnish National Police Board, or a member of the association, declare the association terminated:

(1) if the association acts substantially against the law or good practice;
(2) if the association acts substantially against the purpose defined in its rules; or

282. *See* above, Part II, Ch. 3, §1, III. Fundamental Rights of Legal Persons, C. *Religious Communities as Ideological Associations under Private Law.*

(3) if the association acts in violation of the permission referred to in section 4 or the provision of section 35(3) (The chairperson of the executive committee shall be resident in Finland, unless the Finnish Patent and Registration Office grants an exception to this provision).[283]

538. If the public interest does not require termination of the association, the association may be cautioned rather than terminated.[284]

539. The termination of religious communities as legal entities under private law will be effected by the dissolution of the association according to the decision of its members on the basis of its statutes. Article 45 of the Associations Act reads:

> (1) When an association is declared terminated or its activities are provisionally prohibited, the association shall immediately terminate its activities. The executive committee of the association may nevertheless continue the trade or other economic activity carried on by the association and manage the property of the association until the decision to terminate the association has become final, unless otherwise ordered by the court.
> (2) If the court does not permit the executive committee to manage the association's property in the period referred to in subsection 1, the court shall appoint at least one person, in the capacity of a trustee, to manage the property of the association.
> (3) On declaring the association terminated the court shall, where necessary, appoint one or more liquidators. In such case the provisions of this Act in respect of liquidation and the requisite liquidation measures in the dissolving of an association shall apply mutatis mutandis.

540. To sum up, the association can lose legal entity status through the by decision of the authorities when it endangers the common good by a decision of its members' meeting or by any illegal activity of its board. This will also be the case when a non-profit association takes up profit-making as its dominant aim.

283. Finnish Associations Act, §43.
284. *Ibid.*

Chapter 2. Autonomy of Religious Communities

§1. General Principles

541. All religious communities, regardless of their legal status, enjoy the self-determination of religious communities. The self-determination of religious communities is guaranteed by Article 13(2, 3) of the Constitution and by opinions issued by the Constitutional Law Committee.[285] Every religious community may, to a certain degree, independently regulate and administer its own affairs – normally defined by Church Act, Church Code or Church Order – within the limits of the RFA and of the general law, which applies to everyone. The right of self-determination covers such things as religious dogma (confession) and matters related to religious education and teaching and other spiritual and charitable activities in the community, as well as the selection of religious leaders, priests, and teachers.[286] It also applies to matters concerning important parts of the relationship between church employer and employees,[287] and data protection.[288]

542. At a more profound level, the autonomy of churches is regulated in Finland at three levels:

I. Legislation Affecting the ELCF

543. In the new constitution that came into force in the year 2000 (11 June 1997/731), the position of the Evangelical Lutheran Church remained essentially the same as in the 1919 Constitution. A central feature of the public law position of the Finnish Evangelical Lutheran Church – as already referred to several times – is the explicit reference to the Church law in the Constitution (§76). In terms of the position of the ELCF the direction of the legislation of the Church law (652/2023) is essential (Church Act Chapter 1, section 5 paragraphs 1–3), since it refers to the sole right of initiative of the Church synod and to the non-interference of the legislative bodies of the state in the content of the church legislative requests of the synod. In practice this means that the Church's own organ, the Synod, has the power to adopt initiatives on the enactment of the Church Law and on changes in the text of the law. The final parliamentary vote has only the right to accept or reject a proposal related to a Church Law.[289]

544. As a subject of public law, the ELCF is bound by the Constitution and by other laws in force in the State. Under Article 3(1) of the Constitution, legislative power, including the Church Act, is vested in Parliament. According to the principle

285. PeVL 28/2006 vp, 2, PeVL 20/2003 vp, 2, PeVL 57/2001 vp, 2.
286. *Ibid.*
287. *See* Part VI, Labour Law Within Religious Communities.
288. *See* Part XI, Religion and Culture, Ch. 2. *Religion and Media.*
289. The provision of the Church Act of 14 Apr. 2023 (652/2023, KL) corresponds in substance to the provisions of the earlier Church Acts of 1869, 1964, and 1993.

of legality under Article 2(3) of the Constitution, the exercise of public powers shall be in accordance with the law and all public activities shall be conducted in strict compliance with the law.[290] The basis of the authority held by a public authority must always ultimately be in reference to the law as enacted by Parliament. Although the general principles and functions of municipal autonomy (self-government) are also prescribed by law, the Constitution does not grant the same right of initiative that the Church holds under Articles 76(2) and 2(1) of the Constitution.

545. The Constitution has created a space for the Church to act according to its confession. It is a matter of what is commonly referred to as church affairs. These are the factors in support of which the Church, because of its confession, requires special regulation. It should be noted here that, historically, the Church Law system has been created for the practice of the religion of the members of the Evangelical Lutheran Church in Finland, and in particular according to the confession of the Evangelical Lutheran Church.[291]

546. The new Church Law (652/2023) was presented to Parliament on 2 March 2023. The Church Act entered into force 1 July 2023. The new legislation codifies existing church legislation so that its content is largely retained. Because of its nature as a codification, the reform does not include changes in the relationship between church and state.

547. It is interesting that the Constitutional Law Committee of the Parliament, which in practice interprets the Constitution in terms of the legislative stage, has during the course of its history taken almost no stand on the legal status of the Lutheran Church. Its previous statements have shown an understanding of the need for the Lutheran Church to define the content of the Church Act concerning the Church in accordance with the requirements of a church's confession. The Constitutional Law Committee has considered the Church to have an autonomous role specifically in terms of its doctrine and of the regulation it requires.[292]

548. In fact, in 2019, on the first occasion when a new Church Act proposal (HE 19/2019 vp) was drafted – but not implemented – it was suggested by the parliamentary Constitutional Law Committee and the Administrative Committee of the Parliament that a new Church Act should be interpreted so that it would be better to have a confessional article in the Church Order, decided by the General Synod itself, rather than in a Church Act adopted by Parliament.

549. However, the General Synod of the Evangelical Lutheran Church did not follow the interpretation of the Administrative Committee of the Parliament but held that the freedom of religion guaranteed by the Constitution included a certain degree

290. Article 2(3) of the Constitution reads: 'The exercise of public powers shall be based on an Act. In all public activity, the law shall be strictly observed'.
291. *See* above General Introduction, §3. *Historical Background, II* and *III.*
292. PeVL 57/2001 vp, PeVL 10/2003 vp, PeVL 20/2003 vp, and PeVL 28/2006 vp.

of self-determination for a religious community, including the right to decide on the content of its own confession in the Church Code, which is included in the exclusive right of initiative of the Church Synod guaranteed by Article 76 of the Constitution.[293]

550. In this context, it should be noted, however, that although the ELCF has the right to propose amendments to the Church Act in matters within its administration, the Church is in fact very much bound by various principles and practices generally accepted in society. This applies, for example, to the Church's own civil service law, pension law, civil and collective agreement law, electoral law, equality law, administrative procedure, and the judicial system.

551. In this respect, the Church Act is not as stoned as is often thought in Finland. Generally speaking, the Church cannot give its officials and employees worse benefits, but nor can it give better benefits than those enjoyed by the rest of society. This shows the universally pervasive equality and parity requirement that the Church must actually follow. And it does not (generally) affect the profound religious autonomy of the Church, which is ultimately the purpose of the Church Act. The scope of the Evangelical Lutheran Church Act in Finland is so extensive compared to all other religious communities that the Lutheran Church is confronted with this issue in different ways from those experienced by other religious communities.

II. Legislation Affecting the Finnish Orthodox Church

552. The autonomy of the Orthodox Church is based on the Orthodox Church Law (985/2006), on the one hand, and on the canonical law, on the other. In the new Constitution there is no direct provision for the Finnish Orthodox Church to regulate its position in society. In this regard, the legislative status of the Orthodox Church differs from that of the Lutheran Church. However, the status of the public law relating to the Lutheran Church has been taken into account in the new Church Law.

553. In the Orthodox Church, autonomy refers to the right of a church in a particular state or geographically homogenous area to decide on its internal administrative and partly also on canonical matters. The Autonomous Church is always subject to the spiritual and ecclesiastical law, i.e., to the canonical administration (jurisdiction) of an Autocephalous Church.

554. The OCF is an Autonomous Church under the protection of the Ecumenical Patriarchate. The highest bishop of the OCF is the Ecumenical Patriarch of Constantinople (currently Patriarch Bartholomew I). In practice, the Archbishop of Finland (currently Archbishop Leo) is in charge of the Autonomous Church of Finland.

---

293. For a more detailed discussion, *see* the previous General Introduction, 4, *F. The Church Act Codification Work in 2005–2023, d).*

III. Legislation Affecting the Registered Religious Associations

555. For registered religious communities, their autonomy is based on Article 17 of the RFA, which defines the legal effects of registration more precisely. Article 17 reads:

> A registered religious association and its registered local community can acquire rights, enter into commitments and be a litigant in court and with other authorities.
>
> Members of a registered religious association are not personally liable for the obligations of the community.

556. According to Articles 18, 19, and 20 of the same law, the founding documents must be submitted to the National Patent and Register Board.[294] Article 22 specifies the information to be entered in the religious community register.

§2. Limitations of the Right to Self-Determination and State Court System

557. The self-determination of religious communities does not exist without limitations. By invoking the freedom of religion and conscience, it is not possible to religious communities to participate in activities that violate human dignity or other fundamental rights or are against public law. Nor does the constitutional protection of freedom of religion or conscience prevent the authorities from issuing statutory regulations in accordance with generally accepted moral and ethical values in society, which various religious trends must take into account. In particular, consideration must be given to the fundamental rights of others when interpreting the extent to which the protection of fundamental rights, such as the right to practice a religion, is granted by law.[295]

558. In Finland, the Constitutional Law Committee defines the actual interpretation of the guidelines for applying the laws affecting all of the religious communities. As quoted above, the Constitutional Law Committee has defined its opinion of the concerns that are covered by the right of self-determination, such as religious dogma (confession) and matters related to religious education and teaching, and the selection of religious leaders, priests, and teachers.[296] In addition, the Parliamentary Ombudsman has in recent years played an important role in a number of cases interpreting the role played by religious communities. Previously, Chapter 2 (Part II, §9, I. B) dealt with a legal case where the Deputy Parliamentary Ombudsman determined that the Evangelical Lutheran Parish of Rekola in Vantaa had acted illegally when the parish distributed magazines intended for its members to households that

294. *Ibid.*, §18.
295. *See* above, Part II, §9, I. B. *The Variety of Limitations.*
296. PeVL 57/2001 vp, PeVL 10/2003 vp, PeVL 20/2003 vp and PeVL 28/2006 vp.

were not members. In his discussion of the principles behind his decision the Deputy Ombudsman referred to the provisions on the freedom of religion contained in section 11 of the Constitution and Article 9 of the ECHR, which include the right not to belong to a given religious community.[297]

559. Recent developments also show more broadly that local courts are increasingly prepared to interface with the concerns of religious communities. The media has recently featured prominently in court rulings and law enforcement decisions on the ecclesiastical matters of the Evangelical Lutheran Church that have been linked to the Church's doctrine. The case law has also evaluated the relationship of the Church Act with other legislation in society,[298] although churches have given ample space to the right of self-determination in assessing each individual case.

560. Among other things, the application of discrimination provisions in the Equality Act and the Criminal Code in the Church has raised questions about how discrimination in the Church should be dealt with and how it should be addressed in the Church's own civil service legislation. The most taxing topic in recent times has been the Gender-Neutral Marriage Act, which came into force on 1 March 2017. The Evangelical Lutheran Church, which has the right under secular law to solemnize marriages, has not yet granted its permission for the implantation of the decree of the General Synod (2018) concerning the right of its priests to conduct marriages between individuals of the same sex. Some priests, invoking the general law, have, however, already conducted same-sex marriages. A vitally important, recent precedent is the Decision of the Administrative Court of Northern Finland (2019/0272/29), which found that the appellant (a priest) had not acted within the meaning of the Church Act when he violated the duties of the priesthood and the promise of the priesthood by performing the marriage of a same-sex couple in Oulu.

561. However, the Supreme Administrative Court (KHO: 2020: 97) annulled the decision of the Administrative Court of Northern Finland by four to one votes (19/0272/2).[299] In its assessment, the Supreme Administrative Court took into account that the warning referred to in Chapter 5, section 3, subsection 3 of the Church Act is an administrative sanction for holding a priestly office, which differs in purpose and consequences from the Civil Service Warning referred to in Chapter 6, sections 26 and 50 of the Church Act. The authority of the Diocese Chapter to issue the warning referred to in Chapter 5, section 3, subsection 3 of the Church Act applies to all priests who have been ordained to the priesthood and hold the office of priest. Based on the preliminary work of the provision, the right and authority to supervise

---

297. The decision aroused criticism even in the Constitutional Law Committee, which noted in its report (17/2006), with reference to Art. 9 of the ECHR, that both this document and the Constitution provide powerful protection for freedom of expression in matters of religious and philosophical communication.
298. Kouvola Administrative Court Resolution (HO 6.2.2009 145) concerning the Hyvinkää discrimination case.
299. At https://www.kho.fi/fi/index/paatokset/vuosikirjapaatokset/1600323418463.html.

the court chapter reflect the episcopal structure of the church, according to which the diocesan clergy is under the special direction and supervision of the bishop and the chapter.

562. The Supreme Administrative Court drew attention to the fact that the preliminary work on the amendment to the Marriage Act had emphasized that the amendment was not intended to interfere with the right of religious communities under section 16 of the Marriage Act to prescribe the conditions and form of ecclesiastical consecration. This right is ultimately restored to the freedom of religious association guaranteed by Article 11 of the Constitution, which also includes a certain degree of internal autonomy of the religious community. All religious communities thus have the independent right to decide whether to marry same-sex couples. The Supreme Administrative Court found that, in this warning case, the court could therefore only examine whether the Diocese Chapter, in directing and supervising the diocesan clergy, had considered that the priest in office had against.

563. In view of the above, the Diocese Chapter could not be considered to have acted unlawfully when it had given A the warning referred to in Chapter 5, section 3, subsection 3 of the Church Act. The matter had not been safeguarded by the Constitution, given the internal autonomy of the Church, in this context of the exercise of the priesthood, there was no reason to assess otherwise in the light of the principle of proportionality.

564. The Supreme Administrative Court annulled the decision of the Administrative Court by which the Administrative Court had, on A's appeal, annulled the decision of the Diocese Chapter. The decision of the Diocese Chapter of the Diocese of Oulu to issue a written warning to appellant thus remained in force.[300]

565. One of the most interesting issues in the Gender-Neutral Marriage Act is the future role to be played by the Lutheran Church. Many churches that have been given the right by the state to perform marriages may in the future be able to refuse to marry same-sex couples on the basis of their own principles. For the Orthodox Church and the Free Churches in particular, this will be a difficult issue.

566. The question of how much the state (courts) should give way to church decisions in cases involving religious communities will also remain problematic in the future and will require further discussion. It is obvious that, for the ELCF and the OCF as public law entities, the question of fundamental rights entails an active responsibility to be closely involved in the implementation of civil rights within their own communities.

300. Sources of law used in the explanatory memorandum: Article 11 of the Finnish Constitution; Church Act Ch. 1, s. 2; Ch. 1, s. 1, subs 2; Ch. 5, subs 1, subs 3; Ch. 5, s. 2, subs 1; Ch. 5, s. 5, para. 2; Ch. 12, s. 2, subs 1, para. 6 and s. 3, subs 1–3.

567. Registered religious associations that have no public law status are not, *at least not directly*, obliged to adhere to the human rights guarantees of the Constitution. However, registered religious associations, which are not governed by public law, are subject to the legislation that applies to private corporations and have all of the responsibilities prescribed by other judicial norms (e.g., the law on equality, and labour legislation in general), which in turn oblige them to act in conformity with the actual principles of human rights and fundamental freedoms.

568. Fundamental rights in the Finnish judicial system permeate all areas of common law since they represent a constitutional decision in favour of certain defined values. Human dignity, freedom, and equality must be respected, and this applies not only to religious communities but to relations between individuals.

Part IV. International, Transnational and Regional Impacts on Religious Communities

Chapter 1. The Impact of International Law on Religious Communities

§1. PUBLIC INTERNATIONAL LAW

I. Basic Principles

569. Finland has signed and ratified all important and relevant international treaties concerning freedom of religion. Finland joined the Council of Europe in 1989 and ratified the European Convention for the Protection of Human Rights and Fundamental Freedoms (ECHR) the following year, on 10 May 1990.[301] Joining the ECHR marked a significant move in Finnish Human Rights law and was a major reason for the revision of the Basic Rights and Liberties enshrined in the Finnish Constitution in 1995.

570. In common with the other Nordic countries, Finland has principally adopted a dualistic model with regard to the relationship between international

301. Finland had nevertheless established relatively close relations with the Council of Europe before joining it formally. This had begun in 1963, when representatives first attended meetings on topics such as legal cooperation in an observer capacity and members of the Finnish Parliament were first invited to general parliamentary sessions. Finland had signed the European General Agreement on Culture in 1970, so that this became the first Council of Europe general agreement that it ratified, and it had subsequently signed numerous other such agreements prior to becoming a full council member. Some of these agreements have had a substantial influence on the evolution of the country's internal legislation. Thus, the law on the extradition of persons suspected of having committed a criminal offence (Finnish Law Collection 456/1970) is largely constructed on the model of the corresponding European general agreement (SopS 32/1971; 15/1985), while the Council of Europe's general agreement on data protection (SopS 36/1992) greatly influenced the content of the law on the recording of personal data (471/1987), which had come into force before Finland joined the council and its ratification of that agreement took effect. Finland had also participated in the work of many committees and other bodies responsible to the Council of Europe before achieving formal membership. Matti Pellonpää, *Euroopan ihmisoikeussopimus* (ECHR, Helsinki: Talentum, 4th edn 2005), 6.
The Convention on Human Rights was signed in connection with the act of joining the Council of Europe on 5 May 1989 and ratified a year later, on 10 May 1990 (SopS 18–19/1990).

agreements and the country's internal legislation. The principles laid down in the Constitution and the established practices arising from those oblige the Finnish Parliament to approve international agreements that are binding upon Finland and to grant them the force of law to the extent that they contain provisions that 'are of a legislative nature'.[302] If an agreement does not contain provisions that are of a legislative nature it may be brought into force simply by means of a statute. If, on the other hand, the discrepancy between the provisions of the agreement and the existing Finnish legislation is constitutional nature, it will need to be brought into force by means of a constitutional act of parliament passed with a two-thirds majority (Finnish Constitution §95: 2).

571. The provisions of most treaties and other international obligations are brought into law in Finland in the form of 'blanket laws' which state that they 'shall come into force in the manner agreed upon'. Thus the law obtains its material content from the agreement itself, which is published as an annex to the statute implementing the law. The statute may be purely of a blanket form or it may contain additional regulations, e.g., ones containing reservations regarding the applicability of the agreement.[303]

572. The approval of such a blanket or hybrid law (and/or statute) implies 'incorporation' of the agreement into the internal legislation of Finland, but in addition to this it is possible and quite common for specific alterations to be made to existing legislation in the same sphere, i.e., this incorporation is supplemented with 'transformation'. If all the relevant legislation has been altered prior to approval of the international agreement, it is possible to incorporate the agreement by means of a blanket statute alone. It is nevertheless important in the case of human rights agreements, which have an immediate impact on the legal status of the individual, that these should always be incorporated by means of a law.[304]

573. Once an agreement is brought into force in the manner described above, it becomes a part of Finnish law and applicable in principle in the same manner as any other part of the legislative code.

574. In his comparison of the observance of general human rights agreements in the internal legislation of various countries, Professor Matti Pellonpää notes in the case of Finland that the real significance of such agreements in practical terms is not determined solely by the formal status of the agreement. This claim is supported by the minor significance which this agreement had for a long time in relation to the decisions of the Finnish courts. Pellonpää observes that more than ten years passed before the Agreement on Civil and Political Rights brought into force in 1976 (Law 107/1976 and Statute 108/1976) was referred to in a Finnish high

302. The relevant principles were contained in §33 of the original Constitution and §69 of the Parliament Act. The corresponding paragraphs of the new Constitution are §94 and §95.
303. Pellonpää 2005, 54.
304. PeVL 2/1990 vp, s. 1; Pellonpää 2005, 54.

court for the first time, in the Supreme Administrative Court in 1988.[305] Earlier the same year, the Supreme Administrative Court had issued a ruling concerned with the general agreement on the legal status of refugees (SopS 77/1968) that can be regarded as the first decision by a high court in Finland that was an application of any international agreement that could be described as connected with human rights.[306] References to human rights agreements have, however, become more common in Finnish courts since that time, and it must be noted that the Parliamentary Ombudsman had in practice regularly invoked legal arguments derived from this human rights agreement prior to the court cases.[307]

575. In Pellonpää's opinion one can speak of a breakthrough with regard to human rights that has taken place within Finnish jurisprudence over the last twenty-five years or so (up to 2019). Where the core of the Finnish system of fundamental human rights is concentrated on the legislative organs – as these fundamental considerations have defined a certain order of enactment for the country's laws – it is particularly through international human rights agreements that it has become customary to take questions of civil rights into account in 'everyday' legal practice.[308] It is this, above all, that has been brought about by the ECHR and Fundamental Freedoms.

II. The European Convention of Human Rights and ICCPR-Agreement

A. General Relevance

576. In Finland the minimum basic rights are determined by international human rights agreements,[309] as interpreted by organizations governed by international treaty such as the ECtHR and the UN Human Rights Committee. Both the ECHR[310]

305. The case KHO 1988 A 48 concerned a conflict between the existing statute on passports, since rescinded, and the provisions of §12 of the Agreement on Civil and Political Rights regarding freedom of movement.

306. Pellonpää (2005, 55) points out that, in the case KHO 1988 A 49, the court was simply making use of the refugee agreement that had been brought into force by means of a blanket statute as a tool for interpreting the law on aliens (400/1983), rather in the same way as the European Convention on Human Rights, which had not yet attained a position in the internal legislation of the Nordic countries, had been applied there previously.

307. Pellonpää 2005, 55.

308. *Ibid. See also* Riku Neuvonen & Pauli Rautiainen. 'Perusoikeuksien tunnistaminen ja niiden sisällön määritteleminen Suomen perusoikeusjärjestelmässä' (Identifying and defining fundamental rights in the Finnish system of fundamental rights). *Lakimies* 1 (2015): 28–53.

309. For greater detail, *see* Martin Scheinin, *Ihmisoikeudet Suomen oikeudessa.* (Human rights in Finnish law). (Helsinki: Suomalainen Lakimiesyhdistys), 1991; Jukka Viljanen, *The European Court of Human Rights as a Developer of the General Doctrines of Human Rights Law.* (Tampere, 2003). *Diss.;* Ineke Boerefijn, 'International Human Rights in National 'Law'. In Catarina Krause & Martin Scheinin (eds), *International Protection of Human Rights: A Textbook* (Turku: Åbo Akademi University Institute for Human Rights, 2012), 577–599.

310. *See* Tuomas Ojanen, 'Räppänä raollaan Eurooppaan – Euroopan unionin perusoikeudet Suomen oikeudessa' (Hatch Open into Europe – EU Fundamental Rights in Finnish Law). In Tuuli Heinonen & Juha Lavapuro (eds), *Oikeuskulttuurin eurooppalaistuminen: Ihmisoikeuksien murroksesta*

and the ICCPR-agreement are considered legal norms and may take precedence over national legal norms because of the minimum level of rights stipulated.[311] However, as a matter of Finnish constitutional law, international human rights obligations binding upon Finland feature as a means of protecting minimum standards of rights. Hence, the level of protection of fundamental rights cannot be lower than that provided by international human rights treaties, although this does not prevent Finland from also providing more stringent protection.[312]

577. By amending its basic rights, Finland moved over in 1995 to a system requiring civil servants to interpret basic rights favourably. In practice, this means that a civil servant is required to select the option that best responds to an individual's basic and human rights. *In this situation the ICCPR-agreement provides individuals with greater protection of their religious freedoms in the Finnish judicial system.* It sets the minimum level for religious freedoms for Finland. Juhani Kortteinen terms this 'basic rights pluralism, which guides favourable basic rights solutions even in those cases where the interpretations of international human rights agreements differ from one another'.[313]

578. The code of civil rights in Finland was effectively altered to conform to international obligations – and even to exceed those obligations at certain points – through the transfer of the content of the 1995 reform of the Finnish Constitution of 1919 into a new Constitution, which was approved in the year 2000.[314]

---

kansainväliseen vuorovaikutukseen (Helsinki: Suomalainen Lakimiesyhdistys, 2012). *See also* Steven Greer, *The European Convention on Human Rights – Achievements, Problems and Prospects* (Cambridge University Press, 2006); Jean-François Akandji-Kombe, *Human rights handbooks, No. 7. Positive Obligations under the European Convention on Human Rights. A Guide to the Implementation of the European Convention on Human Rights. Council of Europe* (Belgium, 2007).

311. For further detail, *see* Tuomas Ojanen & Martin Scheinin, 'Kansainväliset ihmisoikeussopimukset ja Suomen perusoikeus–järjestelmä'. In *Pekka Hallberg, Heikki Karapuu, Tuomas Ojanen, Martin Scheinin, Kaarlo Tuori, Veli-Pekka Viljanen, Perusoikeudet* (Fundamental rights). (2nd revised edn WSOYpro, 2011), 171–195. (Ojanen & Scheinin 2011 a). *See also* Tuomas Ojanen, 'Perus- ja ihmisoikeudet Euroopan unionissa' (Fundamental and human rights in the European Union). In *Timo Koivurova & Elina Pirjatanniemi. Ihmisoikeuksien käsikirja.* (Helsinki: Tietosanoma, 2013); Thomas Christiansen, & Christine Reh, *Constitutionalizing the European Union.* (Basingstoke: Palgrave Macmillan, 2009).
312. For greater detail, *see* Tuomas Ojanen, EU-oikeuden perusteita (The Basics of EU Law) (Helsinki: Edita, 2016).
313. Juhani Kortteinen, 'Turbaaneja, huiveja ja ristejä – uskontoperusteisen pukeutumisen rajoittamisesta' (Turbans, Scarves, and Crosses – Restricting Religious Clothing). *Perustuslakiblogi* (The Constitutional Blog). (Helsinki: Suomen valtiosääntöoikeudellisen seuran ajankohtaispalsta 20.12.2013). *See also* Tuomas Ojanen, *The European Way. The Structure of National Court Obligation under EC Law.* (Omakustanne (Author's edition). Saarijärvi, 1998). *See* Robert Alexy, *A Theory of Constitutional Rights.* Oxford, 2002.
314. Hallberg (2011, 48) regards the exceptional code of civil rights, in which both the fundamental freedoms and the economic, educational and social rights of citizens are expressed in connection with the constitution, as a distinctive feature of Finnish jurisprudence. Hallberg, Pekka. 'Kokoontumisvapaus' (Freedom of assembly). In *Pekka Hallberg, Heikki Karapuu, Tuomas Ojanen, Martin Scheinin, Kaarlo Tuori, Veli-Pekka Viljanen, Perusoikeudet* (Fundamental rights). (2nd, revised edition. WSOYpro, 2011).

579. It is laid down in §22 of the new Constitution that the public authorities shall be responsible for guaranteeing fundamental human rights. In accordance with the constitutional reform of 1995, these public authorities, which, as mentioned in §76 of the Constitution, include the ELCF, are obliged and bound to take responsibility for the implementation of civil rights in all forms of public activity, including their legislative, administrative, and executive aspects. It is not (any longer) regarded as sufficient that the public authorities should refrain from interfering with the fundamental rights of citizens through legislative or other measures. They are, instead, expected to take an active role in protecting personal freedoms from external violations and to create conditions that truly foster the practical application of the principles of civil rights.[315] Apart from procedural issues, this is also a question of guaranteeing basic rights in a material sense.

580. For the ELCF[316] and the OCF, as communities governed by public law, the question of fundamental rights entails an active responsibility for the implementation of civil rights within their own communities.

581. Other registered religious associations, on the other hand, since they are not governed by public law, are subject to the legislation that applies to private corporations and have the responsibilities laid down in other judicial norms (e.g., the law on equality and labour legislation), which lead them to act in conformity with the actual principles of human rights and fundamental freedoms.[317]

B. Case Law

582. One of the most visible cases involving Finland prior to the establishment of the ECHR was the case of *Konttinen v. Finland* (1994), in which a man (a Seventh-Day Adventist) rejected working hours for religious reasons (Sabbath); this has been discussed, above, in Part II, §10, Chapter II.1.A.

---

315. This obligation extends to the local authorities and other public sector organizations primarily only in so far as they are assigned responsibilities and jurisdiction with regard to fundamental freedoms. As far as the church is concerned, this applies to it as a statutory public body, so that it can be expected to act in such a way as to ensure the civil rights of its clergy and staff.

316. In the case of the unique rights enjoyed by the Evangelical Lutheran Church of Finland, as laid down in the laws governing that church, one cannot, however, speak of an *active* obligation under the Constitution, as the Finnish Constitution provides for the legislative autonomy of the church, the principal mark of which is the order of enactment of ecclesiastical law (Ecclesiastical Law §2:2, clause 1). This last grants to the Church Assembly (Synod) the exclusive right to propose changes to this law, while barring the state legislative bodies from interfering in the content of any such proposals.

317. No investigations or surveys have been conducted with regard to the implementation of human rights in the churches or religious associations of Finland, as far as decisions of the higher courts are concerned, but Pitkänen (2006) has produced a more general account of human rights in Supreme Court decisions as a whole. Pitkänen, Maija. *On annettava merkitystä--* (Must give meaning–). Tutkimus perusoikeuksien toteutumisesta ylimpien tuomioistuinten lainkäytön näkökulmasta. University of Joensuu: Degree dissertation, 2006.

583. Other cases involving Finland prior to the establishment of the ECHR were mainly connected with the right of individuals and institutions to a fair trial: §6 and §13.

584. Under §6, paragraph 1, of the ECHR every person whose rights and/or obligations are to be determined or who has been accused of a crime is entitled to a fair public trial in a legally constituted, independent, and impartial court within a reasonable period of time.

585. Among the various judgments reached related to the provisions of the ECHR, a number of cases can be regarded as being of at least indirect relevance to the administration of the church. A few of the approximately twenty cases to which the state of Finland has been a party can be examined here.

Infringements recorded:

> Case: *Launikari v. Finland*
> *Launikari v. Suomi* (European Court of Human Rights, Application no. 34120/96). This is an example of the binding nature of international agreements, although actually in the form of a decision reached by the European Court of Human Rights on 5 October 2000 concerning a matter that had already been under discussion among the authorities of the Evangelical Lutheran Church of Finland for a considerable time. The court deemed that Finland had contravened §6, paragraph 1, of the European Convention on Human Rights *regarding the right to a fair trial within a reasonable period of time*. The particular case involved an appeal and an administrative dispute that had been under consideration by the church authorities and in the Supreme Administrative Court between February 1987 and January 1996. No individual stage in its handling was considered open to criticism, but the erroneous instructions for an appeal issued by the Church Council meant that *the state was accused of permitting a delay of unacceptable length in view of the fact that it was a matter of the office held by the appellant and thus of his source of income.*

586. One of the main problems is the compliance of national administrative courts with the reasonable time requirement in Article 6(1) of the ECHR, which has come into use in recent years, including in cases classified as religious.

587. Given the number and distribution of solutions, this is a pan-European phenomenon in which the Court of Human Rights itself cannot escape criticism. Most of the decisions concerning the length of the proceedings concern Italy[318] and, to some extent, France. In the past, Germany was often the subject of complaints

318. *See* Matti Pellonpää, 'Euroopan ihmisoikeussopimus' (ECHR, Helsinki, 4th edn 2005), 332 and Sonja Wolf, 'Trial within a Reasonable Time: The Recent Re-forms of the Italian Justice System in Response to the Conflict with Article 6 (1) of the ECHR'. In *European Public Law* 2003, 189. For greater detail about this, *see* Leena Halila, 'Euroopan ihmisoikeustuomioistuin ja kansallisen hallintoprosessin kehittäminen' (European Court of Human Rights and development of the national administrative process). In *Lakimies* 7–8 (2003): 1300–1305.

against the reasonable time clause. The situation has now changed with the necessary amendments by Germany.[319] Despite national emphases, Finland has also not avoided human rights violations with regard to this requirement, as the case of *Launikari v. Finland* shows.

No infringement:

> Case: *Helle v. Finland*
> *Helle v. Finland*, European Court of Human Rights, 19.12.1997: §6 – The right to a fair trial (the right to a hearing and other legal guarantees in an employment dispute involving the Lutheran Church)

588. The case originally concerned a dispute over the financial losses sustained by a parish verger as a result of his post being reduced to a part-time one. The case subsequently extended to the manner in which the dispute had been handled, including a failure to arrange a hearing in an impartial court.

589. The Supreme Administrative Court had rejected the appeal against the decision of the diocesan chapter in certain respects and had concluded that there were no grounds for altering its verdict. The ECtHR considered that the way in which the court had 'incorporated' the justifications for the verdict was in accordance with the convention that constituted the purpose of the appeal into its own judgment. The ECtHR pointed out that the judgment of the Supreme Administrative Court had been linked to the verdict in each question separately and that the arguments behind the diocesan chapter's original verdict had been adequate.[320]

C. The Right of Self-Determination and the ECtHR

590. In its settled case law, the ECtHR has repeatedly made it clear that, as enshrined in Article 9 ECHR, freedom of thought, conscience, and religion are a major part of the foundations of a 'democratic society' within the meaning of the ECHR.[321]

591. The autonomy, i.e., the self-determination, of the Churches and religious communities is a foremost and integral aspect of freedom of religion. Where the

---

319. On the reform of German administrative process legislation, *see* Bernd Goller & Alexander Schmid, 'Reform of the German Administrative Courts Act'. In: *European Public Law* 1998, 31–44. In Germany, it has been perceived (p. 32) that, in principle, a lack of resources or structural aspects of the judiciary cannot be effectively invoked before the Court of Human Rights. *See* closer https://kluwerlawonline.com/journalarticle/European+Public+Law/4.1/EURO1998004. Accessed 9 Jan. 2024.
320. *See* ECtHR 19.12.1997: §6, *Helle v. Finland*, points 55–61.
321. For further detail, *see* Dimitris Xenos, *The Positive Obligations of the State under the European Convention of Human Rights*. (Baskerville, VA: Routledge, 2012).

organization of the religious community is at issue, Article 9 ECHR[322] must be interpreted in light of Article 11 ECHR,[323] which safeguards the right to associate against unjustified state interference. Seen in this perspective, the community will be allowed to function peacefully and free from arbitrary state intervention. It is self-evident that Finnish case law has taken into account the recommendations of the ECtHR, which are visible in the requirements of the ECHR and other international agreements binding on Finland at all stages in the drafting of legislation. The requirements of Article 9 were also carefully realized in the design of the new RFA (456/2003).

592. In addition to focusing on individual freedom, one of the main tasks of the Committee on Religious Liberty was to investigate how the status of registered religious communities could be strengthened by a new law paralleling the treatment of the Evangelical Lutheran and Orthodox Churches. That is to say, the Committee desired greater insight into how the differences between religious communities could be better tolerated and respected. The Committee felt, for example, that the RFA should no longer include the provision of the Ministry of Education to inspect registered religious communities. At the same time, unnecessary regulations limiting the right of registered religious communities to acquire and own real estate were removed.[324]

593. The Committee also wanted to loosen the precise provisions of the law on the status of religious communities or other local communities. The Committee came to the conclusion that the religious community should itself be able in its by-laws to decide on its possible division into congregations or other local communities. In addition, the legal status of the communities and their relationship with the religious community was to be resolved in terms of the community's autonomy.[325] This applies not only to issues of worship and ritual practice but also to matters of religious beliefs about the way the religious community should be

322. 'Everyone has the right to freedom of thought, conscience and religion; this right includes the freedom to change his/her religion or belief and freedom, either alone or in community with others and in public or private, to manifest his/her religion or belief, in worship, teaching, practice and observance'.
323. (1) 'Everyone has the right to freedom of peaceful assembly and to freedom of association with others, including the right to form and to join trade unions for the protection of his interests'.

(2) 'No restrictions shall be placed on the exercise of these rights other than such as are prescribed by law and are necessary in a democratic society in the interests of national security or public safety, for the prevention of disorder or crime, for the protection of health or morals or for the protection of the rights and freedoms of others. This article shall not prevent the imposition of lawful restrictions on the exercise of these rights by members of the armed forces, of the police or of the administration of the State'.

324. Juha Seppo, *Uskonnonvapaus 2000-luvun Suomessa* (Freedom of Religion in 21st Century Finland), (Helsinki: Edita, 2003), 70.
325. *Ibid.*, 70.

structured. Needless to say, state authorities or other authorities outside the religious community should not be able to compel the religious community to introduce a scale of loyalty obligations into its internal structures and hierarchies.

594. At the time of the enactment of the law, the Committee had not yet reached a position in its interim report on whether the new RFA would provide state aid to registered religious communities. This happened later, at the beginning of 2008 when the registered religious associations received financial aid from the government to support their activities. The Ministry of Education and Culture now grants state subsidies to registered religious communities on a computational basis according to their membership numbers. This aid is based on the State Aid Act.[326]

595. In secular settings, the Finnish national law must take account of the necessity to secure an employee's freedoms under Articles 8, 9, or 10 ECHR or under other relevant human rights guarantees of the ECHR against unreasonable demands made by the employer, even if the demands result from a valid employment contract. While the employer may indeed be a belief organization – a Church or religious community – it is in fact also necessary to protect the collective freedom of religion of the employee in vital matters of doctrine and practice.[327]

III. Other International Instruments

596. Freedom of religion and the autonomy of religious communities are not only closely linked to the UN's Declaration on Human Rights, the ECHR, and the procedures of ECHR but also, to a large extent, to what is commonly referred to as the OSCE process. The crucial moment in the development of human rights issues, and thus in the realization of religious freedom, took place in the aftermath of the 1975 OSCE meeting in Helsinki.[328] The OSCE meetings in Vienna (1986–1989) and Paris (1990) subsequently confirmed this development.[329]

597. The final document of the OSCE meeting in Vienna laid the foundation for the idea that the political system of the state is essential for the protection of human

326. For further information about the details, *see* Part VIII, Church Financing, §4 *State Subsidies.*

327. For further information about the details, *see* Part VI, §4 *Labour Law Within Religious Communities.*

328. The Final Act contains the principles governing interstate relations. Seven of these concern human rights and freedom of religion: 'Respect for human rights and fundamental freedoms, including freedom of thought, conscience, religion or belief'. The ten principles go even further. These state that signatories commit themselves to comply with international law (including human rights) when deciding on national laws and regulations.

However, the Helsinki Final Act was not a legally binding instrument. It expressed the intention of the governments that had emerged from a non-legal, political process. For more about the details, *see* Final Act of the OSCE meeting in Helsinki, 14 ILM 1292 (especially Principles VII, X) 1975.

329. For more about the OSCE process, *see* Matti Kotiranta 2020, Religionsfreiheit im postkommunistischen Europa – Ein historischer Rückblick über die Vergangenheit. Staat – Religion – Recht. Festschrift für Gerhard Robbers zum 70. Geburtstag, 2020, 371–375.

rights and that human rights are not separate issues. Religious freedom created standards and new vocabulary that went beyond the UN standard. For example, the 'human dimension' replaced the term 'human rights'. The term combines human rights, the rule of law, and democratic pluralism. This was an important step forward, as states came to the conclusion that their political system was essential for the protection of human rights and that human rights were not simply internal issues.[330] Principle 16.4 of the Vienna Concluding Document states that public states will respect the right of the religious communities not only to 'organize themselves according to their own hierarchical and institutional structure' but also to 'select, appoint and replace their personnel in accordance with their respective requirements and standards as well as any freely accepted arrangement between them and their state'.[331]

598. In addition, Principle 17 of the Vienna Concluding Document requires that 'participating states recognize that the exercise of this right relating to the freedom of religion or belief may be subject only to such limitations as are provided by law and consistent with their obligations under international law and with their international commitments'.[332]

599. The last obstacles to human rights issues were removed at the OSCE meeting in Paris in November 1990, following the reunification of Germany. Respect for human rights was no longer simply a humanitarian issue, as in the Helsinki (1975) document, but a direct prerequisite for peace and security in Europe. Similarly, human rights were no longer internal issues that others should not interfere with, but governments were responsible to the international community[333] for the way they treated their citizens. It was now the responsibility of States to address human rights violations.[334]

§2. European Union Law

I. Basic Principles

600. Finland joined the European Union in 1995. At the same time, EU law became part of the Finnish legal order, compelling the national authorities to draft

330. Erich Weingartner, *Ihmisoikeuksien suojeleminen. Käsikirja ihmisoikeustyön alkajille. Euroopan turvallisuus- ja yhteistyöjärjestön alueella toimivien kirkkojen ihmisoikeusohjelma* (Protecting Human Rights. A Manual for Practitioners of the Churches' Human Rights Programme in the CSCE) 1994, 15.
331. *Concluding Document of the Vienna Meeting* 1986–1989, 8.
332. *Ibid.*, 9.
333. The international community is legally governed in Europe by the UN International Court of Justice in The Hague, the Court of Justice of the European Communities, and the European Court of Human Rights under the Council of Europe, which oversees compliance with the ECHR.
334. For further information about the politics of international law, *see* Martti Koskenniemi, *The Politics of International Law.* (Oxford and Portland, Oregon: Hart Publishing, 2011).

similar laws and practices. In addition to the Treaties[335] and Acts of the Union, other sources of Union law – legal principles, international agreements concluded by the Union, and the case law of the European Court of Justice (ECJ) – are part of the Finnish national legal order and are binding on the national authorities. With the coming into force of the Accession Treaty, Finland has formally implemented the Treaties and adopted the Union's legal order in its national law.[336]

601. The European Union has Acts directly adopted by its legislators – the European Commission, the European Parliament, and the Council of the European Union – pursuant to a provision of the Treaty, and also Acts of subordinate law adopted pursuant to those acts. Acts adopted by the Union legislature under the Treaty are at the highest level. Below these are Acts based on Acts adopted under the Treaty. These are usually issued by the Commission.

602. There is no hierarchical distinction between the different types of EU Acts – Regulations, Directives and Decisions, but their purpose is related since all of these instruments can be issued under the Treaties or under the powers of the Legislators unless the instrument used is prescribed or provided for in the legal basis.

603. Binding acts are *Regulations* and *Directives*. Union Regulations create uniform legislation. They are directly applicable and their entry into force or applicability within the Member States does not require any specific action to be taken by the Member States.[337]

604. Directives are Acts which are addressed to the Member States and which oblige the Member States to take the measures required by the Directive and to bring their national legislation into line with the content of the Directive.[338] Each Member State is free to choose the way in which it takes the measures required by the Directive, but national regulation must lead to the result sought by the Directive. The Member State may also decide on the form of implementation within the Member State.

605. The main fundamental rights references – EU Treaties and other European and international treaties – that Finland adheres to are the following:[339]

---

335. It is worth mentioning here the main EU treaties: the Maastricht II (1992), Amsterdam (1999), Nice (2001), and Lisbon (2007) treaties.

336. Act on the Approval of Certain Provisions of the Treaty of Finland's Accession to the European Union (SopS 102/1994) and the Decree on the Entry into Force of the Treaty of Finland's Accession to the European Union and Approval of Certain Provisions of the Treaty (SopS 103/1994). *See* Niilo Jääskinen, *Euroopan unioni: Oikeudelliset perusteet* (The European Union: Legal Basis). (Helsinki: Talentum, 2007).

337. *See* TFEU, Art. 288, second paragraph.

338. *Ibid.*, third paragraph.

339. The list of the key references of fundamental rights, is based on the article 'The protection of fundamental rights in the EU: European Parliament achievements during the 2014-2019 legislative term and challenges for the future'. For further information about the details, *see* https://www.europarl.europa.eu/RegData/etudes/BRIE/2019/621911/IPOL_BRI(2019)621911_EN.pdf.

- The *Treaty on European Union* (TEU): especially its Preamble, Articles 2 (Union values), 3.1 (Union objectives), 3.3, second subparagraph (Union objectives), 4.3 (loyal cooperation), 6 (Charter and ECHR),[340] 7 (risk of breach of EU values), 9 (equality, Union citizenship), 19.1 (effective judicial protection).[341]
- The *Treaty on the Functioning of the European Union* (TFEU): especially Articles 8 (equality between men and women),[342] 10 (EU policies and actions to fight discrimination), 18 (anti-discrimination on grounds of nationality), 19 (anti-discrimination), 20 (citizenship), 21 (free movement), 22 (elections), 24 (European Citizens' Initiative, petitions, Ombudsman), 67 (Area of freedom, security and justice (AFSJ), fundamental rights), 167 (EU contribution to the development of the cultures of the Member States while safeguarding their national and regional diversity).
- The *EU Charter of Fundamental Rights* (Freedom of religion or belief is guaranteed in Article 10).[343]
- The UN's ICCPR: The ICCPR agreement contains provisions on, *inter alia*, freedom of expression, association and religion, and the criteria for a fair trial. The agreement also contains a general prohibition of discrimination, minimum criteria for the use of the death penalty, and a provision on the rights of persons belonging to minorities.[344]

---

340. For more detail, *see* Sonya Walkila, 'Euroopan unionin perusoikeuskirja EU:n tuomioistuimen oikeuskäytännössä' (Charter of Fundamental Rights of the European Union in the case law of the Court of Justice). *Defensor Legis* 6 (2011): 813–819; Clare Ovey & Robin C.A. White, *European Convention on Human Rights*. 5th edn (Oxford: University Press, 2010); David Harris & Michael O'boyle & Ed Bates & Carla Buckley. *Law of the European Convention on Human Rights*. (3rd edn Oxford University Press, 2014); Matti Pellonpää & Monica Gullans & Pasi Pölönen & Antti Tapanila. *Euroopan ihmisoikeussopimus* (European Convention on Human Rights). Helsinki: Talentum, 2012. Päivi Hirvelä & Satu Heikkilä. *Ihmisoikeudet. Käsikirja EIT:n oikeuskäytäntöön* (Human rights. A guide to EIT case law, 2nd, revised edn). (Helsinki: Alma Talent, 2017). *See also* Matti Pellonpää, 'Euroopan ihmisoikeussopimuksen tulkintaa koskevasta vuoropuhelusta' (On the dialogue of the interpretation of the European Convention on Human Rights). In *Heinonen – Lavapuro (toim.): Oikeuskulttuurin eurooppalaistuminen. Ihmisoikeuksien murroksesta kansainväliseen vuorovaikutukseen*. (Vantaa, 2012), 69–94.
341. For more on the ECHR and EU Charter of Fundamental Rights, *see* Paavo Nikula, 'Euroopan ihmisoikeussopimus ja EU:n perusoikeuskirja' (European Convention on Human Rights and EU Charter of Fundamental Rights), 238–247. In Nuolimaa – Vihervuori – Klemettinen (eds), *Juhlakirja Pekka Hallberg 1944–12/6 – 2004* (Jyväskylä, 2004).
342. For further detail, *see* Liisa Nieminen, 'Tasa-arvo Euroopan unionin perusoikeuskirjassa turvattuna perusoikeutena' (Equality as a fundamental right protected by the Charter of Fundamental Rights of the European Union). In *Nieminen (ed.), Perusoikeudet EU:ssa*. (Helsinki, 2001), 179–212.
343. For further detail, *see* Koen Leanerts, 'Exploring the Limits of the EU Charter of Fundamental Rights'. *European Constitutional Law Review* Vol. 8 (3) (2012): 375–403; Jasper Krommendijk, 'Principled Silence or Mere Silence on Principles? The Role of the EU Charter's Principles in the Case Law of the Court of Justice'. *European Constitutional Law Review* Vol. 11(2) (2015): 321–356; P.P. Craig, 'The Charter, the ECJ and National Courts'. In Diamond Ashiagbor, Nicola Countouris & Nicola Ionnais Lianos (eds), *The European Union after the Treaty of Lisbon* (Cambridge University Press, 2012); David Anderson & Cian C. Murphy. 'The Charter of Fundamental Rights'. In *Andrea Biondi, Piet Eeckhout & Stefanie Ripley, EU Law after Lisbon* (Oxford: Oxford University Press, 2012).
344. For further information about fundamental rights protection in the EU, *see* Jaakko Husa, 'Perusoikeusvalvonta EU:n alueella – riitasointuinen triangeli?' (Fundamental rights protection in the EU – a controversial triangle?). In *Nieminen (toim.): Perusoikeudet EU:ssa*. (Helsinki, 2001), 43–64.

606. Other relevant EU references include:

- Article 49 TEU (EU accession) and the Copenhagen criteria, notably the political criteria (stability of institutions guaranteeing democracy, the rule of law, human rights and respect for and protection of minorities);
- the *Commission communication of 15 October 2003* entitled '*Article 7* of the TEU: respect for and promotion of the values on which the Union is based' (COM (2003) 0606);
- the Commission communication of 11 March 2014 entitled '*A new EU Framework to strengthen the Rule of Law*' (COM (2014) 0158);
- the Commission communication of 3 April 2019 entitled '*Further strengthening the Rule of Law within the Union*. State of play and possible next steps' (COM (2019) 0163).

607. It can be argued that in Finland the EU Charter of Fundamental Rights, the ECHR, the ICCPR-agreement,[345] and the case law of the ECtHR[346] are the most important legal instruments for the protection of fundamental rights and religious freedom.[347] These four instruments establish the rights that Finland respects, in particular when implementing EU law on fundamental rights and religious issues. At the European level, of significance are also the conventions, recommendations, resolutions, and reports of the Parliamentary Assembly, the Committee of Ministers, the Human Rights Commissioner, the Venice Commission, and other bodies concerned with fundamental rights under the umbrella of the Council of Europe.

608. Due to the large amount of EU legislation that concerns religious issues, EU legislation has also had a significant impact on the development of religious freedom in Finland since it acquired EU membership in 1995. In the first place, it has accelerated the reform of fundamental rights in general, but also the freedom of religion included therein. Although the politically most significant part of the Finnish constitutional reform in 2000 concerned the power relations between key state institutions – such as the Parliament, the President of the Republic, and the Government – the reform also dealt indirectly (§6, §11, §13, and §22) with the religious freedom of churches and other religious communities, and also directly with state-church relations (§76). These issues were further defined in the context of the

---

345. *See* above, Part IV, II. *The European Convention on Human Rights and the ICCPR agreement. See also* Hans Christian Krüger & Jörg Polakiewicz. 'Proposal for coherent human rights protection in Europe. The European Convention on Human Rights and the EU Charter of Fundamental Rights'. *Human Rights Law Review* Vol. 22, No. 1–4 (2011): 1–13.
346. *See* above, Part IV, Ch. 1, II. A. General Relevance and B. *Case Law. See also* Jukka Viljanen, 'The Role of the European Court of Human Rights as a Developer of International Human Rights Law'. *Cuadernos Constitucionales de la Cátedra Fadrique Furió Ceriol* no. 62/63 (2011): 249–265 and Jukka Viljanen, 'Euroopan ihmisoikeustuomioistuin ja yleiset opit' (European Court of Human Rights and general doctrine). *Lakimies* 3 (2004): 521–525.
347. For further detail, *see* Hallberg, Pekka: 'Perusoikeusjärjestelmä' (The Fundamental Rights system). In *Pekka Hallberg, Heikki Karapuu, Tuomas Ojanen, Martin Scheinin, Kaarlo Tuori, Veli-Pekka Viljanen, Perusoikeudet* (Fundamental rights). (2nd revised edn WSOYpro, 2011), 29–59. *See also*, Dorota Anna Gozdecka, *Rights, Religious Pluralism and the Recognition of Difference*. (Oxon & New York: Routledge, 2016).

reform of the RFA (456/2003). In sum, the new constitution protects both the individual and also the communal dimensions of religious freedom by cultivating a positive attitude on the part of religious communities towards democratic society and its legal life course.

609. The judgments of the ECJ are central to the interpretation and application of EU law.[348] In consequence, the content of EU law also requires an examination of the case law practised by the Court of Justice. This principle has also been applied in Finland in civil matters concerning religious freedom.[349]

II. Freedom of Religion or Belief in Primary European Union Law

610. Fundamental rights, including freedom of religion or belief (in the Finnish jurisprudence *conviction*), form part of the common constitutional traditions of the Member States of the EU and as such also form an integral part of EU law itself. Article 6 of the Treaty of European Union reads:

> (1) The Union is founded on the principles of liberty, democracy, respect for human rights and fundamental freedoms, and the rule of law, principles which are common to the Member States. ... (3) The Union shall respect the national identities of its Member States.[350]

611. The idea of the common constitutional traditions of the Member States, which provides a basis for the development of religious law structures and religious freedom, emerged from the Intergovernmental Conference held in Amsterdam in June 1997. The Conference decided to include in the TEU (Maastricht II) a declaration (not an Article) on the status of the churches and religious communities. The Declaration of the Final Act of the Amsterdam Conference on the Relations of the European Union with the Churches and Religious Communities in its Member States reads as follows:

> The European Union respects and does not prejudice the status under national law of churches and religious associations or communities in the Member States.
>
> The European Union equally respects the role of philosophical and non-confessional organizations.[351]

348. *See* Matti Pellonpää, 'Euroopan ihmisoikeustuomioistuin ja Euroopan unioni' (European Court of Human Rights and the European Union). *Lakimies* 7–8 (2005): 1229–1250; Charles F. Sabel & Oliver. Gersterberg, 'Constitutionalising an Overlapping Consensus: The ECJ and the Emergence of a Coordinate Constitutional Order'. *European Law Journal* 5 (2010): 511–550.
349. *See* above, Part II, Ch. 1, § 10, II.1. and Part IV, Ch. 1, §1., II. B.
350. Article 6 Treaty of European Union (TEU). In Finnish: Sopimus Euroopan Unionista (SEU).
351. The Declaration no. 11 on status of churches and non-confessional organizations was attached to the Final Act of the Treaty of Amsterdam.

612. The recognition of the status of churches and religious communities in the intergovernmental treaty has been interpreted as resulting in a reconsideration in the European Union, formerly known purely as an economic and political community. Although this declaration was not included in 1997 in the EU Treaty itself (Maastricht II) as a separate article, which made it less legally relevant than having a specific treaty article devoted to it, it should be noted that this declaration was politically binding. The Treaty came into force on 1 May 1999, following ratification by all of the Member States in accordance with their respective constitutions.

613. Since then, no major changes have been made in the Amsterdam Treaty to this very positive EU guideline for the churches, and religious and philosophical organizations. The Nice Treaty (2001) specifically addressed Amsterdam's 'remnants', that is, the institutional problems of enlargement, which could not be resolved in 1997. The Lisbon Treaty[352] signed in December 2007, although under the influence of slight headwinds, clearly reinforced the role played by churches and religious communities.[353] The Lisbon Treaty made the Declaration on Religious Communities in the Amsterdam Treaty a separate treaty article.[354] This change was also reflected in the introduction to the article on the European Union's value system.

614. It can be argued that the basic structures of European law on religion remain very evident. Religious freedom is, in general, recognized everywhere in the EU as an element of EU law, and religious communities possess institutional independence. Further structural principles – as Professor Gerhard Robbers has explained in detail – include the obligation of the EU to remain neutral in questions of religion and belief, to show tolerance towards different religions and beliefs, and to grant equal treatment to religious and belief communities. Second, Article 4, section 2, Treaty of the European Union (TEU) in turn requires special respect towards the traditionally developed institutions governing civil ecclesiastical law in the Member States. Third, the principle of EU loyalty in the form of respect for the constitutional structure of its Member States prohibits any unilateral assimilation of the law where these matters are concerned. And finally, the principle of subsidiarity, according to Article 5 TEU, requires a reticence on the part of the EU with regard to questions of the law on religion.[355]

352. For more detail about the Lisbon treaty, *see* Wolfgang Weiß, 'Human Rights in the EU: Rethinking the Role of the European Convention of Human Rights After Lisbon'. *European Constitutional Law Review* 7 (2011): 64–95.

353. 2008 was the year of the Lisbon Treaty ratification round. More than half of the twenty-seven EU Member States approved the Treaty of Lisbon by June 2008, including Finland.

354. For the text of the Lisbon Treaty, as well as consolidated versions of the EU and TEU, *see Full text of the treaty*, http://europa.eu/lisbon_treaty/full_text/index_en.htm => EU law/EU treaties.

355. Gerhard Robbers, *Germany.* In *International Encyclopaedia of Laws: Religion*, edited by Rik Torfs. Alphen aan den Rijn, NL (Kluwer Law International, 2013), 184.

III. Amendments by the Lisbon Treaty to the Primary European Union Law Related to Religion

615. The Lisbon Treaty strengthened the Union's fundamental and human rights dimension in its religious policy.[356] Of particular importance to churches was Article 16c of the Treaty or, in its later version, Article 17 (TFEU),[357] which stated that the Union shall respect and not interfere with the position of churches and religious associations or communities in the Member States in accordance with national law. The Treaty of Lisbon has therefore replaced the text of the Declaration contained in the former Amsterdam Treaty with a new Article 16c/17, according to which the Union shall conduct an open and regular dialogue with churches, religious associations or communities, and philosophical and non-confessional organizations.

616. The new Article 17 TFEU reads in its entirety:

(1) The Union respects and does not prejudice the status under national law of churches and religious associations or communities in the Member States.
(2) The Union equally respects the status of philosophical and non-confessional organizations.
(3) Recognizing their identity and their specific contribution, the Union shall maintain an open, transparent and regular dialogue with these churches and organizations.

617. In sum, the Amsterdam, Nice and Lisbon Treaties can generally be considered to promote diversity and pluralism,[358] and also not to strive for greater coherence within or between Member States. Both the Declaration on the Churches and Religious Communities of the Amsterdam Treaty and the new Article 16c of the Treaty of Lisbon, as amended, undoubtedly mean, without the repeal of any human rights instruments of the Council of Europe and the OSCE, the inclusion of legislation within the jurisdiction of the EU Member States, thus observing way to the cultural specificities of the various countries. They also guarantee the exercise of religious freedom in the Member States of the European Union. In this context, it should be mentioned that the dialogue with churches and religious and philosophical communities is based on similar principles, to an open, transparent, and regular

---

356. For further detail, *see* Giancomo Di Federico, 'Fundamental Rights in the EU: Legal Pluralism and Multi-Level Protection After the Lisbon Treaty'. In *Di Federico (ed.), The EU Charter of Fundamental Rights from Declaration to Binding Instrument.* (Dordrecht, 2011), 15–54. *See also* Allan Rosas & Heidi Kaila. 'Euroopan unionin tuomioistuin ja Lissabonin sopimus' (The Court of Justice of the European Union and the Treaty of Lisbon). In Länsineva, Tuomisto, Wikström & Viljanen (eds), *Juhlakirja Heikki Kulla 1950 – 28/8 – 2010.* (Turku, 2010), 261–284.

357. The Treaty of Lisbon amended the two central treaties of the EU, the TEU, and the Treaty establishing the European Community. The name of the latter was changed, and it is now called the TFEU. For the text of the consolidated versions of the EU and TEU, consult Europa (ed.), Full text of the treaty, http://europa.eu/lisbon_treaty/full_text/index_en.htm.

358. In addition, Art. 167 Treaty on the Functioning of the European Union (TFEU) confers responsibility for the protection of cultural variety upon the EU.

dialogue with the representative institutions of civil society.[359] The provisions of Article 17, sections 1 and 2, acknowledge churches and religious communities as factors within community law. The EU respects the Member States' competence in the field of religion. Whenever the European institutions exercise their competence, they must respect and not prejudice the Member States' law on religion within the scope of EU law.

618. A number of new treaty articles or changes to earlier articles in the Lisbon Treaty are linked to the EU's external action to make it more transparent and effective, and also to the EU's foreign, security, and defence policy. The Treaty further emphasizes the obligation of Member States to commit themselves to democracy and to guaranteeing the human rights of all citizens. With respect to religious policy, this means that the State also cannot ignore the religious needs of its citizens. In this regard, the EU bases its thinking on a positive interpretation of religious freedom, which was clearly emphasized in international religious freedom documents after the Second World War. Citizens have the right to religion and its community practice, not just the right to be free from all religions. The negative interpretation of religious freedom in Finland has long been overemphasized as a legacy of 1960s radicalism and proximity to the former Soviet Union. In adopting a positive interpretation of religious freedom, Finland arrives on the second train far behind the rest of Western Europe.[360]

IV. Religion in Secondary European Union Law

A. Provisions of the European Union

619. Secondary law means legally binding acts adopted by the institutions of the European Union, namely regulations, directives, and decisions. They may take the form either of legislative Acts or of subordinate Acts. In addition to binding Acts, the EU institutions may issue recommendations and opinions.

620. Secondary EU law also respects religious requirements and needs. At the European level, it is above all the European Union or EU law regulations and directives that are relevant in relation to 'Community' or 'Community law'. At least the

359. For further detail, *see* Matti Kotiranta, 'Euroopan unionin ja uskonnollisten yhteisöjen suhde tulevaisuuden Euroopassa' (The Relationship between the European Union and the Religious Communities in a Future Europe). A presentation made on 14 May 2009 at the Euro-election candidates' seminar 'Religions and the EU', organized by the Finnish Ecumenical Council. *See* http://www.ekumenia.fi/sen_toimii/opillinen_vuorovaikutus/uskonnot_ja_eu/matti_kotiranta_euroopan_unionin_ja_uskonnollisten_yhteisojen_suhde_tulevaisuuden_euroopassa_/?hitspic=1&hitspage=1. Article also available in *Etsijä* 1/2009, 10–17.

360. On religious freedom in Europe, *see* Robbers, Gerhard. 'Religionsfreiheit in Europa'. In *Festschrift für Joseph Listl*, edited by Josef Isensee, Wilhelm Rees & Wolfgang Rüfner. Berlin: Duncker & Humblot, 1999.

following two should be mentioned: Television Directive (Directive 2010/13/EU) and the directive on equal treatment in employment and occupation (Directive 2000/78/EC).

621. The former protects religious broadcasts with a scheduled transmission time of less than thirty minutes, which must not be interrupted by advertising (Article 20 section 2). In addition, advertising must not violate religious feelings (Article 9 section 1 lit. c) iii).[361]

622. The latter, Directive 2000/78/EC Article 4, has a major impact on the occupational requirements of churches and other public or private organizations:

> in the case of occupational activities within churches and other public or private organizations, the ethos of which is based on religion or belief, a difference of treatment based on a person's religion or belief shall not constitute discrimination where, by reason of the nature of these activities or of the context in which they are carried out, a person's religion or belief constitutes a genuine, legitimate and justified occupational requirement, having regard to the organization's ethos. This difference of treatment shall be implemented taking account of Member States' constitutional provisions and principles, as well as the general principles.

623. As Professor Gerhard Robbers has pointed out, 'this Directive shall thus not prejudice the right of churches and other public or private organizations, the ethos of which is based on religion or belief, acting in conformity with national constitutions and laws, to require individuals working for them to act in good faith and with loyalty to the organization's ethos. The autonomy rights of the religious communities are thus secured to a far-reaching extent'.[362]

B. European Union Law and the Finnish Anti-discrimination Provisions

624. Of the UN instruments relevant to religious discrimination, Finland ratified the ICCPR in 1976 (SopS 7–8/1976), the International Convention on the Elimination of All Forms of Radical Discrimination (ICERD) in 1970 (SopS 37/1970), and the Convention on Discrimination in Education in 1971 (SopS 59/1971). Also relevant is the UN Declaration on the Elimination of All Forms of Intolerance and Discrimination Based on Religion or Belief, as proclaimed by the General Synod resolution 36/55 of 25 November 1981.[363]

---

361. Gerhard Robbers, *Germany.* In *International Encyclopaedia of Laws: Religion*, edited by Rik Torfs. Alphen aan den Rijn, NL (Kluwer Law International, 2013), 187.
362. *Ibid.*, 188.
363. For further detail on the international monitoring of fundamental and human rights, *see* Tuomas Ojanen & Martin Scheinin, 'Perusoikeuksien ja ihmisoikeuksien kansainvälinen valvonta' (International monitoring of fundamental and human rights). In Pekka Hallberg, Heikki Karapuu, Tuomas Ojanen, Martin Scheinin, Kaarlo Tuori, Veli-Pekka Viljanen, *Perusoikeudet* (Fundamental Rights). (2nd revised edn WSOYpro, 2011), 875–905. Ojanen & Scheinin 2011 b, *See also* Tuomas

625. The relevant section of the Finnish Constitution dealing with Equality mirrors the provisions of the European Union Law (TFEU: Articles 8, 10, 18, 20, 67 and 167), the ECHR, and, to a considerable extent, the ICCPR agreement, implementing the minimum level of rights stipulated in the national legal norms.[364]

626. Article 6 (paragraph 2) of the Finnish Constitution contains a list of certain prohibited discriminatory criteria. It specifically mentions gender, age, origin, language, religion, conviction, opinion, health, and disability. Paragraph 2 reads:

> (2) No one shall, without an acceptable reason, be treated differently from other persons on the ground of sex, age, origin, language, *religion*, conviction, opinion, health, disability or other reason that concerns his or her person.[365]

627. Other prohibited reasons related to the individual are likewise treated as being prohibited. These include social status, wealth, participation in associations, family relationships, pregnancy, marital origin, sexual orientation, and place of residence.[366]

628. Equal treatment is also a key feature of the RFA (453/2003) and it is closely linked to the prohibition of discrimination based on religion or belief contained in Article 6 (paragraph 2) of the Constitution.

629. This prohibition, among other things, is accompanied by an obligation on the public authorities to treat all religious communities and world views in a balanced manner.

630. However, equal treatment does not require identical treatment but intends to treat equally what is equal and to treat unequally what is not equal, according to the extent of the differences. For example, a difference of treatment on the grounds of religion or belief of employees of a religious community (regardless of their legal status), follows normal state labour law rules (collective labour agreements). It is, however, modified in many circumstances on the basis of the new Freedom of Religion Act (2003). This will be discussed in greater detail in the next chapter, Part VI. (Labour Law within Religious Communities).

631. In Finnish jurisprudence, the provision prohibiting discrimination does not prohibit any discrimination between persons, even if the discrimination is expressly

---

Ojanen, 'Ihmisoikeusulottuvuuden kehittyminen Euroopan yhteisön oikeuteen' (The development of the human rights dimension in European Community law). In *Scheinin Martin & Taina Dahlgren (eds) Euroopan unioini ja ihmisoikeudet.* (Turku: Åbo Akademin ihmisoikeusinstituutti, 1994), 875–905.

364. *See* Mikko Puumalainen, 'Mitä Euroopan unionin perusoikeudet merkitsevät laillisuusvalvonnalle?' (What do the fundamental rights of the European Union mean for law enforcement?), 265–294. In Heinonen – Lavapuro (eds), *Oikeuskulttuurin eurooppalaistuminen. Ihmisoikeuksien murroksesta kansainväliseen vuorovaikutukseen* (Vantaa 2012).

365. Italics mine.

366. PeVL 11/2012 vp, 2.

mentioned in the provision. What matters is whether the distinction can be justified in a way that is acceptable to the fundamental rights system. The requirements for justification are particularly high in the case of the prohibited discriminatory criteria listed in the provision. In addition to the acceptability of the distinction, the Constitutional Law Committee's practice has paid attention to the proportionality of the method chosen.

632. In its opinions, the Constitutional Law Committee has assessed the acceptability of differential treatment based on, *inter alia*, sex,[367] age,[368] nationality,[369] religion or belief,[370] health and disability,[371] and other personal causes.[372]

633. In principle, the constitutional equality provision applies only to people. However, the principle of equality may also play a role in the assessment of the rules applicable to legal persons, in particular where the legal position of natural persons may be indirectly affected. The more meaningful the perspective, the more distant this connection is.[373] The relationship between the principle of equality and legal personality was discussed in greater detail in Part II, Chapter 3.[374]

634. The prohibition of discrimination also applies to: (a) pure discrimination (segregation); (b) indirect discrimination, that is to say, measures whose effects, albeit indirectly, would lead to discriminatory outcomes;[375] (c) affirmative actions, such as measures to improve the situation and conditions of women, children and minorities;[376] (d) and also provisions on the treatment of children, which ensure the equal status of children.[377] For example, the special treatment of children and young people is very common in criminal law.[378]

---

367. PeVL 38/2006 vp, 2, PeVL 30/2005 vp, 5, PeVL 10/2003 vp, 3, PeVL 13/1995 vp, 3, PeVL 100 21/1994 vp, 1.
368. For a summary of age-based distinctions, *see* PeVL 44/2010 vp, 6.
369. PeVL 26/2010 vp, 2, PeVL 13/2009 vp, 2, PeVL 11/2009 vp, 7, PeVL 31/2008 vp, 2, PeVL 6/2008 vp, 2, PeVL 19/2005 vp, 3, PeVL 28/2004 vp, 3, PeVL 30/2002 vp, 2, PeVL 26/2001 vp, 2.
370. PeVL 9/2007 vp, 6, PeVL 28/2006 vp, 3, PeVL 19/2005 vp, 3–4, PeVL 28/2004 vp, 2, PeVL 103 57/2001 vp, 2.
371. PeVL 60/2010 vp, 3, PeVL 31/2006 vp, 3–4.
372. PeVL 23/2012 vp, 2–3, PeVL 14/2006 vp, 2, PeVL 59/2002 vp, 2, PeVL 18/2001 vp, 8, PeVL 105 36/2000 vp, 2, PeVL 23/2000 vp, 2, PeVL 9/2000 vp, 2–3, PeVL 37/1997 vp, 2.
373. PeVL 60/2010 vp, 3, PeVL 31/2006 vp, 3–4.
PeVL 11/2012 vp, 2.
374. *See* further §1. Basic Principles, III. Fundamental Rights of Legal Persons.
375. HE 309/1993 vp, 44; *see also* PeVL 28/2009 vp, 2, PeVL 40/2004 vp, 2, PeVL 10/2003 vp, 2, PeVL 46/2002 vp, 6–7.
376. HE 309/1993 vp, 44; *see also* PeVL 56/2010 vp, 4, PeVL 38/2006 vp, 2, PeVL 34/2005 vp, 2, PeVL 40/2004 vp, 2, PeVL 10/2003 vp, 3, PeVL 20/1998 vp, PeVL 3/1997 vp.
377. HE 309/1993 vp, 45. The provision on the right of the child to influence his or her own affairs, in line with his or her level of development, demonstrates that each child should be treated as an individual and not merely as a passive subject. *See* closer HE 309/1993 vp, 45, PeVM 25/1994 vp, 7.
378. *See* further. PeVL 21/2005 vp, 4, PeVL 59/2001 vp, 2.

V. The ECJ

635. The European Union's legal principles are partly based on the express provisions of the Treaties and partly on the case law of the Court of Justice. In its case law, the ECJ has established legal principles in various contexts that have a significant influence on decisions affecting religious communities.[379] The principles of case law are as binding as those laid down in the Treaties. The best-known case concerning Finland is *Konttinen v. Finland*, where the ECtHR was in conformity with the line on religious freedom adopted in the former case of *X v. Denmark*.[380] Other important precedents that have proceeded in Finland to the Supreme Court and the Administrative Courts can be regarded as consistent with the decisions of the ECtHR, as expressed in its judgment in the case *X v. Denmark*.[381]

636. The fact that the ECJ deals with explicit religious provisions in EU law also contributes at Member State level to creating a more open and conscious way of dealing with religious issues.

---

379. These principles should be taken into account, as appropriate, in the activities of both the Union institutions and the authorities of the Member States. The binding nature of the principles is not limited to the adoption and application of Union acts but may also apply to the adoption and application of national law. They shall be taken into account both in the drafting of national legislation necessary to implement a Union act and in other national legislation having a bearing on Union law. For further detail on judicial protection before the Court of Justice, *see* Albertina Albors-Llornes, 'Judicial Protection Before the Court of Justice of the European Union'. In Catherine Barnard & Steve Peers (eds), *European Union Law* (Oxford: Oxford University Press, 2014).
380. Case 7374/76 of the European Commission on Human Rights (*X v. Denmark*), decision of 8 Mar. 1976, DR 5.
381. For closer information, *see* above, Part II., § 10, II.1. Cases where §9 of ECHR has been applied, and II.2. *Important precedents which have not proceeded to the Supreme Court and the Administrative Courts.*

Chapter 2. Transnational and Regional Law Effects on Religious Communities

637. There are no transnational or regional law impacts on religious communities, as Finland does not have a federal system.

638. Finland is, however, divided into municipalities whose administration is based on the self-government of their residents. Provisions on the general principles of municipal administration and the duties of the municipalities are laid down by an Act.[382] Municipalities are often important partners of religious communities, as municipalities have the exclusive power to plan for local development; this includes taking into account the religious and cultural needs of the population.

639. Common perspectives emerge from the legal basis and objectives of the municipality and the church. Both have a mission and a vision for the citizens' service, promoting well-being and the perspective of sustainable development. The municipality and the local parishes have traditionally been the creators and bearers of the local identity. A common area, mainly ordinary members, and complementary roles are important for identity.

640. The attitudes of the municipalities have often been positive towards the presence of religion, which is particularly evident in the early education that the municipalities have often done in collaboration with the local parishes.[383] The link between the municipal welfare mission and church's religious mission indicates the effects of a shared history.

382. Article 121 of the Constitution. Local Government Act (410/2015). Also available https://www.finlex.fi/en/laki/kaannokset/2015/en20150410.pdf (410/2015 English – Translations of Finnish acts and decrees).

383. *See* further discussion, *see* Sami Lahtiluoma & Raimo Turunen, *Kunta ja seurakunta – vuorovaikutusta ja yhteistyötä* (Municipality and parish – interaction and cooperation). (Helsinki: Kuntaliitto & Suomen evankelis-luterilainen kirkko, 2011).

Part V. Religion and Politics

Preamble

641. Religious communities in Finland are free to participate in the democratic process. No statutes or case law exist with respect to the involvement of churches and religious communities or members of the clergy in political life. Hence, there is no obstacle to members of the clergy participating in politics in Finland. Similarly, churches and religious communities can and do participate in public debate; the way in which such participation takes place varies between the different religious denominations and religious communities.

642. Churches and religious communities are important institutions in the public debate and have established a number of formalized ways of making their voices heard. The Finnish Ecumenical Council is a forum on which Christian Churches of a wide variety of denominations and religious communities cooperate with a view to developing joint policy. A concrete demonstration of common objective occurred in June 2006, on the eve of the start of the Finnish EU Presidency, when the Finnish Churches published a brief document, *Finnish Churches and the Finnish EU Presidency 2006*, which was drafted by the Finnish Ecumenical Council. It was handed to the Prime Minister and to the Foreign Minister by representatives of the Church Council at the traditional CEC/COMECE Presidency Meeting at the end of June that year. The common objective of the churches and religious communities for the Finnish EU Presidency was, in general, to present their perspectives, and then also to take a stance on the ideological goals that they wanted the EU to represent.

643. The Islamic community as a distinct entity has not thus far been active in Finnish politics, although the state authorities have maintained contact with them.[384] Instead, some individual Muslims have been actively involved in politics

384. The Islamic Council of Finland (Suomen Islamilainen Neuvosto, SINE) was established in November 2006 and was coordinated initially by the Office of the Ombudsman for Minorities. The aim of the authorities was to establish an umbrella organization for Islamic communities and associations, thus providing a liaison body with the authorities. This goal was also shared by the Muslim community, although the communities and organizations outside SINE founded another Islamic umbrella organization that used the old name of the Islamic Federation of Finland. For further detail, *see* Part III, §2., V. *Specific Issues of Organization.*

and city administration, primarily in southern Finland, in Helsinki,[385] Espoo, and Vantaa, and in some of the other main cities.

644. The various political parties represented in the Finnish Parliament have no confessional basis, part from one, the Christian Democratic Parliamentary Group, which, as of 3 May 2018, had five Members of Parliament. Since Parliament has two hundred members in total, elected for a term of four years, the Christian Democrats can be seen to play a relatively minor role in Finnish politics.

385. Finland's first Muslim female deputy mayor, city councillor, and former MP of the Social Democratic Party, Mrs Nasima Razmyar, is responsible for education and training.

Chapter 1. Religious Influence in Politics

§1. Constitutional Law Foundations

645. The political participation of the religious communities is based on a broad understanding of freedom of religion, as guaranteed in Article 11[386] of the Constitution and by the *Electoral and participatory rights* guaranteed by Article 14.

646. Article 14 of the Constitution contains fundamental rights provisions on the right to vote in national elections and referendums (paragraph 1), in European elections (paragraph 2), and in municipal elections and municipal referendums (paragraph 3). Paragraph 4 contains the constitutional mandate for the public power to promote the ability of individuals to participate in other forms of social activity and influence decisions affecting themselves.

647. From a more general perspective, Finnish democracy has evolved into a consensus thinking mode typical of Finnish politics, a democracy of associations such as trade unions, employers' organizations, and consumer associations that have a significant influence on the political process. Churches and religious communities are part of this system as a social partner. This issue is further explored in Part VI, which deals with the Labour Law within Religious Communities.

648. The status of national churches as public law entities does not exclude them from the democratic process; all religious communities, from the legal point of view, take part in the political process in the same way, as do other non-state organizations. As indicated earlier, in Part II (§8. Horizontal Application of Religious Freedom), freedom of religion or conviction is nowadays understood as the right both of the individual and of religious entities (communities). This means that religion is not merely a personal matter but also a public one; it becomes part of the public political process. How these two identities are intertwined in Finland is dealt with in greater detail in sections 5–8 of this chapter.

§2. Religions in Politics Based on Treaty Law

649. There exist no special agreements in Finland between the state and religious communities, concordats[387] between the state and the Holy See as in France or in Poland, or agreements between the state and the Protestant provincial (*Land*) Churches (known as the Loccum Treaty, or *Loccumer Vertrag*) as in Germany,

386. *See* further information, *see* Part II. Religious Freedom in General, §1. *Normative Structures* and §2. *Functions.*

387. The Concordat Treaty makes a legal distinction between state and church, but the country's public law provides guidance on how church-state cooperation can be organized on the basis of a separate agreement.

which would guarantee the political role of religious communities.[388] Finland does not have a federal system, nor does it have Lutheran provincial churches.

§3. The Media and Religions

650. Although technological advances have dominated the contemporary media landscape, it is ultimately the state that has directed the public media in numerous different countries. In particular, public broadcasting includes news broadcasts, sports, culture, programmes for children, and (almost as an afterthought) religious programming. The role of religion and the church in the Finnish media differs from that in many Central European countries, such as the Netherlands,[389] Germany,[390] and the United Kingdom,[391] where religion is a prominent factor in the public media. It is not very common in the Finnish religious landscape for church representatives and theologians to be regularly interviewed on television and radio about current issues and hot topics, as is the case in many other European countries.

651. The marginalization of the Church away from the media is partly due to the line taken by the Finnish media, but is at least as much due to the Church's own attitude towards publicity. Its outward orientation has been restrained, in many cases downright repressive. It is only in recent decades that the Churches and religious communities have adopted a more open approach to publicity. Issues related to globalization and internationalization have emerged, such as concerns about world peace, the gap between rich and poor, and Finland's relationship with development cooperation, refugees, and international terrorism.[392] One historical reason for the earlier, more restrained orientation may be that Finland has had a strong tradition of Christian daily newspapers, which have adopted the role of a consciously religiously oriented speciality.[393]

652. The Finnish broadcasting system combines both public broadcasting institutions (YLE) and private broadcasting enterprises. As far as religious programmes are concerned, broadcasting time is allotted to the broadcasting companies, mainly

388. For further detail, *see* Gerhard Robbers, *Germany.* In *International Encyclopaedia of Laws: Religion*, edited by Rik Torfs. Alphen aan den Rijn, NL (Kluwer Law International, 2013), 163.
389. Hermineke van Bockxmeer, 'The portrayal of religion in the Netherlands: the media and the arts'. In *Norman Doe (ed.), The Portrayal of Religion in Europe: The Media and the Arts Le portrait de religion en Europe: les médias et les arts.* (Leuven: Peeters, 2004), 185–208.
390. For example, Germany has used the principle of transparency to reserve time for churches and religious communities on public radio and national television channels such as ZDF and ARD, as well as on regional provincial channels.
391. James Young, 'Regulation of the representation of religion in the media in the United Kingdom'. In *Norman Doe (ed.), The Portrayal of Religion in Europe: The Media and the Arts Le portrait de religion en Europe: les médias et les arts.* (Leuven: Peeters, 2004), 265–285.
392. For further discussion of international terrorism, *see* Stella Margariti, *Defining International Terrorism: Between State Sovereignty and Cosmopolitanism.* Berlin: Springer-Verlag, International Criminal Justice series, Vol. 12, 2017.
393. For a list of the main Christian daily newspapers, *see* https://kristilliset.com/fi/esittelyt/kristilliset lehdet/. Accessed 9 Jan 2024.

to the national broadcasting TV and radio company known as YLE. Under its current contracts, the Communications Centre of the Lutheran Church co-ordinates the provision of religious programmes on TV and radio channels with YLE. Sunday services and hours of Christian worship on the part of both the main churches and minority denominations are broadcast in accordance with a jointly agreed schedule. Congregations and religious associations may also buy air-time from regional and local TV and radio channels.

653. From a purely legal perspective, the fundamental norms regulating the legal status of the media and religion in Finland are laid down in the Constitution, in section 12 ('Freedom of expression and the right of access to information') and in section 11 of the same Act ('Freedom of religion and conscience').

654. The status of the Evangelical Lutheran Church and the Orthodox Church as public law entities does not mean that they are incorporated into the state body as state institutions. Hence, they do not have a specific media structure guaranteed by the state, as would be the case in some other EU countries. There is also no specific law on Media and Religions for the registered religious communities.

655. In the Constitution of Finland (2000), the Freedom of Expression (§12, HM §10) enjoys a large field of application in the sense that freedom of expression is not bound to any particular method of communication; that is, there is a far-reaching neutrality with regard to the instruments of communication. In addition, by virtue of the Constitutional Act the regulations dealing with freedom of expression are applied to all kinds of communication technology, both those being currently used and those that may be introduced in the future. The sphere of application of the Freedom of Expression Act includes all kinds of data, opinions, and other messages, irrespective of their content (Government bill 309/1993 Parliament, p. 56) or of the purpose of the expression and publication in question; i.e., there is a state of neutrality as regards content and purpose.[394]

656. The articles on freedom of expression in the human rights agreements similarly protect general opinions, information, and ideas. Thus, with respect to the sphere of application of the Constitution's Freedom of Expression Act, in Finland no distinction is made, for instance, between political, *religious*, artistic, scientific, commercial, entertainment-related, and other messages. Instead, the regulations are applied to all forms of communication. Furthermore, with respect to religious communication, it must be noted that §11 (HM §9) of the Constitutional Act, which safeguards freedom of religion and conscience, has specifically confirmed everyone's right to express his or her convictions.

657. Individual members of religious communities (Christian, Jewish, Muslim, etc.), who serve as Members of Parliament may have duties in government bodies

394. For further detail, *see* Matti Kotiranta, 'The Legal Position of Religion and the Media in Finland'. In *Norman Doe (ed.), The Portrayal of Religion in Europe: The Media and the Arts Le portrait de religion en Europe: les médias et les arts* (Leuven: Peeters, 2004), 41–56.

that regulate media activities, such as the Transport and Communications Committee, which deal with matters that concern telecommunications, radio and television functions, and other communications, the information security of communication services, and the Finnish Broadcasting Company.

§4. Religions and State Political Institutions

658. Churches and religious communities are not represented as such in parliament or in any equivalent bodies. Nonetheless, members of religious communities may, like everyone else, exercise political functions. There are no legal restrictions on any such activities in Finnish law.

659. According to state law, the right to vote and to be elected is in no way restricted. Article 14 (paragraphs 2–3) of the Constitution reads:

(2) Every Finnish citizen and every foreigner permanently resident in Finland, having attained eighteen years of age, has the right to vote in municipal elections and municipal referendums, as provided by an Act. Provisions on the right to otherwise participate in municipal government are laid down by an Act.

(3) The public authorities shall promote opportunities for the individual to participate in societal activity and to influence the decisions that concern him or her.

660. Some religious communities, for example the Finnish Orthodox Church, have introduced internal restrictions on their personnel concerning political offices. One case that may be mentioned here concerned Mr Mitro Repo, a priest of the Orthodox Church, who was a Member of the European Parliament from 2009 to 2014. The Synod of Orthodox bishops found Repo's candidacy to be a violation of the canonical tradition of the church and voted by a simple majority of two to one to reject Repo's right to exercise his priestly office during his European election campaign in 2009 and during his subsequent parliamentary term.[395]

§5. Religions and Political Parties

661. Finnish political parties are, in the main, grounded in the basic convictions, ideas, and value systems for which they stand. In many fields, however, the political parties overlap, and people of all faiths and non-denominations can nowadays be found in almost all of the relevant political parties, where religiously oriented members form internal groups with varying degrees of formal organization.

395. Repo appealed against the decision of the Bishops Assembly to the Supreme Administrative Court. In December 2009, Repo's complaint was rejected by the Supreme Administrative Court. The KHO considered it an internal matter of the Orthodox Church and the right of the Church to interpret the doctrine of the Church. Many schooled in Finnish law felt, however, that canon law was given priority over civil law and basic human rights.

662. Many of the political parties explicitly express a basic relation to religious contexts in their programmes. The Cultural Ecclesiastical Parties include the National Coalition Party (Kokoomus),[396] the Centre Party (Keskusta),[397] and the Swedish People's Party (Ruotsalainen kansanpuolue, RKP). Of those, the Centre Party[398] and RKP[399] continue to state in their manifestos that the Christian tradition is an integral part of Finnish culture and that Christian values form the basis of Finnish ethics.

663. The Value Christian parties – the Finns Party[400] and the Christian Democrats (KD)[401] – say that their activities are based on Christian values. Of the Finnish political parties, only the Christian Democratic Party is explicitly based on Christian values, but it is not linked organizationally with any specific Christian denomination. Many of its supporters belong to the so-called 'Fifth Awakening Movement', the free Churches, and the Pentecostals.

664. The SDP remain ambivalent regarding their church relationship. Its party programmes, starting with the Forssa programme (1903), have held the view that religion is a private matter and that church and state should be separated from each other.[402] The relationship between church and state has been the subject of debate in the party throughout its history. The SDP Party Assembly has repeatedly stated that one of their goals is the separation of church and state, but implementation of

---

396. The Coalition Party has been the leading political church force in Finland since the early 1960s. In the new Principle and Value Programme of the Coalition Party 2018, there is no longer any mention of the Christian tradition. It has been replaced by national and cultural identities, which are said to be inter-dimensional and ever-changing. Finnishness is said to be a part of both Nordic identity and Europeanism. *See* https://www.kokoomus.fi/tietoa-kokoomuksesta/arvot-periaateohjelma/. Accessed 9 Jan 2024.

397. On the importance of the Centre Party as a Value Christian ecclesiastical party in the Finnish political field, *see* Jaakko Antila's dissertation, *Keskustapuolueen kirkkopoliittisten tavoitteiden muotoutuminen vuosina 1966–1978* (Politics in the Church. Formation of Centre Party Church Political Objectives, 1966-1978). (University of Helsinki, 2010). *Diss.*

From the 1960s onwards, influence shifted to the Centre Party, which was an important force in church politics until the late 1980s. The Centre Party Principle Programme, 'Principle 101', states in Principle 46: 'We recognize and value the Christian roots of our society. Everyone should have the freedom to recognize and practice their religion or outlook on life in accordance with Finnish law and good practices.' *See* further: https://keskusta.fi/politiikkamme/ohjelmia-ja-linjauksia/periaateohjelma/. Accessed 9 Jan. 2024.

398. From the 1960s onwards, influence shifted to the Centre Party, which was an important force in state politics defending the Church in terms of its Christian values. *See* Antila 2010, 220–230. *See* especially, 230.

399. The RKP party programme also mentions religion in addition to other activities: 'Cultural, sport, homeland, and community activities, and also church and religious activities reinforce identities and play an important role in [Finnish] society'.

400. The first sentence of the Finns Party Manifesto reads: 'The Finns Party is a patriotic and Christian social party that promotes national interests'.

401. As the basis of the Christian Democratic Principles Programme (2017), §1 is the Christian image of humankind: 'The Christian image of man [sic] is the starting point of values'. *See*, https://www.kd.fi/files/2017/08/Periaateohjelma2017_puoluekokouksen-paattama.pdf. Accessed 9 Jan. 2024.

402. The current party programme (23 Aug. 2020) makes no mention of a church or religious view of the world. *See*, https://www.sdp.fi/tutustu/tietoa-sdpsta/periaatejulistuksemme/. Accessed 9 Jan. 2024.

the policy has not progressed.[403] Both the Left Alliance and the Greens (Principle Programme 2012) require that all religious and world-view communities should have equal status within the state. In their 2015–2019 political programme, the Greens aimed to abolish the tax collection rights of the national churches, to delegate the statutory functions of the Church (such as burial services) to the state and municipalities, and to end the special relationship that exists between the state and the churches. The new Objective 2019–2023 programme (Objective 6, §14) aims at 'treating religious communities in the same way as other third sector actors and ensuring the fulfilment of church social functions'.

665. There is no specific Muslim political party. Individual Muslims are members of all major political parties. However, in elections Muslim voters tend to prefer the Social Democratic Party of Finland (SDP) and the Greens (Vihreät). There is no reliable research data concerning this, but among the Finnish parties the SDP and the Greens appear to be most positive towards Muslims in Finland. This is particularly evident regarding the question of the education of imams.

666. The SDP welcomes the education of imams and notes that the growing Muslim population needs its own religious scholars. According to the Greens, the education of imams would be a natural continuation of the training of Islamic teachers already underway at the University of Helsinki. According to the National Coalition Party, the education of imams at Finnish universities must also be considered.

667. Of the parliamentary parties, the Centre Party, the Finns Party, the Left Alliance and the Christian Democrats reject the idea of educating imams using public funding. According to the Centre Party, Islamic communities provide training for their own employees and should not be interfered with by the state as long as the training does not conflict with national law.[404]

668. It is generally accepted in Finland, that religion is a private matter and that politics and religion should not be confused. Most politicians (except Christian Democrats) are alien to God's involvement in political debate. In Finland, the distinction between politics and religion has often been justified by the distinction between earthly and spiritual regimes, although in Luther's ecclesiastical thinking there was historically no idea of a divine reality separate from God: both regimes were regarded as subordinate to the same divine reality. In any case, Finnish policy, largely due to the idea of two kingdoms, has given rise to the general idea that the use of natural reason in secular government is sufficient for the purpose of human creation. For decades, the leadership of the Evangelical Lutheran Church in Finland has also been able to support such an approach to church politics in which the church and the state have their own playing field, their own mission, on the basis of

403. Pikkusaari, Jussi, *Vaikea vapaus. Sosialidemokratian häviö kirkolle 1850-luvulta 1920-luvulle käydyssä Suomen kulttuuritaistelussa* (Hard freedom. The loss of social democracy in the church in the Finnish cultural struggle, 1850–1920). (University of Oulu. Bibliotheca historica 32. Helsinki: Suomen historiallinen seura, 1998), 53–69, 133–137. *Diss.*

404. For further detail *see*, https://www.kotimaa.fi/artikkeli/kokoomus-ja-sdp-suhtautuvat-myonteisesti-imaamikoulutukseen/.

the rule of the kingdom. The danger for the Church in this way of thinking in the increasingly pluralistic society of today is that the Church may unconsciously trip on the threshold of its political influence, even though from time to time it adopts a strong stance on societal issues, both the values represented by economic neoliberalism and also the everyday problems of ordinary people.

669. Religion, however, strongly influences politics in Finland. The history of both national churches, the Evangelical Lutheran Church and the OCF, is living proof that it is impossible to distinguish between church and politics.

670. During the Civil War of 1918, the Lutheran Church settled on the white side. This choice alienated the church's working population and left-wing parties for decades. After the Civil War, church leaders supported the German monarchy in the government dispute, which irritated the Republican Peasant Alliance (Maalaisliitto, the present-day Centre Party). Before the Second World War, the church was also labelled as right-wing. The caricature by the famous Finnish cartoonist, Kari Suomalainen, featuring the Coalition Party as a helmet-headed priest goes back to those early decades.

'Priest – Sacristan – Peasant – (Cupper)' Kari Suomalainen's view of the National Coalition Party (left), the Christian Democrats, the Centre Party, and the Social Democrats. HS. 14 December 1976. Copyright Kari Suomalainen's estate.

671. After the Second World War (the Winter War and the Continuation War, 1939–1944) the political profile of the church changed from being primarily right-wing to universal bourgeois. At the same time, in the 1960s the church began to cooperate with the working class and the left-wing parties. The politicization of the Evangelical Lutheran Church in Finland aroused much debate in the late 1960s and especially during the 1970s. There was a wide spectrum of public perceptions of how party politics marched into the church and the church was becoming a battleground for parties. In church politics, the Centre Party continued its right-wing policy – which in its programme emphasized Christian values, religious education, and family values – and feared that 'social democrats would take over the church'. Concerns about the loss of old supporters of the revival movements, especially on the part of the Christian Union of Finland (now the Christian Democrats), were a major factor in defining the Church's political goals in state decision-making. While fighting with the SDP for political power, the Centre Party also became interested in church appointments, which became the engine of church politics for the party in the 1970s and 1980s.[405]

672. For a hundred years the political pendulum of the Lutheran Church has swept a wide arc from right to left. At present, some even see the red-green clergy sweeping over many issues that divide citizens, such as the controversy surrounding same-sex marriage (the new law came into force on 1 March 2017), the related issues of euthanasia[406] and care, and solidarity with refugees and immigrants.

673. For the OCF, the historical image is also complex. The church was first shaken politically by the dissolution of the Moscow Patriarchate and the establishment in 1923 of the Ecumenical Patriarchate as an autonomous Archdiocese. Directly after the war, the Church fought for its existence in what was known as the canonical controversy between the Finnish Orthodox Church and the Moscow Patriarchate, which threatened to undermine the position of the Finnish Orthodox Church in 1945–1957. In the Finnish Government it was principally the Ministers of Education, Foreign Affairs, and the Interior who were engaged in the re-affiliation process; they wanted to return the Finnish Orthodox Church to the Moscow Patriarchate. The eventual outcome of the canonical controversy was that the Moscow Patriarchate failed to win supremacy over Orthodoxy in Finland.[407]

674. During the war years of 1939–1945 and later, during the period of reconstruction, when the Orthodox population was re-settled from Karelia to Finland, believers faced real difficulties in practising their faith in an alien environment. In many places, the Orthodox Church had to carry the stigma of the Russian Church, and was frequently castigated as the 'Ryssän kirkko' (Russo Church). It was not until 1969, when Parliament approved the Law on the Orthodox Church, that the Church could legitimately see itself as an equal partner standing alongside its Lutheran counterpart.[408] Archbishop Paul and later Archbishop John and Father Ambrosius (later, Metropolitan of the Diocese of Helsinki) had a very important influence on the public image of the Orthodox Church in Finland. In their time, church life

405. *See* Jaakko Antila, *Keskustapuolueen kirkkopoliittisten tavoitteiden muotoutuminen vuosina 1966–1978* (Politics Targeting the Church – the Formation of Centre Party Church Objectives, 1966-1978). (University of Helsinki, 2010), 232–256.

406. On Euthanasia in Criminal Law, *see* Kimmo Nuotio, 'Avustettu potilaan itsemurha ja eutanasia' (Assisted patient suicide and euthanasia). In *Oikeuden historiasta tulevaisuuden Eurooppaan: Pia Letto-Vanamo 60 vuotta* (The History of Justice to Future Europe: Pia Letto-Vanamo 60 Years). (Helsinki: Suomalaisen lakimiesyhdistyksen julkaisuja. E-sarja 26, 2014), 277–294.

407. For greater detail, *see* General Introduction, §3, IV. c. *The Change in Finnish Politics in the Post-war Years – The Paasikivi–Kekkonen Line and Realpolitik vis-à-vis the Former Soviet Union.*

408. Within the Orthodox Church, attention was drawn to the fact that the rules governing the Lutheran Church were set down in the Church Law, the equivalent rules for the Orthodox faith having been adopted only by the Church's own authority, the Regulations of 1925.

stabilized, and Orthodoxy also began to open up to the outside world. The new Valaam (Valamo) monastery became a versatile cultural centre. Orthodoxy also became popular with intellectuals, writers, and artists. The above-mentioned bishops, and also the present Archbishop Leo, have all been closely connected with cultural circles and political decision-makers.

675. As for party politics, the dilemma for the Evangelical Lutheran and Orthodox churches in Finland is compounded by the question of how to proclaim the Bible's social message without being misidentified as a lawyer for any party.

§6. The Political Representation of Religions

676. The major Finnish churches, i.e., the Lutherans and the Orthodox Church, are not represented by any established institutions in the political sphere, and the same is true of the other religious communities. Indeed, the churches and religious communities no longer play a clear political role in society, although it would be over-hasty to think that the largest religious communities in Finland, the Evangelical Lutheran Church and the Orthodox Church, had no effect on the of strengthening of present-day national identity and independence.[409] There has been no tendency to argue politically about key issues of church and religious policy but, as in other Western and Northern Europe democracies, the political focus has been on social and economic policy and on income distribution. The most important political issues have been addressed with the support of the church administrations, and informal contacts have been maintained at a high level.

677. Thus, the ELCF and OCF were decisive factors during Finland's post-war reunification, as has been noted above. It is also notable that the longer the history of Finland's independence has continued to develop, the more the churches and religious communities have been obliged to relocate themselves in society in new ways. Formal changes in the social status of the Church have been happening gradually and are relatively minor, and all have emphasized the independence of the Church from the State. In the new context, the churches have increasingly used their moral voice in society. The context has been one of economic change, the capitalization of society, and globalization, all of which have changed the conditions of everyday life in ways that the Church has found it necessary to address. In the process, the Archbishop's role as President of the Church has been further emphasized. The Archbishops of the ELCF, Mikko Juva, John Vikström, and Kari Mäkinen, have enjoyed

409. This can be seen in the fact that the church leadership is regularly called to the National Defence Courses in conjunction with MPs and the country's most important organizations and corporate leadership.

popularity as the nation's moral voice, while within the Church itself the Archbishops have received support primarily from a church characterized by social and ecumenical openness.[410]

678. Smaller religious communities, the Catholic Church, the Free Churches, and the Jewish and Islamic communities, have played a less prominent role historically in Finnish politics. The Catholic Church in Finland has been in contact with the CEC/COMECE, through which it has been able to promote its views at EU level. The ELCF also maintains an office in Brussels. In addition, the Finnish Ecumenical Council has provided a forum through which Christian churches representing a wide variety of denominations and religious communities cooperate with a view to developing joint policies.

679. Muslim associations have also begun to find a role for themselves in Finnish politics. As noted earlier, the Islamic community as a distinct entity has not yet become active in Finnish politics, although some individuals in the Muslim communities have been actively involved in politics and city administrations. The majority of mosque associations are members of associations that have united within umbrella organizations, such as the Helsinki Islamic Centre (founded in 1995) and the Islamic Centre of Finland (founded in 1994). In addition, there are at least five other Islamic communities in the metropolitan area with their own prayer rooms. These umbrella organizations provide a platform for discussing and developing the integration of Muslims into Finnish society and the platform is considered to be the most important forum between the Finnish state and Muslims living in Finland.

§7. The Political Impact of Religious Communities

680. National churches and other registered religious communities have fully accepted the Finnish democratic system. From time to time, the church has been accused of invading the sphere of politics. It is true that churches and religious communities have not been able to make rapid changes but, for example, in the debate over the status of gender and sexual minorities, the Evangelical Lutheran Church leadership has expressed its support for equality and change. Criticism has also been raised by the Church's encroachment on funding for development cooperation. In the debate on Finland's competitiveness in 2015 and 2016, the Lutheran Church was criticized for adhering to Epiphany and Ascension Day as public holidays, a custom that is alleged to undermine the competitiveness of the national economy. The

410. Mikko Malkavaara (2017, 60), 'Luterilaisuuden vaikutus kulttuuriin ja yhteiskuntaan' (The Impact of Lutheranism on Culture and Society), in *Ruth Illman, Kimmo Ketola, Riitta Latvio & Jussi Sohlberg (Ed.), Monien uskontojen ja katsomusten Suomi.* (Kuopio: Kirkon tutkimuskeskuksen verkkojulkaisuja 48, 2017). Malkavaara states, that 'the conflict has been caused by human rights, which were central to the 1995 Reform of Fundamental Rights and the new 2000 Constitution. The Church has had no objection to this, except for the ecclesiastical minority, which believes that the human rights debate breaks the traditional structures of society that are interpreted as biblical'. *Ibid.*

Church has also been criticized for providing assistance to those who have been denied asylum while awaiting deportation. For the Church, however, it was not a question of politics but of assisting the weak and the marginalized.

681. The ecumenical and international relations of the Finnish churches and religious communities have served a broader church policy in relation to the EU. A concrete demonstration of this was a historic incident when representatives of the churches in Finland (Lutheran, Orthodox, and Roman Catholic, Finnish Free Church Council, and the Finnish Ecumenical Council) together approached the President of Finland at the end of 1995 and suggested that the Finnish delegates adopt a greater religio-political initiative at the intergovernmental conference to be held in 1996. During their visit the representatives of the Finnish churches expressed their entire agreement with the efforts of the German Evangelical Church (EKD) and German Catholic Episcopal Conference to have a statement on the religious communities appended to the founding document of the European Union. This initiative was repeated a year later, in June 1997, at the intergovernmental conference in Amsterdam, when it was decided to include in the agreement of the European Union (Maastricht II) a declaration (not simply an article) on the status of the churches and religious communities (present Article 17, in The Lisbon Treaty).

682. The first step forward in the direction of a detailed church-political EU strategy was taken (at the suggestion of Archbishop Jukka Paarma) on 30 May 2001, when *The Advisory Board on EU Affairs* was established under the auspices of the Church Board. Its task was to create an EU strategy for the ELCF and to seek to monitor the effects of the activities of EU institutions on ecclesiastical life. The Consultative Committee – which *included a strong academic representation*: (1) functions as an advisory expert body in matters related to the EU; (2) participates in the discussion on EU policy vis-à-vis the Church; (3) related to this, makes proposals to the Church Board; and (4) promotes cooperation with Church and State and local authority organs responsible for EU matters as well as with non-governmental organizations. In this connection, in 2002 the ELCF created its own EU strategy which took a stand on the kinds of ideological goals that the Church would want the EU to represent.[411]

683. The second significant moment that produced a detailed EU strategy for the churches was accomplished – as mentioned in the preamble – when Finland held the Presidency of the European Union from 1 July to 31 December 2006. In June, on the eve of the start of the Finnish EU Presidency, the Finnish Churches published a brief document, *Finnish Churches and the Finnish EU Presidency 2006*, which was drafted in cooperation with the Finnish Ecumenical Council. The statement was handed to the Prime Minister, *Matti Vanhanen*, by representatives of the

411. Document in English. For more detail, *see* Matti Kotiranta et al. 'The Teaching and Study of Church–State Relations in the Nordic Countries in the United Kingdom and in Ireland'. In José María González del Valle & Alexander Hollerbach (eds), *The Teaching of Church–State Relations in European Universities – L'enseignement du droit ecclésiastique de l'État dans les universités européennes.* (Leuven: Peeters, 2005), 148–152.

Church Council and to the Foreign Minister, *Erkki Tuomioja*, at the long-established CEC/COMECE Presidency Meeting at the end of June.

684. The Churches wished to support the public administration in issues related to the Presidency. In this respect, the Finnish churches' work in EU affairs had a strong ecumenical dimension. According to the ecumenical declaration *Charta Oecumenica*, signed in 2001, the Churches supported the integration of the European continent and, grounded in their Christian conviction, were working towards a humane, socially conscious Europe in which human rights and the basic values of peace, justice, freedom, tolerance, participation, and solidarity could prevail.[412]

685. The aim of the Finnish churches was also to establish a regular dialogue with the Government Secretariat of EU Affairs on issues that were considered of importance for the Churches and in which they could add value to the general debate.

686. In the document *Finnish Churches and the Finnish EU Presidency 2006*, the Churches emphasized certain key issues that they felt should be prioritized during the Finnish EU Presidency. These included:

- Strengthening the value dimension of the Union and keeping alive the discussion about the future of the Union.
- The need for inter-religious dialogue based on mutual tolerance and respect and knowledge of one's own identity and conviction.
- Enhancing the social and environmental dimension of the Union, combating human trafficking and promoting a consequent human immigration and refugee policy.[413]

687. The latest stage in the detailed church-political EU strategies is represented by the document *The Church and the EU – active participation and commitment to common values* (2009), which articulated perceptions of the aims and priorities of the ELCF in relation to EU affairs.[414] One of the priorities of the Church's work in the field of EU affairs was to take part in the debate over the value dimension of the Union (as already seen in the 2002 document) and to strengthen it. The 2009 document emphasizes the importance that the Treaty of Lisbon should promote respect for human dignity, freedom, democracy, equality, the rule of law, and human rights – including the rights of persons belonging to minorities – as the foundational values of the European Union. According to the Treaty, the Member States can be characterized by pluralism, non-discrimination, tolerance, justice, solidarity, and equality between women and men. According to the document the Evangelical Lutheran Church was strongly committed to these jointly defined values. It desired

412. *Finnish Churches and the Finnish EU-Presidency 2006*, 1.
413. *Ibid.*, 2–4.
414. *See* http://evl.fi/EVLen.nsf/Documents/79D92BD6D45C541CC22575CA0038BEA7/$file/ATTF8EBK.pdf.

to enhance the value dimension within all of the policy areas and affirmed that these values needed to be implemented in practice.

688. The Evangelical Lutheran Church is also of the opinion that thc Lisbon Treaty strengthens the European Union as a community of values, promotes the monitoring and enforcement of human rights, and supports the development of the Union's social dimension. 'In addition, the Treaty creates better possibilities for participatory democracy. For the churches this culminates in the Union's commitment to maintain an open, transparent, and regular dialogue with them (art. 17). The Lisbon Treaty confirms that Church and State relations are also going to be defined in the future at the national level. The Treaty also recognizes the specific contribution of the churches.'[415]

§8. Religious Communities and Election Campaigns

689. During election campaigns the national churches, the ELCF and the OCF, do not openly support specific political parties.

690. However, individual candidates are free to express their beliefs and convictions in their parliamentary election campaigns. The most openly Christian values are those espoused by the Christian Democrats, which can also be clearly seen in their party manifesto (§1).[416]

691. In church, rather than parliamentary, elections, political parties are also openly visible. In the 2018 parish elections, representatives were elected in 384 parishes. The turnout was 14.4%, representing 439,000 voters out of a potential 3,056,000.[417]

415. The Church and the EU – active participation and commitment to common values (2009), 6.
416. *See*, https://www.kd.fi/tutustu/ohjelmat/periaateohjelma/. 9 Jan. 2024.
417. For more detail, *see* https://public.tableau.com/profile/kirkon.tutkimuskeskus#!/vizhome/Seurakuntavaalit2018_TEST/SRKVAALIT_2018_5. Accessed 30 Oct. 2019. (Updated 9 Jan. 2024) *See also* Virpi Sintonen, *Puolueet kirkkoa valtaamassa? – Suomen evankelis-luterilaisen kirkon ja yhteiskunnan suhteet Forssan, Merijärven ja Vihdin seurakuntavaalien 1970, 1974 ja 1978 valossa.* (Parties taking control over the church? – Relations between the Evangelical Lutheran Church in Finland and society in the light of the Forssa, Merijärvi and Vihti parish elections in 1970, 1974 and 1978). (Helsinki: Unigrafia, 2018). *Diss.*

Chapter 2. Political and Legal Interaction Between Religions and the State

692. There are no regular meetings in Finland between the secular authorities and governments (Synods or Councils) of the churches and religious communities to exchange views.

693. Parliamentary hearings on bills are a way of exerting religious influence in general politics. Occasionally, From time to time, religious communities are invited to these hearings for questions related to them. The usual way in which a law is drafted occurs either in Parliament or more often in the competent ministry.[418] Once the first draft has been completed, the various stakeholders in society will be involved in the drafting of the law. A good example of this was the preparation of the new RFA (453/2003), where, in accordance with the decision of the Administration Committee of Parliament, a draft of the RFA was submitted to the Constitutional Law Committee. Prior to the preparation of the report, at several meetings the Committee panel heard a total of nine experts from across government, the religious communities, and administrative law at the University of Helsinki.[419] In addition, the Education and Culture Committee heard various parties. The Association of Free thinkers also gave its opinion on the question of 'teaching about a pupil's own religion'.[420]

694. The most important individual Muslims and Muslim organizations that are representative of the variety of Muslim life in Finland have actively participated in the Islamic Council of Finland (SINE). As indicated above, this Council has been coordinated by the Office of the Ombudsman for Minorities to discuss issues of Muslim life in Finland, and the intention is that it should act in liaison with the authorities. This goal has been also shared by the Muslim community, though the communities and organizations outside SINE founded another Islamic umbrella organization that used the old name of the Islamic Federation of Finland. Some Muslim organizations also actively participate in inter-religious dialogues.

---

418. *See* Jyrki Tala, *Lakien laadinta ja vaikutukset* (Drafting and Impact of Laws). (Helsinki, 2005). About the quality of legislation work, *see* Ahtonen, Riitta & Anssi Keinänen & Mia Kilpeläinen, *Eduskunnan valiokuntien näkemys lainvalmistelutyön laadusta* (The views of parliamentary committees on the quality of legislagion work). (OPTL:n tutkimustiedonantoja 111. Helsinki, 2011); Ilkka Saraviita, 'Lisänäkökohtia perustuslakivaliokunnasta lausunnonantajana ja asiantuntijoiden kuulijana' (Further insights about the Constitutional Law Committee as an expert committee and hearings from experts). *Oikeus* 2 (2012): 299–304.
419. For further detail, *see* Juha Seppo, *Uskonnonvapaus 2000-luvun Suomessa* (Freedom of Religion in 21st Century Finland). (Helsinki 2003), 118–119.
420. *Ibid.*, 120–127.

Part VI. The Labour Law Within the Religious Communities[421]

Chapter 1. Scope of Application of the Labour Law

§1. Factual Situation

695. The large churches – the Evangelical Lutheran Church and the Orthodox Church – in Finland together employ about 16,300 persons.[422] Church employees usually work in connection with congregations, parish unions, cathedral chapters, and Church Councils. These are independent employer organizations that have their own administration and they recruit their staff independently.

696. There are many kinds of work done in the church. About half of the jobs are spiritual work, which includes priests, church musicians, deacons, and employees working with youth and child activities. Churches also have employees working in areas such as administration, office work, communications, IT, and property management.

697. A Church's requirements include actual membership of the Church itself. Such a requirement includes all of the Church offices, and also those relating to worship, ecclesiastical ordinances, deaconess, and teaching. This requirement is the case for the Lutheran, the Catholic, and the Orthodox Church.

698. The terms and conditions of employment for Church personnel, such as salary, annual leave and working hours, are agreed upon by the settlement of collective labour agreements. The major Churches are part of the public sector and their terms of employment are comparable to those of the state and the municipalities.

699. Registered religious communities are covered by civil law and their statutes based on it, as well as by general labour law.

---

421. Part VI. The Labour Law within the Religious Communities is based on a revised and expanded version of the article, Matti Kotiranta 'Law and Religion in the Workplace (FINLAND)'. In *Miguel Rodríguez Blanco (ed.), Law and Religion in the Workplace – Droit et religion au travail.* (Alcalá de Henares: European Consortium for Church and State Research, 2015), 155–175.

422. The Evangelical Lutheran Church of Finland has a total of 354 parishes (15 Nov. 2023) with a total staff of 16,109. The Orthodox Church employs approximately 200 people. For further details, *see* https://www.kirkontilastot.fi/viz.php?id=244.

§2. Labour Law and the Individual's Rights in the Workplace

I. General Principles

700. For the large majority of employees in the service of churches and religious communities, the normal state labour law applies (collective labour agreements). In addition, the RFA (2003) distinguishes between three types of religious communities: (1) the Evangelical Lutheran Church and (2) the Orthodox Church are public law entities, while (3) the registered religious communities are civil law entities. Their different public-law status also governs them as employers. The law has, however, been modified, in accordance with the new Freedom of Religion Act (2003), in many details that distinguished three different types of religious communities.

701. The ELCF, together with the OCF, retains a special status in public law that also includes its own law (Church Act of the ELCF 652/2023 & Church Act of the OCF 985/2006) and a special public status that is implemented in these laws.

702. With reference to the ELCF, a distinction can be seen between a religious office and a minister's office. A religious office (*pappisvirka*, with its full responsibilities and rights) is received upon ordination and is governed by church law and statutes concerning the rights of the office. The office of minister (*papin virka*), for example, refers to employment for which a salary is paid (a position comparable in the secular sphere of employment with that of a civil servant).

703. In contrast, offices no longer exist in the OCF, where all staff, including the clergy, are now considered to be employees.

704. The offices and activities of registered religious communities, comprising both Christian and non-Christian communities, are so varied that it is not possible to describe them in great detail. In the main, however, their employees are under contract. Furthermore, they do not have societal obligations governed by law as do both the ELCF and OCF. These bodies are responsible for certain societal tasks, such as maintaining cemeteries and culturally valuable buildings, which are considered the activities of the ELCF and OCF. However, it is difficult to obtain a clear picture of the frequency and breadth of these activities within the various registered religious communities. But with regard to employment rights, the priests and imams of registered religious communities are covered by civil law and by the statutes that are based on it, as well as by the general labour laws.

II. Religious Freedom and Employees' Rights in the Workplace

705. The following national laws protect religious freedom and employee rights in the Finnish workplace:

I. Section 11 of the Finnish Constitution defines religious freedom as a basic right:

> Everyone has freedom of religion and conscience, implying the right to profess and practice a religion, the right to express one's convictions and the right to be a member of or to decline to be a member of a religious community.
>
> No one shall be under any obligation to participate in the practice of a religion against his or her conscience.

II. Chapter 3, section 8 of the Non-discrimination Act (1325/2014) comprises the prohibition of discrimination. The statute also implicitly covers employee salaries and the acknowledgement of their religious conviction in the workplace:

> Nobody may be discriminated against on the basis of their age, origin, nationality, language, religion, belief, opinion, political activity, trade union activity, family relationships, state of health, disability, sexual orientation or other personal characteristics. Discrimination is prohibited, regardless of whether it is based on a fact or assumption concerning the person him/herself or another.
>
> In addition to direct and indirect discrimination, harassment, denial of reasonable adjustments as well as an instruction or order to discriminate constitute discrimination as referred to in this Act. (1325/2014).
>
> Discrimination means:
>
> (1) the treatment of a person less favourably than the way another person is treated, has been treated or would be treated in a comparable situation (direct discrimination);
> (2) that an apparently neutral provision, criterion or practice puts a person at a particular disadvantage compared with other persons, unless the said provision, criterion or practice has an acceptable aim and the means used are appropriate and necessary for achieving this aim (indirect discrimination);
> (3) the deliberate or de facto infringement of the dignity and integrity of a person or group of people by the creation of an intimidating, hostile, degrading, humiliating or offensive environment (harassment); and
> (4) an instruction or order to discriminate.

III. Section 6 of the Constitution, which also considers non-discrimination, was used as the basis for another separate equality act called the Act on Equality between Women and Men (609/1986), where gender equality was promoted, particularly in working life.

However, section 2 of the above-mentioned act contains restrictions on the applicability of this law to the church and other religious communities. Thus, there is recognition of the fact that it cannot be applied directly to many aspects of the religious observances of the Evangelical Lutheran Church, the Orthodox Church, and other religious groups (on account of restrictions on the priesthood, the nature of religious observances, and confessions, to name only a few of the reasons).

IV. In Chapter 2, section 2 of the Employment Contracts Act (55/2001) it is stated that 'the employer shall not exercise any unjustified discrimination against employees on the basis of religion'.

Later in the same section of the act, reference is made to both the Non-discrimination Act and also the prohibition of discrimination:

> Provisions on the prohibition of discrimination based on gender are laid down in the Act on Equality between Women and Men (1325/2014). The definition of discrimination, prohibition on sanctions and burden of proof in cases concerning discrimination are laid down in the Non-discrimination Act (21/2004). (23/2004).
> Equality and the prohibition of discrimination are governed by the Non-discrimination Act (1325/2014), whereas the prohibition of discrimination based on *gender* is covered by the provisions of the Act on Equality between Women and Men (609/1986).

V. The employee's position is further governed by the Working Hours Act (605/1996), Annual Holiday Act, Occupational Safety and Health Act (738/2002), and also other acts concerned with national and municipal civil servants' rights.

706. Occupational health and safety issues in Finland are considered to take precedence over the rights of the employee. The labour laws oblige the employer and employees to follow safety regulations and instructions. It is possible, for instance, that such instructions would not allow an employee to wear a scarf if that person is working with machinery and wearing a scarf might well be injurious to health. Another common example: it is obligatory to wear a helmet when working in the construction industry.

Which Manifestations of Religious Beliefs Are Protected?

707. When an employee is hired, the starting point of the agreement or contract is that gender, sexual orientation, and religious beliefs will not affect the recruitment process (*see*, above, section 8 of the Non-discrimination Act and the Act on Equality between Women and Men).

708. The employer is obliged to recognize an employee's religious beliefs to a reasonable degree and also their potential need to practise their religion in the workplace. The notion and degree of 'reasonable' depends on the employer, the workplace, and the trade being practised, as well as the ways of practising a variety of different religions. This also takes into consideration the right of the worker to be absent from his or her workstation.

What Is the Rationale of the Approach? Is It 'Equality' or 'Religious Freedom' or Both, or Is There Some Other Basis?

709. When religious beliefs and demands for equality clash in the workplace, it is difficult to declare a 'winner'. In other words, it is difficult to determine which carries more weight: equality or religious freedom.

710. One of Finland's foremost experts on its constitution, Professor Mikael Hidén, who has also frequently served as an expert on the Government's Constitutional Law Committee, has come to the conclusion that religious freedoms sometimes override the demands of equality:

> Religion sometimes allows for small exceptions. Gender should not be a reason to discriminate in hiring, but in the Orthodox Church only men can serve as priests. This gender consideration has also been accepted in the Catholic Church for certain positions seen as central to its religious doctrine. This is all a part of finding an equilibrium between the freedom of religion and equality.[423]

711. Hidén also points out that not all religious points of view can be written in law and that they have to be considered on a case-by-case basis:

> I cannot say that equality in Finland always loses to religious freedom nor can I say the reverse is true. These are difficult and sensitive questions of principle. We have to accept that issues can be evaluated case-by-case.[424]

The Decisions of the ECtHR and Their Impact on the Finnish National Ethos

712. ECtHR decision-making praxis and the ICCPR agreement have affected two areas in the Finnish workplace: (A) with respect to refusing on the basis of religious convictions to carry out certain tasks, and (B) with respect to religiously determined dress codes.

A. Refusal to Carry Out Work Duties Because of Religious Convictions

713. In Finnish high court praxis, anyone employed by a church or other religious community who finds him/herself in conflict with that church or community on an issue of belief or conviction is deemed to have exercised his/her individual religious freedom in the act of taking up such employment. Once he or she has done so, he or she cannot thereafter appeal to the freedom of religion in order to depart

423. The Finnish Broadcasting Company, 26 Jul. 2013, 2:45 pm – Hidén's statement on the provisions in s. 2 of the Equality Act that exclude the Church and other religious communities.
424. *Ibid.*

from the tenets of that religious community.[425] This line of interpretation conforms with the line on religious freedom adopted in the earlier case of *Konttinen v. Finland* in 1994 (ruling of the European Commission on Human Rights in the case of Appeal no. 24949/94).[426]

714. On the other hand, instances of an office-holder (including a church minister) refusing to carry out certain obligations have also been interpreted in Finland as neglect of duty purely on the grounds of administrative law. These decisions of the Finnish Supreme Court have mostly concerned one of two groups of cases: those in which a minister has placed conditions of his or her own on the baptism of a child,[427] and those in which a bishop has refused to ordain women as priests. This was the approach, for example, adopted by the Chancellor of Justice in resolution 561/24 May 1989, where a bishop was regarded as an official of the state, and hence considering his right to refuse to ordain women as priests in the light of this.

715. Regarding other religious communities and beliefs, it must be stated that in Finland, on the basis of religious beliefs one can either refuse employment completely or refuse to perform any part of a job. One can also refuse to do work for a specific period of time. An employee could also, for example, request permission to use a veil or make a similar type of request. This, in turn, raises the question of when an employer has the right to dismiss an employee, and also the problem of when an unemployed person might lose his or her unemployment benefits if they refuse a job offered to them.

716. The Act on Employment Insurance 30 May 2002/1290 states briefly:

---

425. This is also suggested in the statement made by the Parliamentary Constitutional Committee to the Parliamentary Administrative Committee (PeVL 22/1997) on the bill for alterations to §16c of the law on the Orthodox Church in Finland:

   – Every person enjoys the fundamental right of the freedom of speech, although more precise regulations regarding this are given in law. It is in the nature of the offices mentioned in the bill that their holders should teach in accordance with the precepts of the Orthodox Church and that they should be aware of this fact when taking up such an office.

   It is similarly noted in the statement on disciplinary proceedings that:

   – It should also be said that matters concerned with the right to remain in public office have been demonstrated in the practices of the Human Rights Commission to lie beyond the scope of article 6 of the European Convention on Human Rights. Admittedly, no instances of problems or conflicts, or even of differences in interpretation, have arisen with regard to the doctrines of the Orthodox Church of Finland.

426. In the case of referred to as Konttinen, a man (a Seventh Day Adventist) rejected working hours for religious reasons (the Sabbath). For further detail, *see* Part II, above. Religious Freedom in General, Ch. 1, §10.II.A.1.

427. For the details of the case, *see* Part II, above. Religious Freedom in General, Ch. 1, §10.II.B. *See also* cases 1, 2, 3, and 4 in the same chapter.

The job seeker has a valid reason to refuse employment if the employment is against his or her religion or conscience.

In comparison, other accepted non-physical reasons for refusing employment are included in the act as 'obscene or improper' work.

717. There are a number of cases in this area:

- A Muslim wanted to use the veil at work and was not offered employment. Unemployment benefits could not be withheld. The vote was 4 to 1 (*see* Insurance Law 1713:96).
- A non-Lutheran refused to clean a Lutheran Church. According to Insurance Law, unemployment benefits could not be withheld. The vote was 4 to 1 (*see* Insurance Law 05142/96/955).
- A Jehovah's Witness refused clerical work with the Finnish Armed Forces, and unemployment benefits could not be withheld. The vote was 4 to 1 (*see* Insurance Law 12569:95).
- One can also refuse work on grounds other than religious beliefs:

A pacifist who had completed service as a conscientious objector refused to work as a warehouse worker for an Armed Forces Unit and unemployment benefits were not withheld. The vote was 3 to 2 (*see* Insurance Law 4286:99).

718. The definitions of freedom of religion and of conscience were also discussed in 1995 in the context of the Constitutional reform. The Government's bill (309/1993) was somewhat vague in advocating 'systems dividing work'.

719. The provision universally advocates a system of separation that avoids placing an obligation on anyone to execute tasks that contradict his or her beliefs. For example, the conflicts occurring between the freedom of religion or conscience and tasks required in an office have to be resolved on a case-by-case basis. In consequence, the regulation will not lead to a universal right to refuse the obligations of an office on the basis of religious beliefs.

720. Separate from that is still the question of whether offices in the public sphere should have stricter regulations than in private corporations. In principle, the core activities of the state and municipalities are secular; specific laws prohibiting discrimination broaden freedom of religion and at the same time restrict the right of the employer to dismiss an employee. In Finland, there is no strict difference, although fundamental rights are regarded as restricting individual relationships to a certain degree.

B. Religiously Dictated Dress Codes

721. Discrimination in the Finnish workplace is monitored by occupational health and safety inspectors working out of the regional state administration offices.

A handful of cases involving religious headdress and clothing have thus far been tried in Finnish courts. *For example, the uniforms of security guards and police officers are regulated by laws and decrees, and religious headdress is not a part of the uniform.* This neutral uniform easily limits the access of those who use headdress, such as Sikhs and female Muslims, to positions normally requiring them.

722. The Chancellor of Justice and the Ombudsman monitor the activities of the authorities in Finland, and hence they are able to adopt a stance on whether a dress code is constitutional. Before cases can actually reach them, however, a complaint must first be entered, and subsequently the court will reach a decision. Another way for the situation to be changed is to have a Member of Parliament introduce a bill on the matter at hand.

723. Of all of the regional state administrative offices only one, in southern Finland, has handled four cases dealing with religious headdress and clothing. Of these, three concerned the use of the veil and one with the wearing of a turban.

724. A bus driver in Vantaa named Sukhdarshan Singh Gill was refused the right to wear his turban. His employer, Veolia Transport, justified this restriction by citing both the company's uniform dress code and also its occupational safety requirements.

725. Similarly, a hotel manager in Turku defended his/her decision to ban the use of the veil to preserve 'the neutrality of hotel reception', meaning that the veil might detract from the customer service provided.

726. At the end of March 2014, the Helsinki District Court fined a manager employed by the clothing retailer Guess for discrimination because he/she had dismissed an employee who wore the veil. Citing a number of reasons, in the manager's opinion the veil did not suit the image of the store. The District Court ruled that the employee was placed at a disadvantage without cause because of her use of the veil.

727. This ruling was the first of its kind in Finland to involve religious headdress, and hence it will serve in the future as a precedent and also as a guide for employers. Thus the message is simple: an employer must permit religious headdress in the workplace unless there is a valid reason, such as occupational safety, that prevents it.

728. As previously mentioned, occupational health and safety issues overrule employees' rights. An example of this kind of case occurred in 2006 when a prosecutor claimed that a restaurant manager was not guilty of discrimination when he refused to let a female Muslim wear her veil during a customer service internship. The manager justified his/her decision by citing arguments connected with image and also occupational safety. The student was given clear instructions on the dress code for the kitchen and dining room; the same veil could not be used during the cooking as during the serving of the food. He/she further justified the decision by stating that the customers wanted their waiters to use a specific uniform. The student did not remove her veil. Instead, she left the establishment.

III. The Labour Status of Individual Churches and Religious Communities

A. The Evangelical Lutheran Church

729. **The ELCF** collective agreements are governed by the Church Act of the Lutheran Church, public sector collective agreements and the most important laws governing working life (such as the Employment Contracts Act, the Working Time Act, the Annual Holiday Act, and the Occupational Health and Safety Act, as well as national and municipal civil servant statutes) that may affect the legal position of the person holding the office.

730. The Church's employing organizations consist of the congregations, parishes, chapters, and the Church administration itself. These are independent employers that have their own administrations and take care of recruitment independently.

731. The Church's employing organizations have common decrees and conditions of service, such as their system of remuneration. In addition to the Church's employment organization, there are many other ecclesiastical organizations, such as missions, that offer employment. The conditions of service for the employees of the church, such as salary, holiday periods, and working time, are arranged on the basis of collective agreements.

732. The working and holiday times of those employed by the church are laid down by the Working Hours Act, the Church's Working Hours statute, and the Church's collective agreement, and are based on decisions made by the Church's administration. The general definition of an employee's working week is thirty-eight hours and fifteen minutes long, whereas the working week of an office is thirty-six hours and fifteen minutes long. The Lutheran Church and the Orthodox Church negotiate the conclusion of agreements by means of collective bargaining between their own institutions (Kirkon työmarkkinalaitos, Palta) and the trade unions.

733. The Working Hours Act does not apply to those carrying out spiritual work, such as priests, cantors, those holding diaconal offices, and youth workers. Their work is not measured in hours but their work is carried out on five of the seven days of the week. The holiday allocations for church personnel are usually better than those offered generally in the employment market and are based on work experience. At their longest, after fifteen years of service, holidays can amount to thirty-eight days, the equivalent of almost eight calendar weeks.

734. The Competition agreement reached between the various central employment organizations (Kiky) created a number of changes in the church's conditions of office and employees. Working hours were extended in the various areas of church-related work by thirty minutes per week and six minutes per day, with the changes coming into effect on 1 February 2017.

735. The impact of the agreement on the labour market situation has been strongly negative. In the autumn of 2019 and winter of 2020, Finland experienced an unusually widespread series of strikes affecting many sectors, which were primarily motivated by the extension of working hours included in the competitiveness pact.[428]

736. In many 2020 collective agreements, the additional hours taken from the Competitiveness Pact (Kiky) were exchanged for changes that provided equivalent cost benefits, such as by means of flexible arrangements and a reduction in certain compensations. Labour unions emphasized the impact of removing the Competitiveness Pact (Kiky) hours, while employers argued that they merely underwent a transformation.[429]

B. The Orthodox Church

737. **The OCF** is governed by the OCF Act (958/2006), the OCF collective agreement, and also the *most significant laws governing working life* mentioned previously. The OCF Act is referred to during the hiring process. Otherwise, the employer has the right to hire, dismiss and supervise in accordance with the Employment Contracts Act.

738. The stipulations of the collective agreement are normally applied to the personnel of the OCF, the Orthodox seminary, and also other relevant organizations working within the sphere of the Orthodox Church.

739. In contrast, the collective agreement is not applied to archbishops, bishops, and the Church's legal counsel, nor to individuals who are in equivalent supervisory positions in the Church's administration or to monastery staff. Furthermore, it is not applied to those teaching religion.

740. An employee's salary consists of two parts: the level of demand for the tasks required (basic pay) and the employee's performance of those tasks. Basic pay is determined by the level of demand for the tasks, with ten levels present on the scale. An employee's hourly wage can be calculated by dividing the monthly salary by 153, resulting in the regular weekly working time normally consisting of thirty-six hours and fifteen minutes.

---

428. *See* closer, https://www.hs.fi/talous/art-2000006337995.html?share=a6964cfd136894d047ddc452347fb7b2, *Helsingin Sanomat* 10 Dec. 2019 and https://www.hs.fi/politiikka/art-2000006367897.html?share=117454eb977cd78b2a33ba87aed22b11, *Helsingin Sanomat* 10.1.2020. Accessed 19 Dec. 2023.

429. *See*, https://www.hs.fi/politiikka/art-2000006409724.html, *Helsingin Sanomat*. 17 Feb. 2020. Accessed 19 Dec. 2023.

741. Those doing spiritual work (priests, deacons, and cantors) are given two days off per calendar week unless urgent or necessary tasks or other pressing reasons prevent it. However, the days off cannot include Saturdays or Sundays, nor can they be church holidays, except under exceptional circumstances.

742. Working hours are defined as the time used for work where the employee is required to be at his or her place of work and at the disposal of his or her employer. Working time is also counted outside of the workplace when the work is carried out in the name of, and has been approved by, the employer.

C. Registered Religious Associations

743. Registered religious communities are governed by civil laws and according to agreements based on those laws. The employees of these communities belong to trade unions (e.g., Palta) that negotiate collective agreements on behalf of their members. However, the process of unionizing employees working in Muslim religious communities has been weak. Few Muslim communities have full-time imams. In Finland, there is only one paid imam. The rest work on a volunteer basis, some only a few hours a week, although many work more than twenty hours a week.[430]

D. The Labour Status of Religious Ministers When Working in Other Institutions (Chaplains, Teachers of Religions in Schools, Etc.)

744. Religious ministers and chaplains in Finland do not work as teachers of religion in schools. Religious education in Finland is non-confessional and hence teachers do not have to belong to any denomination, while teacher education takes place in universities. Religious education teachers have exactly the same status as the teachers of other school subjects. In other words, they are not employees of the Church or of an equivalent institution but are employed as municipal officials and granted their qualifications by the state universities. The majority of religious education teachers are not ordained priests. In contrast to many European systems, the training is organized by the Department of Applied Sciences of Education and not by the Faculty of Theology.

745. Teachers of religion belong to the Union of Religion Teachers in Finland, which represents its members through the Subject Teachers' Union (AOL) and the body of representatives of teachers' associations in Finland (POE).

---

430. Latvio, Ritva & Satu Mustonen & Ilari Rantakari (eds), *Imaamit Suomessa. Imaamikoulutusselvitys 2013* (Imams in Finland. Imam training survey 2013). (Helsinki: Kulttuuri- ja uskontofoorumi FOKUS ry, 2013), 38.

§3. Collective Labour Law

746. Churches and religious communities are also in a special position in the sphere of collective labour law because their specific religious needs are protected by the freedom of religion and consequently by the right to self-determination.[431] The state is in principle also not allowed to intervene in the internal organizational structures and set-up of the religious communities in the field of collective labour law.

747. The Lutheran Church and the Orthodox Church negotiate the conclusion of agreements by means of collective bargaining between their own institutions (Kirkon työmarkkinalaitos, Palta) and the trade unions. Within the church structure, there is also a right to strike. So far, however, there has been no need to resort to a strike for those carrying out spiritual work, although in 1981 the (Lutheran) Priesthood Association went as far as issuing a strike warning. In the mid-1980s SAK unions were also on strike at church workplaces. The Lutheran Church's Collective Bargaining Law requires that during the course of a strike, the clergy should perform the duties as listed in Chapters 4–13 of the Old Church Act (1964) – i.e., practically all spiritual work. A similar list can now be found in Chapter 3, sections 6–22 of the Church Order (657/2023). These include services of worship, holy communion, baptism, and conducting marriages, burials, confirmation, and confession.[432] All other work has been validated as eligible for inclusion in strike action.

748. The right to strike is based on the Finnish Constitution and on the treaties of the International Labour Organization (ILO), to which Finland as a State is bound. The right to strike is derived directly from a fundamental right, freedom of association (Article 13 of the FC), and, like other fundamental rights, it can only be restricted by law. The right of civil servants is limited by law, but not those who have an employment contract. Notice periods under labour law must be respected, as must the restrictions laid down in collective agreements.

749. The collective agreement system in its current form in Finland was born in the public sector in the 1970s. These agreements were made in the national, municipal, and church sectors (for the ELCF and OCF up until 2005).

750. The conditions of service for those holding ELCF offices are determined in Chapter 6 section 5 of church law, and by collective agreements both for appointments and for contract employment made according to the law governing ELCF collective agreements.

431. *See* Part III, Ch. 1, II, and Ch. 2. §1, A, above.

432. There are, in fact, three different, overlapping rules on the same subject: the 1964 Church Act, the 1990s Enactments, and the 1993 Church Order. These have been consolidated in the new 2023 Church Act (HE 652/2023 vp).

751. Collective agreements are made by the Commission for Church Employers (Kirkon työmarkkinalaitos) for parishes, parish unions, and the Church. This is done according to section 1 of the Evangelical Lutheran Church's statute (827/2005) governing the Commission.

752. The purpose of the agreement system is to improve working conditions and to ensure job security. The collective agreement for appointments represents the minimum and maximum agreement possible, while the agreement for other positions represents the minimum agreement possible. The conditions of service are agreed in these agreements, and the salaries, holidays, leave, and compensation for all those holding Church offices or other positions are also determined through these collective agreements.

753. There are additional rules regarding leave of absence in the statutes governing appointments. There are also further rules on the annual holidays, leave of absence, and leisure time for priests, lecturers, and cantors. These rules are set by the Church's central according to the authority given to it by church law (Collection of Church Provisions no. 68/30.5.1995).

754. Working and leisure time are based on the Working Hours Act and through the collective agreements made possible by the Working Hours Act.

755. In the law concerning the OCF (985/2006), paragraph 1 of section 114 states that the Church's administration is responsible for the collective agreement for the Church, its parishes, and its monasteries. The Union of Service Employers, Palta, negotiates the collective agreement on behalf of the OCF administration and the OCF employees as their representatives. The collective agreement is negotiated by the principal negotiators in lead groups that manage the negotiation process and any other work concerning the development of working conditions.

756. This agreement, as previously mentioned, does not apply to archbishops, bishops, the Church's legal counsel, individuals who work in positions equivalent to Church administration's leadership positions, or to monastery personnel.

757. Registered religious communities, which are governed by civil law, buy services related to work security from Palta, a member of the Confederation of Finnish Industries. Palta has collective agreements for a variety of working conditions, and what is noteworthy about Palta is that was able to agree on universally binding labour decisions on behalf of religious communities.

§4. The Social Security System

I. General Principles

758. Article 19 of the Constitution guarantees the right to basic subsistence. The Constitution's approach is stated quite powerfully:

(2) Everyone shall be guaranteed by the Act to maintain the right to basic subsistence in the event of unemployment, illness, disability and during old-age, and also at the birth of a child or on the loss of a provider.

759. The same article (paragraph 3) continues that the 'public authorities shall guarantee for everyone, as provided in more detail by the Act, adequate social, health, and medical services, and promote the health of the population'.

760. People who work as employees in church or religious communities are, like anyone else, part of the general social system. According to the general principles of the compulsory pension insurance system, the contributions payable are calculated on the basis of defined contributory earnings.

761. The major churches, the Lutheran Church and Orthodox Church have established special social security provisions regarding pension insurance for their priest and special personnel. Personnel who are regarded as public officials are included in pension systems similar to state officials.

762. Other religious communities and non-profit religious associations do not have this kind of pension insurance system but are linked to the general social system.

II. Health Insurance

763. Everyone living in Finland, irrespective of their nationality, is insured from birth so that medical treatment will be available, whenever necessary, for sickness, and for pregnancy and childbirth. Health insurance is a part of social security and is administered by the Social Insurance Institution (KELA). The purpose of state health insurance is to provide everyone with proper care, regardless of their wealth, and to provide financial security during their illness.

764. Statutory health insurance is a social security scheme built on sickness or a health condition that compensates for any work-related incapacity due to illness or accident.

765. Statutory health insurance is paid in the form of a tax-like contribution in connection with taxes paid on wages or salary, with contributions paid by the employer and the employee, each being fixed by the tax authorities. As elsewhere, the payment is termed the social security contribution (sosiaaliturvamaksu).

766. The Finnish Social Insurance Institution (KELA) is responsible for paying the sickness insurance indemnity to any person in Finland who has a personal identification number issued by the Population Register Centre.

767. There are no exemptions from compulsory health insurance in the field of religion. Clerics belonging to religious communities recognized as non-profit associations under public law are not exempt from health insurance. The same applies to statutory members of monastic brother- and sisterhoods (the monasteries of New Valaam and Lintula), deaconesses, and similar persons.

768. In this context, it is worth mentioning that Finland is currently undergoing an unprecedented reform of its healthcare and social care in general. Part of the reform will include legislation for a larger freedom of choice concerning the services available, a policy that was intended to come into force at the same time as the reform. The changes were intended – according to a statement issued by the Ministry of Social Affairs and Health and the Ministry of Finance – in order to improve the accessibility, cost-effectiveness, customer-orientation, and quality of the health services. Prior to the proposed reform, freedom of choice was limited to public sector services, whereas in the future the choices would also include private and third sector service providers. The reform would thus enable the recipient to choose between the public, private, and third-sector providers of the health service. Freedom of choice would be total as far as the basic health services are concerned, while in more specialized healthcare activities such as the various social services, it would be implemented flexibly during the early stages of the reform. In brief, increased freedom of choice would become one of the cornerstones of a future social care and healthcare system.[433]

769. Unfortunately, the proposed reforms did not materialize in 2019 as had been intended but stumbled in the face of a range of constitutional problems.

770. However, the discussions and work on the reform of social and healthcare have continued in Finland since 2019. Various models and legislative proposals have been put forward and the continuation of the reform has been challenging, both politically and in its practical implementation.

771. The aim of the health and social services (SOTE) reform has included such things as the integration of health and social services, improving cost-efficiency, enhancing service accessibility and equality, and also the streamlining of administrative structures. Decisions related to the progress of the reform have, however, been complex, requiring extensive collaboration between the various stakeholders.

772. The health and social services (SOTE) reform stands as one of the most significant administrative reforms in the history of Finland. The reform restructured the organisation of public healthcare and social welfare in Finland. As part of the reform the various rescue services were also restructured. As from the start of 2023, the responsibility for organizing healthcare, social welfare and rescue services was transferred from the municipalities and joint municipal authorities to 21 regional welfare areas, although the municipalities will continue to organise certain services, including child daycare, education, sports and cultural activities. But there is an

433. Ministry of Social Affairs and Health, and Ministry of Finance, 2017.

exception to this, since the city of Helsinki retains responsibility for organizing its social and healthcare services and rescue services. In addition, the Helsinki University Hospital District (HUS) has a separately determined responsibility for specialized healthcare-related tasks in its own area.

III. Pensions Insurance

773. There exist three different forms of pension in Finland. A person's pension may consist of an occupational pension (työeläke), a national pension (kansaneläke), and a guarantee pension (takuueläke).

774. An occupational pension is a pension paid to anyone who has been in employment. It is based on wages and entrepreneurial income. An occupational pension provides protection against old-age and disability, and in the case of death. The occupational pension accrues on the basis of wage income or an entrepreneur's earnings.

775. The national pension provides a minimum level of security for a person who has not accumulated any pension during their working-life or only a small amount of earnings-related pension.

776. The guarantee pension guarantees a minimum pension higher than the national pension for all.

777. The benefits of the occupational and national pension schemes include old-age, disability, and survivors' pensions. The earnings-related pension also includes a partial early old-age pension and an occupational pension. The family pension (perhe-eläke) is paid to the widow and children.

778. As a partial early retirement pension, it is possible take part of one's accumulated earnings before actual retirement. An occupational pension enables the individual to retire shortly before the actual retirement age.

779. In addition, the pension coverage can be supplemented by voluntary supplementary pension provision organized by the employer or the person him/herself. The amount of voluntary pension insurance will then be paid monthly for an agreed period.

780. The employee may increase the pension thus saved at the time of retirement (e.g., two to five years). Voluntary pension provision is not based on earnings, nor is it linked to wage and price changes in subsequent indices. In addition, voluntary pension insurance is not taken into account when calculations are made of invalidity, a survivor's pension, unemployment, or sickness benefit.

781. With regard to the religious communities, the Evangelical Lutheran Church operates a special Pension Fund (Kirkon eläkerahasto, KER). This was started in

1991 when the existing Church pension scheme was replaced by a partially funded pension scheme. The assets not actually used for paying pensions were taken over to cover the pension liabilities of the pension fund.

782. The Board of the Church Pension Fund (KER) is appointed by the Church Council and the director of the Church Pension Fund. The practical operation of KER is overseen by the investment unit. The General Synod, the supreme decision-making body of the ELCF, annually approves the budget of the Church Pension Fund (KER), the action plan and the financial plan, and also the financial statements issued by the plenary assembly.[434]

783. The Church Pension Fund (KER) was separated from the Central Fund on 1 January 2016 to become an independent legal person governed by public law, i.e., when the new law (68/2016) on the Pension Fund came into force.[435] Pursuant to the entry into force of this section, the Church Pension Fund continued to operate the Church Central Fund Pension Fund and the Church Central Fund Pension Fund's assets, rights and obligations that were transferred to the Church Pension Fund on 1 January 2016. In addition, the entry into force provision stipulated that this transfer of assets, rights, and obligations was not subject to any transfer tax or other tax penalty.[436]

784. With the enactment of the new Church Act (652/2023) on 1 July 2023, as part of the comprehensive reform of the Church Act, a new law regarding the Evangelical Lutheran Church's pension fund was also issued (656/2023).[437]

IV. Accident Insurance

785. Accident insurance is a statutory insurance that must be used to cover accidents at work or occupational diseases while working. In practice, the employer – including the churches and registered religious communities – must always take out accident insurance. For very small jobs only, the employer does not need to take out occupational accident insurance on behalf of their workers (in practice, households).

786. Occupational accident insurance rates are calculated in relation to the wages paid to the users and are paid to the employer on top of the gross wages. It therefore becomes part of the employer's ancillary costs.

---

434. For closer information, *see* Collection of Rules for the Central Church Fund and the new law on the Evangelical Lutheran Church's pension fund (HE 656/2023), *See*, https://www.finlex.fi/fi/laki/alkup/2023/20230656. Accessed 19 Dec. 2023.
435. https://www.finlex.fi/fi/laki/alkup/2016/20160068.
436. *See* the Law amending the Church Act of 1054/1993: (1602/2015).
437. *See*, https://www.finlex.fi/fi/laki/alkup/2023/20230656. Accessed 19 Dec. 2023.

787. The cost of accident insurance varies according to the insurance company and the job done. The premium for occupational accident and disease insurance varies between 0.05% and 5%, depending on the danger level of the work performed by the employer (occupational accident and disease risk). On average, in 2021, this comprised roughly 0.7% of salaries.[438]

788. In Finland no exemptions are permissible from compulsory accident insurance for clerics, deaconesses, or statutory members of monastic brother- and sisterhoods.

438. https://www.tvk.fi/uutiset-ja-blogit/uutiset/2021/keskimaaraiset-vakuutusmaksut-vuonna-2021/. Accessed 19 Dec. 2023.

Chapter 2. Ministers of Religion and the Labour Law – Case Law

789. The latest regulations reforming the rules governing ELCF offices came into force on 1 June 2013. Since then, all of the most important labour laws (e.g., Employment Contract Act, Working Hours Act, Annual Holiday Act, Occupational Health and Safety Act, and also the statutes governing national and municipal civil servants), plus the Finnish Constitution, have all been completely overhauled, while the Church law that came into force on 1 January 1994 was still in force. For this reason, some of the rules governing the Church's appointments have been rendered invalid and do not satisfy the requirements of the Constitution.

790. The objective of the reform has been to ensure that the position of those holding Church appointments is covered as collectively and comprehensively as possible, taking into consideration the requirements of the Constitution as well as the developments in civil servants' rights and in the labour laws. In addition, it has been hoped that the legal position of a person holding a Church appointment would be the same as a person holding a civil servant's position in the public sector, unless the Church's organization or activities demand otherwise. The clergy's position in particular is affected by factors stemming from a Church order (e.g., ordination and apostolic guidance), which justifies certain exceptions to civil servant entitlement practices.

791. The most important changes to the labour conditions affecting ELCF employees are those that concern the changes to legislative levels of church law, the requirements of church membership, and requirements preventing discrimination.

792. The reform of the new Church Act (652/2023) includes the complete renewal of Chapter 6 (Office holders and employees) of the former Church Act (1054/1993) as well as other provisions regarding the position of an appointment holder.

793. First, many provisions have been carried over from former Church Act (1054/1993) into new Church Order (657/2023) that affect, for example, the publication of a job advertisement for an appointment, selections to an appointment, the responsibilities of an appointment, leaves of absence, secondary occupations, keeping employee records, and also certain methods for recruiting priests and rules regarding the presentation of the documents of appointment.

In addition, Chapter 6 (Office holders and employees) of the former Church Order (1055/1993) has been completely reformed and carried over the new Church Order (657/2023, Chapter 8, Personnel). The provisions on how parishes and parish federation select candidates for positions as ministers and those governing the presentation of appointment documents have remained largely the same. The Church Council decides on appointments to posts in the parish. In addition to the office of parish priest, the parish may also include the offices of chaplain and parish pastors. The office of vicar will not be subject to the probationary period referred to in §14 of the Act on Officials of the Evangelical Lutheran Church. The vicar cannot be discharged. The certificate of employment of the vicar shall be issued by the cathedral chapter.[439]

In a parish federation the Joint Church Council decides on the offices of the parish federation and the parishes, unless otherwise provided for by law or the statutes. The parish federation may have parish pastors to undertake its functions.[440] The method of selection for cantors has changed in that the verification of the applicant's eligibility and the selection itself no longer require the Cathedral Chapter's approval.

The Cathedral Chapter may decide on the creation or abolition of the office of joint vicar of two or more parishes in its diocese. Parishes belonging to the same diocese may decide on another joint office.[441]

794. Second, although the new law (652/2023) does not contain specific anti-discrimination provisions, it does not mean that discrimination is condoned by the Church. Universal laws such as the Constitution, the Act on Equality between Women and Men, and the Non-discrimination Act are already enforced in churches and parishes.

795. The difference between the proposal for the Church Act (HE 19/2019) and the new Church Act (HE 652/2023), from the perspective of relations between the church and the state, lies in the fact that in the latter case the regulation of church officials, the Commission for the Church Employers and the pension fund have been detached from the Church Act, which is subject to the exclusive right of initiative on the part of the church and moved into the area of so-called ordinary legislation. This means that the state will henceforth be responsible for the development of such legislation (in cooperation with the Evangelical Lutheran Church). Previously, the amendment or repeal of such legislation was also included in the exclusive competence of the Church.

796. The OCF is an autonomous archdiocese connected to the Ecumenical Patriarchate of Constantinople. Hence, the Church is simultaneously both a Finnish organization governed by public law and also a part of an international Orthodox Church. This makes the position in Finnish law of the Orthodox Church both unique and problematic in terms of labour laws.[442] The clergy's job security is weakened because of the Church's right to interpret the employee's position based on Orthodox canons. The Church Council and ultimately, the Synod, led by the Archbishop, have the right to interpret canons to the employee's detriment.

439. Church Order (657/2023), Ch. 8, p. 2.
440. Church Order (657/2023), Ch. 8, p. 3.
441. Church Order (657/2023), Ch. 8, p. 4.
442. The position of the Orthodox Church's canons and other spiritual regulations has been strengthened in the Orthodox Church Act (985/2006). Paragraph 1 of s. 1 states that 'the Orthodox Church of Finland is founded on the Bible, traditional knowledge, Orthodox dogma, canons and other Church regulations'. Paragraph 3 of section 1 also defines the Church canons' relationship to the Ecumenical Patriarchate of Constantinople. This relationship is referenced in the Ecumenical Patriarchate's decision of 6 Jun. 1923 in what is known as the Tomos document.

797. Two interesting cases of this have occurred in Finland. The first concerned Euro-parliamentarian Mitro Repo and the other a priest who was dismissed after remarrying. The Synod found Repo's candidature for the European Parliament to be against the traditional canon and voted two to one against Repo in order to prevent him from practising his priest's duties during his campaign in 2009 and during his term in the European Parliament.[443] The other case concerned a widowed Orthodox priest Kuisma Suopela, who was suspended from service for a year and in November 2012 lost his right to work as a priest and provost because he had become engaged to a widow. The Orthodox Church holds canon in higher esteem than the civil law, although many schooled in Finnish law felt that it should not take precedence over civil law and basic human rights.

798. In an article headlined 'Does religious autonomy trample on fundamental rights?' The daily newspaper *Helsingin Sanomat* (HS) asked legal experts how they would suggest dealing with the potential conflict between religious communities, on the one hand, and Finnish law and fundamental rights, on the other. The experts cite as an example the decision taken by the Ombudsman in the case of Kuisma Suopela.

799. In the Ombudsman's view, the decision that he should forfeit the priesthood falls within the internal autonomy of the Church.

800. Seppo Koskinen, a Professor of Labour Law, states: 'The requirement that a priest remain a widower does not accord with the basic principles of the secularized Finnish system. Kuisma Suopela's case was that of a church employee, which does not contradict the basic principles of society. The Equality Act came into force at the start of 2015, and has greater flexibility in such cases.'

801. Juha Lavapuro, a Professor of Public Law at the University of Turku, emphasized that 'the new equality law would apply in the case of loss of priesthood. The end result might still be that a difference in treatment could be justified if the church's autonomy, which is based on religious freedom, were considered acceptable. In addition, it would not run counter to the position of the European Court of Human Rights in similar cases'. However, great precision must be required on the part of the canons. He wonders 'whether there is evidence of arbitrariness or favouritism if men who have divorced elsewhere have been ordained priests. The Constitution takes a clear position that fundamental freedom and human rights must not be violated on the basis of religious freedom'.[444]

---

443. Repo appealed against the decision made by the Synod to the Supreme Administrative Court (SAC). In December 2009 the SAC denied his appeal. In the SAC's opinion, it was an internal matter of the Orthodox Church and it is its responsibility to interpret Church doctrine. Repo returned to service as a priest in Helsinki's Orthodox parish in August 2014.

444. *See* HS for further details of the interview, https://www.hs.fi/kotimaa/art-2000002814012.html. Accessed 9 Mar. 2021. (Updated 9 Jan. 2024).

Chapter 3. Other Church Employees and the Labour Law

802. As public entities, the Evangelical Lutheran Church and the Orthodox Church are considered to be entitled to grant public appointments. Thus, they are able to have employees who are considered to be civil servants. This means that church administrations are structured along the same lines as their state counterparts. The churches frame their own civil service law along the same lines as the public civil service law, even in terms of salaries and benefits.

803. Priests in the military chaplaincy are regarded as state civil servants and are paid by the state. Teachers in state schools teaching religion are also paid by the municipalities. The same is true of professors of theology at the state universities. All of them share the same specific status as that of their secular colleagues, and they enjoy all of the benefits of state civil servants and have the same duties. The state has, however, no power to determine their religious work in any way, even though the status of military chaplain, teacher of religious instruction at a state school, or professor of theology at a state university refers to the equivalent secular status.

804. Spiritual workers employed by registered religious communities do not hold the status of civil servant.

Part VII. Religious Communities and Protections of the Individual

805. The basic principles of fundamental rights also apply to relations between religious communities and individuals. For the religious communities this presupposes that the general law has been interpreted and applied in a way that is compatible with the values expressed in the fundamental rights guaranteed by the Constitution. In Finland, however, there is no straight application of fundamental rights that would directly impose a wider obligation on religious communities. Only religious communities such as the Lutheran and Orthodox Churches as legal entities governed by public law are required to respect fundamental rights when exercising sovereign power delegated to them by the state, such as the right to levy church taxes or other issues related to the public service status of their officials.

806. From a fundamental rights perspective, individuals who are not members of any religious community must also be taken into account. For the sake of positive religious freedom, everyone has the right to express their religion and convictions in an appropriate manner in accordance with their own religion. On the other hand, in view of negative religious freedom, individuals have the right not to belong to any religious community and the right not to be disturbed by any religious community. The point here is that both rights mentioned here will be balanced appropriately and leave as much space as possible for both considerations. General law – in particular collective labour law and individual rights in the workplace, criminal law (religious peace), marital law, and medical deontology – clarifies these conditions and must also be interpreted and applied in light of the relevant fundamental rights.[445]

807. In the context of Finland the disruptive behaviour of religious communities towards non-religious individuals is relatively marginal. Evening bells on Saturdays at 6 pm and the ringing of church bells every Sunday at 10 am are generally understood to be part of the Finnish national tradition. In contrast, the rights of Islam in relation to the values of the mainstream culture have been the subject of some

445. For further detail about the relationship between human rights and criminal policy, *see* Elina Pirjatanniemi, 'Haastavatko ihmisoikeudet Suomen kriminaalipolitiikan?' (Do Human Rights Challenge Finland's Criminal Policy?). *Oikeus* 2011 (2): 154–174.

debate in the media; in particular, right-wing populist circles have raised the question of whether the state's flexibility with regard to Islam goes too far. Their actions have led to some criminal offences including incitement to religious hatred.[446]

808. One special issue has touched upon the Muslim call to prayer (Azaan) by the Muezzin, from the minaret of a mosque.[447] So far, no minarets exist at the places of worship of the Muslim communities in Finland, but it can be assumed that the possible construction of minarets and the incorporation of Muezzin-calls would also raise the question of their legitimacy in Finland.[448] These issues have caused problems in Switzerland and Sweden, for example. In a referendum the Swiss decided in 2009 not to build minarets as part of mosques.[449] The fact that the people voted this way in Switzerland despite the appeals of the government and most parties is a sign of great distrust in Islam. In the religious history of Sweden, the first Friday Muezzin-call was made on 26 April 2013 from the loudspeakers of a Muslim mosque minaret in Fittja, a suburb of Stockholm in Botkyrka. Since then, Sweden has also pushed the boundaries of how Islam is seen and heard.[450] The controversy over allowing a prayer call on Fridays seems to have been resolved in a surprising way: a phone app has replaced the Muezzin call.[451]

809. The following chapters provide examples of the actual relationships existing between religious communities and individuals in a number of relevant areas, although not all of the issues that arise in practice are covered here.

---

446. Of these, the most recent case concerns Mr Sebastian Tynkkynen, a member of the Finnish Parliament (Finns Party), who was responsible for indicting a group of people in the Oulu District Court on 3 Oct. 2019. The charge brought by the Prosecutor General applies to text and an image published on Tynkkynen's Facebook page in March 2016. Tynkkynen's publication allegedly contains images of the perpetrators of the terrorist attacks, and includes the statement that 'they have one thing in common: they all serve Allah'. The public prosecutor considered this expression against the law. The Prosecutor General justified the charge by stating that 'Tynkkynen's view of the Islamic group of people is deliberately racist and disparaging hate speech that is generally directed towards all Muslims and is self-defining and even religiously intolerant vis-à-vis Muslims'. The prosecutor also emphasized that Tynkkynen's Facebook page had 11,000 followers. For further information, *see* Helsingin Sanomat (HS), 4 Oct. 2019. For more on the legal regulation of hate speech in Finland, *see* Kimmo Nuotio, 'Vihapuheen rikosoikeudellinen sääntely' (Regulating Hate Speech as a Crime), 139-164. In Neuvonen, R. (ed.), *Vihapuhe Suomessa.* (Helsinki: Edita, 2015).
447. *See*, https://yle.fi/uutiset/3-9968587. Accessed 17 Oct. 2019. (Updated 9 Jan. 2024). *See also*, https://www.suomenuutiset.fi/muslimit-haluavat-rukouskutsun-raikaamaan-kaikille-imaamin-huuto-kuumottaa-naapureita/. Accessed 17 Oct. 2019. (Updated 9 Jan. 2024).
448. *See*, Helsingin Sanomat (HS) editorial 'Minaret Is Not a Necessary Part of Islamic Ritual', https://www.hs.fi/paakirjoitukset/art-2000004697383.html. Accessed 17 Oct. 2019.
449. *See*, https://yle.fi/uutiset/3-5963403. Accessed 17 Oct. 2019. (Updated 9 Jan. 2024).
450. For further details, *see* the HS article 'Moskeijan kolmeminuuttisesta rukouskutsusta nousi äläkkä – Ruotsi vetää rajoja sille, miten islam saa näkyä ja kuulua', https://www.hs.fi/sunnuntai/art-2000005607278.html. *See also*, https://www.kotimaa24.fi/artikkeli/muslimien-rukouskutsut-herattavat-huolta-ruotsissa-lupahakemuksesta-virisi-kiivas-keskustelu/. Accessed 17 Oct. 2019. (Updated 9 Jan. 2024).
451. For further details, *see*, https://www.expressen.se/nyheter/flera-moskeer-mobilapp-lika-effektivt-som-boneutrop/. Accessed 17 Oct. 2019. (Updated 9 Jan. 2024).

Chapter 1. Protection of Privacy

§1. General Principles

810. Religious freedom is strong in Finland, and the public authorities have not considered it their duty to control or limit the content of the activities of religious communities. When they acquired official status as a registered religious community – as a church or a registered religious association – according to Finnish law, they will have themselves presented the nature of the core beliefs that constitute their sacred beliefs. The legislation on religious freedom only applies to registered communities that possess such beliefs. However, religious communities may oblige their members to behave in certain ways in their private lives. They may make adherence to certain moral principles conditional on membership and employment. For example, in the Lutheran ordination oath, inherited from Schauman's Church Law of 1869, the dignified performance of service and exemplarism was merged with the oath, as was the Carolinian Church Law of 1686.[452] The present priesthood oath also emphasizes the will to set a good example for all and not to provoke or annoy anyone.[453]

811. In the case of free Christian societies, the introduction of the RFA has allowed religious communities to organize themselves into their own churches, while at the same time the legislation touching civil law corporations has ensured the freedom of individuals to practise religious activities in the form of an ideological association. For example, the need for unification was widely discussed during the early days of the Pentecostal Awakening, and some members of the movement believed that the activities of the Spirit should be free from all official forms, both from churches and from associations. The ideal of the free revival movement was the free operation of individuals without structures defined by society. Alternatives to legal organization were not systematically designed at all, but organizational problems arose as a result of the economic reality demanding a response. There was

452. Esko M. Laine, 'Pappislupaus, pappisvala ja papin velvollisuudet reformaatiosta 1900-luvulle', 5. *See* closer, https://www.akiliitot.fi/liitteet/514/2/papin_rooli_ennen_ja_nyt_(nootitettu_uusin).pdf. Accessed 18 Oct. 2019. The page no longer exists (Updated 9 Jan. 2024).

453. The pastor is expected to live according to the Church's doctrinal life and conduct through the way in which he is committed in his priesthood, both in following and teaching about the Christian life. When the priesthood is full-time and life-sustaining, it is something that cannot be 'privatized' for private life and out of office. Mrs. Eeva-Kaarina Nurmiranta's (1998) doctoral dissertation 'The priest in judgment. A public law study of the control of priestly doctrine, office, and life, 1940-1989', shows that, in the Lutheran practice of priesthood settlement, a priest's obscene or sinful life constituted the largest component of twenty-one judgments. The penalties ranged from one month to one year's suspension from office. The loss of the priesthood, that is, the punishment prescribed by the strictest church law, was applied in one case. In addition, the loss of priesthood was applied in two cases for an offence that made a priest unsuitable for a priesthood office, and in one case for a priesthood dispute and disagreement. The case law showed that the priest's marriage and sexual behaviour were effectively controlled by the lay population. For further detail, *see* the same work.

a need to acquire real estate, hire employees, raise funds, start a mission, and publish magazines and books. The external and individual activities of the religious community had to be adapted to the legal forms of society.[454]

812. Churches and registered religious communities cannot impose sanctions that violate general law, criminal law, or other state laws. No religious community may use physical violence, deprivation of personal freedom, or sexual harassment in order to compel anyone to comply with its internal rules.[455] There have been many cases of abuse in Finland in recent years in connection with certain free-spirited and ecclesiastical revival movements, which, for example, have been disguised as a matter of secrecy of confession and investigated as an internal matter of the movement.[456] However, it is difficult for a state to address the religious sanctions that a religious community may impose on its members, such as exclusion from the sacraments.

§2. Data Protection

813. The protection of privacy is enshrined in Article 10 of the Constitution, which also covers the protection of personal data, which is further regulated by law (1050/2018). Article 10 reads:

> (1) Everyone's private life, honour and the sanctity of the home are guaranteed. More detailed provisions on the protection of personal data are laid down by the Act.
> (2) The secrecy of correspondence, telephony and other confidential communications is inviolable.

454. For more detail *see*, *Lauri Ahonen, Suomen helluntaiherätyksen historia* (The History of the Finnish Pentecostal Awakening), Jyväskylä 2004; *Jouko Ruohomäki, Suomen helluntailiikkeen synty, leviäminen ja yhteisönmuodostus* 1907–1922 (The Birth, Spreading and Community formation of the Pentecostal Movement in Finland, 1907–1922). (Keuruu: Aikamedia, 2014). University of Eastern Finland. *Diss.*

455. However, there are no specific rules governing this in the Act of Religious Freedom. Menace, assault, and coercion are mentioned in the Criminal Code. Of these, menace and coercion appear in Ch. 25 of the Criminal Code (578/1995). Article 7 deals with menace, Art. 8 coercion. Staging a physical an attack can result in up to two years in prison or a fine. If an attack is aggravated, imprisonment up to ten years can be imposed.

456. The new chairman of the board of the conservative Laestadian movement known as the Rauhanyhdistys and the Central Association of Finnish Peace Associations (Suomen rauhanyhdistysten keskusyhdistys) has stated that the secrecy of confession or sin should not be used as a cover for crime. In an interview with a newspaper in Central Ostrobothnia (Keski-Pohjanmaa) he emphasizes that new cases of abuse that may be uncovered are no longer being investigated within the Peace Associations as internal issues. 'In the old days they were sometimes investigated internally and had bad consequences.' Juntunen emphasizes criminal responsibility and says that 'sin or secrecy of confession must not be used as a cover for crime'. 'When sin comes, it also has an earthly responsibility. We must act in accordance with the law.' *See* further, Keski-Pohjanmaa, 6 Jul. 2014. Conservative Laestadianism is the largest branch of the Lutheran revival movement Laestadianism. *See also*, *Ville Niva, Vanhoillislestadiolaisuuden hyväksikäyttötapaukset julkisessa keskustelussa 2010–2014* (Cases of Abuse within Conservative Laestadianism in the Public Debate 2010–2014)'. (Helsinki: University of Helsinki, 2015) *Master's thesis.*

(3) Measures encroaching on the sanctity of the home that are necessary for the purpose of guaranteeing basic rights and liberties or for the investigation of crime may be laid down by an Act. (817/2018, entry into force 15 October 2018).

(4) Limitations of the secrecy of communications may be imposed by an Act if they are necessary in the investigation of crimes that jeopardize the security of the individual or society or the sanctity of the home, at trials and security checks, during deprivation of liberty, and for the purpose of obtaining in the formation on military activities or other such activities that pose a serious threat to national security (817/2018, entry into force 15 October 10.2018).

814. The Finnish Data Protection Act (1050/2018), based on the EU Data Protection Regulation, respects the specific needs of religious communities. The general rules on the protection of the personal data of individuals also apply to religious communities. The authorities have the right to inquire into a person's membership of a religious community only to the extent that their rights or duties may depend upon it or that a statistical survey mandates it by law. These include, for instance, national Population Register Board data on the distribution of citizens' faith and Patent and Registration Office data on registered religious communities. The third party to which the data are transmitted may process or use them for the purpose for which they have been transmitted. Data protection is discussed in more detail in Chapter XVI.

Chapter 2. Freedom to Marry

815. The Finnish Constitution does not directly protect marriage and the family, and hence there is no specific section in the law devoted the topic. However, the constitutional significance of the issue is evident, and it emerged when the new gender-neutral marriage law was adopted. In its opinion expressed in 2001 on formalized partnerships, the Constitutional Law Committee considered that the adoption of marriage law and related laws was a specific solution to the future and values of society, which justified the special status of marriage in law.[457]

816. In December 2014 Parliament approved the law amending Marriage Act (156/2015) so that two people of the same sex could marry in the future. In the Marriage Act, the passages that previously referred to a man and a woman were removed. Other legislation was also amended in 2016 to reflect the amended Marriage Act. The changes came into effect on 1 March 2017.

817. Both religious marriage and civil marriage have the same legal status in Finland. More precisely, the Marriage Act defines those religious communities that have the right to solemnize marriages. The State marriage law does not prohibit the marriage of gay and lesbian couples in any religious community. This is, however, often contrary to the teachings of particular religious communities.

818. The Orthodox Church regards marriage as a sacrament, as does the Roman Catholic Church. For the Orthodox Church, its clergy may marry before ordination, but not thereafter. The Catholic Church does not recognize the right for priests to enter into marriage at all, and the issue of divorce has also been difficult.

819. More recently, the Catholic Church has softened its attitude towards people who have remarried after divorce. According to Pope Francis, unmarried couples are also welcome in the Church, but they will be 'counselled'. By contrast, the Church's strong stance on homosexuality has not changed. According to the Pope, the bishops pondering the issue in two synods did not see any basis for equating homosexual covenants with God's intended marriage and family. According to the current line of the Catholic Church, gay unions are 'in themselves wrong'. However, at more general level all discrimination based on sexual orientation is condemned.[458]

820. The Lutheran and Orthodox churches accept remarriage after divorce, as do most other religious communities.

821. The right of two persons to marry before a Finnish civil authority is governed by Finnish law (156/2015). Article 108 reads:

---

457. *See* PeVL 15/2001 vp, *see also* PeVL 15/2011 vp.
458. *See*, https://yle.fi/uutiset/3-8797681. Accessed 19 Oct. 2019. (Updated 9 Jan. 2024).

> If neither of them is a Finnish citizen and neither of them is resident in Finland, they are entitled to marry before a Finnish authority only if the marriage is allowed under Finnish law and both have the right to marry under the law that they are or have a residence, or under the law of one of the two States applicable to the investigation of obstacles to marriage. The engagement partner is required to provide a satisfactory statement of their right to marry under the law of a foreign country.

822. Marriage as a legal institution and the conditions for marriage are discussed in further detail in Part X. *Matrimonial and Family Law.*

Chapter 3. Freedom of Expression

823. The fundamental norms regulating freedom of expression are established in the Constitution, in section 12 of the Constitutional Act (Freedom of Expression and the Right of Access to Information). The Circle of Freedom of Expression as such covers all kinds of expression, whatever their purpose may be.

824. Article 12. reads:

> Everyone has freedom of expression. Freedom of expression entails the right to express, disseminate and receive information, opinions and other communications without prior prevention by anyone. More detailed provisions related to the exercise of freedom of expression are laid down in an Act of Parliament. Provisions necessary for the protection of children by imposing restrictions related to pictorial programmes may also be laid down by an Act.

825. Documents and recordings in the possession of the authorities are public unless their publication has for compelling reasons been specifically restricted by an Act of Parliament. Everyone has the right of access to public documents and recordings.

826. The provision includes a general clause on freedom of speech, a specification of the rights included in the provision, the prohibition of censorship measures and a reservation to enact more detailed provisions on the exercise of freedom of expression later through an Act of Parliament.[459] In addition to the practice of religion, section 12 of the Constitutional Act makes it possible to incorporate freedom of expression into all views of life, including agnosticism and atheism. In such an interpretation, the word 'faith' includes both its religious and its non-religious dimensions. In the Finnish context, it is more common to use the notion of 'religion' and 'conviction' in conversation when it comes to protection of religious freedom, but also to different ways of life and different world-views.

827. Churches and religious communities are free to demand special respect from their employees for their spiritual and moral teaching. General legislation does not require this. For the major churches, freedom of expression has primarily touched upon the divergent expressions of conscientious priests about the priesthood, the conditions of godliness, and remarriage.

---

459. The Bill of Government of Finland, HE 1/1998 vp, p. 79.

Chapter 4. Due Process Norms and Religious Groups

828. In Finland, as in many other countries, the Occupational Retirement Provision is statutory and compulsory. The earnings-related pension accrues under the same rules for all persons who work in Finland and is calculated from the income earned between the ages of 17 and 67. There is no alternative system for religious communities. This is discussed in more detail in Part VI. §4, *The Social Security System, III. Pension Insurance.*

Chapter 5. Professional Secrecy

829. The secrecy of confession for the clergy is intensely protected.[460] The secrecy of confession is regulated by the Evangelical Lutheran and Orthodox Churches in their Church Acts and by other religious associations in their 'own constitutions' (i.e., Church Orders or Internal Orders). In addition, all of the religious communities mentioned are bound by Chapter 15 section 10 of the Criminal Code. With regard to the Evangelical Lutheran Church, the Church Act (652/2023, Chapter 7 section 9) contains a provision on confidentiality. In a private confession or other pastoral care, the matter entrusted to the priest shall not be expressed, nor shall any person who has confided to the cleric.[461] The provision is limited to situations where (a) the case is a private confession or pastoral care, and (b) the recipient of the confession is a priest or a church lecturer.

830. According to Chapter 8 section 1 of the Church Act, the law on the transparency of authorities and other laws in addition to what is required by the Church Act shall also be applied. Thus, in addition to the Church Act, church employees are bound by other laws that provide for confidentiality.

831. In 2011 the Episcopal Conference issued a code of conduct to guide the priest and the lecturer in reconciling the secrecy of confession with the protection of the child. The guide maintains the absolute confidentiality of the confession but also clarifies children's protection measures. The best interests of the child and the need to protect children are always taken into account. The starting point for church law is that the matter is resolved and taken care of, but the means vary depending on the situation. This must also be the case where the matters brought to light are covered by the obligation of professional secrecy.[462]

832. With regard to the secrecy of confession's connection to criminal law (Chapter 15, §10), the priest must according to the church law encourage the confessor himself to act (report to the police) if the crime or pastoral care reveals that 'there is a common law offence'. If the confessor refuses to report the crime that s/he is planning to the authorities, the priest must inform the authorities of possible

460. For further detail, *see* Johannes Alaranta, 'Rippisalaisuus' (Secrecy of confession). *Edilex:* 12.10.2010. (www.edilex.fi/artikkelit/7328).

461. The earliest provisions on the secrecy of confession date back to the ninth century. The strict obligation of confidentiality applies to the priest and church lecturer who has received the confession. The courts cannot order them to disclose what has been said in the secrecy of confession. If the priest breaks the secret, he commits an offence that, in the most serious of cases, can lead to the loss of his priesthood. *See* Pentti Lempiäinen, *Rippikäytäntö Suomen kirkossa uskonpuhdistuksesta 1600-luvun loppuun.* (Confession practice in the Church of Finland from the Reformation to the late seventeenth century.) (Helsinki: Suomen kirkkohistoriallinen seura, 1963).

462. In addition, the Church Council's 2011 guide to the professional secrecy of the church employee, 'Time to talk – Time to remain silent', deals with the secrecy of confession in relation to the disclosure requirements of the Criminal Code and the Child Welfare Act. *See* further, *Aika puhua – Aika vaieta Rippisalaisuus ja vaitiolovelvollisuus kirkossa.* (Time to speak – Time to remain silent. Confession and confidentiality in the Church). Finnish Evangelical Lutheran Church Board Publications 2011.

danger, but he must not disclose the confessor's identity.[463] With regard to the condition of being involved in criminal projects, the priest's reporting obligation can be considered as extending to cases where criminal activity is prevented. Child abuse cases are often such crimes.[464]

833. The priest must therefore advise the person to inform the authorities or the person in danger. If s/he does not agree, the priest must inform the authorities in a timely and careful manner, but not directly revealing person's identity.

834. The report issued by the Episcopal Conference emphasizes that in situations not covered by private confession or pastoral care, there is a duty to report to child welfare authorities and police in accordance with the Child Welfare Act (417/2007).

835. A priest of an Orthodox Church shall not, as a witness or otherwise, express what has been entrusted to him in the confession of sin or other pastoral care, or a person who has confessed to him. If someone in the confession or otherwise in pastoral care declares that a crime that ought to be reported under general law is being planned, the priest must advise him to report it to the authorities or to the person in danger. If he refuses, the priest shall inform the authorities to a sufficient degree, without any direct or indirect disclosure.[465]

836. The disclosure obligations under Chapter 5 section 25(9) of the Child Welfare Act (417/2007)[466] do not apply to information subject to the secrecy of confession of the priest of the Orthodox Church. Other information and persons other than the priest ('employed' and 'trustees'), on the other hand, are required to report to the child welfare system and the police.

837. Religious communities other than the Evangelical Lutheran Church and the Orthodox Church may have their own regulations concerning the secrecy of confession or other pastoral care. The state does not impose any limitations on secrecy. This means that the disclosure of what has been told in confession to a Roman Catholic priest does not enjoy the same reporting obligation as that of Lutheran priests. Roman Catholic priests are, according to their own tradition, subject to the obligation of non-disclosure, since disclosure of what has been told in confession to a Roman Catholic priest – even if only in an indirect way – would lead to the excommunication of the priest.

463. The Church Act, Ch. 7, s. 9, para. 3. The Church Act provides for the secrecy of the priesthood as follows: 'In private confession or otherwise in pastoral care a matter entrusted to a priest shall not be disclosed nor the identity of any person entrusted to the priest' (The Church Act, Ch. 7, s. 9, para. 1).
464. According to a 2010 survey of priests, two-thirds of priests have never had a non-confidential discussion about child sexual abuse throughout their careers. The priests who had discussed the matter mostly heard about it from the victim or had become aware of the incident in some other way.
465. Law on the Orthodox Church (985/2006), §110.
466. *See*, https://www.finlex.fi/en/laki/kaannokset/2007/en20070417. Accessed 9 Jan. 2024.

838. The other religious communities mentioned in Chapter 5 section 25(9) of the Child Welfare Act are registered religious communities as defined in Chapter 2 of the RFA.

Chapter 6. Medical Deontology

839. Medical treatment in Finnish law is considered to depend on the personal decision of the patient. An adult always has the right to refuse all or part of a course of medical treatment. The reason may be religious, but there is no need to report any specific reason.

840. In matters of medical treatment influenced by religious or belief convictions – such as blood transfusion and circumcision – legal maturity is reached at the age of 18. It is up to the parents or legal guardians to act in these matters on behalf of their children. However, the child cannot be circumcised if the parents disagree with each other on the matter.[467] If parents reject a blood transfusion that would be needed by their child, a transfusion may also be given in cases of emergency by obtaining a swift response on behalf of the child by means of a Supreme Administrative Court decision.[468]

841. Hospitals in Finland are divided into university hospitals, central hospitals, regional hospitals (private districts), and private hospitals. There are no religious hospitals in Finland; for example, there are no Roman Catholic hospitals, which would not be free to provide abortions, as in Germany.[469] Hospitals do not determine the extent of medical treatment on the basis of religious beliefs, but on the basis of professional medical standards. In Finland, healthcare personnel do not have a statutory right to refuse abortions on the basis of personal conviction. The citizens' initiative in this regard (KAA 2/2015 vp) ended on 25 November 2015.

842. Health care is strictly regulated in Finland. Religious or spiritual healing and alternative medicine are not recognized as medical treatment. In recent years, there have been a handful of cases in Finland of false doctors and false nurses, who have been accused of criminal responsibility for their actions.[470]

---

467. *See* above, Part II, §3. II. B. *Practical Implications of Religious Maturity and Solutions*; KKO 2016:25 and KKO 2016:24.
468. KHO 2385/3/99.
469. Gerhard Robbers (2013, 237) mentions many examples in Germany: Basic order of Catholic hospitals in North Rhine-Westphalia (Grundordnung für katholische Krankenhäuser in Nordrhein-Westfalen as of 1 Oct. 1996, as amended, KA 1996, no. 198, 5.203, KA 1999, no. 117, 5.147, KA 2001, no. 80, 5.138), available at Diözesane Arbeitsgemeinschaft der Mitarbeitervertretungen im Bistum Aachen (DiAg MAV) (ed.), https://diag-mav-aachen.de/export/sites/einrichtungen/diag-mav-bistum-aachen/.galleries/downloads/Grundordnung-fuer-katholische-Krankenhaeuser-in-NRW.pdf, 9 Jul. 2012: 'The aims and activities of the hospital have to follow the faith and moral teachings of the Church. The hospital does under no circumstances perform abortions.' Gerhard Robbers, *Germany.* In *International Encyclopaedia of Laws: Religion*, edited by Rik Torfs. Alphen aan den Rijn, NL (Kluwer Law International, 2013).
470. The most notable of these is the case of Esa Laiho, a fake doctor. He was sentenced to five years' imprisonment by the Court of Appeal. Laiho's sentence in the Helsinki District Court was subsequently extended by half a year. He worked as a doctor between 2001 and 2011 in several hospitals and clinics.

Chapter 7. Non-discrimination

843. The Constitution provides explicit rules for equal treatment in relation to religions. Religious equality is made explicit in several provisions of the Finnish Constitution. Article 6(2) of the Constitution contains a list of certain prohibited grounds for discrimination. It specifically mentions religion and belief. Paragraph 2 reads: 'No one shall, without an acceptable reason, be treated differently from other persons on the ground of sex, age, origin, language, *religion, conviction*, opinion, health, disability or other reason that concerns his or her person'. Implicitly, this means, that no one may be disadvantaged by reason of adherence or non-adherence to a particular religious denomination or philosophical creed. In addition, Chapter 2, section 2 of the Employment Contracts Act (55/2001) states that 'the employer shall not exercise any unjustified discrimination against employees on the basis of religion'. In addition, the pursuit of civil and political rights and access to public services is independent of religious affiliation.

844. As indicated above (Part II, Chapter 4), current anti-discrimination legislation in Finland can be characterized by a certain dualism and fragmentation that have given impetus to many amendments of this legislation over a long period of time.[471] The new Non-discrimination Act (1325/2014) covers a wide range of grounds of discrimination. In addition to direct and indirect discrimination, discrimination within the meaning of the new law is harassment, denial of reasonable accommodation and instruction, or instruction to discriminate.[472] The labour law also sets strict criteria regarding discrimination.[473] However, the prohibition of unequal treatment for religion or belief does not prejudice the right of the religious community to oblige its members to behave in certain ways in their private lives. They may, for example, make adherence to certain moral principles conditional on membership and employment, as stated above.

---

471. *See* above, Part II. Ch. 4, §2. *General Non-discrimination.*
472. For further information on the prohibition of discrimination from the point of view of public office, *see* above, Part II. Ch. 4, §3. *Non-discrimination in Public Office. See also* Tuomas Ojanen & Martin Scheinin: 'Yhdenvertaisuus ja syrjinnän kielto, PL 6 §', (Equality and non-discrimination). In *Pekka Hallberg, Heikki Karapuu, Tuomas Ojanen, Martin Scheinin, Kaarlo Tuori, Veli-Pekka Viljanen, Perusoikeudet* (Fundamental rights). (2nd revised edn WSOYpro, 2011), 227–280. (Ojanen & Scheinin 2011 d).
473. For further detail, *see* Part VI. Labour Law Within Religious Communities.

Chapter 8. Penal Law and Religion

§1. Legal Status of Clergy and Members of Religious Orders

845. There is in general no special status in Finnish (State) law for priests, ministers, and members of religious orders. In the major churches, the clergy are subject to both civil and ecclesiastical law. If a minister or bishop/priest/deacon (in the Orthodox and Catholic Churches) acts against the common law or the criminal code, the case is heard in the Court of Justice. If a minister is accused of a disciplinary offence, the case is heard in the Lutheran Church by the Cathedral Chapter and in the Orthodox and Catholic Churches by the bishop who decides upon such cases. In the Lutheran Church, if another church worker, such as a deacon or cantor, is accused of a disciplinary offence, the case is heard by the local Church Council or Parish Board in the particular parish where the defendant is working.

846. In accordance with the Church Law and Church Order of the ELCF, pastors do not have to give evidence, especially in court, concerning events which were made known to them in a personal confession as confessional secret. This regulation is protected by law in the common code of legal proceedings (Code of Judicial Procedure (*oikeudenkäymiskaari*) 17:23, 2). The same applies to the Orthodox and the Catholic Churches in Finland.

§2. Religious Peace

847. Religion enjoys considerable protection in Finnish criminal and procedural law. The current Criminal Code (766/2015)[474] no longer protects God's honour (as did the Criminal Code of 1889/1894), but rather religious convictions and feelings, and religious peace. Religious peace means religious order, related to the general category 'law and order'.[475] The offence of a breach of the sanctity of religion was reformed in 1998.[476] One common provision of Criminal Law (563/1998), Chapter

474. *See* https://www.finlex.fi/en/laki/kaannokset/1889/en18890039_20150766.pdf. Accessed 9 Jan. 2024.

475. Nuotio 2013, 66. Following the 1999 law reform, fifteen people have been convicted of violating the religious peace in Finland. The offence is punished by a fine or by imprisonment for a maximum of six months. In 2012 the most famous case was that of the MP Jussi Halla-Aho, who was fined for blogging and insulting Islam and humiliating the people. The judgment was reached in terms of violations of religious peace and agitation against the people.

476. For more on the reform of the Finnish criminal code, *see* Kimmo Nuotio, 'The Reform Story of the Finnish Penal Code: Ideological Turns and Waves of 'Modernization'. In K. Goodall, M. Malloch, & B. Munro (eds), *Building Justice in Post-Transition Europe?: Processes of Criminalisation Within Central and Eastern European Countries* (Abingdon, Oxon: Routledge, 2012), 78–93. *See also* Kimmo Nuotio & Tapio Lappi-Seppälä. 'Crime and Punishment'. In Pia Letto-Vanamo, Ditlev Tamm & Bent Ole Gram Mortensen (eds), *Nordic Law in European Context.* Ius Gentium: Comparative Perspectives on Law and Justice, No. 73 (Berlin: Springer-Verlag, 2019), 179–199.

17, applies today in the case of both blasphemy against God (Article 10, paragraph 1) and blasphemy against sacred beliefs (Article 10, paragraph 2).[477]

848. Article 10(1) reads:

> A person
> (1) who publicly blasphemes against God or, for the purpose of offending, publicly defames or desecrates what is otherwise held to be sacred by a church or religious community, as referred to in the Act on the Freedom of Religion (267/1998) [nowadays 453/2003], or

849. Article 10(2) reads:

> (2) by making a noise, acting threateningly or otherwise, disturbs worship, ecclesiastical proceedings, other similar religious proceedings or a funeral, shall be sentenced for a breach of the sanctity of religion to a fine or to imprisonment for at most six months.

850. As Prof. Kimmo Nuotio has stated, the fact, that 'the provisions have been placed in Chapter 17 on Offences against public order (563/1998), which means that these provisions have finally lost their position as the opening chapter of the criminal code, as well as their separate nature as offences with a religious content. The specific offence of violation of the sanctity of religion requires intent on the part of the perpetrator, meaning that as the requirement of culpability one form of so-called *dolus* must be present'.[478]

851. It is noteworthy that religion has emerged alongside other 'racist motives' in the Criminal Code, and hence the punishment can be increased if a person has been motivated by an act of religion or belief:

852. Chapter 6, section 5 – Grounds for increasing punishment (564/2015)

853. The following are considered to be grounds for increasing punishment:

(1) the methodical nature of the criminal activity;
(2) commission of the offence as part of the activity of an organized criminal group;

477. Nuotio (2013, 66) emphasizes that 'this structure arose because at a very late stage parliament amended the government bill by reintroducing God as a figure into the provision. The original proposal, which was prepared as part of a larger law reform project, had not provided for such a distinction – the idea being that protection of the Christian God would fall under a single formula. Both the law committee and the constitutional committee of parliament shared this view. The law committee was explicit in mentioning that the penal legislation also needed to be acceptable from the point of view of those who do not share a belief in God (*see*, Report of the Law Committee, 3/1998; Report of the Constitutional Committee 23/1997)'. Kimmo Nuotio, 'Religion in the Criminal Law of Finland'. In Matti Kotiranta, & Norman Doe (eds), *Religion and Criminal Law. Religion et Droit Pénal* (Leuven: Peeters 2013), 67–68.
478. Nuotio 2013, 66.

(3) commission of the offence for remuneration;
(4) *commission of the offence for a motive based on* race, skin colour, birth status, national or ethnic origin, *religion or belief*, sexual orientation or disability or another corresponding grounds;[479] and
(5) the criminal history of the offender, if the relation between it and the new offence, due to the similarity between the offences or otherwise, shows that the offender is apparently heedless of the prohibitions and prescriptions of the law.

854. Other sections of the Criminal Code *directly related* to religion are as follows:

> Chapter 11, Section 8 – *Ethnic unrest* (578/1995)
> A person who spreads statements or other information among the public where *a certain race, a national, ethnic or religious group or a comparable* group is threatened, defamed or insulted, shall be sentenced for ethnic agitation to a fine or to imprisonment for at most two years.[480]

855. Chapter 11, section 10 – *Ethnic agitation* (511/2011) nowadays also refers to incitement against a group of people and also mentions religion:

> A person who makes available to the public or otherwise spreads among the public or keeps available for the public information, an expression of opinion or another message *where a certain group is threatened*, defamed or insulted *on the basis of* its race, skin colour, birth status, national or ethnic origin, *religion or belief*, sexual orientation or disability or a comparable basis, shall be sentenced *for ethnic agitation* to a fine or to imprisonment for at most two years.[481]

856. Chapter 17, section 11 – *Prevention of worship* (563/1998):

> (1) A person who employs or threatens violence, so as unlawfully to prevent worship, ecclesiastical proceedings or other similar religious proceedings arranged by a church or a religious community, as referred to in the Act on Religious Freedom, shall be sentenced for *prevention of worship* to a fine or to imprisonment for at most two years.
> (2) An attempt is punishable.

857. Although legal entities rooted in a religious or philosophical ethos enjoy the same rights of freedom of religion, philosophical associations are not protected by the criminal code.

858. Chapter 17, section 12 – *Breach of the sanctity of a grave* (563/1998):

> A person who

---

479. Italics mine.
480. Italics mine.
481. Italics mine.

(1) unlawfully opens a grave or exhumes a corpse, a part thereof, a coffin or a burial urn,
(2) handles an unburied corpse in a manner giving offence, or
(3) damages or desecrates a grave or a memorial of the dead, shall be sentenced for a *breach of the sanctity of a grave* to a fine or to imprisonment for at most one year.

§3. Religious Property

859. In Finland there is no comprehensive law on cultural monuments and their legal protection as in some EU countries.[482] This issue is handled as a part of the law of 247/2016, where the Evangelical Lutheran Church is obliged to perform certain social tasks funded by the state,[483] which includes maintenance of culturally valuable buildings and movables. However, there is no mention in this law of the criminal offences related to religious property, such as theft, misappropriation, and unauthorized use.

860. 'Religious property' as such is not specifically protected either by the Constitution or by general law. Theft of property is covered by criminal law, but there is no specification of religious property, either.

861. Article 15 of the Constitution (*Protection of Property*) contains a general clause on property protection (paragraph 1) and an expropriation clause (paragraph 2):

(1) The property of everyone is protected.
(2) Provisions on the expropriation of property, for public needs and against full compensation, are laid down by an Act.

862. Constitutional protection of property is established to protect property rights and interests, which include the right to own property. The protection of property includes not only the power of owners to manage, use, and exploit their property as they wishes, but also the power to dispose of it.[484] In addition to the actual ownership, property protection includes, for example, limited rights such as various uses and mortgages.

482. Instead, Finland has a Law on the Protection of Building Heritage (498/2010) which, as such, applies to everyone except the Evangelical Lutheran Church and the Orthodox Church, which have their own regulations on church buildings in the Church Act and the Church Order. The Protection of Building Heritage Act also contains some organizational provisions. There are also certain restrictions and regulations on the exportation of items of cultural and historical value. For further detail, *see* Law on Restricting the Export of Cultural Items (933/2016).
483. Laki valtion rahoituksesta evankelis-luterilaiselle kirkolle eräisiin yhteiskunnallisiin tehtäviin (Government proposal HE 247/2016 to Parliament for Government funding of the Evangelical Lutheran Church for some social tasks) 430/2015, s. 1.
484. PeVL 15/2005 vp, 2, PeVL 41/2006 vp, 2, PeVL 49/2006 vp, 2.

863. Chapter 28 of the Criminal Code, as amended by Law 769/1990, defines in Articles 1–12 the content of theft, misappropriation, and unauthorized use. Neither of these articles deals with the matter of religious property.

864. However, the violation of public order at a place of worship or during a religious practice involves protection of property. Chapter 17, section 3 – *Violent rioting*, reads:

> When a crowd commits an offence referred to in Chapter 16, Section 1, employs violence against a person, or causes significant *damage to property*, a person who actively participates in the acts of the crowd[,] shall be sentenced for violent rioting to a fine or to imprisonment for at most two years.

865. Chapter 17, Section – *Leading a violent riot*, continues:

> A person who incites or leads a crowd referred to in Section 3 shall be sentenced for leading a violent riot to imprisonment for at most four years.

§4. Religious Titles, Garments and Emblems

866. State, municipal, and other government officials are subject to special responsibilities. By law, an official is a person who has an official or comparable employment relationship with a state, a municipality or a federation of municipalities, or any other group of municipalities concerned with cooperation on public law, Parliament, a state enterprise, or *the Evangelical Lutheran Church or the Orthodox Church or its congregation or their parishes*, the Province of Åland, the Bank of Finland, the Social Insurance Institution, the Finnish Institute of Health, the Municipal Guarantee Board, or the Municipal Labour Market Institute.

867. Finland has no Administrative Offences Act, which would provide special protection for official costumes and insignia of religious communities against misuse, for example in German law. These issues are implicitly referred to in Chapter 16 of the Criminal Code (563/1998), which is devoted to *Crimes Against Authorities*. A person who misleads an official or, without authorization, uses titles or emblems is liable to punishment according to Articles 5, 7, 8 and 9 in Chapter 16.

§5. Confessional Secrecy

868. Confession secrecy is widely protected. Clergy are not obliged under any circumstances to report what they have heard in a private confession.[485] However,

485. In addition, the documents relating to secrecy and pastoral care are strictly confidential. *See Kirkkohallituksen lausunto 2003-00939 kansallisarkistolle rippisalaisuutta ja sielunhoitoa koskevien asiakirjojen salassapidosta* (Church Council's Opinion 2003-00939 to the National Archives on the secrecy of documents related to secrecy and pastoral care). Helsinki, 2003.

they are obliged to report of planned serious crimes. The priest must first advise the confessor to report his/her intention to the authorities or to the person in danger. If the confessor disagrees, the priest shall, in good time and with caution, inform the authorities about a potential serious crime and also the person who is in danger, but without direct or indirect disclosure of the identity of the person concerned.[486]

869. The Code of Judicial Procedure (*oikeudenkäymiskaari*) has been slightly reformed and includes a provision requiring the priest to prove:

> The Code of Judicial Procedure 17:16 (June 12, 732/2015)
>
> A priest or other person of a registered religious community within the meaning of the Religious Freedom Act (453/2003) may not testify about what he or she has learned in private confession or private pastoral care unless the person for whom the obligation of secrecy is imposed consents.

870. However, the Finnish Evangelical Lutheran Church and the OCF have separate obligations regarding confidentiality.

871. The connection of confessional secret with the Criminal Code (Chapter 15, §10) was dealt with more specifically in the previous section, above, *5. Professional Secrecy.*

§6. The Position of Religious Communities

872. No special rules apply for religious communities in Finland with regard to criminal prosecution in cases connected with their office-holders, since they are subject to the same criminal law as other citizens.

873. If the offence has been committed against public officials of a religious community in the performance of their duties (e.g., taxation or civil registry office) as public authorities, the provisions of Article 16 of the Criminal Code (536/1992) on *Crimes Against Authorities* shall apply (*see* above §3).

§7. Special Duties of Religious Office-Holders

874. There are no specific obligations or intensified punishments for officials of religious communities under the general law or criminal law. The Evangelical Lutheran and Orthodox Churches of Finland, as subjects of public law, are bound by the constitutional and other legal information in force in the state, which is subject to the same criminal law as other citizens.

---

486. Church Act (652/2023), Chapter 7, section 9, para. 3.

875. In this context it should be noted that the Evangelical Lutheran Church has an autonomous role specifically connected with its doctrine and the regulation it requires. Under the authority of the bishop, the cathedral chapter is in charge of staffing and overseeing the duties and lives of the clergy and other parishioners and employees. Thus, the ELCF administration is characterized by the fact that the legal position of office-holders is extensively regulated by subordinate legislation, the Church Order (657/2023), and by the rules of employment established by the employer. The statutes of the parishes are statutes approved by the parish council in accordance with the Church Act (652/2023), which have been subjected to the approval of the cathedral chapter. The provisions of the Church Act for government officials are narrow.

876. The development of civil law has been strong since the early 1990s. The State Civil Servants Act (750/1994) and the Municipal Officials Act (304/2003) have been completely reformed. At the same time, the content of civil servant legislation has been approximated to that of the Employment Contracts Act. The European Union has introduced new requirements for workplace regulation which, in some respects, extend to the public sector. At the same time, the development of labour law has been rapid. One example is the adoption of the Employment Contracts Act (55/2001), Working Hours Act (605/1996), the Occupational Safety Act (738/2002) and the Annual Holidays Act (162/2005).

877. The Church does not have a separate statute governing the Church's civil service that would be similar to the Act on Government Officials (750/1994) or the Law on Municipal Government Officials (304/2003).

878. As noted earlier, in Finland there is an Administrative Offices Act that would provide specific obligations or intensified punishments for officials of religious communities.

§8. Administrative Misdemeanour

879. The Criminal Code (Chapter 16) does not apply to religions or religious communities in a specific way, but administrative violations within registered religious communities are subject to public law and administrative law.[487]

§9. Crimes Against International Law

880. The Criminal Code, Chapter 11, §1 – *Genocide.*

881. The Code of Crimes against Public International Law protects religion and religions against genocide and against crimes against humanity as well as against prohibited methods of warfare.

487. *See*, above, §1. *Legal Status of Clergy and Members of Religious Orders.*

882. The provisions on genocide in Finland are based on the Convention adopted by the UN's General Assembly in 1948.

883. Genocide is referred to in the Finnish Criminal Code as 'holocaust' (joukkotuhonta) and Chapter 11 – *War Crimes and Crimes Against Humanity* – **section 1** (11.4.2008 / 212) of the Criminal Code provides:

§1 – Genocide (Holocaust)

(1) A person who for the purpose of entirely or partially destroying a national, ethnic, racial or religious group or another comparable group
   (1) kills a member of the group,
   (2) inflicts grievous bodily or mental illness or injuries on members of the group,
   (3) subjects the group to such living conditions that can cause the physical destruction of the group in whole or in part,
   (4) undertakes forcible measures to prevent procreation among the group, or
   (5) forcibly moves children from a group to another, shall be sentenced for *preparation of genocide* to imprisonment for at least four months and at most four years.
(2) An attempt is punishable.

884. The preparation of genocide and a conspiracy to commit genocide are also punishable:

§2. Preparing for genocide

'For any of the purposes referred to in Article 1

(1) conspires with another to commit genocide, or
(2) makes plans for genocide
shall be sentenced for *preparation of genocide* to imprisonment for at least four months and at most four years.

§3. Crimes against Humanity

The Crimes against Humanity Regulations were enacted in Chapter 11 of the Finnish Criminal Code in 2008 (212/2008).

885. Crime against humanity is a widespread and systematic attack on the civilian population, as defined by Finnish law, involving murder, slavery, trafficking in human beings, torture, mutilation, extermination, expulsion and expropriation, imprisonment in violation of international law, rape or other sexual violence, coercion sterilization, segregation, or persecution of a particular group or community on the basis of political opinion, race, nationality, ethnic origin, culture, *religion*, gender or similar.

886. Article 3. reads:

A person who, as part of a broad or systematic assault on a civilian population:

(1) kills or enslaves another, subjects him or her to trade by offer, purchase, sale or rent, or tortures him or her, or in another manner causes him or her considerable suffering or a serious injury or seriously harms his or her health or destroys a population by subjecting it or a part thereof to destructive living condition or in another manner;
(2) deports or forcibly transfers population lawfully residing in an area;
(3) takes a person as a prisoner or otherwise deprives him or her of his or her liberty in violation of fundamental provisions of international law or causes the involuntary disappearance of a person who has been deprived of his or her liberty;
(4) rapes another, subjects him or her to sexual slavery, forces him or her into prostitution, pregnancy or sterilization, or commits other corresponding aggravated sexual violence against him or her;
(5) engages in racial discrimination or persecutes a recognizable group or community on the basis of political opinion, race, nationality, ethnic origin, culture, *religion* or gender or on other comparable grounds,[488] shall be sentenced for a *crime against humanity* to imprisonment for at least one year or for life. Any attempt is punishable.

§4. – Aggravated crime against humanity

If in a crime against humanity:

(1) the offence is directed against a large group of persons;
(2) the offence is committed in an especially brutal, cruel or degrading manner; or
(3) the offence is committed in an especially planned or systematic manner.
and the offence is aggravated also when assessed as a whole, the offender shall be sentenced for an *aggravated crime against humanity* to imprisonment for at least eight years or for life.
(2) Any attempt is punishable.

887. For other Articles of Genocide and Crimes against humanity, §5 – *War crime* (paragraphs 1–14), §6 – *Aggravated war crime* (paragraphs 1–4), §7 – *Petty war crime* (paragraphs 1–2), §7(a) – *Violation of the ban on anti-personnel mines* (paragraphs 1–2), §8 – *Breach of the prohibition of chemical weapons* (paragraphs 1–3), §9 – *Breach of the prohibition of biological weapons* (paragraphs 1–3), §9(a) – *Torture* (paragraphs 1–4), §10 – *Ethnic agitation*, §10(a) – *Aggravated ethnic agitation, see* more detail: https://www.finlex.fi/en/laki/kaannokset/1889/en18890039_20150766.pdf

888. Currently, one can be charged in Finland with incitement if one has publicly threatened, insulted or defamed a group with regard to factors such as ethnic origin, religion, or sexual orientation.

488. Italics mine.

889. Finland needs, however, to tighten its legislation regarding crimes of incitement. The European Commission believes that Finland's current criminal law is not aligned with the general EU Framework Decision that came into effect in 2008 (2008/913/JHA, Article 1, combating serious manifestations of antisemitism[489]) and it has not been fully or precisely implemented the EU rules in all respects in matters such as combating racism and xenophobia by means of criminal legislation. According to the Framework Decision, member states must criminalise the denial and trivialisation of mass atrocities such as the Holocaust.

890. It has been argued in Finland that the sections of the criminal code that address incitement *against ethnic groups* also permit intervention in cases of Holocaust denial[490] or trivialization. Finland has ratified IHRA's (International Holocaust Remembrance Alliance) definition of antisemitism, which includes the denial of the Holocaust, its scale, its mechanisms (such as the gas chambers), and the intentionality of Nazi Germany or its collaborators and supporters during World War II, and of the Holocaust. There have been cases in Finland where convictions for incitement against ethnic groups[491] have been handed down for Holocaust denial, but these cases have frequently involved elements of neo-Nazi ideology.[492] According to the EU Framework Decision, hate speech *targeting individuals* should also be punishable, but Finnish legislation lacks this provision concerning individuals.

489. https://eur-lex.europa.eu/legal-content/fi/ALL/?uri=CELEX%3A32008F0913.

490. The latest publication evaluating Holocaust denial from a Nordic perspective is Kimmo Nuotio's 2023 article titled 'Holocaust Denial as Memory Criminal Law Seen Through the Nordic Lenses, https://doi.org/10.15845/bjclcj.v11i1.4038 . Accessed 29 Sept. 2023.

491. For further detail, see, for instance, the Supreme Court decision in which the Central Council of Jewish Communities requested in August 2012 that the Oulu police should investigate the anti-Semitic content of a magazine called 'Magneettimedia'. The case was transferred to the national prosecutor. The Prosecutor General brought charges and the case was heard in the Ylivieska-Raahe District Court in October 2013. The District Court sentenced the editor-in-chief of the free-distribution magazine 'Magneettimedia', Kärkkäinen, to a 90-day fine for incitement against a group. The articles in the magazine questioned such things as the actual occurrence of the Holocaust and the mass murder of Jews, describing it as a 'mythical story' and 'Holocaust brainwashing'. The articles also associated Israel with ISIS forces, Syrian gas attacks, and drug trafficking. In addition, the retail company J. Kärkkäinen Oy, which published the magazine, was fined EUR 45,000. Kärkkäinen appealed the verdict. The prosecutor also appealed and demanded a harsher sentence of conditional imprisonment. The Rovaniemi Court of Appeal upheld the original judgment, and the Supreme Court did not grant leave to appeal. *See also* two judgments by the Court of Appeal: one dated 25 May 2007 (R 07/629) and the other 18 February 2009 (R 08/607), and the recent judgment of the Helsinki District Court (30 December 2022, 5 June 2023).

492. *See* the Supreme Court decision KKO:2020:68, in which the Police Board demanded the dissolution of an unregistered association on the grounds that the association substantially acted against the law and good practices (Pirkanmaa District Court judgment on 30 November 2017, No. 17/41766).The Police Board referred in the Supreme Court to a printout from the Nordic Resistance Movement's website as new written evidence supporting the claim that the Nordic Resistance Movement had organized a demonstration on 6 December 2018 at which the organisation's leader carried a swastika flag. The Supreme Court found that the association substantially acted against the law, requiring its dissolution. Furthermore, the Supreme Court held that the association's activities did not enjoy protection under freedom of speech or association, since its activities were an abuse of these freedoms.

891. Finland has delayed action on this law, but in a Government statement to Parliament released in early September 2023 on the promotion of equality, gender equality, and non-discrimination in Finnish society, the government pledged to criminalise Holocaust denial. The statement includes a total of 23 different measures.[493] The government commits itself, for instance, to investigating whether the use of Nazi symbols and Communist symbols could be criminalised when used to promote those ideologies (paragraph 18). However, the government's decision was not entirely voluntary as the European Commission initiated infringement proceedings against Finland in February 2021. Alongside Finland, Sweden, Belgium, Bulgaria, and Poland have also come under the Commission's scrutiny and are required to clarify their legislation.

892. In the infringement proceedings, the European Commission requests explanations from the various countries regarding the measures they have taken to rectify their legislation. If the response does not satisfy the Commission, the country may be brought before the Court of Justice of the European Union. By then at the latest, Finland should have introduced the necessary legislative amendments. It is possible that Holocaust denial could be included in the criminal code in the same section as that already containing a provision regarding incitement against ethnic groups (The Criminal Code, Chapter 11, §10).[494]

893. Ultimately, this concerns the message that Finland and the other countries currently under Commission scrutiny wish to convey to the world as a whole. Criminalising Holocaust denial has significant symbolic value. Condemning the atrocities of the Nazi regime and committing to equality have been a defining aspect of European identity since the end of World War II.

493. http://urn.fi/URN:NBN:fi-fe20230829112043.

494. For incitement against a group, *see* Heiskanen 2010, https://oikeus.fi/hovioikeudet/helsinginhovioikeus/material/attachments/oikeus_hovioikeudet_helsinginhovioikeus/julkaisut/painetutjulkaisut/kirjoituksiaviestintaoikeudesta2010/KyEr5bTSB/06_Kiihottaminen_kansanryhmaa_vastaan_Jussi_Heiskanen.pdf. Accessed 10 Sep. 2023.

Part VIII. Church Financing

Chapter 1. Direct Financing of Religious Communities

§1. Protection of Property

894. Article 15(1) of the Finnish Constitution protects everyone's property. The purpose of this provision is, in principle, to protect individuals and their rights. The term *everyone* thus covers all natural persons within the jurisdiction of Finland and also their benefits in value. In addition to natural persons, the property of private legal persons is also protected on the basis of Article 15 of the Constitution.

895. It is generally accepted in Finnish jurisprudence that private legal persons do not have direct property protection but receive constitutional protection of their property indirectly through the natural persons behind them.

896. The property of legal persons governed by public law, such as the State, municipalities or the Evangelical Lutheran or Orthodox Churches, does not enjoy the protection of Article 15 of the Constitution, but their property is protected by ordinary law.[495] With regard to the assets of legal persons belonging to indirect public administrations, such as companies, foundations or organizations performing public law functions, that the applicability of §15(1) of the Constitution has to be examined on a case-by-case basis.[496]

---

495. Pekka Länsineva. *Perusoikeudet ja varallisuussuhteet* (Fundamental Rights and Property Relations) (Jyväskylä, 2002), 566; P. Länsineva, *Omaisuudensuoja*, PL 15 § (Property protection, Article 15). In *Pekka Hallberg, Heikki Karapuu, Tuomas Ojanen, Martin Scheinin, Kaarlo Tuori, Veli-Pekka Viljanen, Perusoikeudet* (Fundamental rights). (2nd, revised edition. WSOYpro, 2011), 549–604; Kalevi Laaksonen, *Kiinteän omaisuuden perustuslainsuoja – Tutkimus eräiden erityisesti maaseutu–kiinteistöihin kohdistuvien oikeudenrajoitusten säätämis–järjestyksestä ja korvattavuudesta* (Constitutional protection of immovable property – Study on the order and substitutability of certain legal restrictions, especially on rural properties). (Helsinki, 1998), 143; Pekka Länsineva, *Perusoikeudet ja varallisuussuhteet* (Fundamental rights and property relations). (Jyväskylä, 2002). Länsineva states, that such a constitutional provision is, for example, section 92 of the Constitution on State Ownership. *Ibid.*, 197.

496. Länsineva 2002, 197. In addition to the personal dimension, property protection can also have institutional dimensions, whereby property protection, for example, protects property rights and contractual freedom, but not as strongly as personal protection. In addition, property protection for the unspecified group of people (collective dimension) has not traditionally been advocated, but has been seen as affecting more individuals. However, this interpretation has somewhat eased off. *See.* Pekka Länsineva, 'Omaisuudensuoja, PL 15 §' (Property protection, Constitution, Art. 15). In

§2. State Subsidies in General

897. When the sources of income of churches and religious associations and the financial support they receive in Finland are examined, it is possible nowadays to distinguish between three different types of religious communities whose different status under public law regulates their sources of income and the financial support they receive from the State. According to the new Freedom of Religion Act (170/2002 vp), such religious communities are: (1) the Evangelical Lutheran Church, (2) the Orthodox Church and, as prescribed by the Freedom of Religion Act, (3) the registered religious communities.

898. The most important source of income for the Evangelical Lutheran and Orthodox Churches is the church tax. Since the beginning of 2008 the registered religious associations have received financial aid from the government to support their activities. Associations had earlier funded their activities principally through donations, membership fees, and their own fundraising activities. According to the State Aid Act, state aid is received by registered religious associations on a numerical basis according to the number of members. State aid is not to be granted to associations with fewer than 100 members and not to associations that in fact do not have any, or have very few, activities.

§3. Church Tax

I. Basic Facts

899. The most important source of income of the Evangelical Lutheran and Orthodox Churches (and their parishes) is the church tax, which is levied from parishioners on the basis of taxable income in municipal taxation.[497]

900. The legal framework of the Evangelical Lutheran Church tax is based on the Church Act (252/2023), Chapter 6 section 2. In the case of the Orthodox Church, the church tax is based on the Orthodox Church Act (985/2006), Chapter 7 section 77.

Pekka Hallberg, Heikki Karapuu, Tuomas Ojanen, Martin Scheinin, Kaarlo Tuori, Veli-Pekka Viljanen, Perusoikeudet (Fundamental rights). (2nd, revised edition. WSOYpro, 2011), 567–568, and Länsineva 2002, 194–196; cf. Jukka Kultalahti, *Omaisuudensuoja ympäristönsuojelussa.* (Property protection in environmental protection). (Jyväskylä, 1990), 172.

497. For further detail about the historical background of 'The development of the church tax system', *see* Matti Kotiranta, 'The Financing of Churches and Religious Associations in Finland'. In Ilkka Huhta & Esko M. Laine (eds), *Kirkkohistorian alueilla* (Helsinki, SKHST, 2011) 217 & Karjalan teologisen seuran julkaisuja 2, 412–423. *See also*, Matti Halttunen 'Die Entwicklung der Beziehungen zwischen der Evangelisch-Lutherischen Kirche und dem Staat in Finnland seit 2000'. Zeitschrift für evangelisches Kirchenrecht 50 (2005): 3.

901. According to the Finnish Constitution, the right of taxation lies with the State (Article 81), the municipalities (Article 121), and the sub-laws of these related to the Evangelical Lutheran and Orthodox Churches.

902. The state does not, however, follow a diverse tax policy between the religious institutions (churches and registered religious associations) and the philosophical or non-confessional organizations. All existing churches and religious communities in Finland are taxed according to the same rules and principles. Income taxation does not recognize any differences between the dominant churches (Evangelical Lutheran Church and Orthodox Church) and any other religious communities. The applicable law in this case is the Income Tax Act (Tuloverolaki 1535/1992).

903. Registered religious communities and associations are considered separate taxable entities.[498]

904. All religious communities are partially exempted from income tax. The Evangelical Lutheran Church, the Orthodox Church, and other religious communities pay tax only to the municipality on business profits and on income from real property used for other than public or non-profit-making purposes.[499] The current tax is 4.78% (2023).

II. Taxable Persons

905. Church taxes are collected only from the members of the two dominant churches, the ELCF and the Finnish Orthodox Church, and two countrywide Lutheran parishes: the German parish in Finland and the Olaus Petri parish for citizens of Sweden living in Finland.

906. Persons that are not members of these churches are exempted from paying church tax. It is also a relatively normal practice for the members of registered religious communities to pay tithes to their churches.

III. Objection to Church Tax

907. Those desiring to be free of the tax can achieve that result by leaving the Church (Evangelical Lutheran or Orthodox Church). In the case of other religious communities, who collect membership fees, withdrawal from the religious community is effected by de-registering with the state officials. This simply means that one has, according to the state classification of the National Patent and Register Board, officially ended one's membership of the particular religious community in question.

---

498. *See* Income Tax Act, s. 3.
499. *Ibid.*, s. 21 paras 2 and 4.

IV. Tax Rate

908. The rate of Church tax is usually determined at between 1% to 2% of the individual's wage and income tax liability.[500] A member of the Evangelical Lutheran Church with an average income pays roughly EUR 356 in church tax per year (2021). But if all Church members are taken into account, the average church tax per head stands at about EUR 247 per year. The Church compensates the state for the expenses involved in collecting the tax itself. In 2019, this compensation amounted to EUR 14,6 million.[501]

V. Administration of the Church Tax

909. The state forwards the income from the church tax. The actual levying of the church tax is carried out by the state tax authorities, but the parishes pay a proportion of the taxation expenses incurred. Each month the Tax Administration distributes revenue to the parishes, which in turn pay a contribution for the cost of tax collection, as defined in the law. The payment of the church tax takes place as part of the regular income taxation.[502]

VI. Religious Communities, Philosophical and Non-confessional Organizations

910. Members of the Evangelical Lutheran and Orthodox Churches pay their churches a church tax, whereas the other religious communities do not have the right to tax. As mentioned above, since the beginning of 2008, the registered religious associations have received financial aid from the government to support their activities. However, registered religious communities and philosophical and non-confessional organizations fund their activities mainly through donations, membership fees, and their own fundraising activities.

§4. State Subsidies

I. The Evangelical Lutheran Church

911. The Evangelical Lutheran Church has a number of social tasks funded by the state. Each year, the Ministry of Education and Culture grants funding to the

500. *See* https://www.vero.fi/syventavat-vero-ohjeet/paatokset/47465/kuntien-ja-seurakuntien-tuloveroprosentit-vuonna-2024/.
501. https://evl.fi/tietoa-meista/kirkon-organisaatio/kirkon-talous/kirkollisvero/ and https://evl.fi/en/our-work/our-finances/church- tax/.
502. For closer detail, *see* Tax Assessment Procedure Act (Laki veromenettelystä 1558/1995), s. 1.

Evangelical Lutheran Church for the statutory tasks related to various burial functions,[503] the civil registry, and the maintenance of culturally valuable buildings and movables.[504] The amount of funding in 2023 was EUR 122,7 million, a sum that is annually increased in line with the change in the consumer price index, as provided in the law. However, as part of the balancing of government finance, this index increase was frozen for the period 2017–2019.[505] The law itself came into force at the beginning of 2016.

912. At the same time, the right of Evangelical Lutheran and Orthodox parishes to raise tax revenue was removed. Originally, the right to raise tax revenue was not linked to the social tasks of the churches. However, this revenue-collection right was later justified by the social tasks of these entities. The level of state funding is defined in such a way that it should cover a fair share of the costs of statutory social tasks. The amount of state funding was based on an estimated sum that would cover roughly 80% of the costs. From the perspective of the state economy, the reform was cost-neutral so that the state funding corresponded to the average amount of the proportion of corporate tax revenue coming to the churches. Thus, the part of burial expenses that falls to the Church is covered by the charges for the burial services. The burial payments are intended to cover the part of the burial costs not covered by state funding, also taking into account other statutory social tasks.[506]

913. The state funding of burial is justified by the fact that the maintenance of cemeteries and caring for the dead are essential social tasks from a health perspective.[507] This responsibility is ultimately a matter for society as a whole. When such an essential social function is entrusted to the Evangelical Lutheran Church, it is justifiable that the state will also take care of the financial preconditions necessary for the performance of the task.

914. Because this revenue is not a business or real estate income, it is exempt from income tax.

II. Registered Religious Associations

915. Since the beginning of 2008, the registered religious associations have received financial aid from the government to support their activities. The Ministry of Education and Culture grants state subsidies to registered religious communities on a computational basis according to their number of members. This aid is based

503. An obligation to maintain public cemeteries where deceased persons with no church affiliation are entitled to obtain a burial plot (*Hautaustoimilaki* 457/2003, Ch. 2, s. 3).
504. Laki valtion rahoituksesta evankelis-luterilaiselle kirkolle eräisiin yhteiskunnallisiin tehtäviin (Government proposal HE 247/2016 to Parliament for the Government funding for the Evangelical Lutheran Church for a number of social tasks) 430/2015, s. 1.
505. *See* the Law on Parliament for further details of the Government funding of Evangelical Lutheran Church for various social tasks, pp. 2–3, s. 2; https://www.finlex.fi/fi/laki/smur/2015/20150430.
506. *Ibid.*
507. For further detail, *see* Part XV. The Burial System.

on the State Aid Act.[508] The purpose of the aid is to support religious freedom by improving the opportunities for the recognition and practice of religion. In 2018, a total of EUR 524,000 was used for grants and thirty religious communities received such grants.[509] The amount of funding appears to be stuck at this level as the allocated sum in the state budget has remained the same from 2019 to 2022 at EUR 524,000, and there have been no discussions within the Ministry of Education and Culture (OKM) concerning any changes. The support is not significant for small religious communities since it involves small amounts relative to their membership numbers.

916. This aid cannot be granted to religious communities functioning in the form of an association (non-profit organization)[510] nor by local or branch communities of registered religious communities.

917. Because this revenue is neither business nor real estate income, it is exempt from income tax.

§5. Examples of Facts and Figures

I. The Evangelical Lutheran Church

918.

Evangelical Lutheran Church of Finland Economy 2022[511]		
Incomes	EUR (in millions)	%
Church tax and parish contribution	936.5	71,8
Credits and subsidies for building maintenance and investments, income from sales	82,3	6.3
Subsidies and contributions received from third persons	8.8	0.7
State donations	109.5	8.4
Fees received for church services, Income from property	153.9	11.8

508. Valtionavustuslaki (Act on Discretionary Government Transfers) 688/2001. *See*, https://www.finlex.fi/en/laki/kaannokset/2001/en20010688.pdf (29 Jun. 2019).
509. *See* https://minedu.fi/documents/1410845/4935909/2019+uskonnolliset+yhdyskunnat/2ec67db4-d499- 05ae-1765-444e9fe42f2e/2019+uskonnolliset+yhdyskunnat.pdf (29 Jun. 2019). Previous years *see* https://minedu.fi/avustukset/avustus/-/asset_publisher/rekisteroityjen-uskonnollisten-yhdyskuntien-toiminta (29 Jun. 2019).
510. *See* above, Chapter 3, III. C *Religious Communities as Ideological Associations under Public Law.*
511. Source: Taloustilasto 2022 (Financial statements of parishes 2022). I am grateful for the most recent data to Juho Laatikainen of the Church Council of the Evangelical Lutheran Church.

Collections, gifts	13.9	1.1
Income total	1304,9	100.0
Expenditure		
Priests and religious education	134.9	11.4
Parish work and work with children and young people	212.9	17.9
Cemeteries	132.4	11.1
Other special church services	18.8	1.6
Kindergartens	48.6	4.1
Diaconal services	77.3	6.5
Other parish diaconal work	20.7	1.7
Ecumenical work and world mission	30.9	2.6
Public and publicity work	34.0	2.9
Education and science	2.1	0.2
Management and administration	168.7	14.2
Administration of property	21.8	1.8
Maintenance of church real property and buildings	244.9	20.6
Other tasks	30.8	3.4
Expenditure total	1110.0	100.0

II. The Orthodox Church

919. With regard to the Orthodox Church and registered religious associations, it is difficult to cite reliable data on the annual amounts of funding that are allocated for religious purposes.

920. There is no similar data to that available from the ELCF that can be applied to the Orthodox Church since such data are published independently for each diocese.

921. OCF and its parishes Economy 2018:[512]

Economy 2022	*EUR (in Millions)*
Incomes	
Church tax and parish contribution	16.7
State donations	2.7

512. For the Orthodox Church of Finland, information was provided by Mrs Henna Mynttinen, Chief Financial Officer. For tax revenue received by individual churches, more detailed statistics can also be found in taxpayers' returns: http://veronsaajat.vero.fi/fi-FI/srk/Sivut/Default.aspx.

Economy 2022	*EUR (in Millions)*
Incomes	
Fees for church services, income from property	10.0
Collections, Gifts	0.1
Income, total	29.5

III. Registered Religious Associations

922. There is no comprehensive data available for other religious communities.

Chapter 2. Indirect Financing of Religious Communities

§1. Non-taxation and Tax Exemptions

923. In principle, churches, religious communities, and non-profit ideological associations as legal persons also have the same opportunities to meet the criteria for tax exemptions. However, because tax exemption may be based on different sections of the Income Tax Act (Tuloverolaki 1535/1992), the requirements for exemption vary. For churches and religious communities, it is sufficient to be classified as registered religious communities. A non-profit organization, on the other hand, must be engaged in non-profit activities.

924. A business activity is interpreted as 'not carrying out the tasks assigned to the church by the Church Act or Church Code'. In consequence, taxable business activities include the sale of ordinary goods or services, such as the sale of flowers, candles, or tombstones.

925. According to the Finnish Tax Administration Guidance, there also exists the possibility of income from real property used for other than public or non-profit-making purposes.[513]

926. Non-taxation and tax exemptions are based on three types of use of real property:

- General or non-profit use (tax-free real property income).
- Other than general or non-profit use (taxable real property income).
- Wholly or predominantly in the course of business (income from business activities).

927. Real property is regarded as being in general use, for example, when the property is used as a public school, library, or church. Real property is in public use when the real property is rented to a non-profit organization, for example, for use in a non-profit activity. A forest is generally considered to be an example of other than general or non-profit use.

928. In addition to religious communities, any non-profit organization can be exempt from income tax.

929. An organization is non-profit if:

- it acts solely and immediately for the common good of a material, spiritual, moral or social purpose;

513. Concerning the income from real property used for other than public or non-profit making purposes, for closer information, *see* Mika Nissinen, 'Tax Law, Religion, Philosophical and Non-Confessional organisations in Europe. Finland'. In Miguel Rodriguez Blanco (ed.), Taxation, Religions and Non-Confessional Organisations in Europe. Granada: Comares, 2023, 68.

- its activities are not restricted to limited personal circles; and
- it does not provide the participant with an economic advantage in the form of dividends, profit share or a salary that is higher than reasonable, nor any other compensation.[514]

930. Non-profit organizations pay tax only to a municipality based on their business profits and income from real property used for other than general or non-profit-making purposes.

931. Thus, the taxation of non-profit organizations, including philosophical and non-confessional organisations, is similar to the taxation of dominant churches and other religious communities.[515]

§2. Tax-Deductible Donations

932. Inheritances, bequests, and collections are the main tax-deductible donations. Religious communities and any non-profit organizations are exempt from inheritance tax when they receive an inheritance or bequest. Under the rules governing an association after its activities have ceased, tax is not paid on inheritance or property that has been transferred to another.

933. In addition, tax is not paid out of assets given to the state or its institution, province, municipality, municipal federation, parish or other religious community, or to a charity or educational institution. The same applies to a non-profit association or other community, institution, or foundation with a public interest purpose.[516]

934. Collections should also be mentioned in this context. A collection is a voluntary gift of money offered at a service or mass, the sum of which is gathered in a dedicated collection bag and determined by the donator himself or herself. Finns are eager to give alms: collections and other gatherings bring in almost EUR 10 million annually.[517]

935. 'Collections are often gathered for the parish's work, going, for example to youth work but also for international aid work and missionary work. In 2016, parishes were instructed to take additional collections particularly for international aid work'.[518]

936. Parishes also receive funding in the form of bequests made for local and international charitable work. In 2015, Lutheran parishes received a total of EUR 2.5 million in bequests.

---

514. Nissinen, 68. *See also* Income Tax Act, p. 23.
515. Nissinen, 69. *See also* Income Tax Act, p. 23.
516. *See* Inheritance and Gift Act s. 2 (Perintö- ja lahjaverolaki 378/1940).
517. *See* https://evl.fi/our-work/our-finances/church-tax => Donations.
518. *Ibid.*

§3. Other Tax Exemptions

937. There are also a number of other tax exemptions granted with respect to religious communities that should be mentioned here:

> Before 31 March 2018 *Communion wine was exempted from alcohol tax*. The exemption did not apply to other taxes, such as VAT on wine. In principle, the exemption covered all religious communities, but in practice the Lord's Supper was used only by Christians, and some of them used berry juice instead of wine. The exemption was abolished in the spring of 2018.[519]

938. Registered religious communities are also exempt from transfer tax. A buyer of immovable property in a secular context will pay a transfer tax of 4%. The exemption does not apply to any other transfer tax, such as the purchase of apartment buildings. The tax exemption was incorporated into a law that came into force in 1997, but similar legislation was already in place under the previous Stamp Tax Act.[520]

939. Desolate churches and monasteries are exempt from property tax. The definition of a 'desolate church' is broad. The most important condition is that the church must be 'absent from regular ward use', that is, not used for weekly worship.[521] All desolate churches are at the moment Evangelical Lutheran, but the law as such would not preclude the classification of a property owned by the Orthodox or Catholic Church as a desolate church. From the church's point of view, the preservation or protection of a cultural heritage can be considered as a burden constraint that causes significant additional costs for the church.

940. Under the Property Tax Act, a municipality may exempt certain properties, including those owned by religious communities. It is not known whether municipalities use this opportunity to support their religions. Property tax in its current form has been in use since 1993 and has been involved from the outset.

---

519. Council Directive 92/83/EEC of 19 Oct. 1992 on the harmonization of the structures of excise duties on alcohol and alcoholic beverages. The taxation of alcoholic beverages was based on the Alcohol and Alcoholic Beverage Tax Act (1471/1994). Article 8(2) also exempts wines and intermediate products used by the Evangelical Lutheran or Orthodox Church or a religious community registered under the Freedom of Religion Act as communion wine, under the conditions laid down in more detail by decree. Thus, registered religious communities other than churches were also exempt. The committee proposed that a new para. 2 be added to Art. 8 of the Alcohol and Alcohol Beverage Tax Act, which maintained the traditional exemption for communion wine. (VaVM 90/1994 vp).

520. Article 10 of the Transfer Tax Act (931/1996) provides for the acquisition of general government. According to that, if the transferee is the province of Åland, the municipality, the association of municipalities, the parish or the registered religious community, no tax is payable. When the law was reformed in 1966, the previous provision of s. 30 of the Stamp Tax Act on Government Procurement of 1943 was retained. This relief also applies to all religious communities.

521. This is governed by the Real Estate Tax Act (654/1992), which provides, in accordance with Article 3(1), that property taxes are to be waived on, *inter alia*, deserted churches, castles, fortifications, and monasteries.

941. Communities, in practice mainly companies, but in principle also associations, pay *a broadcasting tax* on their business income. *Religious communities are exempt from this tax.* This is the newest of the tax exemptions, which came into force in 2013 when tax collection began. The government proposed that state churches be exempt from the broadcast tax, but Parliament extended it to all religious communities.[522]

§4. OTHER ECONOMIC CONTRIBUTIONS

942. The property owned by churches and religious communities is largely tied to church buildings, chapels, parish halls, and camp centres. For example, parishes of the ELCF own roughly 800 church buildings in total.[523] Parishes also own dwellings that provide income from rent.

943. Parishes also have property holdings. In 2023, roughly two-thirds of parishes 236 out of 354, to be specific) of the Evangelical Lutheran Church-owned land, with most of the forest property belonging to parishes in Northern and Eastern Finland. Cemeteries also fall under the category of land owned by parishes.[524] Due to increasing pressure on parish finances, many parishes have sold land in recent years to fund their work. In 2022, the proportion of revenue from forestry with regard to all sources of income for the parishes was on average 1.7%.

522. Of the entities referred to in s. 3 of the Income Tax Act, the State and its body, the municipality, the association of local authorities, the parish, the religious community, the housing company, or the corporation are exempt from income or professional or agricultural activities (s. 3(2) of the Broadcasting Act 484/2012). The provision therefore applies to all religious communities and not only to churches of the Evangelical Lutheran Church or the Orthodox Church.

523. *See* https://evl.fi/our-work/our-finances/church-tax => Property.

524. *Ibid.*

Part IX. Education[525]

Chapter 1. Religious Education in State and Private Schools

§1. Religious Education in State Schools

I. General Principles of Public Education

944. The basic right to education and culture in Finland is recorded in Articles 16 and 17 of the Constitution.[526] Public authorities must secure equal opportunities for every resident in Finland (not simply Finnish citizens) to receive education even after the completion of compulsory education and to develop themselves, irrespective of domicile, sex, economic situation, or linguistic and cultural background.[527]

945. Legislation provides for compulsory education and the right to free pre-primary and basic education.[528] Second, the public authorities are also obliged to guarantee everyone an equal opportunity to obtain other education besides the basic education, according to their abilities and special needs, and to develop themselves without being prevented by economic hardship.[529] Most other qualifying education is also free of charge for the students, including postgraduate education at universities.

946. The provisions of Article 16 are laid down by the Basic Education Act (628/1998), which defines the pupil's rights and obligations. It also sets out the

525. Part IX. Education is based on a revised and expanded version of the article, Matti Kotiranta 'Religious Education in Finland'. In *Gerhard Robbers (ed.), Religion in Public Education – La religion dans l'éducation publique*. (Trier: European Consortium for Church and State Research, 2011), 139–153.
526. *See*: http://www.eduskunta.fi. => In English/The Constitution of Finland.
527. In addition, the public authorities are obliged to provide for the educational needs of the Finnish- and Swedish-speaking population according to the same criteria. Approximately 5.5% of the population have Swedish as their mother tongue. Both language groups have the right to receive education in their own mother tongue. Regulations on the language of instruction are stipulated in legislation concerning the different levels of education. The entirely Swedish-speaking Province of Åland has its own educational legislation. http://www.oph.fi/english/education/overview_of_the_education_system.
528. Article 16(1) of the Constitution states that 'everyone has the right to basic education free of charge'.
529. Article 16(2).

rights and obligations of the guardians separately.[530] It is the responsibility of the guardian to ensure that the child's compulsory education is completed (Article 26).

947. Parents decide, for example:

- on the participation of children in preschool education (Article 26a);
- on the choice of subjects and courses (Article 30).

948. Guardians must be consulted, for example:

- prior to the imposition of a disciplinary penalty (Article 36a);
- before transfer to special education (Article 17).

949. Guardians must be informed, for example, of:

- criteria and their application to student assessment (Basic Teaching Regulation, §13).

950. General education in public schools, that is, schools run and maintained by the municipalities, is religiously neutral. There may be no mission or proselytism; religions must be treated equally.

951. Religious and ethical teaching has been organized as required by the new law of Religious Freedom (456/2003, §6), with the positive content of religious freedom as the right to receive religious instruction as specifically provided for. Whereas the old law only spoke about the basis for the liberalization of religious instruction, the new legislation starts with the positive approach of 'education according to individual religious affiliation'. The law on comprehensive and upper secondary education was replaced with 'teaching the pupil's own religion'[531]

952. The right to receive teaching 'according to the pupil's own religion' is anchored in the definitions of international treaties and declarations on the relationship between religious freedom and education. According to these definitions, everyone has the right, among other things, to learn and teach their own religion or belief. Second, parents or custodians have the right to decide on a child's religious education corresponding to the child's level of development. Third, everyone should be provided with equal societal conditions for learning and studying their own religion or equivalent view of life (ethics).

953. Since Independence, Finnish teaching and jurisprudence has assumed that the religious community of a pupil or student is the reference group within which

530. In Finland the rights and obligations of guardians are often defined in legislation by reference to children's rights. Guardians act as representatives and guardians of their minor child; they have the right to be informed and consulted on matters concerning their own child.
531. *See* https://www.finlex.fi/en/laki/kaannokset/1999/en19990731.pdf § 13 (6.6.2003/454).

he or she has been taught religious education. Until the adoption of the new RFA, this teaching was traditionally referred to as 'denominational religious teaching'.

954. Denominational religious teaching is well suited to describing the teaching practices prevailing before World War II. Religious education in schools at that time was confessional in the true sense of the word. Most of it was ecclesiastical instruction within the school administration. Thus, it can be stated that the RFA (456/2003) marked a major shift towards more neutral and objective religious instruction.

955. School prayers or morning assemblies in state schools are permissible. However, possible restrictions on morning assemblies can be based on the limitation of religion or belief by others. No one is obliged to participate in school prayers against his or her convictions.

956. Opting out of co-educative sports for religious reasons is not possible.[532] Health education (sex education) is also compulsory for everybody in state schools.

957. Crucifixes in state schools have not been a matter of intense public debate in Finland as they have, for example, in Germany and Italy. The only public debate concerning crucifixes was briefly raised by the Finnish media in November 2009 when the ECtHR ruled against the use of crucifixes in classrooms in Italy. The ruling marked the end of an eight-year battle by a Finnish-born mother, Soile Lautsi. She took her cause to court after failing to get crucifixes removed from the school at which her two children were being taught in a town in north-east Italy. The Italian Constitutional Court declared itself not competent to judge the case in 2004 and the Italian Council of State rejected the Lautsi application in 2006. After that, Lautsi appealed in 2006 to the ECtHR, where in 2011 her appeal was eventually rejected.[533]

958. Currently, there is very little discussion in Finland concerning religious symbols (e.g., crucifixes), prayers, or religious services in state schools. Citizens are free to wear religious symbols (e.g., crucifixes or scarves) in schools and public places. There is no law or regulation in Finland that forbids the wearing of a religious garment (e.g., a hijab). Nor is there any legislation that grants permission to use a hijab. Until now there has been no case in either the local or upper courts concerning the wearing of hijabs or burqas (a black garment totally covering the female body, including the head and face) in the basic schools or upper secondary schools. Nor has the question of religious garments been discussed by the Finnish National Board of Education. Consequently, the Board has not issued official instructions to schools.

---

532. *See* above, Part II., Ch. 7, II. Specific Issues, B. Conscientious Objection, 1. *Dress Requirements.*
533. For further detail on the basic information, what the Italian courts have done about the Lautsi case, *see* https://classic.iclrs.org/content/blurb/files/Mancini%20-%20The%20Crucifix%20Rage%20-%20Supranational%20Constitutionalism%20v.%20Counter-Majoritarian%20Difficulty.pdf.

959. There is also no religious aspect connected with the working conditions of teachers or other staff in state schools. In addition, the question of the blessing of school buildings has also never come under discussion.

II. Education Structure

A. The Finnish Educational Path

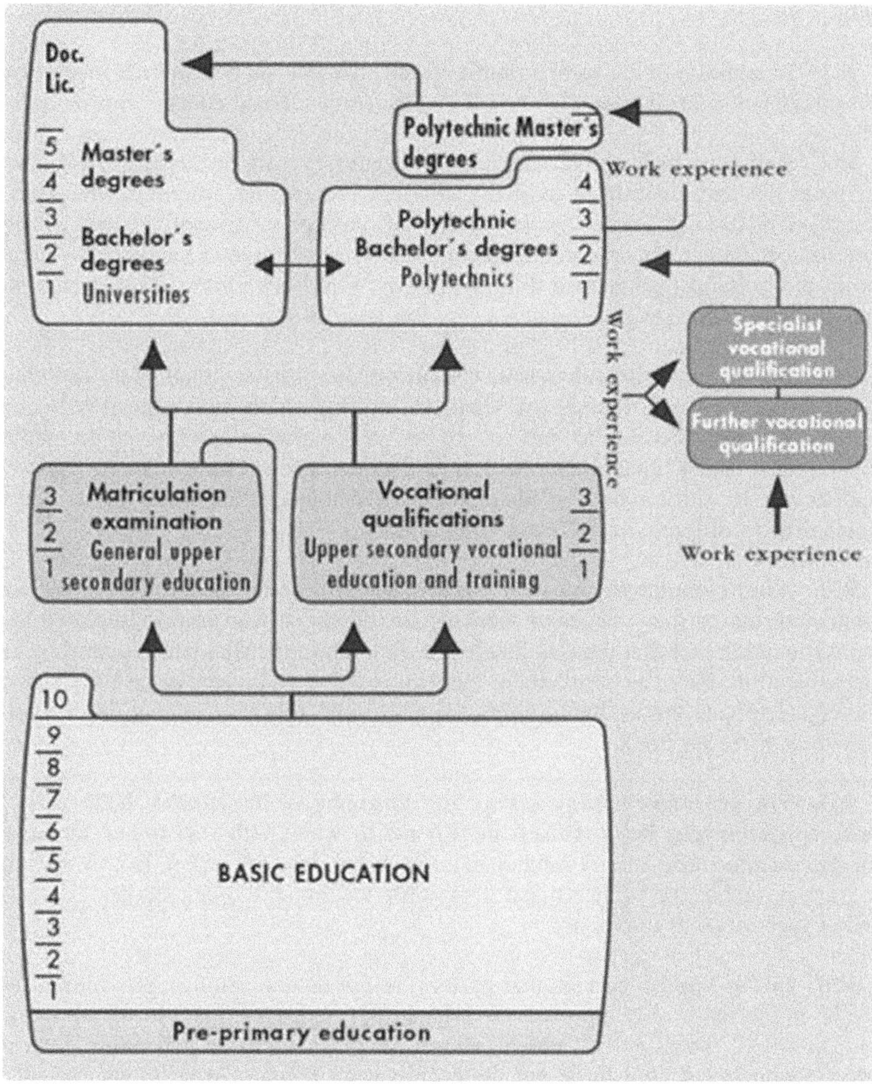

960. **Pre-primary education** (Pre-school education) is provided in schools and daycare centres.[534] Pre-school education starts a year before children go to comprehensive school. The aim of pre-school education is to improve children's capacity and skills for school and learning. Participation in pre-school education is a child's right.

961. In addition to the local authorities and state-owned educational institutions, pre-primary education may also be offered by private basic education providers.

962. Religious and ethical teaching is a statutory part of daycare. In order to facilitate the participation of as many children as possible, religious education is broadly Christian in scope. As the variety of children's nationalities and cultures increases, however, there is an increasing number of children in daycare whose religious and cultural background differs from the Finnish tradition. This creates further challenges for religious education at the level of daycare.

963. **Basic, i.e., comprehensive, education** encompasses nine years and caters for everyone between the ages of 7 and 16, during which time education is compulsory. It is also possible to start school one year earlier or later based on medical psychologist or physician's statement. Schools do not select their students but every student can go to the school of his or her own school district. Students are neither channelled to different schools nor streamed.

964. After complementing their basic education, young people can either continue studying or they can enter working life. If those who have completed their basic education feel that their skills are not quite up to the standard required by further education, they can supplement their knowledge and improve on their school-leaving certificate grades by enrolling for additional voluntary education in what is known as the 10th grade.

965. The government provides for the financing of all schools. Nine years of basic education can be continued in two major ways, either in *upper secondary vocational education* and training or in *upper secondary education.* Both vocational and upper secondary studies make it possible to continue one's studies at a polytechnic school or at university.

966. In the Finnish educational system, religious education is provided at two levels: in the basic or comprehensive education (grades 1–9) and in the upper secondary school (years I–III), which follows on from the basic education.[535] In the upper secondary school there are three obligatory courses in religious education, although a student can choose to take more courses if he or she is willing. There are at least two extra courses available: world religions and religion in Finland. Upper

534. *Source*: http://www.oph.fi/english/education/overview_of_th_education_system.

535. Jakku-Sihvonen, Ritva & Hannele Niemi. *Research-based teacher education in Finland: Reflections by Finnish teacher educators.* Turku: Research in Educational Sciences 25, 2006.

secondary school leads eventually to matriculation. Alternatively, the basic education can be followed by vocational school, where no religious education is provided.

B. Teachers

967. Teacher education in Finland is carried out in the universities and is provided for two types of teachers: classroom teachers and subject teachers. Classroom teachers complete a five-year M.Ed. degree, and the training includes a minimum of 2 credits in religious education. They qualify to teach the full range of subjects at grades 1–6 in the basic education system, including religious education. Their students range in age from 7 to 13 years.

968. Subject teachers qualify to teach basic education in grades 7–9 and in the upper secondary school (years I–III), and their students range in age between 13 and 18. In principle, the requirement for a Religious Education subject teacher is a master's degree in Theology. The subject teachers major in Systematic Theology, Church History, Bible Studies, Practical Theology, or in Comparative Religion. Religious Education teachers are of exactly the same status as the teachers of other school subjects. In other words, they are not employees of the Church or of an equivalent institution but are employed by the municipalities and have received their qualifications from the state. It can also be added that the majority of Religious Education teachers are not ordained priests.[536]

969. The teacher training for subject teachers consists of sixty credits and takes a year. In contrast to many European systems, the training is provided by Departments of Applied Sciences of Education rather than by a Faculty of Theology. It includes studies such as Educational Philosophy, Psychology of Learning, Special Education, Didactics in Religious Education, and three periods of teaching practice. This kind of teacher training is popular among theology students. For instance, at the University of Helsinki only a third of the participants in the teacher training entrance examination are accepted to take this course.[537] In public (i.e., State) schools the qualifications of teachers are paramount. Religious communities have no right to decide on a teacher's qualifications or his/her religious affiliation.

---

536. Excellent national data on Religious Education in the Finnish education system is available in Antti Räsänen & Martin Ubani, 'Finland: The Finnish RE Teacher – A Modern 'Traditionalist'. In Hans-Georg Ziebertz and Ulrich Riegel (eds), *How Teachers in Europe Teach Religion. An International Empirical Study in 16 Countries* (Berlin: Lit Verlag, 2009). The article analyses the Finnish data related to the empirical results of the educational goals, pedagogical methods used, and the educational orientation towards religion, values, politics, and institutions. For further details, *see* Räsänen & Ubani 2009, 61–67.

537. *Ibid.*, 2009, 59.

III. Religious Instructions in Public Schools

A. Preamble

970. Religious Education has a long tradition in the Finnish education system.[538] At the present moment Religious Education is a compulsory school subject both in the Finnish comprehensive schools (7–16 years) and in the senior/upper secondary schools (16–18/19 years).[539] In the literature, the current Religious Education solution in Finland has been rated as 'weakly confessional'. Students *study Religious Education according to their own religious tradition.* As a result, Religious Education includes contents based on the various traditions but does not include the elements of religious practice.[540]

971. In brief, the purpose of Religious Education is described as follows:

> 'The main purpose of religious education is to offer stimuli for the construction and development of students' own religious view on life by teaching them about their own religion, life and thinking of various religions, and by giving students the readiness to understand different world-views.' Therefore Religious education as a subject gives an opportunity to study and discuss main questions in religion and life. And students in all Religious education at school are respected as independent and truth-seeking individuals.[541]

972. As quoted above, in Religious Education the religious dimension of life comes under scrutiny from the standpoint of the pupil's own growth as a broader social phenomenon. Religion is understood as a cultural factor within Finnish culture. Instruction in religion emphasizes religious knowledge and a readiness to encounter new religions and world-views. In primary education the objectives of the instruction are: (1) to familiarize the pupil with his or her own religion, (2) to familiarize the pupil with the Finnish spiritual tradition, (3) to introduce the pupil to other religions, (4) to help the pupil to understand the cultural and human significance of religions, and (5) to educate the pupil in ethical living and to help him or her understand the ethical dimension of religion.[542]

---

538. For more about A Historical Overview of the Finnish education system, *see* http://www.oph.fi/english/education/overview_of_the_education_system/historical_overview.
539. According to the *Basic Education Act (628/1998)*, all children permanently residing in Finland are subject to compulsory education. Compulsory education starts in the year when a child becomes 7 years of age and ends when the syllabus of basic education has been completed or 10 years after the start of compulsory education.
540. Martin Ubani, 'Young, gifted and spiritual: the case of Finnish sixth-grade pupils'. (Research report/University of Helsinki, Department of Applied Sciences of Education, 2007), 21; Antti Räsänen & Martin Ubani, 'Finland: the Finnish RE Teacher – A Modern 'Traditionalist'. In Hans-Georg Ziebertz & Ulrich Riegel (eds), *How Teachers in Europe Teach Religion. An International Empirical Study in 16 Countries* (Berlin: Lit Verlag, 2009), 58.
541. At http://www.suol.fi.
542. Juha Luodeslampi, 'Religious Education in Finland'. In *Religious Education in Europe. Situation and Current Trends in Schools*, edited by Elza Kuyk (Norway: IKO Publishing House, 2007), 67.

B. Courses in Lutheran Religious Education

973. Religious education is presented in terms of the religion of the majority. Because the majority of Finns are members of the ELCF, in practice the instruction in Religious Education is taught mostly according to the Lutheran majority. Religious education in relation to other religious denominations will be organized if three conditions hold. First, the denomination must be a registered religious community in Finland. Second, the denomination must have a curriculum (referred to as National Framework Curricula) approved by the National Board of Education. The system is not automatic, since some Christian minority groups do in fact participate in the Lutheran Religious Education classes. And, third, instruction is implemented if there is a minimum of three pupils in one municipality who belong to the community and who agree to participate in this study. If Religious Education oriented towards their own religion or denomination is available, pupils have no right to opt out of it. The status of Orthodox instruction differs from that of other religious minorities. If there are at least three Orthodox children in a municipality school then teaching is automatically provided and a parent's request is not needed.

C. Teaching of Religious Doctrines Other Than Lutheran

974. At the moment, National Framework Curricula are written for Lutheran, Orthodox, Catholic, Islamic, Adventist, Buddhist, People of God (Protestant society), Free Church, Krishna Society (ISKCON), Anthropological Society, and Bahai. All of them are labelled Religious Education, but, officially, preference is given to teaching whichever expression of faith can best be included in the curriculum. Because Religious Education is related to one's own religion, each variety of the course on offer has its own name, such as Catholic Religious Education. *Pupils who do not belong to any religious community are taught Ethics, in addition to which there is an alternative subject referred to as 'Life Questions and Ethics'.* The National Board of Education has established its own general aims and principles for the subject, and in general, in Finland, the notion of 'exempted from Religious Education' is no longer in use.

D. The Possibility of Neutral Teaching on Religions and Beliefs

975. In the course of the past thirty years the interpretation of the term 'confessional' has become increasingly problematic in Finland since there has been a sea-change in the meaning in its religious sense. The previous law established freedom *from* religion. In contrast, the current law creates a positive right: freedom *for* religion. Within the Religious Education curriculum, the confessional and denominational concepts were ambiguous and caused problems under the old legislation. In contrast, the new legislation has helped to clarify good practice.[543]

976. The concept of 'according to one's religion' is new, a product of the new Act of Religious Freedom in force since 2003. Although Religious education has been defined as denominational, in the past twenty years or so the Finnish Lutheran denominational the Religious Education under the denominational rubric of Finnish Lutheranism has been understand to be non-confessional in its spiritual or religious meaning. Hence, the term confessional underlines its educational content.

977. The introduction of a new RFA in 2003 meant, above all, the removal of certain restrictions Thus far this has ensured that no cases of infringements of the First Supplementary Protocol to the ECHR (§2)[544] with respect to education in accordance with one's religion and convictions have yet been brought before the Supreme Court. The law differs in many respects from its predecessor passed in 1922.[545] The new law and the consequent changes in the compulsory education law and the law on upper secondary schools[546] have meant a considerable strengthening of the position of Religious Education in schools and a clarification of its nature and purposes. This is clearly reflected not only in the laws themselves but also in a statement issued by the Parliamentary Education Committee and a report drawn up by

543. Juha Seppo, *Uskonnonvapaus 2000-luvun Suomessa* (Freedom of Religion in 21st Century Finland). (Helsinki: Edita, 2003); Juha Luodeslampi, 'Religious Education in Finland'. In *Religious Education in Europe. Situation and current trends in schools.* (Norway: IKO Publishing House, 2007), 66.

544. Article 2 provides for the right not to be denied an education and the right for parents to have their children educated in accordance with their religious and other views.

545. It is, however, very similar in structure, being divided into four main sections, the first containing provisions of a general nature, mostly connected with the individual's freedom of religion and the use to be made of it; the second dealing with registered religious communities, their purpose, foundation procedures, and forms and conditions of activity; the third containing regulations for application of the law in a public assembly to practise of religion and setting out sanctions for infringements of the law on requiring the communication of data on the membership of religious communities to the authorities; while the fourth contains details of when and how the law should come into force, together with transition regulations.

546. §13 of the law on compulsory education and §9 of the law on upper secondary schools contain both old and new provisions on the rights of individuals and certain groups to receive instruction in their own religion or philosophy of life. As heretofore, the authorities responsible for arranging compulsory education are obliged to ensure that those belonging to the majority religious group receive appropriate instruction. A new feature, however, is the provision that pupils or students who do not belong to any religious community should attend classes in the majority religion only if they so desire, as indicated by their parents in the case of compulsory schooling or the students themselves at upper secondary school.

Teaching in their own religion will also be guaranteed to minority groups of at least three pupils belonging to either the Evangelical Lutheran Church or the Orthodox Church, while corresponding teaching will be arranged for groups of at least three pupils belonging to some other religious group only on application from a parent or guardian or from the students themselves at upper secondary school. The upper secondary school legislation grants students entering that level of schooling the right to choose between Religious Education or teaching in the philosophy of life. Seppo 2003, 183.

the Constitutional Committee. It may be concluded from these and from the discussions held in Parliament that a very large majority of representatives were extremely favourably disposed towards pupils receiving teaching in their own religion.[547]

978. It was noted that the right to instruction in religion or the philosophy of life had been clearly defined in the Constitution, and hence the individual's receiving of such instruction could be seen to be in agreement with the Constitution. Second, a distinction was made between instruction in one's own religion and religious observance per se, as referred to in the Constitution. Those who emphasized the nature of religious instruction as a form of religious observance during the preparation of the new law were of the opinion that teaching of this kind should be made optional, with the alternative of teaching in the philosophy of life, or even that it should be replaced by a form of teaching about world religions that would be common to everyone. The minimum requirement was the right to opt out if the teaching contained events or rituals of a kind that could be regarded as religious observances.[548]

979. Parliament nevertheless firmly established that *religious instruction should not be equated with religious observance* and quashed all interpretations to that effect. This also brought years of wrangling on the subject to an end and removed the uncertainty experienced on this point in schools. It is important that no one among those obliged to attend classes in Religious Education should be able to demand exemption on the grounds of it taking on the nature of religious observance.[549]

980. Parliament also laid down that all syllabuses should be examined upon the new law coming into force to ensure that they met the requirement for instruction in the pupils' own religion in an impartial manner,[550] and also to ensure that the religion and philosophy of life syllabuses for the upper secondary school contained 'the

547. Juha Seppo, *Uskonnonvapaus 2000-luvun Suomessa* (Freedom of Religion in 21st Century Finland), (Helsinki: Edita, 2003), 182–183.

548. Seppo 2003, 183.

549. *Ibid.*

550. The aim of the Parliamentary Committee on Religious Freedom was to emphasize religious freedom in line with the modern international interpretation of the positive dimension of religious freedom. This was most evident in the provision concerning religious education in the bill. The reference provision included in the Religious Freedom Act (453/2003), which dealt with participation in the 'teaching of one's own religion', formed an integral part of the new positive interpretation of religious freedom (the right to religious education) in Finland. Religion had to be understood both as the choice of the individual and also as part of the tradition of the community. Communal religious freedom focused on the central importance of religion as a cultural factor. This became clear in the subsequent round of statements on the matter.

After completing its work in February 2001, the round of statements was set up the Parliamentary Committee on Religious Freedom. The Ministry of Education requested a total of 147 statements and in response received 93.

In their estimation, a majority of the commentators considered the draft proposal justified. For example, the Government's Chancellor of Justice, the Ministry of Education, the Ministry of Defence, the Ministry of Labour and the Advisory Board for Ethnic Relations (ETNO), the provincial governments of Western and Eastern Finland, the Research and Development Centre for Welfare and Health (STAKES; Since 2006, the National Institute for Health and Welfare [THL]),

foundations of the major religions of the world to the extent required for a good general education'. This latter aim has now clearly been taken into account, at least as far as instruction in the majority religion is concerned.[551]

981. The new law is also clearer than its predecessor from a material point of view, in that it transfers the regulations applying to individual detailed issues from the RFA to the relevant points in the general legislation.

E. Opting Out of School Obligations for Religious Reasons, Current Developments and Challenges

982. There are in Finland no general provisions that give a pupil the right to be off school on religious holidays. The working year of the schools is normally divided into an autumn and a spring semester, allowing holidays for Christmas and New Year. Within the semesters, the Finnish National Board of Education decides on holidays, normally including Easter holidays. On the other hand, the parents of a pupil have the possibility in the primary and secondary school of taking the child out of school for some days per year. The permission for absence of this kind is granted by the school's head teacher.

983. The current Finnish Religious education situation was only recently established. Finnish teacher training has been reformed in the present century. As a result, research-based teacher education has been accepted as the guiding principle for Finnish teacher education. Research-based teacher education consists of the opportunity to gain a profound knowledge of the object of study and the internalization of

---

the Faculty of Law at the University of Lapland and the Faculty of Theology at the University of Helsinki and the Faculty of Theology at Åbo Akademi University all considered the reform work justified and necessary.

Most of the political parties also agreed with the reasoning of the Committee on Religious Freedom. The committee's basic policy also was praised by many of the religious communities. The Finnish Evangelical Lutheran Church Assembly considered the performance as a whole to be a success. The Orthodox ecclesiastical government also regarded the bill as largely positive. The Swedish-speaking Free Church communities, *Finlands svenska baptistsamfund* (FSB), FS, and *Vörå frikyrkosamling* (VFF) were satisfied and hoped that the new law would come into force swiftly.

The statements received from the religious communities could be divided into two distinct groups. Lutheran and Orthodox commentators – as noted above – were quite satisfied with the bill, with the exception of a few of its details. In contrast, several registered religious communities, notably the Catholic Church in Finland and the Confederation of Free Churches (SVKN), were dissatisfied because, in their opinion, the bill did not provide a positive solution to the weaker legal status of registered religious communities in comparison with the Lutheran and Orthodox Churches. The Catholic Church also suggested that the proposal permitted state interference in the internal affairs of religious communities.

Atheist and anti-church organizations, with their smaller membership bases, clearly produced a negative line and used the harshest language in their criticism of the bill. However, at the crucial political level for the final enactment of the law, the bills were adopted as they stood. For further detail on the discussion, *see* Seppo 2003, 92–143, especially 92–93, 101–102, 116–118, 127–134.

551. Seppo 2003, 183.

a research-oriented attitude to teaching.[552] In practice this means that there is no possibility of opting out of Biology, for example on the grounds of a belief in Creationism.

984. New national curricula (encompassing eleven different religions) were published in 2004, in light of which the schools re-designed their syllabuses. Parliament has reached a clear decision on Religious Education. There was a political idea to unite all Religious Education into a single subject. Parliament took a vote and 75% were against the single-syllabus Religious Education model and in favour of the 'own religion' model. Thus, the new Act on Religious Freedom (2003) was passed in positive terms, since it creates a situation where everyone should have the right to religious education and not simply to opt out of it.[553]

985. The development of multi-cultural religious education could be remarkable in the future. At the present time there are now multi-faith schools in the largest cities, especially in some areas of the capital, Helsinki. If this leads to more religions that have their own Religious Education curricula then the costs incurred in providing such a multiplicity of courses will rise. As Dr *Juha Luodeslampi* has emphasized, this might again increase the pressure to introduce integrated Religious education, but parliament's opinion is currently clear. The right to 'one's own religion' has been affirmed in the recent debate and the cost implications are not a major consideration in determining that approach.[554] Nevertheless, the system and its specific features will still be subject to discussion. Changing ideas on education and religious pluralism and also on state intervention will all have an impact on the future education system in Finland.[555]

---

552. For further detail, *see* Jakku-Sihvonen, Ritva & Hannele Niemi. *Research-based teacher education in Finland: Reflections by Finnish teacher educators.* Turku: Research in Educational Sciences 25, 2006.
553. *See* notes 510–515, above (Seppo, 2003); Juha Luodeslampi, 'Religious education in Finland'. In *Religious Education in Europe. Situation and current trends in schools.* (Norway: IKO Publishing House, 2007), 66.
554. Luodeslampi 2007, 69.
555. For further detail, *see* Martin Ubani. Inkeri Rissanen & Saila Poulter (eds), *Contextualising dialogue, secularisation and pluralism. Religion in Finnish public education.* (Münster: Waxmann, 2019).

Chapter 2. Religious Schools

986. Private schools are permitted to contribute their specific educational, religious, and philosophical approaches to the general state school system. Private schools have the freedom to organize – within the defined boundaries of the school laws – according to their own convictions.

987. There are only a few private schools in Finland. Compared with the total number of schools, the proportion of licensed private schools is small, and the majority of them are not based on religion or supported by a particular religion. Licences have also been granted for a few comprehensive schools that are based on religious faiths. For example, the English school in Helsinki is a Catholic foundation. There are seventeen Christian schools and two other faith-related schools. For children attending these schools, the teaching and educational equipment are free of charge. There are also some twenty-five religious pre-schools.[556]

556. At https://kristillinenkoulu.fi/briefly-in-english/.

Chapter 3. Theological Faculties and Other Religious Training

988. The university system in Finland is predominantly maintained by the state. Universities are state universities with a status of autonomy in matters of their economy,[557] science, research and teaching. Article 16 section 3 of the Finnish Constitution guarantees the autonomy of science: 'The freedom of science, the arts and higher education is guaranteed.' Universities Act 558/2009 defines more profoundly independent academic research as well as academic and artistic education.[558]

989. Theological education is provided by faculties of theology at the University of Helsinki[559] and Åbo Akademi[560] (Turku), and also by the School of Theology, formerly a faculty within the University of Joensuu, which was re-established in 2002 within the University of Eastern Finland (UEF) in 2010 when the Universities of Joensuu and Kuopio merged into the unitary UEF. The UEF School of Theology includes units of Western Theology and Orthodox Theology where the latter is also responsible for the education of priests and church musicians for the Orthodox Church. The two theological faculties in Finland are themselves non-confessional and non-denominational.[561]

990. The origins of theology faculties go back to the Middle Ages and the fourteenth century, when the first Finnish students went to universities in Europe to study. In this process Finland became linked more closely joined to Europe, becoming a part of the Latin-based culture of the time. It was with its universities and its prevailing school system that Finland became, in a broad sense, the heir of the Christians and humanists of the ancient Greco-Roman tradition, including all of the values referred to repeatedly as today's united Europe gradually takes root.

991. The University of Paris became the most important destination for Finnish theological students. The first occasion on which Finnish students are mentioned is in the written record of 1313 at the University of Paris.[562] At the end of the century,

557. The operating environment of Finnish universities has changed dramatically in recent decades. The keywords of the present order are autonomy and competition. State funding for universities is linked to outputs measured by pre-agreed indicators. Universities are also freer to use the funding they receive as they see fit. Behind these reforms is the vision that autonomous universities are the most flexible in responding to the changing needs of society. At the same time, the total funding for universities has been cut and part of the core funding has been transferred to competitive funding.
558. The Universities Act 558/2009 (Amendments up to 644/2016 included). *See*, https://www.finlex.fi/en/laki/kaannokset/2009/en20090558_20160644.pdf. Accessed 9 Jan. 2024.
559. The Theological Faculty of the University of Helsinki was until 1924 the only university institution providing theological education in Finland.
560. Åbo Akademi was founded with private funding in 1918 and started theological training in 1924 primarily for its Swedish-speaking students.
561. For further information on Finnish theological education, *see Ilkka Huhta, From State-Church to non-denominationalism public authorities and theological education in Finland*, in: *Francis Messner (ed.)*, Public Authorities and the Training of Religious Personnel in Europe, (Granada: Comares, 2015), 257–269.
562. Jussi Nuorteva 1997, 523–553, *Suomalaisten ulkomainen opinkäynti ennen Turun akatemian perustamista 1640* (Finnish Study Abroad before the Foundation of the Royal Academy of Turku [Academia Aboensis] in 1640), Bibliotheca Historica 27, Helsinki, 1997.

when the university system spread to Germany, the situation improved significantly for Finns to study abroad. From the 1530s, the University of Wittenberg became the most important destination for Finnish students travelling abroad,[563] especially because, with the Reformation of Sweden, a province of which it then was, Finland had adopted a Lutheran state church system. With the university reform of Sweden in the early fifteenth century, the focus of studying and the total number of students shifted to the University of Uppsala. The first university in Finland (the Academy of Turku) was founded considerably later, in 1640.

992. In the eighteenth century the education of the Lutheran clergy took place at the Academy of Turku. In that time the university awarded no final academic theological degree, but the actual ordination examination was taken in the cathedral chapter at Turku.[564] In the early nineteenth century the influence of the Enlightenment in its moderate form, Neology, was seen in the way the Finnish university theology followed the main trends in Enlightenment theology,[565] especially in the thinking of Professor (later Archbishop and vice chancellor of the university) Jacob Tengström (1755–1832).

993. The era of the autonomous Grand Duchy (1809–1917) in turn marked a change in the political situation in Finland, which in turn resulted in numerous future developments in theological education. A highly significant event must also be mentioned, namely the transfer, after the Fire of Turku in 1827, of the university (the Academy of Turku) to the new national capital, Helsinki, becoming the imperial Alexander University. Even though the state was financially responsible for maintaining the university, in the early nineteenth century the teaching was principally in the hands of the Church. The change occurred in 1828, when the statutes governing the theological disciplines came into force at the same time as a substantial transformation in the European ideal of science and the university. The change was especially clear in the development of the nature of the professorial chairs in the faculty of theology. According to the new statutes, the faculty of theology had four professorships: biblical exegesis, dogmatics, ecclesiastical history, and moral theology. The chair of practical theology was established in 1846.[566]

994. At the end of the period of autonomy, the significance of Lutheranism for the developing Finnish state strengthened. It was clearly in the interests of Finns to have a strong Lutheran Church, and the influence of this political issue may be seen in the Church's attempts to increase its independence in relation to the state, since the Orthodox professing the 'Czar's faith' already enjoyed his special protection. This political situation caused the position of theology in the university to remain

563. S. Heininen, Die Finnischen Studenten in Wittenberg 1531–1552, Schriften der Luther-Agricola-Gesellschaft A 9, Helsinki, 1980.
564. Eino Murtorinne, The History of Finnish Theology 1828–1918. (Helsinki: Societas Scientiarum Fennica 12, 1988).
565. Murtorinne 1988, 12; Ilkka Huhta, 'From State-Church to non-denominationalism public authorities and theological education in Finland'. In *Francis Messner (ed.), Public Authorities and the Training of Religious Personnel in Europe*. (Granada: Comares, 2015), 258–259.
566. Murtorinne 1988, 21.

strong, and it became a task of the theology faculty to serve the needs of the Lutheran Church. This can be seen clearly in the formulation of the statute (1886) concerning the 'education of future pastors at the Alexander University', a statute that remained in force until 1938.[567]

995. Finnish independence in 1917 meant a redefinition of the legal status of Lutheran theological education, and eventually a new decree came into force in 1938. The earlier formulation of the 'education of future pastors at the Alexander University' was replaced in the new decree with 'a degree to be passed at the theological faculty of Helsinki University (459/1938)'. Paragraph 9 of the decree stated that the diploma awarded to a student should cite whether the student 'has the moral seriousness required by Church Law §108 to obtain pastoral ordination'. This regulation was finally omitted from the degree in 1947.[568]

996. A state-financed Orthodox seminary was founded in 1918 and until 1988 it provided education for Orthodox clergy, teachers of religion, and church musicians (cantors). In the 1960s a serious debate was initiated that resulted in the transfer of Orthodox education to the universities, a process that was related to the reform of Finnish higher education as a whole.[569] After several preparatory phases, orthodox theology achieved the academic character of a university system of study towards degrees. Thus, the decree of 1988 provided for an Orthodox theological programme within the Faculty of Humanities at the University of Joensuu. At the same time, the Orthodox Seminary itself was not closed, but its primary function remained to organize applied studies, i.e., practical training related to theological studies at the University of Joensuu. The programme of Orthodox theology in Joensuu also gave a new educational boost to plans to found a second Finnish-language-based faculty. The economic requirements for the new faculty were met at the beginning of 2000, and on 1 January 2002 an administratively independent faculty was established in Joensuu (now part of the UEF), housing two study programmes or units consisting of Western theology and Orthodox theology.

997. University studies of theology are non-denominational and open to everyone, with no requirement of membership of a church or religious community. The main employers of the graduates are the Lutheran and Orthodox Churches. The second largest group of graduates consists of teachers of religion in schools. The third sector consists of media, research, and various international fields of theological work, for example in ecumenical contexts. Both the Lutheran and the Orthodox Church include a university degree in theology in their qualification criteria for the

567. Murtorinne 1988, 22; Ilkka Huhta, 'From State-Church to non-denominationalism public authorities and theological education in Finland'. In *Francis Messner (ed.), Public Authorities and the Training of Religious Personnel in Europe*. (Granada: Comares, 2015), 259–261.

568. Report 1977:21, Church–State Committee, 195–201; Huhta 2015, 262.

569. Jaakko Numminen, 'Yliopistolaitoksen hajasijoitus' (Decentralized placement of a university institution). In *Keränen, Seppo (ed.), Omalla pohjalla Euroopassa. Juhlakirja päätoimittaja, professori Kari Hokkaselle 2. tammikuuta 2003*. (Vaasa: Etelä-Pohjanmaan Lehtiseura ry, 2003), 73–83.

priesthood.[570] The criteria set by the Conference of Bishops of the Lutheran Church for those to be ordained include individual study modules as an obligatory part of the master's degree. In addition, churches have a separate ordination training programme that is granted after graduation and does not form a part of the graduates' university education.

998. The qualification requirements for teachers (professors, university lecturers, lecturers etc.) in the theological faculties are in line with the general qualification requirements of universities and are not linked to the requirements of any specific denomination. In addition, the teacher training is provided by a Department of Applied Sciences in Education, and not by the faculties of theology.[571]

999. The changes brought by multi-culturalism have not only been reflected in the development of the membership of the various denominations and religious communities but have also gained new dimensions that will undoubtedly affect theology at university level into the future. For example, Finnish Muslims have in several contexts expressed their concern to secure trained imams.[572] This would mean a guarantee that an imam and spiritual workers have a proper knowledge of the Islamic sciences.

1000. The teaching of Islamic theology began at the University of Helsinki Faculty of Theology in the Autumn of 2018. Bachelor's studies in Islamic theology are open to all applicants and may be followed by a Master's degree. The aim has been to launch the full programme of study in Autumn 2019.

1001. The purpose of studies and research is to have a multi-dimensional understanding of both Islamic texts and practical Islam. 'We strive to develop a research-based curriculum and study that will provide students with a multi-disciplinary understanding of Islamic textual tradition and its complex role and meaning in contemporary Muslim life. It combines both textual research and ethnographic approaches', says a lecturer in the discipline, Mrs Mulki Al-Sharmani,[573] the first holder of such a post.

---

570. The (Lutheran) Church Act (Kirkkolaki, 652/2023), Ch. 7 §1 and Church code (Kirkkojärjestys, 657/2023), Ch. 7 §4, para. 2. Orthodox Church Code (Ortodoksisen kirkon kirkkojärjestys) 174/2007, §132.
571. *See* above, Ch. II, Education Structure, B. *Teachers.*
572. Latvio, Ritva & Satu Mustonen & Ilari Rantakari (eds), *Imaamit Suomessa. Imaamikoulutusselvitys 2013* (Imams in Finland. Imam training survey 2013). (Helsinki: Kulttuuri- ja uskontofoorumi FOKUS ry, 2013), 38.
573. Helsinki.fi/News of the University of Helsinki, 23 Jul. 2018.

Part X. Matrimonial and Family Law

Chapter 1. Legal Position of Religious Marriage

§1. The Right to a Religious Marriage

1002. In Finland, secular law recognizes the legal impact of actions based on religious law.

1003. After the declaration of Finnish independence in 1917, the register office wedding became an alternative to the church wedding through the Laws on Civil Marriage of 1917, on the Freedom of Religion of 1922, and on the Marriage Act of 1929 (234/1929).[574] Both marriages are equally valid. Married couples are subject to the same laws, regardless of the manner in which they are married.

1004. *Church weddings* (ecclesiastical weddings) are conducted by priests of the Evangelical Lutheran or Orthodox Churches. Generally speaking, the initiator will be a priest from the bride's church. The requirement for a church wedding is that both of those intending to marry are members of the Church and both have attended a confirmation school. If one of the spouses is not a member of the Church, an ecclesiastical wedding is not possible, but it will still be possible to obtain a church blessing of the marriage.

1005. A *civil ceremony* is conducted by a district court official, a Judge, or a Registrar.[575] The ceremony usually takes place on the facilities of the office concerned. Colloquially, it is often referred to as a 'registry office wedding' (maistraatissa vihkiminen).

1006. The marriage may also be conducted by a person from a religious community authorized by the Ministry of Education.[576] Such communities include, for

574. For an unofficial English translation of the Marriage Act (234/1929) issued by the Ministry of Justice, *see* www.finlex.fi/pdf/saadkaan/E9290234.PDF *See also* He 14/2008. For more on the history of marriage, *see Jyrki Knuutila,* Matrimonial and Family Law. In: State and Church in the European Union, (Berlin: Nomos 2nd edn, 2005), 530–532.

575. Section 17 (411/1987) of the Matrimony Act states that: (2) A civil marriage ceremony shall be performed by: (1) the Chief Judge of a District Court, a District Judge, or (2) a District Registrar. (1428/1992).

576. Section 17 (411/1987) of the same Act reads: (1) A religious marriage ceremony may be performed: (1) in the Evangelical Lutheran Church by a priest; (2) in the Greek Orthodox Church by

example, the Catholic Church, the Pentecostal churches, and Jehovah's Witnesses and Mormon congregations. The Roman Catholic Church, which regards marriage as a sacrament, blesses the marriage according to its own practices.

1007. According to Finnish law, spouses older than 18 years may enter into matrimony. There are two main requirements for those who intend to get married: they must not be close relatives, and they must not be married if a previous marriage of one of the intending spouses is still in force. Likewise, no person shall marry if his or her registered partnership is in force. Cousins are not regarded as close relatives by law, and hence they are permitted to marry each other.[577]

1008. In some cases, a person under the age of 18 may, however, for special reasons be granted a dispensation to marry. In that case, he or she needs to acquire an exemption. An exemption can be applied for, for example, if the bride is expecting a child. Exemptions were previously granted by the President, but nowadays the process is overseen by the Ministry of Justice. Before reaching its decision, the Ministry of Justice also consults with a custodian, preferably the parents, of the person(s) seeking an exemption.[578]

1009. Before a marriage, the preconditions of the marriage itself are examined. This will include an examination of potential impediments to the marriage,[579] which will require further details from the local parish or district register office clarifying whether there may be any obstacles to a couple legally marrying. One obvious obstacle may, of course, be the discovery that one of the intending spouses is already married to someone else.

1010. The right of the Evangelical Lutheran and Orthodox Churches to solemnize marriages is directly based on the law. Permission has also been granted to other (registered) religious associations under subsection §14 of the Matrimony Act (234/1929) by the Ministry of Education and Culture. The Act governs the preconditions of marriage (e.g., the capacity to marry, the publication of the banns), the legal position of family members, and divorce.

1011. The cohabitation of persons of the same sex was agreed by the Finnish Parliament in 2001, gaining same legal status as marriage (having reached the age of 18). In accordance with this law (950/2001), which came into force on 1 March 2002, persons of the same sex are now permitted to formalize their partnerships by

---

a priest; and (3) in another religious community by a person who, under the rules of the community, has the right to perform marriage ceremonies.

577. Section 7 (411/1987) of the same Act reads: (1) No person shall marry her father, his mother, his or her grandparent or other direct ascendant, nor his or her child, grandchild or other direct descendant; (2) Siblings or half-siblings shall not intermarry.

578. Chapter 2, s. 4 states: The Ministry of Justice may, however, for special reasons grant a person under 18 years of age a dispensation to marry. Before the matter is decided, the custodian of the applicant shall be reserved an opportunity to be heard if his or her whereabouts can be determined with reasonable measures.

579. Marriage Act, Ch. 3, Examination of Impediments to Marriage (411/1987).

contracting a civil partnership.[580] The main differences between marriage and registered partnership concern the presumption of paternity, adoption (§9, paragraphs 1–3), and the use of each other's surnames (§8, paragraphs 4). Another difference in the 2002 law was that, unlike a heterosexual marriage, a partnership registration cannot occur in a church, and for marriage no residency or citizenship requirements apply.

1012. By the amendment to the Marriage Act, persons of the same sex have been able to enter into marriage since 1 March 2017 (HE 104/217).[581] At the same time, the registration of partnerships was abolished. Along with the amendment, persons in a registered partnership can change their partnership into a marriage by making a joint notification at the local register office concerning it.[582] The Equal Marriage Act, which came into force in March 2017, resulted in a total of 2,460 Finns changing their registered partnership into a marriage in 2017. In 2018 more than 250 people converted their registered partnership, of which approximately 63% were women.[583]

1013. The Evangelical Lutheran Church, which has the right under secular law to solemnize marriages, has not yet granted its permission, with reference to a decree of the General Synod (2018), for its priests to exercise a right to conduct marriages between persons of the same sex. However, many priests have done so. Certain Lutheran congregations have also adopted an active role by allowing the marriage of same-sex couples on their church premises.

1014. With the approval of the new Marriage Act, both majority and minority churches and also certain religious communities (both Christian and non-Christian) have been confronted with a challenging situation. One of the most interesting issues in the Gender-Neutral Marriage Act is the future role of the Church. Many churches that have been given the right by the state to perform marriages may, according to their own principles, be able in the future to refuse to marry same-sex couples. The older minority churches – the Orthodox and Catholic churches, and the free Christian denominations such as Adventist, Baptist, Methodist, and Pentecostal congregations – have adhered to strictly conservative interpretations, emphasising marriage as solely a relationship between a man and a woman, which cannot be equated with any other form of cohabitation.

---

580. Registered partnership is only open for same-sex partners. *See* the Act on Registered Partnerships (Laki rekisteröidystä parisuhteesta) 950/2001 of 9 Nov. 2001. *See* www.finlex.fi/pdf/saadkaan/E0 010950. PDF of an unofficial English translation by the Ministry of Justice of the partnership law.
581. *See* www.finlex.fi => 104/2017.
582. Concepts of Family, cohabitation of couple, and marriage, *see* closer http:www.stat.fi => Quality description, families 2017.
583. *See* http://tilastokeskus =>Artikkelit =>2019, Marjut Pietiläinen & Kirsti Pohjanpää: *Lakimuutokset näkyvät sateenkaariväen tilastoinnissa – samaa sukupuolta olevan kanssa avioliitossa 4 000 suomalaista.*

1015. Until now, the Cathedral Chapters of the ELCF have been able to issue a written warning to any priest who performs marriage ceremonies involving homosexual couples, or to suspend them from their post either temporarily or permanently as a result of conflicting interpretations of the priesthood. The priest may, in turn, appeal against the decision of the Chapter to the Administrative Court and against its subsequent decision to the Supreme Administrative Court.

1016. A vitally important and recent precedent has been set by the Decision of the Administrative Court of Northern Finland (19/0272/2), which stated that a priest was not guilty of misconduct, since he had complied with a law approved by the Finnish Parliament and approved by the President of the Republic. The priest had exercised public authority at his installation, and the judicial evaluation of the exercise of public authority did not constitute a part of the Chapter's powers.

1017. In this case (19/0272/2), the question was whether the Cathedral chapter could have given a written warning to a priest who on 5 August 2017 had conducted a church wedding for a same-sex couple. Here the priest would have acted contrary to the duties of the priesthood and the promise of the priesthood within the meaning of Chapter 5, section 3, paragraph 3 of the Church Act.

1018. The Administrative Court found that since the amendment of section 1(1) of the Marriage Act on 1 March 2017 no provision had been made in the Church Law or the Church Order for the sex of married couples in any way that would reject the right of same-sex couples to marry. In addition, the Church Synod had not redefined the terms of an ecclesiastical wedding in light of this change. The report of the Episcopal Conference was based on previous statements made by the Ecclesiastical and Bishopric Conferences on the concept of marriage that were issued prior to the coming into force of the new Marriage Act. Even if the Church's own understanding was based on interpretation of marriage between a man and a woman, the Administrative Court considered the situation to be unregulated.

1019. In view of the unclear and unregulated state of the matter, the Administrative Court held that the priest had not violated the priesthood duties and the priesthood promise conducting a same-sex marriage and the Cathedral chapter could not have warned him. The decisions of the cathedral chapter had to be overturned as unlawful.

1020. Although the Supreme Administrative Court (KHO: 2020: 97) annulled the decision of the Administrative Court of Northern Finland (19/0272/2) by four to one votes, this precedent was significant in the sense that, for example, the Diocese of Helsinki has followed the lines indicated by the decision of the Administrative Court of Northern Finland. It is, however, problematic from the point of view of the supreme legislator and also for the unity of the Evangelical-Lutheran Church if the Cathedral chapters of the different dioceses may have different interpretations of the matter.

1021. The final stage of the marriage debate is presented in the proposal draft, which was approved by the bishops' conference on 12 March 2024 regarding two parallel understandings of marriage. The bishops propose a model in the church order for two parallel and generally accepted understandings of marriage. In the first, marriage is understood (according to the traditional stance of the church) as existing between a man and a woman, and in the second as between two persons. The proposal includes the freedom of conscience of the priest and the obligation of the congregation to ensure that all couples are able to marry.

1022. The bishops' proposal is recognized as a compromise acknowledging the current situation and as such is not perfect. It has faced strong opposition both from the church's conservative movements and also from liberal values advocates, who see the proposal as discriminatory within the framework of the church order. Currently, it does not mention man and woman but only membership of the church and having undergone confirmation as the prerequisites for marriage. In future, however, it would include mention of a different marriage model with respect to genders.

1023. The bishops' proposal has been discussed at the General Synod of from 13th–17th May 2024. Although, in a survey of the church's academic members, 71% of priests supported the marriage of same-sex couples, its passage at the General Synod seems uncertain because it requires a three-quarters majority, which will be almost impossible to achieve.

§2. The Civil Effects of Marriage

1024. Marriage brings legal responsibilities to spouses. By law, spouses must act in the best interest of the family.[584] Marriage is, therefore, a partnership for the benefit of the family, in which both spouses participate according to their abilities and capabilities. The law also states that both should contribute to the maintenance of their spouse and children to the best of their ability.[585]

1025. The property of the spouses is private, i.e., each spouse owns his or her own property. The spouses may also have jointly acquired property. For example, housing is often purchased together. Each spouse is responsible for his or her own debts. The debts of one spouse cannot be recovered from the assets of the other spouse.[586]

584. For further detail, *see* Liisa Nieminen, *Perus- ja ihmisoikeudet ja perhe* (Fundamental and human rights and the family). (Helsinki: Talentum, 2013).
585. *See* the Marriage Act, Chapter 1, s. 2, para. 1.
586. Part II, Ch. 2, ss. 34–39.

1026. The spouse has a matrimonial right to the property of the other. Divorce is taken into account when family property is divided after divorce or death.[587] Marriage law means that they both receive the same amount of property. The division of matrimonial property is, in principle, as follows: the debts of each of the spouses are deducted, the remaining assets are added together, and the amount is divided equally (tasinko). Marriage law also imposes obligations on the spouse. For example, a spouse cannot sell most of his or her property without the permission of the other spouse.[588]

1027. Matrimonial property law does not apply to property that has been made subject to a prenuptial agreement. In this situation, it is usually agreed that a spouse is not entitled to the property of the other spouse. Thus, the spouses' property remains separate after the divorce and after the death of one of the spouses.

1028. If either of the spouses wants a divorce, he or she must apply to the local district court. The District Court does not investigate the reasons for the divorce or the relationship between the spouses, and a divorce is granted even if one of the spouses does not want the divorce.

1029. Both parents of a child or children must support their offspring. If the parents of the family divorce, a child is entitled to maintenance from the non-resident parent.[589] Parents can make a maintenance agreement with the municipal social welfare office for the services of a child-minder. If the parents cannot agree on the maintenance, the district court will issue its own decision.

§3. The Civil Impact of Religious Marriages Other Than Lutheran or Orthodox or Registered Religious Associations

1030. The right to solemnize marriages can be granted only to registered religious associations. The right to solemnize marriages is granted to associations and not to individuals:

> Concerning marriage – and also in wider sense – Sharia law plays no role in Finland. Especially in Muslim and some other ethnic communities, there have been cases of forced marriages. According to a study prepared by the Institute of Criminology and Legal Policy 2017, there are no exact figures on the number of forced marriages, but it is clear that they do occur. In practice, such marriages are conducted, for example, by exerting pressure on an under-age girl

587. Part IV, Ch. 2, ss. 98–103.
588. Part II, Ch. 2, s. 38.
589. Part III, Ch. 2, ss. 78–79.

living in Finland to be sent abroad to marry a man who may have been completely unknown previously to the girl. This may happen, for example, when a girl travels to visit the country of her family.[590]

1031. Forced marriage is defined as a violation of human rights in a number of international treaties, including the so-called Istanbul Convention on the Prevention of Domestic Violence. Finnish law on causing forced marriages can currently be punished as trafficking in human beings or coercion. However, Finnish law does not recognize a separate criminal offence for forced marriage, unlike, for example, in Swedish and Norwegian law.

1032. The Council of Europe and various human rights organizations have criticized Finland's current legislation as insufficient. Most recently, in early September 2019 the Council of Europe's Expert Group on Violence against Women and Domestic Violence (GREVIO), strongly recommended in its report that Finland should consider separate criminalization of forced marriages.

1033. During Prime Minister Sanna Marin's term of office (2019–2023), a development project hosted by the Ministry of Justice examined the criminalisation of forced marriage. At the same time, initial steps were taken towards a more comprehensive reform of the Finnish Criminal Code in order to base the criminal offence of rape on the absence of consent rather than the use of force. A Memorandum on the Punishability of Forcing a Person to Enter into Marriage, drawn up by the Ministry of Justice, was circulated for comments between 17 November 2021 and 14 January 2022. A total of 46 stakeholders issued an opinion or stated that they had no comment to add.

1034. The majority of those consulted considered it necessary to specify the current provisions of the Criminal Code or to add a separate provision on coercion into marriage to the Criminal Code. In its opinion, the Prosecutor's Office raised the possibility of introducing a reference to the provisions of the Criminal Code on trafficking and coercion in the Marriage Act. This could make the offence easier to detect, even if there is no specific criminal offence of forced marriage in the Criminal Code. Individual B (who wanted to conceal his identity) also stated in his opinion that if the criminalisation of forced marriage is necessarily to be more visible in the law, one option could be to provide for the criminalisation of forced marriage in a non-criminal law and to punish it under the trafficking or coercion sections of the Penal Code.

590. For further information on the types of forced marriage detected in Finland, *see* http://www.ihmiskauppa.fi/en/human_trafficking/forms_of_human_trafficking/forced_marriages. Accessed 2 Oct. 2019. This page no longer exists. *See* new website, https://ihmiskauppa.fi/en/. Accessed 9 Jan. 2024.

1035. Of the alternatives discussed in the memorandum, the most popular options were to add a separate provision to the Criminal Code and to specify the provision on trafficking in human beings laid down in Chapter 25, section 3 of the Criminal Code.

1036. Some of the stakeholders consulted felt that it was justified that 'marriage' should refer only to a legally valid marriage in the provisions concerning coercion into marriage, as proposed in the memorandum. On the other hand, some respondents considered that, in the context of the provisions concerning coercion into marriage, the concept of marriage should also cover religious unions that have not been concluded in a legally valid manner.

1037. Consultations (Memorandum of the Prosecutor's Office on the Punishability of Forcing a Person to Enter into Marriage VN/4063/202, 12 December 2021,[591], and Memorandum of the Ministry of Justice on the Punishability of Forcing a Person to Enter into Marriage, Description sheet 17 April 2023[592]) *did not lead to a separate criminalization of forced marriages.* Instead, on 15 February 2023 Parliament adopted an amendment to the Marriage Act permitting the dissolution of a forced marriage. The law was adopted by a vote of 125–36. No one abstained and 38 MPs were absent.

1038. The amendment (He 172/2021[593]) concerns the Marriage Act, the Code of Procedure and the Court Fees Act. The provisions adopted allow for the annulment of a marriage contracted by force. The law provides that a marriage must be annulled if the spouse has been forced to marry. The legal effects of an annulment are similar to those of a divorce, except that the civil status of the spouse at the time of the annulment is recorded in the civil status register.

1039. In future, a marriage contracted abroad when the spouses were under 18 years of age will be recognized only for a special reason if at least one of the spouses was resident in Finland at the time of the marriage.

1040. The bill on the annulment of forced marriages was linked to the Government Programme's reference to the annulment of forced marriages as part of the development of a secure rule of law and the improvement of the situation of victims of crime.

1041. The new Act on the Modification of Marriage (HE 484/2023 vp[594]) entered into force on 23 March 2023. Sections 27a and 27b of the Act state that (a) A marriage shall be annulled if the spouse has been forced into marriage and (b) The annulment of a marriage has the same legal effects as a divorce.

---

591. https://api.hankeikkuna.fi/asiakirjat/141ff90b-9cb5-4428-8fc0-14ab4e658e69/f0959a10-7f02-4e51-86bd-a504f71a0a60/LAUSUNTO_20211216145352.PDF.
592. https://julkaisut.valtioneuvosto.fi/handle/10024/164850.
593. https://www.eduskunta.fi/FI/vaski/HallituksenEsitys/Sivut/HE_172+2021.aspx.
594. https://www.edilex.fi/saadoskokoelma/20230484.pdf.

Part XI. Religion and Culture

Chapter 1. Religion and Art

§1. Religious Monuments

1042. Churches and religious communities in Finland own a considerable number of cultural and historical monuments. However, no separate law exists that is concerned solely with cultural monuments. The issue is instead handled as a part of law 247/2016, where it is stated that the Evangelical Lutheran Church is obliged to perform certain social tasks funded by the state.[595] Thus the Ministry of Education and Culture grants annual funding to the Evangelical Lutheran Church for statutory tasks related to a number of burial functions, various tasks related to the civil registry, *and the maintenance of culturally valuable buildings and movables.* The law does not, however, apply to religious monuments of other denominations and religious communities. The total funding in 2023 came to EUR 122,7 million, and, as provided in the law, the total amount of funding is increased annually in line with changes in the consumer price index. In 2022 the cost of maintaining cultural heritage, in the broadest sense, required EUR 23 million of this amount.[596]

1043. Chapter 14, section 5 of the Church Act (652/2023) provides for the protection of church buildings. The purpose of protecting a church building is to safeguard the church's built cultural environment as part of its cultural heritage, to preserve its distinctive character and special features, and to promote its culturally sustainable care and use. Church buildings constructed before 1917 are directly protected by law.[597] The Church Government may also propose a church building for protection that has been subsequently used for non-religious purposes if such action can be justified by the history of the building, its art, its building technology, or

595. Laki valtion rahoituksesta evankelis-luterilaiselle kirkolle eräisiin yhteiskunnallisiin tehtäviin (Government proposal HE 247/2016 to Parliament for Government funding of the Evangelical Lutheran Church for certain social tasks) 430/2015, s. 1.
596. *See* closer, https://www.finlex.fi/fi/esitykset/he/2023/20230047.
597. Church Act (652/2023), Ch. 3, s. 22.

other particular environmental values. The protection of the building also includes its interior fixtures, paintings and other works of art, and the immediate surroundings of the building.[598]

1044. Church buildings form a significant part of Finland's national building heritage. Churches and chapels were originally constructed using the best knowledge and materials of their own time. Most of the surviving medieval and seventeenth and eighteenth century cultural and historical artefacts are ecclesiastical property owned, operated, and maintained by parishes. Churches have developed building heritage strategies and materials aimed at managing the financial challenges posed by the need to renovate an ageing property stock.[599]

1045. The costs involved in maintaining the national cultural heritage of the Evangelical Lutheran Church are carefully controlled. The cost of heritage management includes renovations that help to preserve not only a building itself but also renovations that help to restore the character and historical authenticity of a building, including its surroundings, and engaging work methods and traditional building materials that are consistent with the original construction of the building.

§2. Religion in the Arts

1046. Ecclesiastical objects and church art form a significant part of Finland's cultural heritage. They help to connect people to the continuum of the generations, they carry the spiritual and cultural heritage of the churches, and they form an integral part of the history and cultural heritage of each community. Ecclesiastical artefacts and art increase both knowledge and an understanding of the history of a community and of the ecclesiastical identity of the churches and religious communities.

1047. The Church Act and the Church Order of the ELCF do not take a direct stand on the fine arts or musical performances. The works of art and objects in

598. According to the Church Government of ELCF, heritage work means: (a) maintenance and management of church buildings of value, including repairs, conservation, and restoration; (b) appropriate and good use and care of church art, objects, and other movable property; (c) preserving the cultural values of the cemeteries; and (d) monitoring the costs of heritage management. http://evl.fi => kulttuuriperintö+/Kulttuuriperintötyö.

599. For further detail, see the Church Government Strategy 2017 of the ELCF and the Cultural Heritage Strategy of the OCF 2023–2031, Suomen ortodoksisen kirkon kulttuuriperintöstrategia.pdf. These building heritage strategies are, however, fairly general. The publication issued by the Evangelical Lutheran Church 'Under One Roof '(Saman katon alle, Kirkkohallitus 2019) explicitly aims to manage change and, for example, to ensure that the churches, in particular, would be preserved and, where necessary, serve other needs of the congregation in addition to worship; *see* Kirkkohallitus 2019, e.g., pp. 21–24. For further detail, *see* Aleksi Heinilä, 'Kirkollisten rakennusten suojelu ja rakennussuojelua koskevien lakien keskinäiset suhteet' (Protection of church buildings and the interrelationship of laws concerning the protection of buildings). In: *Oikeustiede–Jurisprudentia-vuosikirja* (Law–Jurisprudence yearbook) Vol. 54, no LIV (2021), 65–139. Https://journal.fi/oikeustiede-jurisprudentia/issue/view/10602.

churches are particularly affected by archiving guidelines that date back to the 1686 Caroline Church Act.[600] The vicar, for his part, authorizes productions of the performing arts on church premises. Churches and religious communities also have some special rights in relation to copyright law; shorter musical works, for example, hymns and other musical compositions are protected by copyright. The special permission of the author will be needed when music is broadcast on Sunday services on TV or the radio. The composer may well also have the right to receive appropriate remuneration.[601]

1048. Many parishes have art councils that, in cooperation with the local Church Council, decide on the art to be obtained for the church. Occasionally, there has been lively discussion in Finland about the kind of art most suitable for the churches for instance, such as an altar painting, a mural, or a simply woollen wall-hanging. Thus, discussion will centre on the identity of an appropriate artist from whom an artwork can be commissioned on behalf of a church, including such questions as the fame of the artist versus the intrinsic quality of the item itself. Sometimes it is also important to discuss whether church art differs from other art, and if so, what makes it different. There may also be discussion of whether the cross or an image of Christ, for example, needs to be present in the art displayed in a church, rather than a decision based simply on taste or appropriateness in general. Without taking a closer look at these issues, it can be stated that the meanings associated with objects are stratified, changing over time, and may convey conflicting meanings.

1049. The performing arts have occasionally resulted in legal cases. The only major case involved a 1969 work by the pop artist *Harro Koskinen* in which he depicted a crucified pig-like Jesus with a halo around his head.[602] The pig affair surrounding the 'Pig Messiah' is remembered mainly for its blasphemy charge, which eventually led to the imposition of fines on Koskinen and his exhibitors.[603]

1050. Finally, it is difficult to estimate how much of their income the major churches use in support of cultural activities.

---

600. *Kircko-Laki ja Ordningi* 1686/1986 (Church Law and Order 1686). (Helsinki: Suomalaisen kirjallisuuden seura, 1986) 52, Ch. 16 §1 and Ch. 17 §301. Section 145 required the parish priest to take care of all the movable and immovable property of the church. Later, the disposal of documents relating to the destruction of archival material, in particular movable property, is mentioned in the 1967 Archives Regulations. The churches' archive rule of 1985 also pays special attention to the cataloguing of ecclesiastical objects such as communion items, church textiles, works of art, furniture, candlesticks, vases, etc.
601. Copyright Act 404/1961.
602. The work has been owned by the Finnish National Gallery since 1990 and is now housed in the collections of the Museum of Contemporary Art Kiasma in Helsinki.
603. KKO 178/90 V.D.

Chapter 2. Religion and the Media

1051. The fundamental norms regulating the legal status of the media and religion in Finland are established in the Constitution, in section 12 of the Constitutional Act ('Freedom of expression and the right of access to information') and in section 11 of the same Act ('Freedom of religion and conscience').

1052. The wide scope of the Freedom of Expression Act also regulates religious communications. It has a large field of application in the sense that, on the one hand, freedom of expression is not bound to any particular method of communication (neutrality as to instruments). In addition, through the Constitutional Act, the regulations dealing with freedom of expression are applied to all kinds of communication technology, both those currently used and those to be introduced in the future. On the other hand, the scope of the Freedom of Expression Act has been understood to include all kinds of data, opinions, and other messages, irrespective of their content or purpose (neutrality as to content and purpose). Moreover, with regard to the scope of the Freedom of Expression Act, it is essential that no distinction is made in Finland between political, *religious, artistic,* scientific, commercial, entertainment-related, or other messages. Instead, the regulations are applied to all forms of communication.

§1. The Press

1053. In the press, freedom of expression is seen to be realized most fully when journalism is free and truthful and treats different social groups equally.[604] The independence of the mass media has been understood to be safeguarded best when legislation only defines the exterior framework for the use of freedom of expression and by leaving responsibility for content to the media themselves. There are no principles or guidelines concerning the access of religious groups to the press or the possibility of press consultation with religious groups. However, it is obvious that the larger newspapers take into account religious matters when sharing responsibilities among their editorial departments.

1054. Besides juridical norms, the operation of the media is regulated by what is termed *self-regulation*, an autonomic control seeking to maintain standards of quality in communication. The Council for Mass Media in Finland (*Julkisen Sanan Neuvosto*) and its resolutions regulate those media that have signed the basic treaty of the Council. The Council for Mass Media in Finland is not a court of justice nor does it exercise public authority. However, its decisions are carefully observed in

604. For further details on this, *see* Christina Snellman, 'Suomalaisten sanomalehtien sananvapaus 1990-luvulla – oikeudellisten normien ja eettisten sääntöjen sääntelemänä' (Freedom of expression in Finnish newspapers in the 1990s – governed by legal norms and ethical rules). (University of Helsinki: Master's thesis, 2000). *See also* Veli-Pekka Viljanen, 'Onko sananvapaus poliittinen persuoikeus?' (Is freedom of expression a political right?) In *Heikki Kulla & alii., Viestintäoikeus.* (Communications Law) (Helsinki: WSOY, 2002).

Finland. They form a soft law in the regulation of the freedom of expression and practices which may have significance even in court in situations involving interpretation of freedom of expression provisions. The Council for Mass Media in Finland expresses in its decisions what it considers to correspond to journalistic ethics. Its decisions express what customary law in freedom of expression is.[605]

1055. There are several differing opinions concerning the meaningfulness and efficiency of the self-regulation of the mass media. Dissatisfaction with the press's own capacity to do so, and opportunities to guarantee a responsible use of words, have led to demands for increasing the efficiency of official control. In addition, in Finland, there is occasionally debate about the efficiency of the Council for Mass Media and the competence of its decisions. The establishment of a new kind of institution called the Press Secretary, i.e., an organ monitoring the press, has been alluded to.

§2. Internet, Radio and Television

1056. The Internet and the opportunity it has created for new uses of freedom of expression also raise the possibility of misusing this same freedom.[606] The presentation of baseless claims to a large audience is technically easier through the Internet than through traditional media. Juridical regulation often follows only at a late stage in the development, adopting development processes that have already taken place. This is also happening with the Printing Responsibility Act, which became outdated and impractical with the advent of the Internet. The Internet and other new communication technologies have been taken into account in the new Freedom of Expression Bill which is intended to replace the Printing Responsibility Act, the Radio Responsibility Act, and the Cable Broadcasting Act. The bill drafted by the Freedom of Expression Commission assumes the principle of neutrality regarding instruments, targeting all dissemination of information with the same kind of regulation, irrespective of the distribution technology.

1057. Already the Radio and Television Broadcasting Act (744/1998) has reformed the regulation of electronic communication and abolished the Radio Equipment Act (8/1927) and the Cable Broadcasting Act (307/1987) which earlier regulated the licence system of television and radio broadcasting. According to the new Act, nowadays broadcasting is subject to licence, i.e., the exercise of television and radio broadcasting through radio waves freely propagating in space. However, cable broadcasting and other television and radio broadcasting no longer require a

605. Juridically, the basic treaty of the Council for Mass Media in Finland and journalistic ethics do not bind the hands of those who have not signed the Council's basic treaty. However, it can be seen that deviation from practices created by the Council would require clear justification in order to be acceptable.
606. For further details on this, *see* Part XVI. *Data Law.*

licence but only the provision of a notice to the Finnish Communications Regulatory Authority. The Finnish Broadcasting Company (*Oy Yleisradio Ab*) may lawfully carry out television and radio broadcasting directly without a licence. The reform has thus led to the abolition of the licence regulation contemplated earlier in the Cable Broadcasting Act and has preserved the licence system only in the field of broadcasting under the regime of the new Act.[607]

1058. A broadcasting licence is granted by the Council of State, which, according to the Television and Radio Broadcasting Act's §10, must in its consideration of the licence seek to promote freedom of expression and to safeguard the versatility of programming and the needs of special audience groups. Moreover, it must take into account in its entirety the television and radio broadcasting being carried out in the respective areas.

1059. The Finnish Broadcasting Company (*Oy Yleisradio Ab*) has indeed also been largely responsible for religious radio and television programming. Radio devotions, along with radio worship services, represent the oldest tradition in spiritual programming in the Finnish Broadcasting Company. The first morning devotion was broadcast on the radio in March 1932. The Finnish Broadcasting Company has transmitted the morning devotion practically every weekday morning for seventy years.[608] The Finnish Broadcasting Company also broadcasts on television the acts of worship of various churches and religious communities. Moreover, some regional local radio stations also broadcast religious programmes.

1060. In summary, it can be stated that the Finnish approach to regulating the communication of religion in the media is based on the wide sphere of application of the Constitution's Freedom of Expression Act (Constitutional Act §12). This sphere of application has been understood to include all kinds of data, opinions, and

607. Manninen (1999, 396) points out that radio and television broadcasting being subject to licence does not unreservedly fit into the framework prohibiting prior hindrance, which is confirmed by the constitutional Freedom of Expression Act when it refers to the regulation of broadcasting. On the other hand, the preliminary works of the Reform of Basic Rights, the Committee on the Constitution's earlier statement of practice (Committee on the Constitution 8/1961 Parliament, Committee on the Constitution 2/1986 Parliament), has led to the understanding that the Freedom of Expression Act does not prevent the preservation of the licence system in the area of electronic communication, if the necessity of regulation by licence can be justified in an acceptable way from the perspective of the materialization of freedom of expression. In fact, the licence system can be considered as a means of safeguarding the widest possible practical materialization of freedom of expression in broadcasting. In broadcasting, regulation by licence may also be required in order to distribute the radio frequencies equitably between various broadcasting agencies (HE 309/1993 Parliament, 57–58). Sami Manninen, 'Sananvapaus ja julkisuus, PL 12 §' (Freedom of expression and publicity). In *Pekka Hallberg, Heikki Karapuu, Tuomas Ojanen, Martin Scheinin, Kaarlo Tuori, Veli-Pekka Viljanen, Perusoikeudet* (Fundamental rights). (WSOYpro : 2nd, revised edition, 2011), 459–491.

608. For more information on this, *see* Heikki-Tapio Nieminen's doctoral dissertation on the '*Morning Radio Devotionals on Finnish Radio', The structure and content of Lutheran morning broadcasts transmitted by the Finnish Broadcasting Company – YLE between 1932 and 1997* (Suomalainen radiohartaus: Yleisradiossa vuosina 1932–1997 lähetettyjen luterilaisten aamuhartauksien rakenne ja sisältö). (Helsinki: STKSJ 221, 1999). *Diss.*

other messages, irrespective of their content and purpose. As a result, the churches and religious communities enjoy broad legal opportunities to communicate their message to the public. In Finland the dissemination of the Christian message is carried out mainly through the church-related press, public service radio and television broadcasting, local radio broadcasting, and the Internet. The ELCF also has its own Church Communication Centre which disseminates information about church-related matters to the press and also monitors what the press writes about the church. Indeed, in Finland, the churches have responded actively to the development of mass communication. The churches have also pronounced the birth of the modern information society and the ethical problems caused by it.[609]

609. For more details on this, *see* Raine Haikarainen's doctoral dissertation *Informaatiosta kommunikaatioon: ekumeeninen keskustelu viestinnästä 1948–2000.* (From Information to Communication. Ecumenical Discussion on Communication, 1948–2000). (Helsinki: STKSJ 234, 2002). *Diss.*

Chapter 3. Religion and Civil Society

1061. Religious communities are a basic part of Finnish civil society. Civil society consists mainly of the following actors and entities: (a) civic activities (*kansalaistoiminta*); (b) organizational activities (*järjestötoiminta*); (c) churches and religious organizations; (d) trade union activities;[610] (d) political parties;[611] (e) small-scale cooperative activities; (f) foundations; and (g) free adult education.

1062. Civic and organizational activities form a natural part of civil society in all of the EU countries, not least in Finland, where, in terms of their volume and importance, they form the core of civil society. The major part of Finnish civic activity is performed by NGOs. In addition to registered associations, there are many unregistered groups, clubs, and people's associations, all of them voluntary associations of citizens.

1063. From the point of view of Finnish civil society the organization of religious activities has its own national characteristics. As stated previously, the State and the Church are formally separate. The present-day ELCF is clearly a separate institution from the state, along with its own legal status. However, the Evangelical Lutheran Church and the Orthodox Church also have their own law, the Church Law, and the statutory right to collect church tax. As a result, *their extensive parish activities are excluded from Finnish civil society*, although many of the parish activities, including diaconal work by volunteers, are the most typical activities within civil society. From the perspective of the law, it is in fact more important to identify the specific position of religious communities, and their rights and duties, in light of public law. For the ELCF and the OCF, as communities governed by public law, the question of fundamental rights entails an active responsibility for the implementation of fundamental civil rights within their own communities.[612]

1064. Other churches, including the Pentecostals, the Free Church, the Mormons, the Jehovah's Witnesses, etc., are instead regarded as part of civil society since their activities are organized mainly in the form of associations. Similarly,

---

610. In all EU countries trade union activities are not considered to be part of civil society. In Finland the interpretation is not inconsistent due to the fact that the trade union movement has a major influence on Finnish legislation and, in addition to collective agreements, concludes profit-making agreements at national level with employers' organizations and the national government. However, the trade union movement is made up of trade unions with their local branches and members, which is why they are organized in the same way as other Finnish associations. Like other associations, they also have members and volunteers.

611. In many countries, parties are also excluded from the definition of civil society. This could also be done in Finland since parties occupy a special position in the parliamentary system. The parties nominate candidates for election, form a government, and nominate representatives for state and municipal elected bodies. However, the local and regional divisions of parties are organized in the same way as other associations. Their activities are also governed by the Associations Act. In this way, parties in Finland can be considered on good grounds to belong to civil society. They represent the political sphere of civil society.

612. *See* above, Part IV, Ch. 1. The European Convention of Human Rights and ICCPR-agreement, A. *General Relevance.*

civil society encompasses the activities of various Christian organizations such as children's and youth organizations, the Missionary Society, the Seamen's Church abroad, and revival movements within the Church.

Chapter 4. Religion and Public Debate

1065. In the ongoing public debate, religions – and religions per se – are a topic that is widely debated in Finland. Religion is generally viewed positively in the media, especially during church festivities such as Christmas and Easter.

1066. Over the last few years three main clusters of topics related to religion have emerged in the public debate. First, there has been widespread discussion of the cultural significance of religion in Finland. This has raised a variety of questions. Are Christmas hymns, plays, and customs in our national culture possible in the public space? Do they consist of religious or cultural heritage? Do they violate the beliefs of a non-religious person?[613] The public debate has also raised the question of whether it is part of the mission of state schools to provide religion instruction and how this aim can be achieved in a multi-religious situation. Of particular concern have been the practical difficulties encountered by the school actors in implementing the required teaching.

1067. A range of solutions to these issues have been found in various EU countries. In France, for example, all religions have been transferred equally to the private space. According to this view, the public space is impartial and religiously neutral. Faith can be practised at home or on religious premises and does not belong to the sphere of the state. The contrast in Finland is noticeable. The Finnish starting point has been to promote positive religious freedom, and hence it is the duty of the State to promote the practice of all religions on an equal basis. The modern multicultural situation makes no difference. The way this 'official interpretation' passes through the media varies greatly.

1068. Contributions to the debate outside Finland, such as the controversy surrounding the display of the crucifix in public space in Italy[614] and France and the question of the use of the Muslim veil have contributed to the Finnish debate. How do we address the role played by various religious symbols and customs in the public space in a multi-cultural context? Are the cultural meanings of religion excluded from the public space in the name of equality?

1069. The debate on female circumcision has also come onto the agenda. Finnish law does not permit the practice of circumcision by granting separate rules, nor

613. The most recent case is the decision reached by the Deputy Ombudsman Pasi Pölönen, in which he outlined that an elementary school closing ceremony (a Christmas party in the city of Kouvola) should not be held in a church. Pölönen's criticism focused on the fact that the school's religious celebration was organized as a religious event. Several politicians criticized the Deputy Ombudsman's decision. However, the Church Council of the Evangelical Lutheran Church of Finland understood the policy of the Deputy Ombudsman and pointed out that 'events held at Christian churches should be religious and voluntary in nature'. For further details, *see* the news coverage provided by *Helsingin Sanomat* (HS) news 13 Nov. 2019 (p. A 8).

614. With regard to the *Soili Lautsi* case, *see* Part IX., Ch. 1. Religious Education in Public and Private Schools, §1. *Religious Education in Public Schools*. Lautsi appealed to Strasbourg in 2006 when her case was thrown out by Italy's constitutional court.

does it prohibit the practice explicitly. Instead, with regard to the religious circumcision of female minors, the Articles of the penal code apply to all abuse or gross misconduct. In addition, the circumcision of male minors has occasionally triggered intense public debate.

1070. Another significant topic has been that of immigration and the public and political debate directly or more loosely related to religion as a factor involved in the immigration. Since the migrant crisis that arose in Europe in the spring 2015, and since the Westminster Bridge attack (22 March 2017) and the London Bridge and Borough Market attacks (3 June 2017), the public debate has also focused on the possibility of religiously motivated terrorism originating with the asylum seekers who in recent years have arrived in Finland from conflict areas of the world. The first Islamist terrorist attack took place in Finland (in Turku) on 20 August 2017, carried out by an individual actor who had been radicalized within a very short period of time.[615] This understandably and inevitably grew into one of the most heated discussions of the year.

1071. In the public debate violent religious extremism is seen in Finland mainly in terms of Islam. In part, this also concerns what are frequently regarded as extreme right-wing groups that possess strong anti-immigration sentiments. In this context, however, it is worth mentioning that the tension between religion and secularity does not normally play a significant role. For Finns, religion is a private affair and is not of great importance in any political debate; tensions nevertheless arise more frequently from a neglect of religion in the public domain.[616]

1072. A third main topic has touched on issues related to sexual ethics and sexual harassment. First, it should be noted that the law of gender-neutral marriage, which came into effect on 1 March 2017, has divided the Evangelical Lutheran Church internally and, to some extent, also the general public. And it should also be noted that the numerous sexual abuses that have occurred widely within church revival movements have undoubtedly formed part of the agenda of the mass media.

615. For more detail, *see* Matti Kotiranta, 'Securitization of Religious Freedom: Religion and the Limits of State Control in Finland'. In Merilin Kiviorg (ed.), *Securitization of Religious Freedom: Religion and the Limits of State Control in Europe* (Granada: Comares 2020), 2020, 199–218.
616. *Ibid.*

Part XII. Religious Assistance in Public Institutions

Chapter 1. General Principles

1073. There is a long history of religious services and religious assistance in the public institutions in Finland.[617] The national churches, the Lutheran and the Orthodox, have, as public entities, the right to provide religious assistance in the armed forces, penal institutions, hospitals, and other public institutions.

1074. The Constitution does not in any way regulate or determine religious assistance in the Public Institutions. Religious activities within the armed forces, penal institutions and hospitals are governed by the ordinary law, church law, and regulations between the State and churches.

1075. In this context, it is noteworthy to add that it is not only the law but mainly the historical reasons that, through the course of history, have given the Lutheran Church and the Orthodox Church a special position on pastoral care in hospitals (Hospital Chaplaincy) and pastoral work with the defence forces (Military Chaplaincy) and in prisons.

Defence Forces

1076. The status of religious assistance in the defence forces is regulated by the following laws: The Defence Forces Act (551/2007), the Church Act (652/2023) and the Church Order (657/2023), the Government Decree on the Defence Forces (1319/2007), the Presidential Decree on Military and Service Values, and the Armed Forces Emblem (1490/2007).

1077. The military priests are appointed by the Commander of the Defence Forces. The Field Bishop is appointed by the President of the Republic in conjunction with the Government (Act on the Defence Forces 551/2007, § 38). The Church Order (657/2023), the Government Decree on the Armed Forces (1319/2007), and

617. Part XII. Religious Assistance in Public Institutions is based on a revised and expanded version of an article: Matti Kotiranta, 'Religious Assistance in Public Institutions: Finland'. In Ringolds Balodis & Miguel Rodrígues Blanco (eds), *Religious Assistance in Public Institutions – Assistance spirituelle dans les services publics* (Granada: Comares, 2016), 105–117.

the Armed Forces Act (551/2007) define the nomination practice and the role of the military clergy as part of the church administration.

1078. When serving as a priest, the military priest is under the command of the field bishop. The Field Bishop directs and oversees the spiritual work of the Armed Forces. The Field Bishop belongs to the Archdiocese (Turku/Åbo) and, along with the other military priest, to the Diocese within whose territory he is actually employed (Church Order 657/2023, Ch. 7, § 8, para. 3).

1079. Regarding the religious assistance of the Evangelical Lutheran Church, more detailed instructions are specified in the Church Order.

1080. The status of priestly positions in the Defence Forces is laid down in the Church Order, Chapter 8, section 16:

> The military priest is subordinate to the field bishop in the provision of the priesthood. The powers of the Diocese Chapter in connection with the military priest's office are laid down in Chapter 7, section 8, and in the Church Act, Chapter 7, sections 4 and 5.

Penal Institutions

1081. The responsibility for arranging pastoral care in penal institutions lies with the state. Because the state is responsible for the religious freedom of the prisoners, the Correctional Services Department are supposed to arrange the prison conditions so that the prisoners have effective access to worship and other religious events and can meet a qualified representative of their own religion.

1082. At present, the posts of prison priests belong to the staff of the Correctional Services Department in the administrative branch of the Ministry of Justice and the positions of prison deacons to the staff of the ELCF in the dioceses. The salaries of prison priests are paid by the Correctional Services Department, while those of deacons are paid by the church.

1083. In the current model, the qualification of prison priests and deacons is determined by the (Lutheran) confession affiliation. A priest or deacon should be an employee of the ELCF, with the exception of the Orthodox prison priesthood, which requires a qualification as a priest of the OCF. In sum, it can be stated, that the status of priestly positions in the penal institutions is laid down in greater detail in the Church Order, Chapter 8, section 17, which reads:

> The prison chaplain shall be subject to the jurisdiction of the diocese chapter in respect of the duties of the priesthood.
>
> The office of a priest established in a prison shall be filled by the Diocese Chapter after he or she has applied for the post and obtained the opinion of the applicants from the relevant authority. If necessary, the Diocese Chapter shall appoint a temporary administrator and a senior official.

1084. Compared to other European systems – in Sweden, England, Wales and the Netherlands – the pastoral care in prisons is organized by the various professions on a full-time, part-time, and part-time basis. The Dutch model also takes into account the spiritual needs of unbelievers. However, the religious diversity of prisoners in these countries is significantly higher than in Finland, and even in the Nordic countries the situation of prisoners on religious grounds is remarkably homogeneous: Christianity and the Evangelical Lutheran Church as a religious background for prisoners are more typical than in the case of the general population.[618]

1085. According to the *Report on the Practice of Religion in Prisons 2015*, the experience of inter-church cooperation has been largely good, and the cooperation is extensive and appropriate. The religious practice of Muslim prisoners is hampered by the absence of a central representative body in Finland that would allow for Muslim prisoners' spokespersons or representatives from some Muslim communions. According to the Report, the majority of Muslim prisoners have in fact been in discussions with an Evangelical Lutheran priest and have been pleased with the support they have received.[619]

Hospitals

1086. According to the *Act on the status and rights of patients* (785/1992), a hospital chaplain is a bystander in the care community because he or she is not a health care professional and does not carry out nursing work. The hospital priest is an employee of the Church and also abides by the Church Law and the Church Order.

618. *Report on the Practice of Religion in Prisons* (Uskonnonharjoittaminen vankiloissa – Selvitys uskonnonharjoittamiseen vankiloissa liittyvistä kysymyksistä). (Helsinki, 2015), 81–92.
619. *Ibid.*, 91.

Chapter 2. Institutions

§1. A Question of Clarification – What Does the Concept 'Chaplain' Mean in the Finnish Context

1087. Historically, the Finnish State has not sought to organize any chaplaincy. The model of a chaplaincy in public institutions in Finland has never really been planned for. No attempts have been made on a constitutional or governmental level to reach any proposals or comprehensive decisions on the notion of a chaplaincy. Instead, the State has left it to the major churches to organize chaplaincies in public institutions.

1088. There is no single Finnish word for the phenomenon.[620] The Finnish words 'sairaalasielunhoito' (Hospital Chaplaincy – literally Pastoral Care in Hospitals), or 'sotilassielunhoito' (Military Chaplaincy – literally Pastoral Care/Work with the defence forces) or 'vankilapappi' (Prison Chaplain) have been translated into English simply as chaplaincy, but they don't cover the whole meaning of the concept of a chaplaincy, i.e., in the way that 'chaplaincy' is understood, for example, in the Anglican world.[621]

1089. Nevertheless, there are – in Finland as well as in other countries – chaplains within the public institutions, in the defence forces, in hospitals, in prisons, and so on. To a large extent, 'the development of chaplaincy' in Finland mirrors the religious development that the country as whole has undergone, from a predominantly Evangelical Lutheran country towards a modern society characterized by diversity in religions and in non-religious beliefs.[622]

1090. As mentioned above, Finland has, no comprehensive legal or factual perspective on chaplaincy or priesthood. The Constitution of Finland or the Government Statutes do not contain any specific provisions addressing the issue. In

620. This is similarly so with the Swedish term 'institutionssjälavård' – literally 'soul cure in institutions'. *See* Lars Friedner's report Chaplaincy – Sweden. In Ringolds Balodis & Miguel Rodrígues Blanco (eds), *Religious Assistance in Public Institutions – Assistance spirituelle dans les services publics* (Granada: Comares, 2016), 349–356.

621. For further detail, *see* the online edition of the Oxford English Dictionary, www.oed.com, ***Chaplain n.*** a1100: **1.** *gen.* The priest, clergyman or minister of a chapel *n.*; in Middle English a chantry priest. 2. *spec.* A clergyman who conducts religious service in the private chapel of a sovereign, lord, or high official, of a castle, garrison, embassy, college, school, workhouse, prison, cemetery, or other institution, or in the household of a person of rank or quality, in a legislative chamber, regiment, ship, etc. The OED adds: 'Thirty-six clergymen of the Church of England, and six of the Church of Scotland have the office and title of *Chaplain in Ordinary to her* (or *his*) *Majesty*; there are also several *Honorary Chaplains*; and among other official positions are those of *Chaplain to the Forces*, *Chaplain of the Fleet*, *Army Chaplains*, *Navy Chaplains*, etc., etc.'

Chaplaincy, *n.* a1745*:* **Etymology:** < chaplain *n.* + -cy *suffix*: a modern term, which probably originated in the Army; compare *captaincy*, etc. The office or position of a chaplain; = the earlier **chaplainship *n*.**

622. *See* Kääriäinen, Kimmo & Kati Niemelä & Kimmo Ketola, *Religion in Finland. Decline, Change and Transformation of Finnish Religiosity*. (Jyväskylä: Publications of the Church Research Institute 54, 2005).

addition, there is no national recognition or regulation concerning the various forms of chaplaincy in the major churches and religious communities mentioned in the Freedom of Religion Act (453/2003). The Constitution establishes only the freedom of religion and conscience as stated in §11 of the Finnish Constitution. Nor does the Freedom of Religion Act specify the character of chaplaincy in any way.

1091. In Finland, as in other countries, there is significant variation concerning forms of chaplaincy among the various Churches and religious communities. Hence, no all-embracing view of chaplaincy in Finland can be provided in this context. Suffice it to say that the traditional Churches, i.e., the Finnish Orthodox Church and the Catholic Church in Finland, have interpreted chaplaincy under the regulatory level of the Church Acts (Canon Law) and Church Orders (§2 of Orth. Church) within the traditional threefold office of bishops, priests, and deacons.

1092. In turn, the **Church Act** (Chapter 7, §1. para. 1 and 2) and the **Church Order** (Chapter 7, §1 and § 2) of the ELCF do not use the term 'chaplaincy' but prefer such concepts as 'ministry' or 'minister's office'. In addition, in discussions of the positions in the ELCF, a distinction is made between a 'religious office' (pappisvirka) and a 'minister's office' (papinvirka).[623] A religious office (with its full responsibilities and rights) is received upon ordination and is governed by church law and statutes concerning the rights of the office. A minister's office refers to employment for which anyone receiving a salary, and is similar in many ways to the position of a civil servant).

1093. There are no court decisions or other legal sources in Finland that regulate the various forms of chaplaincy practised by the major churches or religious communities. The only factor that may affect the issue is that if an office-holder (including a minister/chaplain) refuses to carry out certain obligations, this may be interpreted in Finland purely on the grounds of administrative law concerning neglect of duty. In Finnish Supreme Court praxis, a person (chaplain) who is employed by a church or other religious community, and finds him/herself in conflict with that church or community on an issue of belief or conviction, may be deemed to have exercised his/her individual religious freedom in the act of taking up such employment. Once s/he has done so, s/he cannot thereafter appeal to the concept of freedom of religion in order to depart from the tenets of that religious community.[624]

---

623. For further detail on the religious office, *see* Jyrki Knuutila, 'Kirkkolainsäädäntö ja kirkon virka Suomessa kanonisesta oikeudesta vuoden 1993 kirkkolakiin ja -järjestykseen' (Church legislation and church office in Finland, from canonical law to church law and order, 1993). *Edilex* 15.9.2010 (www.edilex.fi/ artikkelit/7258).

624. This is also suggested in the statement made by the Parliamentary Constitutional Committee to the Parliamentary Administrative Committee (PeVL 22/1997) on the bill for alterations to §16c of the law on the Orthodox Church in Finland:

> '– Every person enjoys the fundamental right of freedom of speech, although more precise regulations regarding this are provided in law. It is in the nature of the offices mentioned in the

§2. Chaplaincy in Hospitals

History, Status, Appointment, Funding etc.

1094. The first hospitals – devoted to the care of people suffering from leprosy – were established in Finland in the Middle Ages. In the old capital, Turku, the Hospital of St George (Turun Pyhän Yrjänän hospitaalissa), which was first mentioned in records in 1355, had room for some fifty patients to be treated, while at St. Magdalena's Hospital in Vyborg (Viipurin Maria Magdaleenan hospitaali), which was founded in 1475, the capacity was a little higher. Both cities also had almshouses (vaivaistupa), i.e., the Houses of the Holy Spirit, which took care of the poor and the sick. In Helsinki a small hospital was established shortly after the foundation of the city by Gustav Vasa in 1550, which was first mentioned in the records in 1555.[625] Hospitals were run by the Church, which at that time meant the Roman Catholic Church. Finland, being under Swedish rule, shared the same Church Orders (1571, Kyrko-Ordning) and Church Acts (1686) as Sweden. In this system every hospital had a chaplain. The system remained after the Reformation up until 1809, when Finland was incorporated into the Russian Empire as an autonomous Grand Duchy.[626]

1095. The first Church Law of Finland, which was issued when Finland had become an autonomous Grand Duchy of the Russian Empire, was promulgated in 1869. The law was in force for almost a hundred years, until 1964. It contained 8 provisions (§62, §92, §95, §96, §97, §154, §159, §249) covering the treatment of the sick.

1096. In the nineteenth century, the number of hospitals grew rapidly. Following Finland's independence, pastoral care was organized by Evangelical Lutheran parishes as early as in 1925. However, it was not until the 1940s that modern pastoral care was not organized in hospitals and other medical institutions.

---

bill that their holders should teach in accordance with the precepts of the Orthodox Church and that they should be aware of this fact when taking up such an office.'

It is similarly noted in the statement on disciplinary proceedings that:

'– It should also be said that matters concerned with the right to remain in public office have been demonstrated in the practices of the Human Rights Commission to lie beyond the scope of Article 6 of the European Convention on Human Rights.'

625. Arno Forsius, 'Descriptions of the History of Medicine', Leprosy, *see* http://www.saunalahti.fi/arnoldus/haklaa.html.
626. For further detail, *see* Matti Kotiranta, 'Religious Assistance in Public institutions: Finland'. In Ringolds Balodis & Miguel Rodrígues Blanco (eds), *Religious Assistance in Public Institutions – Assistance spirituelle dans les services publics* (Granada: Comares, 2016), 111–114.

1097. Training in pastoral care and counselling has been offered since 1952, when the first training course for parish pastors in providing marital counselling was offered. The training of hospital chaplains was developed at the same time as the training of family counsellors.[627]

1098. Nowadays, the hospital chaplaincy is maintained by the ELCF and works hand in hand with the healthcare system.[628] The aim of health care is the promotion of health, the prevention and treatment of disease, and the alleviation of suffering. The objective of pastoral care is to address the religious, spiritual, and life-view questions of the sick and those who are suffering. A pastoral caregiver respects the human dignity, beliefs, and integrity of the patient regardless of his/her background or view of life.[629] In order to work as a hospital chaplain, one must pass an aptitude test and complete a specialization programme approved by the Church. Self-determination is clearly stated in the Constitution of Finland and in the Act on the Status and Rights of Patients.

1099. The ELCF has 120 full-time and 17 part-time hospital chaplains at the present time, with more than half of them women. In addition, more than half of hospital chaplains also act as supervisors.

1100. In 2022 hospital chaplains had 25,873 pre-arranged encounters and 8,221 occasional encounters. They made 3,464 on-call or visiting visits and held groups on 916 occasions. Hospital chaplains held 2,471 devotions or prayer meetings and 1,234 private communion meetings. Hospital chaplains blessed 847 people and baptised 102 infants.[630]

1101. Unit of Diaconia and Pastoral Counselling (Kirkon diakonian ja sielunhoidon yksikkö, KDS) is an expert and cooperative body that plans and develops pastoral care in hospitals, institutions and outpatient care. It maintains contact with the healthcare field. It belongs to the Department for Parish Services at the Office of the National Church Council of the ELCF, and it is a member of the *European Network of Healthcare Chaplaincy.*

627. For more detail, *see* Pirjo Hakala, *Learning by Caring. A Follow-Up Study of Participants in a Specialized Training Program in Pastoral Care and Counseling.* (Helsinki, 2000), 11. *Diss.*
628. The latest stage in the detailed specialization of the hospital chaplaincy is represented by the document *Hospital Chaplaincy Specialisation Program,* which was accepted by the Bishops' Council on 13 Sep. 2011.
629. *Principles for Hospital Chaplaincy* were accepted by the National Church Council in its the plenary session on 17 Aug. 2011.
630. *See*, https://evl.fi/plus/seurakuntaelama/sielunhoito/sairaalasielunhoito/kirkon-sairaalasielunhoito-numeroina/. The statistics on the activities of the Church's hospital mental health services for 2022 can be found at https://www.kirkontilastot.fi/viz.php?id=208.

I. Main Legal Components of the Act on the Status and Rights of Patients (785/1992)

1102. According to the Act on the Status and Rights of Patients *(785/1992)*, Chapter 2, section 3, paragraph 1, every person who is permanently resident in Finland is without discrimination entitled to the health and medical care required by his/her state of health within the resources available to healthcare at the time in question. Concerning the right to treatment of persons who are staying in Finland temporarily, what has specially been provided for or what has been agreed upon reciprocally between states shall apply.

1103. Provisions on the obligation of municipalities and the state to provide healthcare services are laid down, in addition, in the Act on Primary Healthcare, the Specialized Medical Care Act, the Healthcare Act (1326/2010), the Communicable Diseases Act (583/1986), the Mental Health Act (1116/1990), the Act on Criminal Sanctions Agency and the Act on Arranging Healthcare in the Defence Forces (322/1987). (1335/2010).

1104. The second and third paragraphs of section 3 of the same Act (785/1992) are of great importance for religious freedom and human rights. Paragraph 2 reads:

> The patient has a right to good quality healthcare and medical care. The care of the patient has to be arranged, and he/she shall also otherwise be treated, so that his/her human dignity is not violated and so that his/her conviction and privacy are respected.

1105. And paragraph 3 continues:

> The mother tongue, individual needs, and culture of the patient have to be taken into account as far as possible in his/her care and other treatment.

II. The Law on the Patient's Autonomy

1106. Chapter 2, section 6, paragraph 1 of the Act *(785/1992)* states that the patient has to be treated in mutual understanding with him/her. If the patient refuses a certain treatment or measure, he/she has to be treated, as far as possible, in other medically acceptable ways in mutual understanding with him/her.

1107. Paragraph 2 sharpens the content of self-determination when it states:

> If an adult patient, because of mental disturbance or mental retardation or for other reason, cannot decide on the treatment given to him/her, the legal representative or a family member or other close person of the patient has to be heard before making an important decision concerning treatment to assess the kind of treatment that would be in accordance with the patient's wishes. If this

matter cannot be assessed, the patient has to be given treatment that can be considered to be in accordance with his/her personal interests.

1108. When a patient is incapable of making an independent decision regarding his/her state of health, paragraph 4 of the same Section shall apply:

> Provisions on treatment given irrespective of the will of the patient are included in the Mental Health Act (1116/1990), the Act on Social Work with Substance Abusers (41/1986), the Communicable Diseases Act (583/1986), and in the Act on Special Care for the Mentally Handicapped (519/1977).

III. Objection to Medical Treatment of Adults

1109. In Finland, an adult always has the right to refuse all or part of a medical treatment. The cause may be religious, but there is no need to report any particular reason.

IV. Objection to Medical Treatment of Minors

1110. Regarding any objection to medical treatment of minors, the Act on the status and rights of the patient (785/1992), Article 7(1) states as follows:

> The opinion of a minor patient on a care or treatment measure should be investigated where possible, taking into account the patient's age or development. The care of a minor patient must be done in agreement with the patient, if s/he can make decisions about the care, taking into account age or development.

And Article 7(2) continues:

> If a minor patient cannot make a decision on the care, he or she shall be cared for in consultation with his or her guardian or some other legal representative.

§3. The Chaplaincy in the Penitentiaries

History, Status, Appointment, Funding etc.

1111. The earliest references to pastoral care in Finnish prisons can be founded in the Finnish reformer Mikael Agricola's manual (1500), which describes in detail how a priest should prepare people who have been sentenced to death. A later document is the Church Order of 1571, which ordered priests to take care of persons in prison. The Church Act of 1686 further stated that the prison chaplains should be well qualified for their special duties. Emphasized was placed on the chaplains' work with those who had been sentenced to life imprisonment or capital punishment.[631]

1112. Finland's centuries-long state connections with Sweden were severed in 1809, and Finland was incorporated into the Russian Empire (though still maintaining its own laws). The Grand Duchy of Finland inherited the Swedish prison network structure, which was supplemented during the period of Autonomy, when several new prisons were built. The Helsinki County Prison ('Helsingin lääninvankila' in Finnish) in the Katajanokka area of Helsinki functioned as a prison from 1837 to 2002. It was established in 1837 by Tsar Nikolai I to function alongside the Helsinki Crown Prison, which had operated since 1749.[632]

1113. After Finnish independence, the exceptional wartime (the 1918 Civil War and the two wars against the Soviet Union between 1939 and 1944) and post-war conditions also left their mark on Finnish criminal policy. *Tapio Lappi-Seppälä* has pointed out that in the 1960s the Nordic countries experienced heated social debate on the results and justifications of involuntary treatment in institutions, both penal and otherwise (such as in healthcare and in the treatment of alcoholics). At the time in Finland:

> the criticism of the treatment ideology was merged with another reform ideology that was directed against an overly severe Criminal Code and the excessive use of custodial sentences. The resulting criminal political ideology was labelled as 'humane neo-classicism'. It stressed both legal safeguards against coercive care and the goal of less repressive measures in general. In sentencing, the principles of proportionality and predictability became the central values. Individualized sentencing, as well as sentencing for general preventive reasons or perceived dangerousness, were consigned to the background. Between 1970 and 1990 all the main parts of the Finnish criminal legislation were reformed from these starting points. The common denominator in several law-reforms was the reduction in the use of custodial sentences. A tangible result of this policy was a long-term systematic reduction of incarceration.[633]

1114. In 1925 the ELCF integrated the prison chaplaincy into its regular organization. The very first prison chaplaincies were founded in the 1820s, during the period of Autonomy. In a statute from 1925 concerning the prison administration,

631. Forsback & Nordström in Svärd (ed.), *Jag var i fängelse – en studiebok om den andliga vården vid fångvårdsanstalterna.* (Stockholm: Klippan 1970).
632. The prison museum in the town of Hämeenlinna functions in the former premises of the provincial prison of Häme. When the building was completed in 1871, it was the first prison in Finland with cells, and remained in use until 1993. The museum was opened to the public in June, 1997. The building was designed by the architect L. I. Lindqvist. *See* http://www.visithameenlinna.fi/en/services/prison-museum/.
633. Tapio Lappi-Seppälä: 'Imprisonment and Penal Policy in Finland'. *In Scandinavian Studies In Law* 1999–2012, 334. *See also* Sakari Melander, *Kriminalisointiteoria – rangaistavaksi säätämisen oikeudelliset rajoitukset* (Theory of Criminalization – Legal Limitations of Criminalization). (Vammala, 2008).

the old title 'a prison preacher' was changed to 'a prison chaplain'.[634] The position of pastoral care in prisons was strengthened in the 1970s and 1980s.

1115. The State funds the salaries of the prison chaplains and the Evangelical Lutheran Church funds the prison deacons. In 2012 the Correctional Services Department proposed transferring the hiring of prison chaplains from the state to the Church. However, the Ministry of Justice decided to continue hiring prison chaplains as employees of the Correctional Services Department.

1116. In 2015 there were fourteen full-time prison chaplains and three deaconesses in the largest prisons. All full-time prison chaplains are ministers of the Evangelical Lutheran Church. In prisons the pastors are employees of the Correctional Services Institution and are part of the prison's rehabilitation activities. Prison deaconesses hold offices in the dioceses. In addition, there were three part-time chaplains and one deacon who maintained contact with prisons over and above the duties of their own parishes. Free churches and different religious organizations also have their own widespread network for providing prison work. Each year they organize an average of more than 100 sessions in the prisons, fifty to eighty group meetings, and also more than 100 individual meetings with prisoners.[635]

1117. According to the report *Church in Change* (2005), 'Work for those with criminal convictions was also done elsewhere than in prisons, with those released from prison and those serving their sentences in the community or who had conditional sentences need support.' The report strongly emphasized that aftercare is one of the most important aspects of the Church's work with criminals. The church is expected to provide support especially with regard to prisoners' families, couple relationships, substance abuse problems, and housing.[636]

§4. Military Chaplaincy

History, Status, Appointment, Funding etc.

1118. Chaplains have served Finnish soldiers in the armed forces since the sixteenth century, which at that time meant within the Swedish armed forces. During the period of Autonomy (as part of the Russian Empire), the formation of the field

634. For further information, *see* Publications of the Correctional Services Department, http://www.rikosseuraamus.fi/material/attachments/rise/julkaisut-monisteetjaraportit/6XRN2xbYF/1-2006_Oikeus_uskontoon.pdf, pp. 12–16.

635. Sami Puumala, 'The study of pastoral care and ecclesiastical work in prisons, 2011–2012' (Selvitys vankilasielunhoidosta ja kirkollisesta vankilatyöstä 2011–2012), *see* in electronic form: http://sakasti.evl.fi/julkaisut.nsf/05892BAE40E8902DC2257E2E0012D529/$FILE/S%20Puumala%20-%20Selvitys%20vankilasielunhoidosta%20ja%20kirkollisesta%20vankilatyöstä%202011-2012.pdf.

636. *See* Kimmo Kääriäinen, Maarit Hytönen, Kati Niemelä & Kari Salonen. *Church in Change. The Evangelical Lutheran Church of Finland from 2000 to 2003*. (Tampere: Publications of the Church Research Institute, no. 545), 2005.

chaplain office and its duties in the Finnish army were formed based on Finnish laws, especially the ecclesiastical law (Schauman's Church Law of 1869), and based on the heritage of the long period of Swedish rule. For example, the custom of granting the honorary title of war dean (sotarovasti) originates from the time of Swedish rule. The Russian field chaplain system only had a minor influence on the field chaplain's office. The only significant Russian influence was that Lutheran chaplains were exempted from military service.

1119. The basis of the duties of field chaplains during the period of Autonomy are to be found in the war articles. The war articles also required a Christian education. Both field chaplains and parish priests were obliged to teach the Christian Doctrine to the professional military battalions. Cooperation between the Lutherans and the Orthodox was trouble-free. As part of the Russian military establishment, the Finnish army represented a small Lutheran minority that was not in complete harmony with the Russian establishment. Furthermore, the supreme military command was in Russian hands. Cooperation nevertheless created confidence between the Czar and the Lutheran Church. For its part, the Finnish army and its priests consolidated the union between the throne and the altar.[637]

1120. Following Finnish Independence in 1917, the chaplaincy work started officially in 1918, when the assessor *Hjamar Svanberg* presented a plan to *General Mannerheim* for pastoral work in the defence forces.

1121. In modern times, the chaplaincy work done in the FDF is mainly the task of the Lutheran and Orthodox Churches and their chaplains. Services are available for all conscripts, regardless of denomination or conviction. *The FDF employs Lutheran and Orthodox chaplains, while the Evangelical Church of Finland and the Orthodox Church have taken financial responsibility for the costs of the military deacons.*

1122. The purpose of the work is to support those serving in the Defence Forces and Border Guard both mentally and spiritually and to maintain their ethical ability to function under all circumstances.[638]

1123. There is also cooperation with other churches and Christian organizations and with the civil defence organizations. In 2015 there were twenty-eight members

637. For more on the Finnish chaplaincy during the period of Autonomy, *see* Kari Vappula, *Sotilaspapin virka Suomen ruotujakoisessa sotaväessä 1812–1880* (The Office of Field Chaplain in the Finnish Military Tenure Establishment from 1812 to 1880). (Helsinki: SKST, 123, 1982), *Diss.*; Kari Vappula, *Sotilaspapin virka Suomen asevelvollisessa sotaväessä 1881–1905* (The Office of Field Chaplain in the Finnish Conscript Army 1881 to 1905). (Helsinki: SKST, 146, 1989).

638. With regard to recent research, special mention should be made of Ms Tiia Liuski's doctoral thesis (2023), 'The Finnish military chaplaincy', which examines the profession of the Finnish Lutheran military chaplaincy in the changing operational environment of the 2020s. *See* more detail, https://erepo.uef.fi/bitstream/handle/123456789/29748/urn_isbn_978-952-61-4877-9.pdf?sequence=1&isAllowed=y.

of the Lutheran and Orthodox clergy in the service of the military and a further fifteen serving on a part-time or fee-paying basis; four of these were Orthodox. Church sector conscripts and reserve military chaplains and military deaconesses are also used on military refresher courses and among crisis management troops.[639]

1124. Religious assistance in the armed forces is subordinated to the general chaplain (military bishop), who is comparable in rank to generals. In the organization of the FDF military, chaplains have the status of officers. During military service chaplains use uniforms, but at masses and services they are dressed in liturgical attire.

1125. In the FDF engaged in international missions there is always a chaplain or chaplains working among the UN peacekeeping forces. Finnish peacekeepers have served in Kosovo, Afghanistan, Bosnia-Herzegovina, Chad, Ethiopia and Eritrea, Lebanon, Macedonia, and Somalia.[640]

§5. The Chaplaincy in Other Public Institutions: Police, Airports, Parliament, Municipalities

1126. Finland has examples of chaplaincies in other public institutions than those already mentioned. These consist, in the first instance, of chaplaincies within universities, commercial centres, the police force, and airports.

1127. There are chaplains at the Finnish universities and also at the Universities of Applied Sciences. Most are priests who belong to the Evangelical Lutheran Church. At some of the larger universities, such as the UEF, the Lutheran priests include full-time university chaplains who are normally paid by the local parishes. There is also a formal association for university chaplains *Kirkon oppilaitostyöntekijät ry*, which has operated for twenty years. Helsinki University's chaplain *Ms Leena Huovinen* also participated at the Rio de Janeiro Olympic Games in 2016 as the Finnish Olympic team counsellor.

1128. In the Helsinki metropolitan area (Helsinki, Espoo, and Vantaa) there have also been chaplains, funded by local parishes, who work at some of the large shopping centres and alongside the police. For more than ten years there has also been a protracted discussion about organizing pastoral activities at Helsinki–Vantaa Airport.

639. About Pastoral work of the Defence Forces, *see* more detail http://www.sakasti.evl.fi/sakasti.nsf/0/4D9073DDB9C38745C22576F20030A70E/$FILE/16.%20services.pdf, 188–190.
640. *Ibid.*

§6. Special Questions: State Chaplaincy, Islam, and Other Religions

1129. There is no State Chaplaincy in Finland, nor are there Chaplaincy Trade Unions. In addition, Finnish Muslims do not yet have Islamic chaplains. In a number of contexts Finnish Muslims have expressed their desire to secure trained imams so that their communities can maintain their spiritual life and to remain a community of faith. That means guaranteeing that an imam and spiritual workers have a proper knowledge of the Islamic sciences. It is noteworthy that, according to a survey on *Imams in Finland*, the need for this type of formal education has arisen from within the Islamic communities in Finland and from the imams themselves.[641]

1130. **The Anglican Chaplaincy of St Nicholas**, Helsinki, was founded by those who fled from Saint Petersburg during the Russian Revolution in 1917. Nowadays, the Chaplaincy is part of the Church of England's Diocese of Gibraltar in Europe and works closely with the ELCF under the auspices of the Porvoo Agreement.

1131. Since there are now three independent Anglican congregations in Finland, the Chaplaincy has moved away from the use of its previous name, the Anglican Church in Finland, and instead refers to its official name under the Church of England: the Diocese of Gibraltar in Europe. The Chaplaincy serves Anglicans living in the greater Helsinki area and is an inclusive community of word and sacrament.[642]

641. The study was written in Finnish with an English summary. An open-access document is available from an email address published online at: http://www.kulttuurifoorumi.fi/fin/julkaisut/?id=125.
642. *See* https://www.achurchnearyou.com/helsinki-st-nicholas-church/.

Part XIII. Religions in the Social Field

Chapter 1. Basic Principles and Activities

§1. Preamble

1132. Modern studies have compared the differences set up by religious ethics in terms of their ambient social reality. Social policy solutions in Catholic southern Europe have diverged from those in Lutheran northern Europe. The conclusion that has been drawn is that the notion of a Nordic welfare state would inevitably be a Lutheran creation. According to the notion, there would have to be a difference between the two parallel ways of thinking in Catholic and Lutheran social studies. This can be illustrated by stating that one of the starting points of Catholic social science[643] is the principle of subsidiarity,[644] according to which people must be able to make decisions that concern them personally. Society can lend its support, but the citizens themselves are left to determine the details. Another point of departure for the discussion is the importance of the family and the provision of support by the family.

1133. In contrast, the Nordic countries are accustomed to thinking that the state has the right to levy taxes and to direct people's lives through its decisions. Emphasis has been placed on coherence and individual responsibility, whereby forms of support are also directed at the individual. Finland has become accustomed to *seeking an equally good model in social and health services, which the state must*

643. Since the end of the nineteenth century, the Roman Catholic Church has an official, constantly evolving and Catholic social doctrine based on natural law, which defines, among other things, the roles and responsibilities of the individual, human communities and the state.

644. The European Union has adopted the principle of subsidiarity in Roman-Catholic social studies. In Finnish it is called the principle of proximity or decision-making. Professor Antti Raunio (1999, 48) has pointed out, that the principle of subsidiarity does not necessarily include all aspects of the Catholic principle of subsidiarity. 'Subsidiarity to the prevailing liberalist thinking now receives interpretations different from those of Catholic social science. Another problem with the principle of subsidiarity is that it is inherently incompatible with societies whose understanding of institutional, community, and individual relationships is based on a different interpretation from Roman Catholicism.' For more detail, *see* Jaana Hallamaa & Simo Knuuttila & Matti Kotiranta & Antti Raunio. *Rahan teologia ja Euroopan kirkot. Lopun ajan sosiaalietiikka* (Theology of Money and the European Churches. The end times of social ethics) (Jyväskylä: Atena, 1999), 45–63. *See also* Antti Raunio, *Järki, usko ja lähimmäisen hyvä* (Reason, Faith, and the Good of Your Neighbour). (Helsinki: STKSJ 252, 2007).

approve by parliamentary decisions and by means of financial sanctions make everyone live according to the decisions reached.

1134. As a result of the Second World War, Finland was slower than other Nordic countries in building up its welfare services. Since the post-war period, however, all of the major political groups in Finland have adopted the idea of a welfare state, and the Evangelical Lutheran Church has explicitly considered the welfare state to be in a Lutheran mould and has argued that the Nordic model is the best guarantee of well-being.[645] At the same time, in the midst of economic liberalism the Church has criticized the weakening of social security and has pointed out that new forms of diaconal work – e.g., food subsidies and social services that should belong to the state – function only as emergency measures. The *Deacon Barometer* of 17 September 2022 strongly emphasizes that the current diaconal work of the Church in fact guides and controls the work of Kela (Social Insurance Institution) on financial matters.[646]

1135. A new type of third-sector, volunteer-based welfare society model is now emerging that pursues its aims that are apparently based on a Lutheran Golden Rule ethical help model,[647] but the undeveloped model is still in its infancy. Come what may, it can be justly claimed that in the Nordic countries Lutheranism has provided a strong ideological basis for universally accessible welfare services. But there is a danger that, if the social ethical tradition of Lutheranism diminishes, the motivation for large-scale income transfers will diminish and there will be a shift towards a more competitive society.

1136. The largest project in the field of welfare state services in Finland in recent decades has been the reform of the social and health care service structure, a reform that was most recently attempted to solve during the government led by Prime Minister Juha Sipilä (2015–2018) and referred to as the SOTE-reform. The aim of the reform was to reduce inequalities in people's well-being and health, to improve equity and access to services, and to reduce costs. The responsibility for organizing the public social and health services was intended to be transferred from the municipalities and municipal federations to eighteen provinces on 1 January 2021. The social and provincial reform did not, however, materialize during the Sipilä government, since on 8 March 2019 the Constitutional Law Committee failed to complete

---

645. *See* closer the document of the ELCF *Kohti yhteistä hyvää: piispojen puheenvuoro hyvinvointiyhteiskunnan tulevaisuudesta* (Towards the Common Good: Bishops' Speech on the Future of a Welfare Society of the Evangelical Lutheran Church of Finland). (Helsinki: SR-kustannus, 1999). About the Nordic model of welfare state, *see* Jørn Henrik Petersen, 'Nordic Model of Welfare States', 21–39. In Pia Letto-Vanamo, Ditlev Tamm & Bent Ole Gram Mortensen (eds), *Nordic Law in European Context.* Ius Gentium: Comparative Perspectives on Law and Justice, No. 73 (Berlin: Springer-Verlag, 2019).

646. At https://julkaisut.evl.fi/catalog/Tutkimukset%20ja%20julkaisut/r/4309/viewmode=previewview. Accessed 10 Feb. 2024.

647. The Golden Rule is the principle of treating others as you want to be treated (also called the law of reciprocity). It is the ethical Maxim that is found in many Religions and Cultures.

its preparations for the provincial reform.[648] The outcome was that the SOTE-reform also failed, and its preparation was interrupted because the two processes were interlinked.

1137. Discussions and work on the reform of social and healthcare have continued in Finland since 2019. From the beginning of 2023, responsibility for organizing healthcare, social welfare and rescue services was transferred from the municipalities and joint municipal authorities to 21 regional welfare areas.[649] The municipalities will continue to organise certain services, including child daycare, education, sports and cultural services.

1138. The organizational structures and practices within the welfare areas are undergoing development to create human-centred service entities. The goal is to achieve better interoperability between primary and specialized services and also seamless coordination between social and healthcare services and rescue services. Public services organized by the welfare area include primary healthcare, specialised medical care, social services, dental care, mental health and substance abuse services, disability services, and housing services for the elderly.

1139. The reform is intended to be carried out in a people-oriented manner, with a particular focus on services. However, when society is changing, its services need to change with it. The main challenge is that the Finnish population is ageing and hence the need for care is increasing. At the same time, the birth rate is falling, and the working-age population will decline in the future. A further result will be that tax revenue will also decrease year by year.

§2. Basic Principles and Activities

1140. It is predominantly the national churches that cooperate with the state institutions and municipalities and other organizations in maintaining the social system in Finland.

1141. As indicated earlier (Part IV, Chapter 2), Finland is divided into municipalities whose administration is founded on self-government practised by their residents. Provisions on the general principles of municipal administration and the duties of the municipalities are laid down by an Act.[650] Municipalities are often important partners of religious communities, since the municipalities have the

648. The SOTE-reform encountered many problems at the level of the Constitution. *See* for instance Maija Dahlberg, 'Perustuslain reunaehdot lainvalmistelulle – ajankohtaisena esimerkkinä sosiaali- ja terveysuudistusta koskenut lakihanke' (Basic limits for draft legislation – a recent example of a bill on social and health reform). *Oikeus* 3 (2015): 321–337.

649. For more detail, *see* https://fi.wikipedia.org/wiki/Suomen_hyvinvointialueet. Accessed 9 Feb. 2024.

650. Article 121 of the Constitution. Local Government Act (410/2015). Also available at: https://www.finlex.fi/en/laki/kaannokset/2015/en20150410.pdf (410/2015 English – Translations of Finnish acts and decrees).

exclusive power to plan local development. This includes taking into account the religious and cultural needs of the population. This cooperative system of social care and culture is a key factor of pluralism.

1142. Common perspectives emerge from the legal basis and objectives of the municipality and the church. Both have a mission and a vision for the benefit of the citizens, including the promotion of well-being and a belief in sustainable development. The municipality and the local Lutheran and Orthodox parishes have traditionally been the creators and bearers of local identity, and it is widely acknowledged that a shared location, populated principally by ordinary members, whose roles are complementary are all important in the construction and maintenance of identity.

1143. The attitudes of the municipalities have frequently displayed a positive attitude to the presence of religion, something that is particularly evident in the early education that the municipalities have often conducted in collaboration with the local parishes.[651] The link between the municipal welfare mission and the churches' religious mission indicates the effects of a shared history.[652]

1144. It must, however, be remembered that cooperation between the Finnish social state, i.e., the municipalities, and the churches and religious communities is not defined in any way by the Finnish Constitution as it is in some European countries, such as Germany.[653] Nor do the churches and religious communities run numerous hospitals, homes for the elderly, nursing homes, or kindergartens, schools, and academic institutions (universities are non-confessional and are maintained by the state). In brief, the churches and religious communities do not have a social monopoly in Finland.

1145. The *Finnish Caritas Association* (Suomen Caritas ry) is the aid organization of the Roman Catholic Church in the country. Caritas Finland is a member of Caritas Internationalis and Caritas Europa. In Finland, the Caritas Federation has no welfare associations as it does, for example, in Germany.[654] Caritas works in the

651. *See* further details, *see* Sami Lahtiluoma & Raimo Turunen 2011, *Kunta ja seurakunta –vuorovaikutusta ja yhteistyötä* (Municipality and parish – interaction and cooperation, in Finnish). (Helsinki: Kuntaliitto & Suomen evankelis-luterilainen kirkko, 2011).
652. The Evangelical Lutheran Church has played a significant role in local and international disasters. These include the Lapua cartridge factory explosion in 1976, many school shootings, the sinking of the cruise ship Estonia in 1994 (at the time of the accident, there were 989 people on board, 852 of whom were killed), and the South-east Asian tsunami disaster.
653. Gerhard Robbers, *Germany.* In *International Encyclopaedia of Laws: Religion*, edited by Rik Torfs. Alphen aan den Rijn, NL (Kluwer Law International, 2013), 309–310.
654. Gerhard Robbers (2013, 310) notes that 'The German Caritas Union (Deutscher Caritasverband) is the welfare organization of the Roman Catholic Church in Germany. It is the largest German welfare association. Caritas has 24,646 centres and institutions in Germany where people can obtain professional support and guidance to help them cope with and overcome their problems. These services are intended for everyone who is socially disadvantaged, regardless of skin colour, religion or nationality.'

field of development cooperation and disaster relief and also immigrants, in cooperation with the Catholic parishes in Finland. In order to finance its activities, Caritas organizes bazaars and takes part in various events such as the World Village Festival. A great part of the work of Caritas is voluntary. Disaster relief is channelled through Caritas Internationalis, whose 165 member organizations represent some 200 countries and regions.[655]

1146. The *Unit of Diaconia and Pastoral Counseling* (KDS) is an expert collaborative body of the ELCF. Its mission is to develop diaconal and pastoral care and to perform specific missions in association with churches, dioceses, and organizations. The mission of the unit is to promote the well-being of the most disadvantaged people and to influence social development from the standpoint of the values of the Church. It is also an expert collaborative body that plans and develops pastoral care in the context of hospitals, institutions, and outpatient care, and maintains contact with the healthcare field. It belongs to the Department for Parish Services at the Office of the National Church Council in the ELCF, and works as a member of the *European Network of Healthcare Chaplaincy*. In its areas of responsibility the Unit aims to maintain contact with the State and with other social and ecclesiastical bodies, churches, and international organizations in the field.[656]

1147. The Finnish Orthodox Church has also its own welfare association, *Philanthropy* (Filantropia). In 2018, philanthropic activities were focused on supporting church work in Kenya, development cooperation in Uganda, channelling humanitarian aid to Syria, and promoting the domestic human rights debate within the Orthodox Church.[657]

1148. Muslim social care is gradually developing. A recent study from 2017 shows that while Finnish society aims to integrate immigrants into their new home environment, integrate them into society, and promote well-being through a variety of measures, there are still immigrants from Muslim backgrounds who are at risk of exclusion or may not receive the social services that they need. A researcher, Ms *Shahram Hatami*, says that they have also received insufficient support from the Muslim community and their own ethnic community. No single authority, organization or community can meet the needs of a radicalized immigrant who is at risk of exclusion or who is already marginalized. It is therefore important that the public sector, the private sector, and the third sector together create the necessary framework for delivering aid.[658]

---

655. *See*, https://www.caritas.fi.
656. *See*, https://evl.fi/ota-yhteytta/kirkkohallituksen-yhteystiedot/toiminnallinen-osasto/diakonia-ja-sielunhoito.
657. *See* further, https://filantropia.fi/eng.
658. Shahram Hatami, 'Need for social services and community support for Muslim immigrants' (Muslimitaustaisten maahanmuuttajien sosiaalipalvelujen ja yhteisön tuen tarve), University of Jyväskylä, 2017, 27. *See*, http://urn.fi/URN:NBN:fi:jyu-201803221809. Accessed 12 Oct. 2019.

Chapter 2. Kindergartens

1149. Churches and religious communities operate numerous kindergartens, which form part of the general educational system as well as part of the social system. Alongside the municipal kindergartens and nurseries, there are also private playschools and parish day clubs.

1150. The staff at municipal kindergartens includes both educational and nursing professionals. A kindergarten is run by a kindergarten teacher who must hold the formal qualifications of the profession. Kindergarten teachers receive their education either at a university or at universities of applied sciences.[659]

1151. The focus of kindergarten activities and the ideological background communities vary. In Finland, the majority of kindergartens are communal social services for families, while some are private. The underlying ideological background may be, for example, Montessor or Steiner pedagogy. Pre-schools often operate in kindergartens, and there are some twenty-five religious pre-schools.[660] 'Language baths' can also be provided in different languages. All Finnish kindergarten nowadays construct an early childhood education plan known as a 'Vasu', and there are educational discussions annually with the parents of each child. This discussion may also address the child's religious beliefs and convictions that parents, as custodians, can decide on.

1152. The system of cooperation between municipalities and religious communities in the field of kindergartens is an expression of cooperation between the state and religious communities in that religion is part of many children's upbringing and education.

---

659. *See*, for example, the Degree Programme in Kindergarten Teacher Education at the University of Eastern Finland, http://www.uef.fi/en/web/skope/lastentarhanopettajakoulutus. Accessed 12 Oct. 2019. *See also*, https://www.sool.fi/opettajaksi/varhaiskasvatuksen-opettaja/. Accessed 9 Feb. 2024.

660. At https://kristillinenkoulu.fi/briefly-in-english/.

Part XIV. Sunday and Religious Holiday Protection

Chapter 1. General Protection of Sundays and Religious Holidays

1153. Sunday and religious holidays recognized by the state are protected by law as days of rest from work. As indicated earlier (in Part II., §9 II. B. Structural limitations), these holidays are not inevitably identified as such within the Finnish legal system, but they have their basis in the Finnish calendar and labour market as historical, cultural, and traditional days of rest. From the legal point, the State has no particular interest per se to provide them with special state protection or to define a certain number of religious holidays that should be protected. The legal status of the national Lutheran and Orthodox Churches does not reflect the state's more positive attitude towards religious values, as evidenced, for example, in the liberalization of Sunday trading hours under international competitive pressure, despite the Lutheran Church's support for the traditional day of rest.

1154. Church holidays for which the Sunday regulation is applied are New Year's Day, Epiphany, Long Friday, the Second Day of Easter, Ascension Day, Midsummer Day, Independence Day, Christmas Eve, and the First and Second Days of Christmas.[661] In addition, the actual public holidays are New Year's Day, Epiphany, the First of May, and Independence Day, and also Christmas Eve and Christmas Day when they fall on days other than a Saturday or Sunday. Of the Labour Market holidays, the First of May (in Finnish, Vappu) is by far the most important in the Finnish context.

1155. The question of public holidays became more pressing on the transition to a five-day working week in Finland at the start of the 1970s. The General Synod of the ELCF, which under Church Law was responsible for laying down the feast days and holidays to be observed, acceded to the proposals coming from the employers' organizations. This resulted in the Synod agreeing to move both Epiphany and Ascension Thursday to the nearest Saturdays, but little more than a decade later, in 1985, these holidays were moved back to their former positions.

1156. In 2014 the central labour market organizations and the Church Council restarted their work on rescheduling the celebration of Epiphany and Ascension

661. Chapter 1, s. 6, of the Church Act (652/2023) prescribes the ecclesiastical holidays.

Day. The aim was to illustrate the theological background and the social and economic significance of the public holidays and the legislation related to Sundays.[662] The arrangement itself was both old and familiar. The labour market, led by Confederation of Finnish Industries (EK), was seeking revenge for the 1985 settlement that had restored Epiphany and Ascension Day to their original biblical positions in the calendar. The then President of the Republic, Mr Mauno Koivisto, had also become involved in the reform. He postponed signing the law into force until 1991, despite it having been enacted by Parliament, thus teasing the church for five whole years. In his own view, Koivisto wished to show that he understood the labour market more better than did the Lutheran national church, for which the holiday was a 'deep cultural structure on which the Finnish way of life is built', as the former Archbishop Kari Mäkinen put it.[663] The Confederation of Finnish Industries brought the public holidays into the spotlight shortly after the central organizations had signed an employment and growth agreement that would have put the Finnish economy on a healthy growth path. It is, however, difficult to imagine that any labour market leader would seriously consider moving 1 May as a public holiday to the closest weekend.

1157. The right to object to working on religious days of rest is part of freedom of religion. Working on Sundays or religious holidays can be ordered only with the consent of the employee, if the work of a type also regularly performed on Sundays or by previous agreement in the employment contract. Many employers are ready to consider the employees' religious needs. Compensation for work done on religious (public) holidays is also determined by collective agreements in the field. Sunday work must pay a salary that has been increased by 100%.

1158. For historical reasons, therefore, Christian holidays prevail and enjoy more intense protection than the holidays of other religions and creeds, which are not protected by the law in any specific way.

662. At http://notes.evl.fi/vanhasak.nsf/0/42B9759B6625F355C2257D7E0031D593/$FILE/arkipyhaselvitys.pdf. Accessed 14 Oct. 2019.
663. Editorial, Turun Sanomat 6 January 2014. Accessed 14 Oct. 2019.

Chapter 2. Sundays, Religious Holidays and Shop Closing

1159. The public debate in Finland concerning keeping retail shops open on Sundays has long been a topic in social debate, especially around the turn of the millennium. Traditionally, the opening hours of shops on Sundays have been legally restricted in Finland for hundreds of years.[664]

1160. The relevant legislation and opening hours have been influenced at various times mainly for economic, legislative (working-time), and trade-related reasons, but also for religious reasons. The biggest changes took place between 1969 and 1997, when the opening hours of shops on Sundays were extended by numerous changes in the legislation.

1161. In the course of the debate, the legislation on opening hours has been amended several times. Restrictions on weekday opening were only introduced in the early twentieth century and have been closely linked to working time legislation. Between 1969 and 1997 opening hours were permitted from 8 am to 8 pm on weekdays and from 8 am to 6 pm on Saturdays. At that time, the Retail Business Act (435/1969), Article 1 stated:

> Unless otherwise provided in this Act, professional retailing is permitted from 8 am to 8 pm on weekdays, except on Saturdays and church holidays, and from 8 am to 6 pm on Independence Day and the First of May.

1162. The 1969 law (453/1969) permitted the unregulated opening of kiosks.[665] The sales area of the kiosk was not precisely defined in this Act. Instead, the decree set out very precisely what items could be sold at kiosks for them to qualify as

664. In Finland when it was still a province of Sweden, Ch. 3, s. 8, of the Penal Code of the 1734 Law ('The Arch of evil doing', 'Pahategon Caari' in old Finnish) was in force. It insisted that the 'trinket merchants' (rihkamakaupat) should be closed on Sundays and ecclesiastical holidays. However, food and drinks could be sold on public holidays once worship was over. A fine of five thalers was imposed for violating the ban. For further detail, *see* Kauppakaari 3/1734, https://www.finlex.fi/fi/laki/alkup/1734/17340003000 and missing text of the Act (III. Lucu. Kirouxista ja Sabbatin ricoxesta), https://agricolaverkko.fi/vintti/julkaisut/julkaisusarja/kktk/lait/1734/l175916.html. Article 8 reads: 'Rihcama-cammiot, eli muut puodit, ei pidä Sunnundaina ja Juhlapäiwinä awattaman, myymisen tähden: Ruoca ja juoma mahta myytää hätätarpexi, sitten cuin Jumalan palwellus on ohitze. Älkön kelläkän olco walda näinä päiwinä cauppaa tehdä laiwois, eli muisa aluxisa. Jos jocu ricko näisä tiloisa; maxacon sackoa Sabbatin ricoxesta, cuin sanottu on. Sama sacko olcon; jos jocu matcaa eteens otta, maalla eli wedellä, caupungisa eli maalla, ennen cuin Jumalan palwelus on lopetettu. Jocainen cuin hewoisen eli wenhen sijhen wuoro; tehkön sackoa wijsi talaria. Jos jocu on matcalla; asettacon itzens Jumalan palwelluxeen sijhen Kirckoon, cuin tien wieresä on.' https://agricolaverkko.fi/vintti/julkaisut/julkaisusarja/kktk/lait/1734/l175916.html. Accessed 15 Oct. 2019. (Updated 9 Jan. 2024).

665. Article 6 of the same law stated that unregulated opening hours were also extended to: (1) pharmacies; (2) sales at airports and ports in areas reserved exclusively for international traffic and on means of transport for passengers; (3) market and market trading; (4) sales from accommodation and catering establishments; (5) the sale of engine fuels and lubricants, liquefied gas, vehicle spare parts and accessories, in the open air at petrol and service stations and from car repair shops and comparable outlets.

kiosks.[666] In 1989 an amendment of the law permitted Sunday opening for shops in sparsely populated areas. In the autumn of 1994 Sunday opening was also permitted in urban areas in December and on six separate Sundays. At the same time, opening hours on weekdays were extended to 9 pm.

1163. Since Parliament had rejected unrestricted shop hours on Sundays in 1998, in the following year the Government narrowed its proposal to permitting shop opening on Sundays mainly in the summer months and in December. In this form, the law was approved by Parliament.[667] Prime Minister Lipponen's second government, with the intention of expansion, returned to the issue of keeping shops open on Sundays. In May 2000 the Government, after a lively debate, presented a bill (1297/2000) designed to regulate the opening hours and practice of the retail trade. According to the new bill, opening on Sundays should be permitted to shops with a maximum of 400 m^2 of operational space. The situation of larger stores was also further clarified by the abandonment of permitted opening on individual Sundays and allowing opening hours on Sundays in May-August and November-December.[668]

1164. In August 2008 the Minister of Finance, Mr Jyrki Katainen, presented possible annual reductions in the VAT on foodstuffs in order to extend the opening hours of stores and thus to regulate their opening. In November 2008 the Representative Council of the Trade Union of Service Industries (PAM) approved a preliminary proposal to reform the opening hours, and in spring 2009 a bill was passed by Parliament (HE 84/2009).[669]

1165. The approval of the bill raised strong opinions in both secular and ecclesiastical circles. Archiater (the eldest in the medical community) Risto Pelkonen stated 'that it would be good for people to calm down and be quiet and not always go somewhere'. He pointed out that 'trade creates needs that are not really there'. Archbishop Paarma in turn described the change as 'Sunday openings to bend the knees to the consuming god'. He stressed that the 'Lutheran work ethic has always included a strong defence of the day of rest, the day off. It is essential for rest and recreation and self-care, but the time it gives to family, friends, and acquaintances is also significant for the community. It is from this point of view that even today

---

666. Alcohol was one of these products. Bringing it to kiosks was considered impossible. However, in late 1980 the 'Middle Beer to R-Kiosk convenience store movement' called for beer with an alcoholic content between 2.8%–4.7% of its volume to be sold from kiosks. 'Almost 300 citizens are deeply concerned about the alcohol policy in our country', stated Markku Juhani 'Mato' Valtonen in his civic address to parliamentary representatives. For further details, *see* https://yle.fi/aihe/artikkeli/2010/08/25/keskikaljaa-vaadittiin-r-kioskeihin-ja-takaisin-alkoon. Accessed 15 Oct. 2019. (Updated 9 Jan. 2024).
667. On the law related to shop opening hours 1997, *see* Seppo, J. 'Church and State in Finland 1997', European Journal for Church and State Research – Revue européenne des relations Églises-État, 5 (1998), 123–125.
668. Act on opening hours of Retail Business and Hairdressing 1297/2000, Article 1, para. 2, 1–2. This repealed an earlier Act 276/1997.
669. The proposal was accepted on 29 May 2009.

the Church is keen to defend the preservation of a common holiday as far as possible. It is for the sake of supporting the community of employees and employers, their families, and our society'.[670]

1166. According to the 2009 Retail Law (1297/2000), shops, hairdressers, and hair salons were generally open from 7 am to 9 pm on weekdays, from 7 am to 6 pm on Saturdays, and from 12 am to 6 pm on Sundays, except on Christmas Eve, when shops could be open from 12 pm to 9 pm. On church holidays as well as on the First of May, Independence Day, Mother's Day, and Father's Day shops had to be kept closed. In addition, they had to close at 18.00 on New Year's Eve and on May Day, and at 12.00 on Christmas Eve and Midsummer's Eve. Pharmacies, kiosks, car dealerships, petrol stations, florists, art shops, and shops open only for passengers at ports and airports were not subject to the law (as had already been stated in the law of 1969).

1167. The 2009 law also extended completely unrestricted opening for larger stores. Previously, only shops (kiosks) of less than 100 m^2 had completely unrestricted opening, but now this was extended to stores of less than 400 m^2, although holiday restrictions were maintained. The Sunday opening hours of the larger stores were extended throughout the year but shortened to 6 pm (November-December at 9 pm). The opening hours at Midsummer and on Christmas Eve were shortened so that shops closed at 12 noon, whereas previously they had closed at 1 pm.

1168. The law on retail opening hours was finally abolished completely at the beginning of 2016 (HE 88/2015), and since then there is no longer any provision in the law (sic!). As a rule, shops are closed on only two days a year: at Midsummer and Christmas. At the same time, however, a provision was added to the Act on unfair business practices, which allows a small entrepreneur in a shopping mall or similar store to remain closed one day a week, and this right cannot be removed by contract.[671]

1169. The debate surrounding Sunday opening hours is also indirectly linked to the overall reform of the Working Hours Act (HE 158/2018 and the law 872/2019 adopted on the basis of the Government proposal).[672,673] The new Working Time Act has come into force on 1 January 2020. It brings with it many reforms that make the law better suited to today's mobile and 'off-the-job' work.[674]

---

670. *Editorial,* Länsi-Suomi 24.7.2017 and *Opinion* on *Rest day, shopping and consumption*, Länsi-Suomi 1.8.2017.
671. Amending to the Act on unfair business practices 596/2018. This Act repealed Arts 4, 6(3) and 10 of the Unfair Commercial Practices Act (1061/1978), as amended by Art. 6(3) of Law 405/1986 and Art. 10 of Law 810/1990.
672. Other related Acts: 873 / 2019–886/2019.
673. The Government's proposal HE 158/2018 to Parliament on working hours and certain related laws was issued on 27 Sep. 2018.
674. Regarding the main principles, the legislative reform abstained from the regulatory approach of the earlier Working Time Act. The most significant innovation is flexibility in work regardless of time and place. In the case of flexible working time, the employee decides on his own working time (also

1170. It is interesting to note that in a debate on Sunday opening hours the trade union Service Union United, or PAM, which works in private service sectors, and the social work of the Evangelical Lutheran Church shared a number of similar perspectives. In brief, the rhetoric of both noted that the third Commandment, 'Keep the Sabbath day to sanctify it' could also be termed the world's first labour protection law.

1171. In sum, it can be stated that the question of sanctifying the Sabbath (Sunday), on the one hand, and the question of Sunday opening hours, on the other, cannot be oversimplified in order to match the demands of contemporary society.

---

whether he or she is ready to work on Sundays) and the place where he works, and the employer defines the tasks and their objectives as well as the overall schedule.

Part XV. The Burial System

1172. The maintenance of cemeteries has long belonged to the Evangelical Lutheran and Orthodox Churches in Finland. When freedom of religion was expanded, burial was also required for those outside the two dominant denominations. The current RFA (453/2003) contains no provisions for burials as did the previous law of 1922.[675] Nowadays, burials are regulated by the Burial Management Act (475/2003), prepared by the Ministry of Education and Culture. The BM Act (Chapter 1, Article 3) starts out from the assumption that cemeteries in the Lutheran parishes would continue to function as general public cemeteries,[676] and those not belonging to the Lutheran Church would still have the right to receive a burial plot in them.[677]

1173. In addition, registered religious communities and registered foundations[678] could maintain cemeteries with the permission of the Regional State Administrative Agency for Eastern Finland (Itä-Suomen aluehallintovirasto).[679] The parishes of the Orthodox Church, the State, the municipalities, and the federation of municipalities are also free to establish a cemetery.[680] The status of Evangelical Lutheran and Orthodox Church cemeteries differs from other cemeteries in that sense that they are still specifically regulated by church law, in accordance with Chapter 3, section 28 of the Church Act (652/2023) of the ELCF and Chapter 8, sections 81–86 of the Orthodox Church Act (925/2006). The community or foundation applying for a cemetery maintenance permit must have adequate facilities to maintain the cemetery, and an individual cannot establish a cemetery.

1174. Since burial is usually accompanied by a religious perspective, fundamental and human rights provisions on freedom of religion or belief have an important role to play in the organization of a burial. In addition to Article 11 of the Constitution, the principle of equality enshrined in Article 6 of the Constitution, which is

675. Article 10(2) of the Old Religious Freedom Act (267/1922) also required Evangelical Lutheran parishes to provide a burial ground for non-members.
676. Burial Management Act (*Hautaustoimilaki*), Chapter 1, Art. 3.
677. *Ibid.*, Arts 4 and 5.
678. *Ibid.*, Ch. 3, Art. 8.
679. The Regional State Administrative Agency for Eastern Finland (AVI) is responsible for the approval, control, and land registry issues within the territory of Finland and for the military cemeteries in the ceded Ladoga region of Karelia (an area previously belonging to Finland before 1945).
680. Burial Management Act, Ch. 3, Art. 7.

considered to mean, among other things, that public authorities must treat all religious communities and world-views equally. This also applies to the funeral places and to the imposition of the same payment criteria in burial management. An egalitarian system of payment criteria requires that fees may not exceed the cost of providing the service, and the fees must be the same for anyone who has the right to be buried in a church cemetery.[681] In addition, frontline veterans and their spouses may be exempted from paying grave charges in whole or in part.

1175. The special non-denominational cemetery is an important religious- or belief-neutral alternative. In this kind of cemetery, the church acts as a technical administrator. This means that the establishment of non-denominational cemeteries remains an obligation of the Lutheran parishes, although this does not mean that every Lutheran parish should separately establish a cemetery. Rather, it is a question of joint regional responsibility. The cemetery needs of other religious communities have been somewhat eased by the fact that some Evangelical Lutheran parishes have voluntarily reserved graveyards separate from their cemeteries for non-religious communities. This kind of burial areas would not be consecrated as cemeteries and there would be no Christian or ideological symbols.

1176. The Burial Management Act also contains provisions concerning the cremation of the deceased.[682] The burial and cremation of the deceased's body and the handling of the ashes must respect the views and wishes of the deceased. The body of the deceased must be buried or cremated without undue delay. The body and ashes of the deceased should be treated in a valued and respectful manner. The ashes of the deceased must be buried or permanently disposed of in a single place within a year.[683] The ash recipient must inform the crematorium in writing where the ashes are to be disposed of before dispensing with the ashes.[684] The consent of the owner or possessor of the area is required for the disposal of the ash. If a memorial or other visible signs are to be placed, permission must be sought from the Regional State Administrative Agency to establish a private tomb.[685] A crematorium may be established by the same communities as in the case of cemeteries. However, its establishment always requires an environmental permit, in accordance with the Environmental Protection Act.

1177. The exercise of burial management as a whole is ultimately the responsibility of society. As indicated earlier, the Ministry of Education and Culture each year grants funding to the Evangelical Lutheran Church for the statutory tasks related to certain burial functions, certain civil registry tasks, and the maintenance

681. *Ibid.*, Ch. 2, Art. 6.
682. *Ibid.*, Ch. 17, Arts 17–20.
683. *Ibid.*, Art. 19.
684. *Ibid.*, Art. 20.
685. In general, permission to establish a private grave is required. According to Art. 16, the permit is applied for from the Provincial Government, which may, for special reasons, grant permission for the burial of a named deceased in a suitable location. The location of the grave must be clearly marked. Private burial land may be restored to its previous function no earlier than twenty-five years after the burial.

of culturally valuable buildings and movables.[686] The amount of funding in 2023 was EUR 122,7 million, a sum that is increased annually in line with changes in the consumer price index as provided in the law.[687]

1178. In addition, it should be mentioned that the Regional Administration of Eastern Finland – which is responsible for the approval, control, and land registry issues of all burials in the territory of Finland – supports with the aid of state subsidies the renovation of the war, field, and civilian cemeteries remaining in Russia (the former Soviet Union) after the Second World War.

1179. In the course of Finnish independence, war cemeteries (sankarihautausmaa) have included the graves of both sides involved in the Civil War (1918) – the Whites and the Reds – who fell, were executed, or died in prison camps, and also the graves of Finns who died as a result of the Winter War, the Continuation War, and the Lapland War (1939–1945). Some of Finland's war cemeteries have official state recognition. They are maintained by the public authorities in order to prevent their destruction with the passing of time.[688] The fact that the Finnish war cemeteries are located within the same places as the public cemeteries is due to the custom during the Civil War of sending the deceased back to his home municipality, a tradition that continued during World War II.

1180. The respectful and dignified care given to the war cemeteries has attracted international acclaim.

---

686. Laki valtion rahoituksesta evankelis-luterilaiselle kirkolle eräisiin yhteiskunnallisiin tehtäviin (Government proposal HE 247/2016 to Parliament for the Government funding of the Evangelical Lutheran Church for some social tasks) 430/2015, s. 1.
687. *See* above, Part VIII. *Church Financing.*
688. For further detail, *see* https://www.sotasampo.fi/en/cemeteries/list.

Part XVI. Data Law

1181. The new EU Data Protection Regulation came into force on 25 May 2018. The purpose of the regulation is to harmonize the regulation of the processing of personal data within the EU. In Finland the previously existing Personal Data Act (523/1999) was repealed by a new Data Protection Act (1050/2018).[689] This Act – as Chapter 1, Article 1 states – 'specifies and supplements Regulation (EU) 2016/679 of the European Parliament and of the Council on the protection of natural persons with regard to the processing of personal data and on the free movement of such data, and repealing Directive 95/46/EC (General Data Protection Regulation), hereafter the Data Protection Regulation, and its national application'.[690]

1182. The personal data directive currently in force has been implemented in very different ways across the EU. What has been allowed in Finland may not be allowed in Germany, for example. The objectives of the new Data Protection Act are to strengthen the rights of the individual, to take into account the global dimension of data protection, and to enhance the enforcement of data protection rules. It also aims to contribute to the development of the EU digital single market, allowing the safe and free transfer of information within the European Union.

1183. Almost all private business corporations and companies have access to personal information. This also applies to the churches and religious communities that maintain membership records.

1184. In Finland, data subjects have the following rights:

- The right to request access to their personal data and the right to have that personal data corrected or deleted.
- The right to request limited processing of their personal data and the right to exercise their rights to object and to use portable data.
- When the processing of personal data is based on consent, the right exists to request the withdrawal of consent at any time. The withdrawal of consent does not affect the lawfulness of processing based on consent before its withdrawal.

689. In addition to this law, there is a special Act on the Processing of Personal Data in Criminal Matters and in Connection with Maintaining National Security (1054/2018). For further detail, *see* https://www.finlex.fi/fi/laki/kaannokset/2018/en20181054.pdf.
690. For further detail concerning the Data Protection Act 1050/2018, *see* the translation from Finnish at https://www.finlex.fi/en/laki/kaannokset/2018/en20181050.pdf. Accessed 9 Jan. 2024.

- The right to lodge a complaint regarding the processing of personal data to the national supervisory authority if the data subject believes that the processing of his or her data violates the EU's General Data Protection Regulation. Exercising this right does not restrict the judicial redress described in the Church Act (652/2023) of the ELCF.

1185. The general challenge especially for companies is that they may not be at all familiar with the full extent of the information that they possess, where and how it is stored, handled, and maintained, or who is responsible for it. Almost every company stores both employee records and also many of those pertaining to their customers and marketing. In a different vein, registered religious communities – especially the ELCF and the Finnish Orthodox Church as public law entities responsible for long-term civic records – have a long tradition of handling, preserving, and maintaining records.[691]

1186. Together with the civil registrars, the Evangelical Lutheran Church and the Orthodox Church maintained civic records until 1999, when they were required simply to keep a register of their members, while the registrars maintained the population records system.

1187. The demographic data is currently maintained by the Population Register Centre and the local authorities. Data registration is based on statutory notifications from citizens and authorities.[692] The demographic information system serves a wide range of societal functions, such as election management, taxation, justice, administrative decision-making and planning, statistics, and research. Businesses and communities also have access to the demographic information collected.

1188. Concerning the Evangelical Lutheran Church and the Orthodox Church, the legal grounds for processing personal data under the EU's General Data Protection Regulation are:

- Religious Membership Register Act (614/1998).
- Church Act (652/2023), Chapter 8, sections 8, 9, 10 and 11.
- Orthodox Church Act (985/2006), §§72–74.

---

691. The current population information system in Finland is based on the combination of two sets of data collected for different purposes. Population records have been kept in Finland for the needs of both the state and the church since the sixteenth century. From 1634, census lists started to be kept in Finland. Until 1652 it was the responsibility of the clergy to keep the population register, after which it was commissioned by the commissars of assessment units (mantaali komissaarit) until 1779 and thereafter by the registrars. The last census registration was held in 1989. Church books in Sweden-Finland are among the oldest in Europe. Finland's first population statistics – population tables – date from 1750. The next major change in population records occurred more than 200 years later, in the 1950s and 1960s. In recent times, the aim has been to reform the legislation related to the population register and to set up a centralized computerized register in order to overcome the problems of the dual and decentralized system that had evolved over the centuries.
692. Law on the Population Information System and Certification Services of the Population Register Centre 661/2009.

– Law on the Population Information System and Certification Services of the Population Register Centre (661/2009) §§23–27, 42, 48.

1189. The purpose of the processing of personal data is to provide personal information for the purposes of society as required by law and for the normal running of the Lutheran and Orthodox Church parishes and the Population Register Centre's population information system and certification services. The personal data register is a member register (maintenance of member information) within the meaning of the Religious Membership Register Act. The data is not used for the purposes of automated decision-making or profiling. No one is required to disclose his or her religious convictions. The authorities have the right to inquire into a person's membership in a religious community only to the extent that rights or duties may depend upon it or that a statistical survey mandated by a law so requires. These include Population Register Centre data on the distribution of citizens' faith adherence[693] and Patent and Registration Office data on registered religious communities.[694]

1190. The legal basis for processing the data for the Evangelical Lutheran Church is the legitimate interest stated in Article 6.1.f of the EU's General Data Protection Regulation,[695] which is based on each data subject's declaration and consent given in connection with placing an order for a civil status document, joining the Church, requesting an intercessory prayer, providing feedback, or subscribing to a newsletter.

1191. The Church Council is responsible for the general and shared content of the website publishing system of the ELCF. Each parish of the ELCF is responsible for its own introduction, contact information, event details, responding to requests for certification of civil status, joining the Church, signing up for events, providing feedback, etc. The site user provides the personal data required for the form or activity in question. Data submitted through the site are not disclosed to third parties. The maintenance of the site's technical environment has been outsourced to an operational service and application provider whose operations meet the requirements of the EU's General Data Protection Regulation. In addition, data are not disclosed beyond the borders of the EU or EEA.[696]

---

693. Statistics Finland's Classification Services on population and religion, *see* Statistics Finland 31 Dec 2022. For details, *see* https://www.tilastokeskus.fi/tup/suoluk/suoluk_vaesto_en.html#Population%20structure%20on%2031%20December. Accessed 23 Nov. 2023.
694. For further detail on the purpose of and legal basis for processing personal data, *see* https://www.prh.fi/en/presentation_and_duties/processing_personaldata/how_we_process/privacystatement_religiouscommunities.html. Latest update 17.07.2023. Accessed 23 Nov. 2023.
695. For further detail concerning the regulations, *see* §4 (Lawfulness of processing 1–4) and §6 (Processing of special categories of personal data), which handles issues for which §9(1) of the Data Protection Regulation does not apply.
696. For further detail about the website publishing system of the Evangelical Lutheran Church of Finland, *see* https://evl.fi/tietosuoja/privacy-policy. Accessed 23 Nov. 2023.

1192. The data protection policy, approved by the Orthodox Church Council of Finland, defines the principles, policies, responsibilities, and controls that are followed by the Central Government, parishes, and monasteries of the OCF. To date, the following documents have been compiled from the privacy records for the personal registers maintained by the OCF: Registry Information Request Form, The Privacy Policy of the OCF, Privacy Statement Certificate of Identity, Privacy Statement for Church Communication and Publication Services, Register of Investigators of the Board of Directors of the Ecclesiastical Board, and Representatives of the Church Assembly.[697]

1193. It is not possible to deal with the privacy practices of the various registered religious communities in the present context; suffice it to say that they are covered by the same EU data protection rules.

697. *See* further (in Finnish) https://ort.fi/hallinto-ja-paatoksenteko/tietosuoja and https://ort.fi/sites/default/files/2018-06/Tietosuojaseloste%20Status%20Papinkirja%201.6.2018.pdf. Accessed 23 Nov. 2023.

Part XVII. The Law on Aliens

1194. The central legal provision governing residence and immigration in Finland is the Aliens' Act (301/2004). The law incorporates into the Aliens' Act all of the European Council's directives and legislative instruments regarding the Common European Asylum System, together with the directive on family reunification.[698]

1195. The Aliens' Act was amended on 1 June 2019 by a new law (437/2019). Most significantly, the changes took into account the availability of labour. Other changes to the Aliens Act included confirmatory applications submitted by asylum seekers, asylum seekers' employment rights, travel documents, and family reunification.

1196. Article 9(4) of the Constitution includes the principle of *non-refoulement*: 'no one shall be deported or extradited or returned to another country if in consequence he or she is in danger of death sentence, torture or other treatment violating human dignity'. The Aliens Act also contains the principle of non-refoulement in its provisions on refusal of entry and expulsion.

1197. It is important to notice that Article 9 of the Constitution does not explicitly refer to religion or religious affiliation in the principles of non-refoulement. There is no explicit reference to the fact that a foreign person should not be deported, for instance, for religious or political reasons. However, it is natural to assume that the act of 'violating human dignity' mentioned in the Constitution also encompasses race, religion, nationality, membership of a specific social group, and religious or political conviction; fuller definitions are provided in Article 6 of the Constitution (Equality).

1198. **Finnish citizenship** is stipulated in the Finnish Constitution and the Finnish Nationality Act (359/2003),[699] which contains more detailed provisions on the matter. A person may obtain Finnish citizenship at birth or through the citizenship of his/her parents, or acquire it by application or declaration.

698. These include: Council Directive 2005/85/EC; Council Directive 2004/83/EC; Council Directive 2001/55/EC; Council Directive 2003/86/EC; Council Directive 2003/109/EC and Council Regulation EC No. 343/2003.

699. For further detail, *see* unofficial translation of the Ministry of the Interior, Finland: https://www.refworld.org/pdfid/3ae6b51614.pdf. Accessed 23 Nov. 2023.

1199. The criteria for acquiring Citizenship on application are based on Article 13 of the Finnish Nationality Act and its general requirements for naturalization. Article 13 states:

> An alien is granted Finnish citizenship on application if, when a decision is made based on the application,
>
> 1) he or she has reached the age of 18 years or has married prior to that;
> 2) he or she is and has been permanently resident and domiciled in Finland (period of residence):
>   a) for the past six years without interruption (continuous period of residence); or
>   b) for eight years after reaching the age of 15 years, with the last two years being without interruption (accumulated period of residence);
> 3) he or she has not committed any punishable act nor has a restraining order been issued against him
>   or her (integrity requirement);
> 4) he or she has not materially failed to provide maintenance or to meet his or her pecuniary obligations under public law;
> 5) he or she can provide a reliable account of his or her livelihood; and
> 6) he or she has satisfactory oral and written skills in the Finnish or Swedish language, or, instead, of similar skills in the Finnish sign language (language skills requirement).
>
> Exceptions to the general requirements for naturalisation may be made only as stipulated below.

1200. From a religious point of view, the most interesting topic consists of the legal requirements on asylum. The Aliens Act of 2004 provides the criteria for granting asylum and also the procedures involved. These are in conformity with the respective EU legislative documents. The asylum application includes a residence permit application, and hence the procedure combines both. Section 52 of the Aliens Act of 2004 reads:

> A residence permit can be issued for individual humanitarian reasons when rejection of the application would be unreasonable given the state of health, ties with Finland or other individual humanitarian reason, and in such circumstances he or she would end up in his or her home country or would be in a vulnerable state.

1201. Since numerous wars and conflicts have broken out around the world in the last twenty years, many refugees have come to Finland, for political reasons, to find a safe place to live until the situation in their home country stabilizes. In the 1990s, most refugees came from Eritrea and Somalia, and most of them were Muslims. In the wake of humanitarian crises and wars in Afghanistan, Iraq, Syria, and the former Yugoslavia, the number of asylum seekers has increased, especially from Iraq and from the former Yugoslavia. The record number of asylum seekers in 2015 (over 32,000 asylum seekers, mainly from Iraq) has influenced the ways in which Finland will deal with migration for years to come. The increase in the number of migrants granted residence permits will probably be reflected by an increase in the number of applications for citizenship and family reunification. The significance of return and removal will continue to be emphasized.[700]

1202. As one of the stated grounds for seeking asylum, religion has been an issue to varying degrees. According to Sari Sirva's study, 'Iranian Bahá'ls and Christians have been the most successful'. Although Finland has had 'very few asylum seekers from Eritrea, those whose applications have been based on their Pentecostal faith have been successful. In general, religion is not the most important factor in seeking asylum in Finland'.[701]

1203. On various occasions, representatives of the ELCF have pleaded for a more humane asylum and immigration policy and voiced concerns over how the increasingly strict criteria for bringing families together affect the well-being of families and children. Indeed, the ELCF, the Finnish Orthodox Church, and some of the Free Churches, such as the Pentecostal Church, have provided asylum to failed asylum seekers pending their deportation. This has been a much-discussed topic in the Finnish media, not least because there are no legal provisions for this kind of response. Legally speaking, the authorities and the police have the right to deport the person enjoying church shelter (i.e., enjoying security 'within the walls of the church').[702]

1204. The ELCF has openly proclaimed church protection, which means that parishes offer spiritual and material support to rejected asylum seekers, for example, and help them plead their case with the authorities. Church shelter is an open activity that aims to ensure the rightful treatment of migrants living in Finland. However, it is important to note that the Church does not hide people or maintain a parallel asylum system. The former Archbishop, Mr *Kari Mäkinen* (in office 2010–2018), who while serving as Archbishop was socio-ethically sensitive, has emphasized that 'the Church has a good working relationship with the authorities and stated that parishes are bound to secrecy and confidentiality in their work'. Mäkinen sees 'collaboration with the authorities as vital and essential but believes it must always be based on the needs and consent of the person in need'.[703]

---

700. For further detail, *see* Matti Kotiranta, 'Securitization of Religious Freedom: Religion and the Limits of State Control in Finland'. In *Merilin* Kiviorg, *Securitization of Religious Freedom: Religion and the Limits of State Control in Europe*. (Tallinn: European Consortium for Church and State Research. Editorial Comares 2020), 2020, 199–218.
701. Sari Sirva, 'Immigration and Religion in Finland'. In *Augustin Motilla (ed.), Immigration, National and Regional Laws and Freedom of Religion*. (Leuven: Peeters, 2012), 72.
702. 'Church shelter' is the centuries-old Christian tradition of permitting marginalized groups to seek refuge in churches. The Finnish Ecumenical Council has published a booklet 'Church as Asylum', which gives guidelines for church shelter. The guidelines emphasize that they are not legally binding, but they provide an impetus for ways of working together with the asylum seeker and his or her lawyer.
703. *See* further https://evl.fi/current-issues/undocumented-migrants-and-church-shelter. Accessed 23 Nov. 2023.

1205. Regarding migration, the public debate has touched on three issues affecting the protection of women and children in the migration crisis: (a) the rights of women and children in the crisis, (b) fears about unfair deportations of women and children to conflict areas, e.g., Afghanistan, Syria, or Iraq, and (c) forced marriages as a basis for family reunification.

1206. (a) In 2015 over 32,000 asylum seekers arrived in Finland. In the past, asylum seekers in Finland were, to a large extent, young men. The situation has now changed in many ways. A typical asylum seeker is no longer a young, solitary traveller. Instead, 60% of those leaving conflict areas are women or children. In addition, it should be noted that children are at high risk of becoming victims of human trafficking.

1207. The Dublin Regulation is the cornerstone of EU legislation concerned with international protection. Finland is committed to observing the Council of Europe Convention on Action against Trafficking in Human Beings. Recently, the Finnish Immigration Service (FIS) has received much public criticism for setting the bar too high when evaluating whether a person is in a vulnerable or highly vulnerable position. It has been argued, for example, that a child's poor health or being in a parent's sole custody is not sufficient for that child to be granted a residence permit on the grounds of being in a highly vulnerable position or of potentially becoming a victim of human trafficking. The FIS has stressed that the authorities in a victim's home country must be unwilling or unable to protect the victim from threats posed, for example, by criminal organizations.

1208. The FIS has also been criticized for not knowing what happens to victims of human trafficking who are refused entry. The FIS has responded to this, emphasizing the following:

> no Finnish authority has a statutory obligation, not to mention the right, to track the citizens of other states abroad. If it had, this would violate (individuals') legal protection. Finland is bound by non-refoulement. We do not return people if they may be subject to the death penalty, torture, persecution or other inhumane or degrading treatment. We are not aware of a single case in which an asylum seeker who has been refused entry to Finland has fallen victim to such acts or conditions of non-refoulement.[704]

1209. Each application for asylum in Finland is handled individually, and the FIS decides in exceptional cases to examine individual applications more closely. Health problems do not usually mean that an applicant is refused entry and returned to another EU Member State. However, if for some reason, the applicant is, for example, unable to take care of his or her child, the application for asylum can nevertheless be processed in Finland if this is in the best interests of the child.

704. Esko Repo, Director of the Asylum Unit, Finnish Immigration Service. Press releases, 18 Aug. 2016.

1210. The latest decision (2019) reversed by FIS was the subject of a judgment of the ECtHR. Finland was found guilty of violating the ECHR, said the ECtHR. The case concerned an Iraqi asylum seeker for whom Finland issued a return decision in 2016. The person returned to Baghdad in winter 2017 and was killed weeks after his return.

1211. Finland defended its return decision to the ECtHR on the grounds that Ali had returned to Iraq 'voluntarily' and Finland could not be responsible for his fate. In stating this, Finland was referring to the *voluntary* return programme that it offers to those who have been issued a return decision. Asylum seekers will receive money from Finland if they return to their homeland without protest. Ali returned to Iraq through a voluntary return programme in November 2017.

1212. The ECtHR did not accept the justification. In practice, the alternative to 'voluntary return' for those who have been returned is to be forcibly detained and returned by the police, followed by an order refusing re-entry into the Schengen area. If the person to be returned is forced to return, his or her alternative fate would be to remain in Finland without a residence permit or legal status.

1213. Thus, the appellant's father had no genuine freedom of choice between these options and his return could be considered a forced return, the ECtHR indicated.[705]

1214. The man, Ali, who was supposed to be dead, has turned out to be very much alive. The public prosecutor brought in accusations of aggravated fraud and aggravated forgery in what is referred to as the fake Iraqi case. The charges have been brought against a woman born in 1996 and a man born in 1984. The woman is the daughter of a man alleged to be deceased, while her co-accused is her ex-husband.

1215. The preliminary investigation of the two suspected ECtHR scammers was completed in August 2020 and was subsequently taken to court at a later date. According to the prosecutor, the deported man's daughter and her ex-husband claimed the woman's father had died as the victim of a homicide in Iraq after Finland had rejected the woman's application for asylum in December 2017. The Iraqi man suspected of ECtHR fraud denies knowing anything about his death – he is still unreachable. The prosecutor has demanded the imprisonment of the daughter and the former son-in-law of the 'fake dead' Iraqi man – with the charge that the accused lied about the death of the woman's father in order to pervert the course of justice.[706]

1216. Finland has asked the ECtHR to review the judgment. On 13 July 2021, the European Court of Human Rights (ECtHR) overturned Finland's conviction in

705. Yle-News, *see* https://yle.fi/uutiset/3-11068247. Accessed 14 Nov. 2019. (Updated 23 Nov. 2023).
706. For more detail, *see* https://yle.fi/uutiset/3-11731120 and https://yle.fi/uutiset/3-11586765. Accessed 19 Mar. 2021. (Updated 23 Nov. 2023).

the case of a falsely deceased Iraqi man. The ECtHR found that the applicant had deliberately misled the court. Hence, the Court held that the 2019 decision must be annulled and the appeal dismissed. The Court's decision was unanimous. The criminal trial of the daughter and the former son-in-law of the 'fake dead' Iraqi man is still pending in Finland. The 2021 Helsinki District Court judgment on fraud is not final, and since 15 September 2022 it has been continued at the Helsinki Court of Appeal.

1217. (b) Fear about unfair deportations of women and children to conflict areas such as Afghanistan, Iraq, and Syria has led to a heated public discussion in the Finnish newspapers.[707]

1218. Despite the strict policy of the FIS, it has done invaluable precious work with minors who arrive in Finland without a guardian. The FIS describes its policy on this matter in the following manner on its website:

> Unaccompanied minors under the age of 16 are accommodated in group homes. The training of the staff and the services provided in these group homes are the same as in Finnish child protection facilities. Most of the occupants are children who have already obtained a residence permit, but who do not have family in Finland.

1219. Asylum seekers between 16 and 17 years of age are accommodated in supported housing units, while asylum seekers who have reached the age of 18 are accommodated in reception centres for adults and families. Unaccompanied minors can also be accommodated in other appropriate locations intended for children.

1220. In addition to accommodation, other basic needs of children who do not have a guardian in Finland are taken care of in group homes and supported housing units. The children receive social and healthcare services such as professional care, food, and financial support. The services also include professional care and fostering plans. The children receive schooling and other education according to their age and educational level. They also receive legal aid, and interpreter services are available if required.[708]

1221. According to the FIS's protocol, every child without a guardian is assigned a representative whose duties include looking after the child's interests in

707. *See*, for example, Helsingin Sanomat 4 Apr. 2016: http://www.hs.fi/kotimaa/art-2000005154727.html; and Helsingin Sanomat 5 Apr. 2017 http://www.hs.fi/paivanlehti/05042017/art-2000005155854.html. (Updated 23 Nov. 2023).

708. At http://www.migri.fi/asylum_in_finland/reception_activities/reception_services/children_without_a_guardian.

every situation. The representative uses the right of action that belongs to the guardian of a minor child and helps the child with official matters. The representative is present, for example, at the interview that is part of the processing of an asylum application.[709]

1222. (c) Forced marriage does not constitute a basis for family reunification.[710] Pursuant to Finnish matrimonial law, marriage is a consensual legal act. In addition, polygamous marriages are not recognized pursuant to EU Council Directive 2003/86/EC (Articles 4, paragraphs 4 and 5) on the right to family reunification. Polygamy accepted by a certain religion or religious community is not respected apart from marriage with the first spouse.

1223. Migration does not, simply involve asylum seekers. In accordance with the government's programme, Finland will continue to promote labour force migration that strengthens its national employment and public finances. This was no doubt the main reason for the preparation of the new Aliens Act (437/2019).

1224. As indicated above, the change in the new Aliens Act took into account of the availability of labour supply. Other changes in the Aliens Act included confirmatory applications submitted by asylum seekers, asylum seekers' employment rights, travel documents, and family reunification.[711]

1225. The Ministry of the Interior is working on several national legislative projects related to labour migration. On 14 June 2017 the Ministry set up a project to prepare the government's migration policy programme. It was intended to lay down migration policy guidelines for the whole government term (in office 2015–2018). The policy was completed in 2018, with its programme aiming to confront radicalization by means of an effective migration policy that would combat extremism and terrorism.

---

709. *Ibid.*

710. For further detail, *see* Part X. *Matrimonial and Family Law.*

711. According to the FIS, the first change is necessary if the asylum seeker submits a confirmatory application with a new justification claiming that he or she has had a reason for not providing appropriate justifications previously.

Another change features in the asylum seekers' employment law. From the beginning of June 2019, the right of an asylum seeker to work will cease at the moment when he or she can be legally expelled. If the asylum seeker has received a negative decision or a confirmatory application on the basis of an earlier enforceable decision, he will no longer have the right to work.

If the asylum seeker receives a positive decision, he or she will in most cases be able to continue working in Finland. Even if the asylum seeker has stayed in Finland for three to six months after submitting his/her application for asylum, he/she can still work without seeking permission.

A third change means that from June 2019 the authorities can confiscate an asylum seeker's passport or other travel document until the asylum seeker either obtains a residence permit or leaves the country. *See* YLE-News, https://yle.fi/uutiset/3-10811540. Accessed 10 Oct. 2019. (Updated 23 Nov. 2023).

1226. With respect to the struggle against radicalization, a glance at Finnish legislation might give the impression that, in the fight against extremism and religiously motivated terrorism, legislators have no real interest in entering into conflict with the constitutional norm of religious freedom.[712] There are no general prohibitions of certain religious communities. A specific prohibition of a particular religious association is possible only if criminal law (e.g., Chapter 34a of the Criminal Code on terrorist offences) is violated. It is also noteworthy, that the reasons stated for prohibitions are not related to religious beliefs but solely to violations of criminal law.

1227. Nevertheless, a new chapter (Chapter 34a [HE 188/2002]) on terrorist offences was added the Criminal Code in February 2003. It contains provisions on the penalties awarded for offences committed with terrorist intention (section 1)[713] and for the preparation of such offences (section 2), the offence of directing a terrorist group (section 3), the facilitation of the activities of a terrorist group (section 4),[714] and the financing of terrorism (section 5).[715] It also contains a definitions provision (section 6),[716] a provision on the right of prosecution (section 7),[717] and a provision determining the liability of legal entities (section 8). Certain minor amendments were also made to the Criminal Code, and the Coercive Measures Act was adjusted accordingly. The law was updated with supplements on 3 April 2014, 1068/2014 (HE/2014)[718] and 2 June 2016, 919/2016 (HE 93/2016).[719] Neither of these laws deals with the subject of religious beliefs.[720]

---

712. On the relationship between terrorism and criminal law, *see* Kimmo Nuotio, 'Terrorism as a Catalyst for the Emergence, Harmonization and Reform of Criminal Law'. In Katja L.H. Samuel & Nigel D. White (eds), Counter-*Terrorism and International Law* (Abingdon, Oxon: Routledge, The International Law of Peace and Security, 2016), 145–163; Katja L.H. & Nigel D. White (eds), *Counter-Terrorism and International Law* (Abingdon, Oxon: Routledge, The International Law of Peace and Security, 2016).
713. Section 1 of the new chapter on terrorist offences provides for such offences for which an increased sentence may be passed when the offence has been committed with terrorist intentions. The list of offences in s. 1 corresponds to the list of offences included in the Framework Decision and, almost without exception, such offences were already subject to punishment before the enactment of the new provisions.
714. The provisions relating to terrorist groups (ss. 3 and 4) are entirely new. 'Facilitation of the activities of a terrorist group' means certain acts that are committed with the intention of facilitating the criminal activities of a terrorist group as referred to in ss. 1 and 2.
715. Section 5 is the earlier s. 9b of Ch. 34 concerning the financing of terrorism, with certain adjustments, which is partly based on the International Convention for the Suppression of the Financing of Terrorism and partly on the aforementioned Framework Decision.
716. Section 6 defines 'terrorist intention', 'terrorist group' and 'international organisation'.
717. Under s. 7, a decision to prosecute with regard to offences referred to in this chapter must be made by the prosecutor general.
718. Added to Ch. 34a of the Criminal Code Art. 4c (Recruitment for a terrorist offence) and Art. 5a (Funding a terrorist group).
719. Added to Ch. 34a of the Criminal Code was Art. 5b (Travelling to commit terrorist offences).
720. For further detail on 'Legislation Relevant to Tackling Extremism and Radicalization', *see*, Matti Kotiranta, 'Securitization of Religious Freedom: Religion and the Limits of State Control in Finland'. In Merilin Kiviorg, *Securitization of Religious Freedom: Religion and the Limits of State Control in Europe*. (Tallinn: European Consortium for Church and State Research; Granada: Comares, 2020), 199–218. *See also* Kimmo Nuotio, 'Security and Criminal Law: A Difficult Relationship'. In Massimo Fichera, Jens Kremer (eds), *Law and Security in Europe: Reconsidering the*

1228. The war of aggression waged by Russia against Ukraine has placed the Finnish state in a completely new situation in terms of asylum decisions involving Russia's hybrid influence on Finland's eastern border, although no one is in any doubt that a Russian hybrid operation is indeed underway on Finland's eastern border. Foreign and security sources have reported that Russian embassies in the Horn of Africa have begun issuing visas to local people to enter Russia and then, with the help of the FSB, to continue their journey as far as the Finnish border. Those brought to the border by Russia are in most cases the same kind of people who would in any case seek asylum in the West.

1229. The government has closed the eastern border on several occasions and in several stages, concentrating first on asylum applications in November 2023 in the northern part of Finland at the Raja-Jooseppi border crossing. However, this did not put an end to the incidents, which resulted in the border being closed for a month from the beginning of 2024, which was then extended by a government decision. When the decision to partially close the eastern border was taken on 22 November 2023, leaving Raja-Jooseppi as the only border crossing point, it was noted that this was allegedly not without legal problems. In the explanatory memorandum to the decision, the government stated that it was taking a legal risk but that it was a risk it was prepared to take:

> The centralisation of the application for international protection as referred to in the Decision is in tension with Union law, in particular the EU Procedures Directive 2013/32/EU. There is no case-law in existence at the Court of Justice concerning any situation of State interference similar to the present situation, where the Court of Justice has accepted exceptions made by a Member State to its rights under the Procedures Directive.
>
> In the present case of State interference, however, accurate and precise restrictions which are necessary, demonstrable and proportionate may be considered justified and at least acceptable in fact and in practice. However, the interpretation of EU law is ultimately a matter for the Court of Justice.[721]
>
> 28 November 2023 the Chancellor of Justice Tuomas Pöysti confirmed the decision by means of which Prime Minister Orpo's government closed the entire eastern border. The decision sparked some controversy, with many legal scholars and the Left Alliance leader Li Andersson wanting the government to clarify how international obligations regarding asylum would be fulfilled when the entire eastern border was closed.

Security Constitution. (Cambridge: Intersentia, 2013); Tuomas Ojanen, 'Perus- ja ihmisoikeudet terrorismin vastatoimissa Euroopan unionissa' (Fundamental and human rights in the fight against terrorism in Europe). *Lakimies* 7–8 (2007): 1053–1074.

721. The Government's decision on the temporary closure of border crossing points and the centralizing of applications for international protection. Memorandum 28.11.2023. For more detail, *see* https://intermin.fi/ajankohtaista/paatos?decisionId=214 and https://valtioneuvosto.fi/paatokset/paatos?decisionId=491. *See also*, https://www.ssj.news/p/finland-closes-entire-eastern-border and https://www.iltalehti.fi/politiikka/a/f8d66e48-8a21-4b4e-b8ea-a1be57e66130.

1230. The Constitutional Law Committee plays a completely central role in the interpretation of the Constitution and enforcing the law in Finland. A new interpretation in the reasoning of the Constitutional Law Committee is that the total closure of the eastern border is in fact a safeguard for asylum applications. The idea is that the Russian-manipulated asylum-seeking is a hybrid effect that prevents appropriate and proper asylum-seeking at the eastern border. This interpretation suggests that when asylum-seeking at the eastern border has been completely blocked, the Russian hybrid operation will end and the border can be reopened for proper asylum-seeking.

1231. The latest turning point in the asylum debate is represented by the Border Security Act, the so-called Refoulement Act (*käännytyslaki*) (HE 53/2024 vp),[722] which is an emergency law that was approved by Parliament on 12 July 2024 by 167-31 votes and confirmed by the President of the Republic, Alexander Stubb, on 16 July 2024. The law came into force on 22 July and may remain in force for one year.

1232. The Act contains four main elements: (1) the introduction of the Refoulement Act is decided by the President and the Council of State; (2) a border guard will have the power to assess the removal of individuals from the country, the final decision to be taken by his or her superior; (3) asylum applications can be accepted from individuals in certain exceptional groups; and (4) an asylum seeker who has been removed from the country may request a review of the decision within thirty days.

1233. The Finnish solution is controversial and if the border were to be opened, the threat of actually having to use the emergency law is real. The Refoulement Act will not destroy Finland's rule of law, but it is historic. The hand seems to be moving to a new point on the scale In Finland's human rights policy. Finland has traditionally taken a strictly binding approach to its international commitments. While human rights treaties are both absolute and relative, the adoption of the Refoulement Act proves that it is possible to apply human rights pragmatically, according to need. The legislative process is also a reminder that the parliamentary Constitutional Committee is also influenced by political power relations. During the current government term, the national Coalition Party has held sway in the committee on a number of notoriously difficult legislative projects, such as cuts to social security, the reform of the law on preparedness, the export-driven wage model and amendments to the law on foreigners. While the opinion of the Constitutional Committee was being driven through, the Social Democrats replaced members of the committee as necessary. The Chancellor of Justice deployed her expertise in the committee. The Ombudsman, for his part, suggested that Finland could influence the interpretation of international treaties. However, admitting contradictions in the drafting of legislation does not remove critical questions about the parties' relationship with the

722. *See also* key documents: the committee document HaVM 15/2024 vp (Report of the Administrative Committee 15/2024) and PeVL 26/2024 vp, and PeVL 29/2024 vp (Opinion of the Constitutional Law Committee PeVL 26/2024, and PeVL 29/2024).

Constitution, EU law and international commitments. The Refoulement Act demonstrated the expeditious manner in which the rule of law can be contravened in the name of national security.

Part XVIII. The Law on Foundations

1234. The new Foundations Act (487/2015), the Act on the Implementation of the Foundations Act (488/2015), and other amendments to the Foundations Act came into force on 1 December 2015.[723]

1235. Foundations are legal entities that have property that is intended for a specific purpose. The foundation supports or conducts useful activities to promote its purpose. The purpose cannot be to conduct a business or provide financial gain to a person affiliated with the Foundation, to the community, or to the Foundation.[724]

1236. The Foundations Act does not apply to public law foundations in Finland. Public law foundations are legal entities that are assigned assets as communities and perform a public function. As such, the Bank of Finland and the Social Insurance Institution are constantly transforming. Pension funds that provide statutory occupational retirement funding, which are governed by the Pension Funds Act (1774/1995), are also excluded from the Foundation Act.

1237. Establishing a foundation is a way of permanently allocating funds for a specific purpose determined by the founder.[725] There are several types of foundation in Finland. The most common foundations mentioned in the Finnish legal literature comprise registered foundations[726] and unregistered non-profit foundations, together with private law foundations and public law foundations. With regard to the financing of the activities of foundations, the foundations are divided into capital foundations, non-profit foundations, and combinations of these, usually referred to as mixed foundations.

723. The previous Foundations Act dates back to 5 Apr. 1930 (109/1930).
724. The activities must be directly related to the purpose of the foundation. The activities may be directly defined in the statutes either in detail or as a limited liability company.
725. A more detailed list on account of the assets, income, and use of foundations can be found in the Ministry of Justice publication, 'Reforming Foundation Legislation. Report on the Rules and Practices of National Foundations' (OMSO 47/2012, http://www.oikeusministerio.fi/en/index/publication/publication archive/1354109655883/Files/Response.pdf).
726. The tax status of a registered foundation is based on tax law. Article 22 of the Income Tax Act (1535/1992) provides for the definition of a non-profit corporation, while Art. 23 provides for the tax liability of a non-profit corporation.
According to the *National Audit Office of Finland*, NAOF, approximately 90% of registered foundations are considered by the taxpayer to be public benefit entities within the meaning of the Income Tax Act.

1238. In addition to registered independent foundations, non-independent foundations (epäitsenäinen säätiö)[727] and other special purpose funds also exist, which are not subject to the Foundations Act. A non-independent foundation is also referred to in the accounting and financial statements as a 'self-managed investment fund' ('omakatteinen rahasto'), while funds set up for other purposes may be referred to as 'other tied funds' ('muu sidottu rahasto').[728] The foundations of the ELCF and its parishes are mainly self-managed investment funds. Religious organizations that operate as non-profit organizations, whether registered or unregistered, may also be supported by a foundation that backs the group, such as the Salvation Army.

1239. Registered ecclesiastical foundations in Finland include *inter alia* the Finnish Salvation Army Foundation, the Finnish Orthodox Church Museum Foundation, the Finnish Orthodox Cultural Centre Foundation, the Helsinki Deaconess Institution Foundation, and the Oulu Deaconess Institution Foundation.[729]

1240. The central fund of the Evangelical Lutheran Church of Finland has, throughout its history, been dependent on two autonomously managed funds – the Church Central Fund (KKR) and the Church Pension Fund (KER) – each having its own regulations and an independent decision-making body. The Church Pension Fund (KER) was separated from the Central Fund into its own legal entity governed by public law on 1 January 2016.

1241. The Church Pension Fund investments as of 31 December 2023 totalled EUR 1,852,000,000, of which direct equity investments amounted to EUR 138,115,000 (Finland) and EUR 562,965,000 (abroad).[730]

1242. Additionally, congregations belonging to the ELCF have their own self-financing funds, primarily related to cemetery maintenance funds. The total balance of these cemetery maintenance funds was EUR 308,900,042 by the end of 2023.

---

727. A non-independent foundation and other dedicated fund are not legal entities but are managed by the beneficiary in their own name. An independent foundation does not require the establishment of its own organization for the management of foundation assets. The liability for the liabilities of such a fund shall not be limited to the assets transferred for the intended purpose but shall be borne by the beneficiary with all his assets.
728. Accounting Board, KILA, Opinion 1334/1995.
729. For more about 100 largest foundations by total assets *see* Matti Virén, *Yleishyödylliset yhteisöt Suomessa. Verot, lahjoitukset ja avustukset tutkimuksen kohteena* (Non-profit organizations in Finland. Taxes, donations and public support under scrutiny). Forskningsrapporter från Svenska handelshögskolan Hanken (School of Economics Research Reports) 74. (Helsinki 2014), 110–112; *see also* about non-profit foundations qualifying for tax relief, *ibid.*, 118–120.
730. I am deeply grateful for the most recent data to Juho Laatikainen of the Church Council of the Evangelical Lutheran Church.

The Church Pension Fund (KER) Investments 31.12.2023

Asset	Market value	Share of the portfolio (%)
All assets	1,852,000,000	100.0
Equities	852,380,000	46.0
Liquid equities	701,080,000	37.9
Finland	138,115,000	7.5
Europe	145,050,000	7.8
North America	150,300,000	8.1
Japan	20,115,000	1.1
Developing Markets	136,400,000	7.4
Global/Sectors	111,100,000	6.0
Other equities	151,300,000	8.2
Capital funds	151,300,000	8.2
Fixed income	531,110.000	28.7
Liquid assets	381,830.000	20.6
Capital market investments	53,150,000	2.9
Finnish Government Bonds	26 740,000	1.4
Investment Grade	95 000,000	5.1
High Yield	47 310,000	2.6
Evolving markets	45 000,000	2.4
Short term bonds	114 630,000	6.2
Other fixed-income investments	149 280,000	8.1
Alternative fixed income	149 280,000	8.1
Alternative assets	468 510,000	25.3
Real assets	428 100,000	23.1
Absolute return funds	39 190,000	2.1
Derivatives	1 220,000	0.1

Country allocations of the equity investments of The Church Pension Fund (KER) 31.12.2023

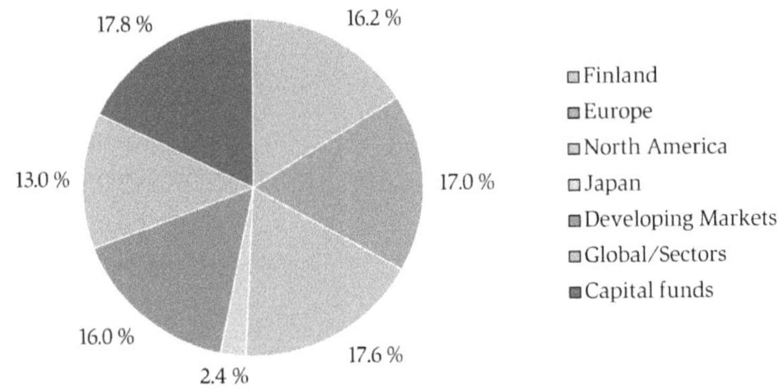

Country allocations of fixed income investments of The Church Pension Fund (KER) 31.12.2023

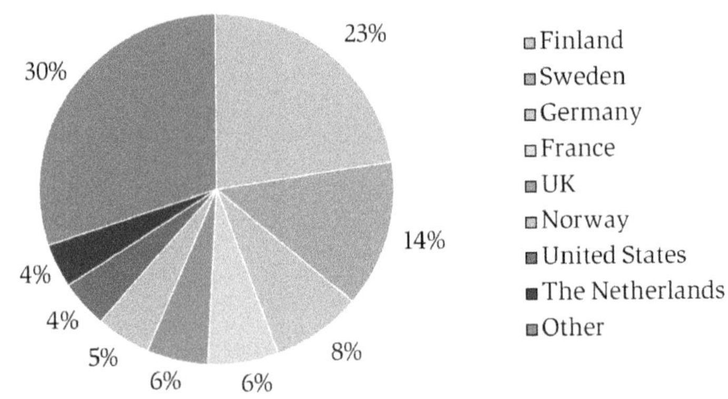

1243. The primary national foundation authority in Finland is the National Patents and Registration Board, which is responsible for supervising the administration of the foundations in accordance with the law and the rules of the foundations (Article 13 of the Foundation Act). The foundations to be registered should be entered in the register of foundations maintained by the NPRB (Chapter 2, Articles 2, 5 and 6 of the Foundations Act). In December 2022 the NPRB held 1,909 registered foundations.[731] It is important to note that, as self-managed funds, church

731. https://vuosikertomus.prh.fi/2022/fi/index/toimintajapaajohtajankatsaus/yhdistyksetjasaatiot.html.

foundations are not directly under the control of the state foundation authority and thus the state cannot require the dismissal of members of the foundation's bodies for serious misconduct or incompetence.

1244. Under the new Foundations Act, the foundation will dissolve itself, and the district court of the seat of the foundation will decide on the dissolution of the foundation. Under the Foundations Act in force, the Foundation terminates itself after obtaining permission from the National Patents and Registration Board.

Selected Bibliography

General and Comprehensive References

References in the English Language

Doe, Norman. *Law and Religion in Europe: A Comparative Introduction.* New York: Oxford University Press, 2011.

Doe, Norman & Russel Sandberg (eds). 'Law and Religion: New Horizons'. In *Law and Religion Studies*, Vol. 7. Leuven: Peeters, 2010.

Durham Jr., W. Cole & Silvio Ferrari (eds). *Laws on Religion and the State in Post-Communist Europe.* Leuven: Peeters, 2004.

European Consortium for Church-State Research (ed. Lina Papadopoulou). *Islam and Human Rights in the European Union – Islam et droits de l'homme dans l'Union européenne.* Granada: Comares, 2022 (2021 Meeting).

European Consortium for Church-State Research (ed. Miguel Rodríguez Blanco). *Philosophical and Non-Confessional Organisations in Europe – Fiscalités, religions et organisations philosophiques ou non confessionnelles en Europe.* Granada: Comares, 2022 (2019 Meeting).

European Consortium for Church-State Research (ed. Marco Ventura). *The Legal Status of Old and New Religious Minorities in the European Union – Le statut juridique des minorités religieuses anciennes et nouvelles dans l'Union européenne*, Granada: Comares, 2021 (2018 Meeting).

European Consortium for Church-State Research (ed. Merilin Kiviorg). *Securitisation of Religious Freedom: Religion and Limits of State Control – Sécurisation de la liberté religieuse – La religion et les limites du contrôle de l'Etat.* Granada: Comares, 2020 (2017 Meeting).

European Consortium for Church-State Research (eds. Ringolds Balodis & Miguel Rodríguez Blanco). *Religious Assistance in Public Institutions – Assistance spirituelle dans les services publics.* Granada: Comares, 2018 (2016 Meeting).

European Consortium for Church-State Research (ed. Miguel Rodríguez Blanco). *Law and Religion in the Workplace.* Granada: Comares, 2016 (2015 Meeting).

European Consortium for Church-State Research (eds. Richard Potz & Wolfgang Wieshaider). *Juridictions religieuses et l'Etat – Religious Adjudication and the State.* Granada: Comares, 2015 (2014 Meeting).

European Consortium for Church-State Research (ed. Francis Messner). *Public Authorities and the Training of Religious Personnel in Europe – La formation des cadres religieux en Europe.* Granada: Comares, 2015 (2013 Meeting).

Selected Bibliography

European Consortium for Church-State Research (ed. Balázs Schanda). *The Mutual Roles of Religion and State in Europe – Interférences mutuelles des religions et de l'État dans l'Union Européenne*. Trier: European Consortium for Church and State Research, 2014 (2012 Meeting).

European Consortium for Church-State Research (ed. Mark Hill QC). *Religion and Discrimination Law in the European Union – La discrimination en matière religieuse dans l'Union Européenne*. Trier: European Consortium for Church and State Research, 2012 (2011 Meeting).

European Consortium for Church-State Research (ed. Gerhard Robbers). *Religion in Public Education – La religion dans l'éducation publique*. Trier: European Consortium for Church and State Research, 2011 (2010 Meeting).

European Consortium for Church-State Research (ed. Agustín Motilla). *Immigration, National and Regional Laws and Freedom of Religion*. Leuven: Peeters, 2012 (2009 Meeting).

European Consortium for Church-State Research (eds. Matti Kotiranta & Norman Doe). *Religion and Criminal Law – Religion et Droit Pénal*. Leuven: Peeters, 2013 (2008 Meeting).

European Consortium for Church-State Research (ed. Achilles Emilianides). *Religious Freedom in the European Union: The Application of the European Convention on Human Rights in the European Union*. Leuven: Peeters, 2011 (2007 Meeting).

European Consortium for Church-State Research (eds. Brigitte Basdevant-Gaudemet & Salvator Berlingò). *The Financing of Religious Communities in the European Union – Le financement des religions dans les pays de l'Union européenne*. Leuven: Peeters, 2009 (2006 Meeting).

European Consortium for Church-State Research (ed. Lars Friedner). *Churches and Other Religious Organisations as Legal Persons*. Leuven: Peeters, 2007 (2005 Meeting).

European Consortium for Church-State Research (eds. Richard Puza & Norman Doe). *Religion and Law in Dialogue. The Covenantal and Non-Covenantal Cooperation of State and Religions in the Members States of the European Union – Religion et droit en dialogue: collaboration conventionnelle et non-conventionnelle entre l'État et religion en Europe*. Leuven: Peeters, 2006 (2004 Meeting).

European Consortium for Church-State Research (eds. José María González del Valle & Alexander Hollerbach). *The Teaching of Church and State Relations in the European Union Countries – L'enseignement du droit ecclésiastique de l'État dans les universités européennes*. Leuven: Peeters, 2005 (2003 Meeting).

European Consortium for Church-State Research (ed. Norman Doe). *The Portrayal of Religion in Europe: The Media and the Arts – Le portrait de religion en Europe: les médias et les arts*. Leuven: Peeters, 2004 (2002 Meeting).

European Consortium for Church-State Research (eds. Richard Potz, Wolfgang Wieshaider). *Islam and the European Union. Proceedings of the Meeting, Wien, November 15–17, 2001*. Leuven: Peeters, 2004 (2001 Meeting).

European Consortium for Church-State Research (ed. Francis Messner). *Le statut des confessions religieuses des États candidats à l'Union européenne – The Status of Religious Confessions of the States Applying for Membership to the European Union.* Milan: Giuffrè Editore, 2002 (2000 Meeting).

European Consortium for Church-State Research (ed. Inger Dubeck, Frands Ole Overgaard). *Social Welfare, Religious Organizations and the State – Les établissements d'assistance, l'État, les Églises et la société.* Milan: Giuffrè Editore, 2003 (1999 Meeting).

European Consortium for Church-State Research (ed.). *New Religious Movements and the Law in the European Union.* Brussels: Bruylant, Milan: Giuffrè Editore, Baden-Baden: Nomos, 1999 (1997 Meeting).

European Consortium for Church-State Research (ed.). *Religions in European Union Law.* Brussels: Bruylant, Milan: Giuffrè Editore, Baden-Baden: Nomos, 1999 (1996 Meeting).

European Consortium for Church-State Research (ed.). *'New Liberties' and Church and State Religionships in Europe.* Brussels: Bruylant, Milan: Giuffrè Editore, Baden-Baden: Nomos, 1999 (1995 Meeting).

European Consortium for Church-State Research (ed.). *The Constitutional Status of Churches in the European Union Countries.* Paris: Litec, Milan: Giuffrè Editore, 1995 (1994 Meeting).

European Consortium for Church-State Research (ed.). *The Legal Status of Religious Minorities in the Countries of the European Union.* Thessalonoki: Sakkoulas Publications, Milan: Giuffrè Editore, 1994 (1993 Meeting).

European Consortium for Church-State Research (ed.). *Marriage and Religion in Europe.* Milan: Giuffrè Editore, 1993 (1991 Meeting).

Ferrari, Silvio., W. Cole Durham Jr. & Elisabeth A. Sewell (eds). *Law and Religion in Post-Communist Europe.* Leuven: Peeters, 2003.

Nemec, D. *Concordat Agreements Between the Holy See and the Post-Communist Countries (1990–2010).* Leuven: Peeters, 2012.

Robbers, Gerhard. 'State and Church in the European Union'. In *State and Church in the European Union*, edited by Gerhard Robbers. 2nd edn. Baden-Baden: Nomos, 2005.

Robbers, Gerhard. 'State and Church in the European Union'. In *State and Church in the European Union,* edited by Gerhard Robbers. 3rd edn. Baden-Baden: Nomos, 2019.

Torfs, Rik (ed.). *European Journal for Church and State Research.* Leuven: Peeters, 1994–2003.

Commentaries

Commentaries on the Constitution of Finland

https://www.finlex.fi/en/laki/kaannokset/1999/en19990731.pdf . English translation of the Finnish Constitution.

Lainkirjoittajan opas. Oikeusministeriö, lainvalmisteluosasto (*Guide to the Law Writer.* Ministry of Justice, Law Enforcement Division). *See*, http://urn.fi/URN:

ISBN:978-952-259-318-4. (The guide describes the constitutional significance of the Constitution and other general legislation and provides guidance on how to write legally clear regulations).

Saraviita, Ilkka. *Perustuslaki* (*The Constitution*). (The Constitution compiles interpretive practices available to the reader by context and by background. The book is a comprehensive commentary on the content of the Constitution – including interpretations and policy practices that do not appear in the legal text). Helsinki: Alma Talent, 2011.

Salminen, Janne. *Suomen valtiosääntö ja Euroopan unioni.* Helsinki: Helsingin yliopiston Oikeustieteelinen tiedekunta, 2019. (The book examines the relationship between the Finnish constitution and the European Union legal order. The discussions focus on the constitutional amendment of Finland on the one hand and the Treaty of Accession of Finland on the other, and the national treatment and overlapping of amendments to the Treaties on which the European Union is founded).

Perusoikeudet (*Fundamental Rights*). Pekka Hallberg, Heikki Karapuu, Tuomas Ojanen, Martin Scheinin, Kaarlo Tuori, Veli-Pekka Viljanen, Perusoikeudet (*Fundamental Rights*). 2nd rev. edn. WSOYpro, 2011.

Niemivuo, Matti. *Kansallinen lainvalmistelu* (*The Preparation of the National Law*). (The study examines the preparation of constitutional and administrative law projects under four different governments 1987–2002). Helsinki: Talentum, 2008.

Jansson, Jan-Magnus, *Grundlagsutskottets funktioner vid riksdagarna 1939–1953* (*The Functions of the Constitutional Committee at the Riksdag 1939–1953*). Helsingfors, 1954.

Meres-Wuori, Ora, *Jurisdictional Relations in the Conclusion of International Agreements*. Jyväskylä, 1990.

Merikoski, Veli: *Muuttomaton, muuttava valtiosääntömme: Suomen hallitusmuoto 1919–19/7–1969* (*Our Immutable, Changing Constitution: The Finnish Constitution*). Helsinki, 1969.

Riepula, Esko. *Eduskunnan perustuslakivaliokunta perustuslakien tulkitsijana* (*Parliamentary Constitutional Law Committee as Interpreter of the Constitutions*). Vammala: Suomalainen lakimiesyhdistys, A 101, 1973.

Sasi, Kimmo. *Asiantuntijat perustuslakivaliokunnan lausuntotyössä* (*Experts in the Constitutional Law Committee's Opinion Work*). In Suomalainen lakimiesyhdistys (toim.): Juhlajulkaisu Mikael Hidén 1939 – 7/12 – 2009. Jyväskylä, 2009.

Books

The following lists works in the English language that were used for this book.[732]

Ahonen, Lauri K. *Suomen helluntaiherätyksen historia* (*The History of the Finnish Pentecostal Awakening*). Jyväskylä: Päivä osakeyhtiö, 2004.

732. A comprehensive list of Finnish legal literature on constitutional and fundamental rights can be found in the book 'Perusoikeudet' (Fundamental Rights). Pekka Hallberg, Heikki Karapuu, Tuomas Ojanen, Martin Scheinin, Kaarlo Tuori, Veli-Pekka Viljanen, Fundamental Rights. (2nd revised edn WSOYpro, 2011), pp. 989–1001.

Ahtonen, Riitta., Anssi Keinänen & Mia Kilpeläinen. *Eduskunnan valiokuntien näkemys lainvalmistelutyön laadusta* (*The Views of Parliamentary Committees on the Quality of Legislation Work*). OPTL:n tutkimustiedonantoja 111. Helsinki, 2011.

Aika puhua – Aika vaieta Rippisalaisuus ja vaitiolovelvollisuus kirkossa (*Time to Speak – Time to Remain Silent. Confession and Confidentiality in the Church*). Helsinki: Finnish Evangelical Lutheran Church Board Publications, 2011, 2.

Akandji-Kombe, Jean-François. *Human Rights Handbooks, No. 7. Positive Obligations under the European Convention on Human Rights: A Guide to the Implementation of the European Convention on Human Rights*. Belgium: Council of Europe. 2007.

Alexy, Robert. *A Theory of Constitutional Rights*. Oxford: Oxford University Press, 2002.

Antila, Jaakko. *Keskustapuolueen kirkkopoliittisten tavoitteiden muotoutuminen vuosina 1966–1978* (*Politics Is in the Church: Formation of Central Party Church Political Objectives from 1966–1978*). Helsinki: SKHST 213, 2010. *Diss.*

Balodis, Ringolds & Miguel Rodrígues Blanco (eds). *Religious Assistance in Public Institutions – Assistance spirituelle dans les services publics*. Granada: Comares, 2016.

Bogdan, Michael. *Comparative Law*. Stockholm: Norstedts Juridik, 1994.

Böse, Martin., Frank Meyer & Anne Schneider (eds). *Conflicts of Jurisdiction in Criminal Matters in the European Union: Vol. I*. Baden-Baden: Nomos, 2013.

Christiansen, Thomas & Christine Reh. *Constitutionalizing the European Union*. Palgrave: Macmillan, 2009.

Dembour, Marie-Bénédicte. *Who Believes in Human Rights? Reflections on the European Convention*. Cambridge: Cambridge University Press, 2006.

Finska, Elina. *Perusoikeuksien rajoittamistestien vertailu Euroopan unionin tuomioistuimen ja Euroopan ihmisoikeustuomioistuimen ratkaisukäytännöissä* (*Comparison of Fundamental Rights Restriction Tests in the Case Law of the European Court of Justice and the European Court of Human Rights*). Tampere: University of Tampere, 2014.

Forsback & Nordström in Svärd (ed.). *Jag var i fängelse – en studiebok om den andliga vården vid fångvårdsanstalterna* (*I Was in Prison – A Study of Spiritual Care in the Prison Institutions*). Stockholm: Klippan, 1970.

Gozdecka, Dorota Anna. *Rights, Religious Pluralism and the Recognition of Difference*. Oxon & New York: Routledge, 2016.

Greer, Steven. *The European Convention on Human Rights – Achievements, Problems and Prospects*. Cambridge: Cambridge University Press, 2006.

Habermas, Jürgen. *Between Facts and Norms – Contributions to a Discourse Theory of Law and Democracy*. Cambridge: Cambridge University Press, 1996.

Haikarainen, Raine. *Informaatiosta kommunikaatioon: ekumeeninen keskustelu viestinnästä 1948–2000*. (*From Information to Communication. Ecumenical Discussion on Communication, 1948–2000*). Helsinki: STKSJ 234, 2002. *Diss.*

Hakala, Pirjo. *Learning by Caring. A Follow-Up Study of Participants in a Specialized Training Program in Pastoral Care and Counseling*. Helsinki, 2000. *Diss.*

Selected Bibliography

Hallamaa, Jaana, Simo Knuuttila., Matti Kotiranta & Antti Raunio. *Rahan teologia ja Euroopan kirkot. Lopun ajan sosiaalietiikka* (*Theology of Money and the European Churches. The End Times of Social Ethics*). Jyväskylä: Atena, 1999.

Halttunen, Matti., Pirjo Pihlaja & Risto Voipio. *Kirkkolainsäädäntö 2008 – Kirkkolain, kirkkojärjestyksen ja kirkon vaalijärjestyksen kommentaari* (*Church Law 2008 – Commentary on Church Law, Church Order and Church Election Order*). Helsinki: Kirjapaja, 2010.

Hämynen, Laura. *Suomen vaikuttaminen Euroopan unionin lainvalmisteluun ja direktiivien kansallinen täytäntöönpano* (*Finland's Influence on European Union Lawmaking and the National Implementation of Directives*). Helsinki: Oikeuspoliittisen tutkimuslaitoksen tutkimustiedonantoja 108, 2011.

Harris, David., Michael O'Boyle., Ed Bates & Carla Buckley. *Law of the European Convention on Human Rights*. 3rd edn. Oxford: Oxford University Press, 2014.

Hatami, Shahram. *Muslimitaustaisten maahanmuuttajien sosiaalipalvelujen ja yhteisön tuen tarve* (*Need for Social Services and Community Support for Muslim Immigrants*). University of Jyväskylä, 2017. http://urn.fi/URN:NBN:fi:jyu-201803221809.

Hautamäki, Veli-Pekka. *Perustuslain auktoritatiivinen tulkinta – Oikeusvertaileva tutkimus perustuslain tulkinnan auktoritatiivisista instituutioista ja niiden käyttämästä argumentaatiosta Suomessa ja Norjassa* (*Authoritative Interpretation of the Constitution – A Comparative Study of the Institutional Interpretation of the Constitution and Its Argumentation in Finland and Norway*). Helsinki: Suomalaisen lakimiesyhdityksen julkaisuja, A, No. 232, 2002. *Diss.*

Heikkilä, Markku & Simo Heininen. A History of the Finnish Church. Helsinki: SKS, 2016.

Heikkilä, Tuomas. *Pyhän Henrikin legenda*. Helsinki: SKST 1039, 2005.

Heininen, Simo. *Die Finnischen Studenten in Wittenberg 1531–1552*. Helsinki: Schriften der Luther-Agricola-Gesellschaft A 9, 1980.

Helin, Matti. *Uskonto Skdl:n politiikassa 1944–1961* (*Religion in Skdl Politics, 1944–1961*). Turku: Annales Universitatis Turkuensis, Ser C, 121, 1996.

Hiekkanen, Markus. *Suomen keskiajan kivikirkot* (*Finnish Medieval Stone Churches*). Helsinki: SKS (87), 2014.

Hirvelä, Päivi & Satu Heikkilä. *Ihmisoikeudet. Käsikirja EIT:n oikeuskäytäntöön* (*Human Rights. A Guide to EIT Case Law.* 2nd r Edn). Helsinki: Alma Talent, 2017.

Hoikka, Mikko. *Sananvapaus Euroopan unionin oikeudessa* (*Freedom of Expresson in European Union Law*). Helsinki: Suomalainen lakimiesyhdistys, A 289, 2009. *Diss.*

Husa, Jaakko. *Non liquet? Vallanjako, perusoikeudet, systematisointi – oikeuden ja politiikan rajankäyntejä* (*Non Liquet? Power Sharing, Fundamental Rights, Systematization – The Boundaries Between Law and Politics*). Vammala: Suomalainen lakimiesyhdistys, 2004.

Husa, Jaakko & Teuvo Pohjolainen. *Julkisen vallan oikeudelliset perusteet – johdatus julkisoikeuteen.* (*Legal Basis of Public Power – Introduction to Public Law.* 4th Revised Edn). Helsinki: Talentum, 2014.

Hyvärinen, Anna. *Suomen mahdollisuudet vaikuttaa valmisteilla olevaan EU-lainsäädäntöön* (*Finland's Ability to Influence EU Legislation; in Preparation*). Helsinki: Oikeuspoliittisen tutkimuslaitoksen tutkimuksia 241, 2009.

Jääskinen, Niilo. *Euroopan unioni: Oikeudelliset perusteet* (*The European Union: Its Legal Basis*). Helsinki: Talentum, 2007.

Jaatinen, Heikki. *Oikeushenkilön rangaistusvastuu* (*Liability of Legal Persons*). Jyväskylä: Kauppakaari- Lakimiesliiton Kustannus, 2000.

Jakku-Sihvonen, Ritva & Hannele Niemi. *Research-Based Teacher Education in Finland: Reflections by Finnish Teacher Educators*. Turku: Research in Educational Sciences 25, 2006.

Jutikkala, Eino & Kauko Pirinen. *Suomen historia* (*History of Finland*). Helsinki: Weiling & Göös, 1966.

Juusten, Paavali. *Suomen Piispain kronikka, Chronicon Episcoporum Finlandensium*. (*According to Henrik Gabriel Porthan in Finnish*), edited by Helmer Winter. Helsinki: Otava, 1956.

Jyränki, Antero & Jaakko Husa. *Valtiosääntöoikeus* (*Constitutional Law*, 2nd edn). Vantaa, 2015.

Kääriäinen, Kimmo & Kati Niemelä & Kimmo Ketola. *Religion in Finland. Decline, Change, and Transformation of Finnish Religiosity*. Jyväskylä: Publications of the Church Research Institute 54, 2005.

Kääriäinen, Kimmo, et al. *Church in Change. The Evangelical Lutheran Church of Finland from 2000 to 2003*. Tampere: Publications of the Church Research Institute, no. 545, 2005.

Kaitaranta, Reea & Maarit Kankarisalo. *Mitä maahanmuuttajapotilas voi syödä? Opaskirjanen Hatanpään puistosairaalan henkilökunnalle muslimien, buddhalaisten, kungfutselaisten ja taolaisten kulttuureista sekä niihin sisältyvistä ravitsemus- ja ruokailutavoista* (*What Can an Immigrant Patient Eat? A Guide Booklet for Staff at Hatanpää Park Hospital on Muslim, Buddhist, Confucian, and Taoist Cultures and the Nutrition and Eating Habits They Contain*). Tampere: Opinnäytetyö, Tampereen ammattikorkeakoulu (Master's thesis, Tampere University of Applied Sciences), 2010.

Ketola, Kimmo. *Uskonnot Suomessa 2008. Käsikirja uskontoihin ja uskonnollisiin liikkeisiin* (*Religions in Finland 2008: Handbook for Religions and Religious Movements*). Kirkon tutkimuskeskuksen julkaisuja 102 (Tampere: Kirkon tutkimuskeskus, 2008).

Kircko-Laki Ja Ordningi 1686 (*Church Law and Order 1686*). Näköispainos ja uudelleen ladottu laitos, edited by Lahja-Irene Hellemaa, Anja Jussila & Martti Parvio. Suomalaisen kirjallisuuden seura. Helsinki: SKS, 1986.

Kirkkohallituksen lausunto 2003-00939 kansallisarkistolle rippisalaisuutta ja sielunhoitoa koskevien asiakirjojen salassapidosta (*Church Council Opinion 2003-00939 on the National Archives Devoted to the Secrecy of Documents Relating to Secrecy and Pastoral Care*). Helsinki, 2003.

Kohti yhteistä hyvää: piispojen puheenvuoro hyvinvointiyhteiskunnan tulevaisuudesta (*Towards the Common Good: Bishops' Views on the Future of the Welfare State*). Helsinki: SR-kustannus, 1999.

Koskenniemi, Martti. *The Politics of International Law.* Oxford and Portland, Oregon: Hart Publishing, 2011.

Kultalahti, Jukka. *Omaisuudensuoja ympäristönsuojelussa* (*Property Protection in Environmental Protection*). Jyväskylä: Suomalainen Lakimiesyhdistys, 1990.

Laaksonen, Kalevi. *Kiinteän omaisuuden perustuslainsuoja – Tutkimus eräiden erityisesti maaseutukiinteistöihin kohdistuvien oikeudenrajoitusten säätämisjärjestyksestä ja korvattavuudesta* (*Constitutional Protection of Immovable Property – A Study of the Order and Substitutability of Certain Legal Restrictions, Especially in Rural Properties*). Helsinki: Kauppakaari Oyj, 1998.

Laasonen, Pentti. *Novgorodin imu. Miksi ortodoksit muuttivat Venäjälle Käkisalmen läänistä 1600-luvulla* (*The Pull of Novgorod. The Reasons for the Orthodox Migration from the Province of Käkisalmi to Russia in the 17th Century*). Helsinki: SKS, 2005.

Laasonen, Pentti. *Suomen kirkon historia. Vuodet 1593–1808* (*History of the Church of Finland. 1593–1808*). Helsinki: WSOY, 1991.

Lahtiluoma, Sami & Raimo Turunen. *Kunta ja seurakunta – vuorovaikutusta ja yhteistyötä* (*Municipality and Parish – Interaction and Cooperation*). Helsinki: Kuntaliitto & Suomen evankelis-luterilainen kirkko, 2011.

Länsineva, Pekka. *Perusoikeudet ja varallisuussuhteet* (*Fundamental Rights and Property Relations*). Jyväskylä: Suomalainen Lakimiesyhdistys, 2002.

Lavapuro, Juha. *Uusi perustuslakikontrolli* (*New Constitutional Control*). Helsinki: Suomalainen Lakimiesyhdistys, 2010.

Latvio, Ritva, Satu Mustonen & Ilari Rantakari (eds). *Imaamit Suomessa. Imaamikoulutusselvitys 2013* (*Imams in Finland. Imam Training Survey, 2013*). Helsinki: Kulttuuri- ja uskontofoorumi FOKUS ry, 2013.

Lehtonen, Risto. *Story of a Storm. The Ecumenical Student Movement in the Turmoil of Revolution, 1968–1973*. Grand Rapids: MI: Wm. B. Eerdmans, 1998 and Helsinki: the Finnish Society of Church History, 1998.

Lehtonen, Tuomas M.S. *Suomi, Ruotsi ja läntinen kirkko* (*Finland, Sweden, and the Western Church*). Helsinki: Brill, 2002, 84.

Leino, Pekka. *Kirkko ja perusoikeudet* (*The Church and Fundamental Rights*). Helsinki, 2003.

Lempiäinen, Pentti. *Rippikäytäntö Suomen kirkossa uskonpuhdistuksesta 1600-luvun loppuun.* (*Confession Practice in the Church of Finland from the Reformation to the Late 17th Century*). Helsinki: Suomen kirkkohistoriallinen seura, 1963.

Margariti, Stella. *Defining International Terrorism: Between State Sovereignty and Cosmopolitanism*. Vol. 12. Berlin: Springer-Verlag, International Criminal Justice series, 2017.

Melander, Sakari. *Kriminalisointiteoria – rangaistavaksi säätämisen oikeudelliset rajoitukset* (*Theory of Criminalization – Legal Limitations of Criminalization*). Vammala: Suomalainen lakimiesyhdistys, 2008.

Murtorinne, Eino. *The History of Finnish Theology, 1828–1918*. Helsinki: Societas Scientiarum Fennica 12, 1988.

Nieminen, Heikki-Tapio. *Suomalainen radiohartaus: Yleisradiossa vuosina 1932–1997 lähetettyjen luterilaisten aamuhartauksien rakenne ja sisältö* (*Morning Radio Devotionals on Finnish Radio, the Structure and Content of Lutheran Morning Broadcasts Transmitted by the Finnish Broadcasting Company – YLE Between 1932 and 1997*). Helsinki: STKSJ 221, 1999. *Diss.*

Nieminen, Liisa. *Perus- ja ihmisoikeudet ja perhe* (*Fundamental and Human Rights and the Family*). Helsinki: Talentum, 2013.

Niva, Ville. *Vanhoillislestadiolaisuuden hyväksikäyttötapaukset julkisessa keskustelussa 2010–2014* (*Cases of Abuse by Conservative Laestadianism in the Public Debate, 2010–'2014*). Helsinki: Master's thesis, University of Helsinki, 2015.

Nuorteva, Jussi. *Suomalaisten ulkomainen opinkäynti ennen Turun akatemian perustamista 1640.* (*Finnish Study Abroad Before the Foundation of the Royal Academy of Turku (Academia Aboensis) in 1640*). Helsinki: Bibliotheca Historica 27, and Helsinki: SKST 177, 1997.

Nurmiranta, Eeva-Kaarina. *Pappi tuomiolla. Julkisoikeudellinen tutkimus papin opin, virkatoiminnan ja elämän valvonnasta vuosina 1940–1989* (*The Priest in Judgment. A Public Law Study on the Control of Priestly Doctrine, Office, and Life, 1940-1989*). Helsinki: Suomalaisen Lakimiesyhdistyksen julkaisuja A 215, 1998.

Ojanen, Tuomas. *EU-oikeuden perusteita* (*The Basics of EU Law*), 3rd Revised edn. Helsinki, 2010 and Helsinki: Edita, 2016.

Ojanen, Tuomas: *Johdatus perus- ja ihmisoikeusjuridiikkaan* (*Introduction to Fundamental and Human Rights Law*). Helsinki: Oikeustieteellinen tiedekunta (Helsingin yliopisto), Forum Iuris, 2009.

Ojanen, Tuomas: *Perusoikeudet ja ihmisoikeudet Suomessa* (*Fundamental and Human Rights in Finland*). Helsinki: University of Helsinki, 2003.

Ojanen, Tuomas. *The European Way: The Structure of National Court Obligation under EC Law*. Saarijärvi: Omakustanne: (Author's Private Edition), 1998.

Ovey, Clare & Robin C.A. White, *European Convention on Human Rights*. 5th edn. Oxford: University Press, 2010.

Pellonpää, Matti, et al. *Euroopan ihmisoikeussopimus* (*European Convention on Human Rights*). Helsinki: Talentum, 2012.

Pellonpää, Matti. *Euroopan ihmisoikeussopimus* (*The European Convention on Human Rights*). Helsinki: Talentum, 1996 (4th edn., 2005).

Pietiläinen Marjut & Kirsti Pohjanpää. *Lakimuutokset näkyvät sateenkaariväen tilastoinnissa – samaa sukupuolta olevan kanssa avioliitossa 4 000 suomalaista* (*Law Changes Show in the Rainbow Statistics – 4,000 Finns Who Are Married as Same-Sex Couples*). Helsinki: Tilastokeskus/Tieto*Et*tredit/Asiantuntija-artikkelit ja ajankohtaisblogit, 24.6.2019.

Pikkusaari, Jussi. *Vaikea vapaus: Sosialidemokratian häviö kirkolle 1850-luvulta 1920-luvulle Suomen kulttuuritaistelussa* (*Hard Freedom: The Loss of Social Democracy to the Church in the Cultural Battle in Finland, 1850–1920*). Oulu: Bibliotheca historica 32; Helsinki: Suomen historiallinen seura, 1998. *Diss.*

Pitkänen, Maija. *On annettava merkitystä---* (*Must Give Meaning ---*). Tutkimus perusoikeuksien toteutumisesta ylimpien tuomioistuinten lainkäytön näkökulmasta. Joensuu: Degree dissertation, University of Joensuu, 2006.

Puumala, Sami. *Selvitys vankilasielunhoidosta ja kirkollisesta vankilatyöstä 2011–2012* (*The Study of Pastoral Care and Ecclesiastical Work in Prisons 2011–2012*). Available in electronic form: http://sakasti.evl.fi/julkaisut.nsf/05892BAE40E8902DC2257E2E0012D529/$FILE/S%20Puumala%20-%20Selvitys%20vankilasielunhoidosta%20ja%20kirkollisesta%20vankilatyöstä%202011-2012.pdf.

Raunio, Antti. *Järki, usko ja lähimmäisen hyvä* (*Reason, Faith, and the Good of One's Neighbour*). Helsinki: STKSJ 252, 2007.

Riikonen, Juha. *The Church in the Embrace of Politics. The Canonical Controversy between the Finnish Orthodox Church and the Moscow Patriarchate, 1945–1977*. Joensuu: University of Joensuu Publications in Theology, JYTJ 2007, 2007. *Diss.*

Robbers, Gerhard (ed.). *State and Church in the European Union*. 3rd edn. Baden-Baden: Nomos, 2019.

Robbers, Gerhard. 'Germany'. In *International Encyclopaedia of Laws: Religion*, edited by R. Torfs. Alphen aan den Rijn, NL: Kluwer Law International, 2013.

Rosas, Allan & Lorna Armati. *EU Constitutional Law – An Introduction*. 2nd edn. Bloomsbury: Hart Publishing, 2012.

Ruohomäki, Jouko. *Suomen helluntailiikkeen synty, leviäminen ja yhteisönmuodostus* 1907–1922 (*The Birth, Spread, and Community formation of the Pentecostal Movement in Finland, 1907–1922*). Diss. University of Eastern Finland. Keuruu: Aikamedia, 2014.

Scheinin, Martin. *Ihmisoikeudet Suomen oikeudessa* (*Human Rights in Finnish Law*). Helsinki: Suomalainen Lakimiesyhdistys, 1991.

Schütze, Robert. *European Constitutional Law*. 2nd edn. Oxford: Oxford University Press, 2015.

Seppinen, Jukka. *Suomettumisen syövereissä* (*In the Abyss of Finlandization*). Jyväskylä: WSOYpro Oy, 2011.

Seppo, Juha. *Uskonnonvapaus 2000-luvun Suomessa* (*Freedom of Religion in 21st Century Finland*). Helsinki: Edita, 2003.

Sintonen, Virpi. *Puolueet kirkkoa valtaamassa? – Suomen evankelis-luterilaisen kirkon ja yhteiskunnan suhteet Forssan, Merijärven ja Vihdin seurakuntavaalien 1970, 1974 ja 1978 valossa* (*Parties Taking Control over the Church? – Relations Between the Evangelical Lutheran Church in Finland and Society in the Light of the Forssa, Merijärvi and Vihti Parish Elections in 1970, 1974, and 1978*). Helsinki: Unigrafia, 2018.

Snellman, Christina. *Suomalaisten sanomalehtien sananvapaus 1990-luvulla – oikeudellisten normien ja eettisten sääntöjen sääntelemänä* (*Freedom of Expression in Finnish Newspapers in the 1990s – Governed by Legal Norms and Ethical Rules*). Helsingin yliopisto: Master's thesis, 2000.

Tala, Jyrki. *Lakien laadinta ja vaikutukset* (*Drafting and Impact of Laws*). Helsinki: Edita Pubishing Oy, 2005.

Tuomi, Marita. *Rauhaa ja politiikka. Suomen evankelis-luterilaisen kirkon ja Venäjän ortodoksisen kirkon käsitykset rauhasta kirkkojen oppineuvotteluissa 1970–1986 ja 1995*. (Peace and Politics. The Understanding of Peace in the Bilateral Negotiations between the Evangelical Lutheran Church of Finland and the Russian Orthodox Church in 1980–1986 and 1995). Joensuu: Dissertations in Education, Humanities, and Theology 191, 2022. *Diss.*

Tuori, Kaarlo. *Kriittinen oikeuspositivismi* (*Critical Legal Positivism*). Helsinki: Werner Söderström lakitieto, 2000.

Ubani, Martin, Inkeri Rissanen & Saila Poulter (eds). *Contextualising Dialogue, Secularisation and Pluralism: Religion in Finnish Public Education*. Münster: Waxmann, 2019.

Ubani, Martin. *Young, Gifted and Spiritual: The Case of Finnish Sixth-Grade Pupils*. Helsinki: Research report/University of Helsinki, Department of Applied Sciences of Education, 2007.

Vappula, Kari. *Sotilaspapin virka Suomen ruotujakoisessa sotaväessä 1812–1880* (*The Office of Field Chaplain in the Finnish Military Tenure Establisment from 1812 to 1880*). Helsinki: SKST, 123, 1982. *Diss.*

Vappula, Kari. *Sotilaspapin virka Suomen asevelvollisessa sotaväessä 1881–1905* (*The Office of Field Chaplain in the Finnish Conscript Army 1881 to 1905*). Helsinki: SKST, 146, 1989.

Vihavainen, Timo. *Kansakunta rähmällään. Suomettumisen lyhyt historia* (*The Nation Bows to the East: A Brief History of Finlandization*). Helsinki: Otava, 1991.

Viljanen, Jukka. *The European Court of Human Rights as a Developer of the General Doctrines of Human Rights Law*. Tampere University Press, 2003. *Diss.*

Viljanen, Veli-Pekka. *Perusoikeuksien rajoitusedellytykset* (*Conditions for the Limitation of Fundamental Rights*). Helsinki: Sanoma Pro Oy, 2001.

Virén, Matti. *Yleishyödylliset yhteisöt Suomessa. Verot, lahjoitukset ja avustukset tutkimuksen kohteena* (*Non-profit Organizations in Finland. Taxes, Donations, and Public Support under Scrutiny*). Forskningsrapporter från Svenska handelshögskolan Hanken (Swedish School of Economics Research Reports) 74. (Helsinki 2014)

Weingartner, Erich. *Ihmisoikeuksien suojeleminen. Käsikirja ihmisoikeustyön alkajille. Euroopan turvallisuus- ja yhteistyöjärjestön alueella toimivien kirkkojen ihmisoikeusohjelma* (*Protecting Human Rights. A Manual for Practitioners for the Churches' Human Rights Programme in the CSCE*) 1994. Editor and translation of the Finnish language version: Eeva Kemppi-Repo.

Xenos, Dimitris. *The Positive Obligations of the State under the European Convention of Human Rights*. Baskerville, Virginia: Routledge, 2012.

Articles

Articles in Books

Albors-Llornes, Albertina. 'Judicial Protection before the Court of Justice of the European Union'. In *European Union Law*, edited by Catherine Barnard & Steve Peers. Oxford: Oxford University Press, 2014.

Anderson, David & Cian C. Murphy. 'The Charter of Fundamental Rights'. In *EU Law after Lisbon*, edited by Andrea Biondi, Piet Eeckhout & Stefanie Ripley. Oxford: Oxford University Press, 2012.

Arffman, Kaarlo. 'Katolisesta lähetysalueesta Ruotsin luterilaisen kirkon osaksi' ('From the Area of the Catholic Mission to the Swedish Lutheran Church'). In *Kristinuskon historia 2000. Kristinusko Suomessa*, edited by Anssi Mäkinen, Veikko Kallio & Rakel Kallio. Porvoo: Weiling & Göös, 2000, 8–52.

van Bockxmeer, Hermineke. 'The Portrayal of Religion in the Netherlands: The Media and the 'Arts'. In *The Portrayal of Religion in Europe: The Media and the Arts* (*Le portrait de religion en Europe: les médias et les arts*), edited by Norman Doe. Uitgeverij: Peeters, 2004, 185–208.

Selected Bibliography

Boerefijn Ineke. 'International Human Rights in National 'Law'. In *International Protection of Human Rights: A Textbook*, edited by Catarina Krause & Martin Scheinin. Turku: Åbo Akademi University Institute for Human Rights, 2012, 577–599.

Craig, P.P. 'The Charter, the ECJ and National Courts'. In *The European Union after the Treaty of Lisbon*, edited by Diamond Ashiagbor, Nicola Countouris & Nicola Ionnais Lianos. Cambridge: Cambridge University Press, 2012.

Di Federico, Giancomo. 'Fundamental Rights in the EU: Legal Pluralism and Multi-Level Protection After the Lisbon Treaty'. In *The EU Charter of Fundamental Rights from Declaration to Binding Instrument*, edited by *Di Federico*. Dordrecht: Springer, 2011, 15–54.

Forsius, Arno, *Descriptions of the History of Medicine*, Leprosy, see http://www.saunalahti.fi/arnoldus/haklaa.html.

Garde, Peter. 'Ret og tro'. Indlaeg ved Kirkeretlig Konference 2. Oktober 1999 på Logum-kloster Hojskok. In *Om norm & rätt i trosamfunden.* Uppsala: Nordisk Ekumenisk Rådet, 2001, 75–86.

Hallberg, Pekka. 'Kokoontumisvapaus' ('Freedom of Assembly'). In *Perusoikeudet* (Fundamental Rights), edited by Pekka Hallberg, Heikki Karapuu, Tuomas Ojanen, Martin Scheinin, Kaarlo Tuori & Veli-Pekka Viljanen. 2nd revised edn. WSOYpro, 2011, 48, 861.

Hallberg, Pekka. 'Perusoikeusjärjestelmä' ('The Fundamental Rights System'). In *Perusoikeudet* (*Fundamental Rights*), edited by Pekka Hallberg, Heikki Karapuu, Tuomas Ojanen, Martin Scheinin, Kaarlo Tuori & Veli-Pekka Viljanen. 2nd revised edn. WSOYpro, 2011, 29–59.

Heikkonen, Johannes & Pamela Slotte. 'Religion and Discrimination Law in the European Union: Finland'. In *Religion and Discrimination Law in the European Union* (*La discrimination en matière religieuse dans l'Union Européenne*), edited by Mark Hill QC. Trier: European Consortium for Church and State Research, 2012, 125–143.

Heiskanen, Jussi. 'Kiihottaminen kansanryhmää vastaan' ('Incitiment against an ethnic group'). In *Kirjoituksia viestintäoikeudesta*, edited by Päivi Tiilikka & Jukka Siro. Helsinki: Helsingin hovioikeus, 2010, 25–40. https://oikeus.fi/hovioikeudet/helsinginhovioikeus/material/attachments/oikeus_hovioikeudet_helsinginhovioikeus/julkaisut/painetutjulkaisut/kirjoituksiaviestintaoikeudesta2010/KyEr5bTSB/06_Kiihottaminen_kansanryhmaa_vastaan_Jussi_Heiskanen.pdf

Huhta, Ilkka. 'From State-Church to Non-denominationalism Public Authorities and Theological Education in Finland'. In *Public Authorities and the Training of Religious Personnel in Europe*, edited by Francis Messner. Granada: Comares, 2015, 257–269.

Husa, Jaakko. 'Perusoikeusvalvonta EU:n alueella – riitasointuinen triangeli?' ('Fundamental Rights Protection in the EU – A Controversial Triangle?'. In *Nieminen (toim.): Perusoikeudet EU:ssa.* Helsinki: Lakimiesliiton Kustannus, 2001, 43–64.

Jokipii, Mauno. *Ensimmäinen ristiretki Suomeen ja sen lähin jälkimaine.* In *Muinainen Kalanti ja sen naapurit (The First Crusade to Finland and Its Immediate Aftermath. Ancient Kalanti and Its Neighbours),* edited by Veijo Kaitanen, Esa Laukkanen & Kari Uotila. Helsinki: SKS, 2003, 300–342.

Karapuu, Heikki. 'Perusoikeuksien käsite ja luokittelu' ('Concept and Classification of Fundamental Rights'). In *Perusoikeudet* ('Fundamental Rights'), edited by Pekka Hallberg, Heikki Karapuu, Tuomas Ojanen, Martin Scheinin, Kaarlo Tuori & Veli-Pekka Viljanen. 2nd revised edn. WSOYpro, 2011, 63–87.

Knuutila, Jyrki. 'Matrimonial and Family Law'. In *State and Church in the European Union*, edited by Edited by Gerhard Robbers. 2nd edn. Baden-Baden: Nomos, 2005, 530–532.

Kotiranta, Matti. 'Uskonnollisten vähemmistöjen oikeusasema Suomessa. Uskonnonvapauslaki 100 vuotta' ('The Legal Status of Religious Minorities in Finland. 100 years of the Freedom of Religion Act'). In *Kirkko yhteiskunnassa: suhteet ja rajapinnat. Uskonnonvapauslaki 100 vuotta.* Helsinki: Suomen ev.-lut. kirkon tutkimusjulkaisuja 143, 2023, 41–86.

Kotiranta, Matti. 'FINLANDE. Fondements contemporains des relations Églises-État en Finlande'. In: Dictionnaire Droit des Religions (2nd. ed. 2022), pp. 357–365.

Kotiranta, Matti. 'FINLAND'. In *Atlas of Religious or Belief Minority Rights*, htt ps://atlasminorityrights.eu/countries/Finland.php, 2022.

Kotiranta, Matti. 'Islam, Human Rights, and State Policy in Finland'. In *Islam and Human Rights in the European Union*, edited by Lina Papadopoulou. Granada: Editorial Comares 2022, 161–202.

Kotiranta, Matti. 'The Specific Role and Equal Rights of Religious Minorities in Finland'. In *The Legal Status of Old and New Religious Minorities in the European Union*), edited by Marco Ventura. Granada: Editorial Comares, 2021, 275–291.

Kotiranta, Matti. 'Religionsfreiheit im postkommunistischen Europa – Ein historischer Rückblick'. In *Staat – Religion – Recht. Festschrift für Gerhard Robbers zum 70. Geburtstag*, 2020, 369–392.

Kotiranta, Matti. 'Securitization of Religious Freedom: Religion and the Limits of State Control in Finland'. In *Securitization of Religious Freedom: Religion and the Limits of State Control in Europe*, edited by Merilin Kiviorg. Tallinn: European Consortium for Church and State Research. Granada: Comares, 2020, 199–218.

Kotiranta, Matti. 'State and Church in Finland'. In *State and Church in the European Union*, edited by Gerhard Robbers. 3rd edn. Baden-Baden: Nomos, 2019, 613–640.

Kotiranta, Matti. 'Finnland, Staat und Religion'. In *Lexikon für Kirchen und Religionsrecht*, edited by Heribert Hallermann, Thomas Meckel, Michael Droege & Heinrich de Wall, Band 2, F–K, 2019, 54–57.

Kotiranta, Matti. 'Religious Assistance in Public Institutions: Finland'. In *Religious Assistance in Public Institutions (Assistance spirituelle dans les services publics*), edited by Ringolds Balodis & Miguel Rodrígues Blanco. Granada: Comares, 2016, 105–117.

Kotiranta, Matti. 'Finland'. In *Encyclopedia of Law and Religion* 4 (2016). Also available in Brill's Online edition (2016), 108–119.

Kotiranta, Matti. 'Law and Religion in the Workplace (Finland)'. In *Law and Religion in the Workplace*, edited by Miguel Rodrigues Blanco. Granada: Editorial Comares, 2015, 155–175.

Selected Bibliography

Kotiranta, Matti. 'Religion and the Secular State in Finland'. In *Religion and the Secular State: National Reports. Reports issued for the occasion XVIIIth Congress of the International Academy of Comparative Law*, edited by Donlu D. Thayer. Washington, 2010 (2015), 108–119.

Kotiranta, Matti. 'Finland'. In *Brill's Encyclopedia of Law and Religion*, edited by Gerhard Robbers (Vol. 4) (2015), 108–119 (also available at Brill's online series).

Kotiranta, Matti. 'The Recent Developments in the Relationship Between State and Religious Communities in Finland'. In *Neuere Entwicklungen im Religionsrecht europäischer Staaten*, edited by Wilhelm Rees, María Roca & Balázs Schanda. Berlin: Duncker & Humblot, 2013, 303–332.

Kotiranta, Matti. 'Religious Education in Finland'. In *The Routledge International Handbook of Religious Education*, edited by Derek Davis & Elena Miroshnikova. London & New York: Routledge, 2013, 104–112.

Kotiranta, Matti. 'The Application of the Freedom of Religion Principles of the European Convention on Human Rights in Finland'. In *Religious Freedom in the European Union*, edited by Achilles Emilianides. Leuven/Paris/Dudley: Peeters, 2011, 129–152.

Kotiranta, Matti. 'The Financing of Churches and Religious Associations in Finland'. In *Kirkkohistorian alueilla.* Edited by Ilkka Huhta & Esko M. Laine. Helsinki, SKHST 217 & Karjalan teologisen seuran julkaisuja 2, 411–429.

Kotiranta, Matti. 'Religious Entities as Legal Persons in Finland'. In *Churches and Other Religious Organisations as Legal Persons*, edited by Lars Friedner. Leuven: Peeters, 2007, 51–72.

Kotiranta, Matti. 'Euroopan unionin ja uskonnollisten yhteisöjen suhde tulevaisuuden Euroopassa' ('The Relationship Between the European Union and the Religious Communities in a Future Europe'). Presentation made on 14 May 2009 at the Euro-election candidates' seminar 'Religions and the EU', organized by the Finnish Ecumenical Council. Article also available in *Etsijä* 1/2009, 10–17.

Kotiranta, Matti, et al. 'The Teaching and Study of Church-State Relations in the Nordic Countries in the United Kingdom and in Ireland'. In The Teaching of Church-State Relations in European Universities (L'enseignement du droit ecclésiastique de l'État dans les universités européennes), edited by José María González del Valle & Alexander Hollerbach. Leuven: Peeters, 2005, 110–138.

Kotiranta, Matti. 'The Legal Position of Religion and the Media in Finland'. In *The Portrayal of Religion in Europe: The Media and the Arts* (*Le portrait de religion en Europe: les médias et les arts*), edited by Norman Doe. Leuven: Peeters, 2004, 41–56.

Länsineva, Pekka. 'Omaisuudensuoja, PL 15 §' ('Property Protection, Consitution, Article 15'). In *Perusoikeudet* (*Fundamental Rights*), edited by Pekka Hallberg, Heikki Karapuu, Tuomas Ojanen, Martin Scheinin, Kaarlo Tuori & Veli-Pekka Viljanen, 2nd rev. edn. WSOYpro, 2011, 549–604.

Lappi-Seppälä, Tapio. 'Imprisonment and Penal Policy in Finland'. In *Scandinavian Studies in Law* 1999–2012.

Lavapuro, Juha. 'Perusoikeusargumentaation kontrolloitavuudesta' ('On the Controllability of the Fundamental Rights Argument'). In *Heinonen – Lavapuro (toim.): Oikeuskulttuurin eurooppalaistuminen. Ihmisoikeuksien murroksesta kansainväliseen vuorovaikutukseen*, edited by Tuuli Heinonen & Juha Lavapuro. Vantaa: Suomalainen lakimiesyhdistys, 2012, 143–177.

Luodeslampi, Juha. 'Religious Education in Finland'. In *Religious Education in Europe. Situation and Current Trends in Schools*, edited by Elza Kuyk. Norway: IKO Publishing House, 2007.

Malkavaara, Mikko. 'Luterilaisuuden vaikutus kulttuuriin ja yhteiskuntaan' ('Impact of Lutheranism on Culture and Society'). In *Monien uskontojen ja katsomusten Suomi*, edited by Ruth Illman, Kimmo Ketola, Riitta Latvio & Jussi Sohlberg. Kuopio: Kirkon tutkimuskeskuksen verkkojulkaisuja 48, 2017, 46–64.

Manninen, Sami. 'Sananvapaus ja julkisuus, PL 12 §' ('Freedom of Expression and Publicity'). In *Perusoikeudet (Fundamental Rights)*, edited by Pekka Hallberg, Heikki Karapuu, Tuomas Ojanen, Martin Scheinin, Kaarlo Tuori & Veli-Pekka Viljanen. 2nd revised edn. WSOYpro, 2011, 459–491.

Nieminen, Liisa. 'Tasa-arvo Euroopan unionin perusoikeuskirjassa turvattuna perusoikeutena ' ('Equality as a Fundamental Right Protected by the Charter of Fundamental Rights of the European Union'). In *Perusoikeudet EU:ssa*, edited by Liisa Nieminen. Helsinki: Kauppakaari, 2001, 179–212.

Nikula, Paavo. 'Euroopan ihmisoikeussopimus ja EU:n perusoikeuskirja' ('European Convention on Human Rights and EU Charter of Fundamental Rights'). In *Juhlakirja Pekka Hallberg 1944–12/6 – 2004*, edited by Risto Nuolimaa, Pekka Vihervuori & Hannele Klemettinen. Jyväskylä, 2004, 238–247.

Nissinen, Mika. 'Tax Law, Religion, Philosophical and Non-Confessional organisations in Europe. Finland'. In Miguel Rodriguez Blanco (ed.), *Taxation, Religions and Non-Confessional Organisations in Europe.* Granada: Comares, 2023, 65–81.

Numminen, Jaakko. 'Yliopistolaitoksen hajasijoitus' ('Decentralized Placement of a University Institution'). In *Omalla pohjalla Euroopassa. Juhlakirja päätoimittaja, professori Kari Hokkaselle 2. tammikuuta 2003*, edited by Seppo Keränen. Vaasa: Etelä-Pohjanmaan Lehtiseura ry, 2002, 73–83.

Nuotio, Kimmo. 'Sananvapausrikosten sääntelyn ja soveltamisen kehitystrendejä ja kehittämiskohtia eräiden kotimaisten oikeustapausten valossa' ('Trends and development details in the regulation and application of freedom of expression offences in the light of several domestic cases') In *Viestin viemää: Viestintäoikeuden vuosikirja 2021*. Korpisaari, P. (ed.). Forum iuris: Helsingin yliopiston oikeustieteellisen tiedekunnan julkaisuja (Forum iuris: Publications of the Faculty of Law of the University of Helsinki), 2022 Helsinki, 47–63.

Nuotio, Kimmo. 'Terrorism as a Catalyst for the Emergence, Harmonization and Reform of Criminal Law' (Previously published in the Journal of International Criminal Justice, 2006 84, 998–1016). In *Counter-Terrorism and International Law*, edited by Katja L.H. Samuel & Nigel D. White. Abingdon, Oxon: Routledge, The International Law of Peace and Security, 2016, 145–163.

Nuotio, Kimmo. 'Vihapuheen rikosoikeudellinen sääntely' ('Regulating Hate Speech as a Crime'). In *Vihapuhe Suomessa*, edited by R. Neuvonen. Helsinki: Edita, 2015, 139–164.

Nuotio, Kimmo. 'European Criminal Law. The Oxford Handbook of Criminal Law'. In *The Oxford Handbook of Criminal Law*, edited by M.D> Dubber & T. Hörnle. Oxford: Oxford University Press, 2014, 1115–1137.

Nuotio, Kimmo. Avustettu potilaan itsemurha ja eutanasia (Assisted patient suicide and euthanasia). In *Oikeuden historiasta tulevaisuuden Eurooppaan: Pia Letto-Vanamo 60 vuotta* (*The History of Justice to Future Europe: Pia Letto-Vanamo 60 Years*). Helsinki: Suomalaisen lakimiesyhdistyksen julkaisuja. E-sarja (26), 2014, 277–294.

Nuotio, Kimmo. 'Between Denial and Recognition: Criminal Law and Cultural Diversity'. In *Criminal Law and Cultural Diversity*, edited by W. Kymlicka, M. Matravers, & C. Lernestedt. Oxford: Oxford University Press, 2014, 67–88.

Nuotio, Kimmo. 'Rikosoikeudellisesta laintulkinnasta eurooppaoikeudellisten oikeuslähteiden vaikutuspiirissä' ('On the Interpretation of Criminal Law Where the Sources of European Law Need to Be Taken into Account'). In *Suomalainen kriminaalipolitiikka: Näkökulmia teoriaan ja käytäntöön. Tapio Lappi-Seppälän juhlakirja*, edited by Ville Hinkkanen & Leena Mäkipää. Helsinki: Helsingin yliopiston oikeustieteellinen tiedekunta, 2013.

Nuotio, Kimmo. 'Security and Criminal Law: A Difficult Relationship'. In *Law and Security in Europe: Reconsidering the Security Constitution*, edited by Massimo Fichera & Jens Kremer. Cambridge: Intersentia, 2013.

Nuotio, Kimmo: 'Religion in the Criminal Law of Finland'. In *Religion and Criminal Law* (*Religion et Droit Pénal*), edited by Matti Kotiranta & Norman Doe. Leuven: Peeters, 2013, 63–74.

Nuotio, Kimmo. 'The Reform Story of the Finnish Penal Code: Ideological Turns and Waves of 'Modernization'. In *Building Justice in Post-Transition Europe?: Processes of criminalisation within Central and Eastern European Countries*, edited by K. Goodall, M. Malloch & B. Munro. Abingdon, Oxon: Routledge, 2012, 78–93.

Nuotio, Kimmo & Tapio Lappi-Seppälä. 'Crime and Punishment'. In *Nordic Law in European Context*, edited by Pia Letto-Vanamo, Ditlev Tamm & Bent Ole Gram Mortensen. Ius Gentium: Comparative Perspectives on Law and Justice, No. 73. Berlin: Springer-Verlag, 2019, 179–199.

Nuotio, Kimmo, Sakari Melander & Merita Huomo-Kettunen (eds). *Introduction to Finnish Law and Legal Culture*. Helsinki: Helsingin yliopiston oikeustieteellinen tiedekunta, Forum Iuris, 2012.

Ojanen, Tuomas. 'Perus- ja ihmisoikeudet Euroopan unionissa' ('Fundamental and Human Rights in the European Union'). In *Ihmisoikeuksien käsikirja*, edited by Timo Koivurova & Elina Pirjatanniemi. Helsinki: Tietosanoma, 2013.

Ojanen, Tuomas. 'Räppänä raollaan Eurooppaan – Euroopan unionin perusoikeudet Suomen oikeudessa' ('Hatch Open into Europe – EU Fundamental Rights in Finnish Law'). In *Oikeuskulttuurin eurooppalaistuminen: Ihmisoikeuksien murroksesta kansainväliseen vuorovaikutukseen*, edited by Tuuli Heinonen & Juha Lavapuro. Vantaa: Suomalainen Lakimiesyhdistys, 2012.

Ojanen, Tuomas & Martin Scheinin. 'Kansainväliset ihmisoikeussopimukset ja Suomen perusoikeusjärjestelmä' ('International Human Rights Treaties and the Finnish System of Fundamental Rights'). In *Perusoikeudet* (Fundamental Rights), edited by Pekka Hallberg, Heikki Karapuu, Tuomas Ojanen, Martin Scheinin, Kaarlo Tuori & Veli-Pekka Viljanen. 2nd revised edn. WSOYpro, 2011, 171–195 (Ojanen & Scheinin 2011 a).

Ojanen, Tuomas & Martin Scheinin. 'Perusoikeuksien ja ihmisoikeuksien kansainvälinen valvonta' ('International Monitoring of Fundamental and Human Rights'). In *Perusoikeudet (Fundamental Rights)*, edited by Pekka Hallberg, Heikki Karapuu, Tuomas Ojanen, Martin Scheinin, Kaarlo Tuori & Veli-Pekka Viljanen. 2nd revised edn. WSOYpro, 2011, 875–905 (Ojanen & Scheinin 2011 b).

Ojanen, Tuomas & Martin Scheinin. 'Suomen valtiosäännön perusperiaatteet, PL 1 § (Basic principles of the Finnish constitution, C 1§)'. In *Perusoikeudet* (*Fundamental Rights*), edited by Pekka Hallberg, Heikki Karapuu, Tuomas Ojanen, Martin Scheinin, Kaarlo Tuori & Veli-Pekka Viljanen. 2nd revised edn. WSOYpro, 2011, 217–226 (Ojanen & Scheinin 2011 c).

Ojanen, Tuomas & Martin Scheinin. 'Yhdenvertaisuus ja syrjinnän kielto, PL 6 §'. In *Perusoikeudet* (*Fundamental Rights*), edited by Pekka Hallberg, Heikki Karapuu, Tuomas Ojanen, Martin Scheinin, Kaarlo Tuori & Veli-Pekka Viljanen. 2nd revised edn. WSOYpro, 2011, 227–280 (Ojanen & Scheinin 2011 d).

Ojanen, Tuomas. 'Ihmisoikeusulottuvuuden kehittyminen Euroopan yhteisön oikeuteen' ('Development of the Human Rights Dimension in European Community Law'). In *Euroopan unioini ja ihmisoikeudet*, edited by Scheinin Martin & Taina Dahlgren. Turku: Åbo Akademin ihmisoikeusinstituutti, 1994, 875–905.

Pauha, Teemu, Suaad Onniselkä & Abbas Bahmanpour. 'Kaksi vuosisataa suomalaista Islamia' ('Two Hundred Years of Finnish Islam'). In *Monien uskomusten ja katsomusten Suomi* (*Finland – A Country of Many Religions and Beliefs*, edited by Ruth Illman, Kimmo Ketola, Riitta Latvio & Jussi Sohlberg. Helsinki: Kirkon tutkimuskeskuksen verkkojulkaisuja 48 (2017), 104–115. See, https://evl.fi/documents/1327140/45386794/Ktk+-+Monien+uskontojen+ja+katsomusten+Suomi/c8c8d8be-e49b-5998-3539-6b2a29a4903d.

Pellonpää, Matti. 'Euroopan ihmisoikeussopimuksen tulkintaa koskevasta vuoropuhelusta' ('On the Dialogue over the Interpretation of the European Convention on Human Rights'). In *Heinonen – Lavapuro (toim.): Oikeuskulttuurin eurooppalaistuminen. Ihmisoikeuksien murroksesta kansainväliseen vuorovaikutukseen*, edited by Tuuli Heinonen & Juha Lavapuro. Vantaa: Suomalainen lakimiesyhdistys, 2012, 69–94.

Petersen, Jørn Henrik. 'Nordic Model of Welfare States'. In *Nordic Law in European Context*, edited by Pia Letto-Vanamo, Ditlev Tamm & Bent Ole Gram Mortensen. Ius Gentium: Comparative Perspectives on Law and Justice, No. 73. Berlin: Springer-Verlag, 2019, 21–39.

Puumalainen, Mikko. 'Mitä Euroopan unionin perusoikeudet merkitsevät laillisuusvalvonnalle?' ('What Do the Fundamental Rights of the European Union Mean for Law Enforcement?'). In *Heinonen – Lavapuro (toim.): Oikeuskulttuurin eurooppalaistuminen. Ihmisoikeuksien murroksesta kansainväliseen vuorovaikutukseen*, edited by Tuuli Heinonen & Juha Lavapuro. Vantaa: Suomalainen lakimiesyhdistys, 2012, 265–294.

Petkoff, Peter. 'Forum Internum and Forum Externum in Canon Law and Public International Law with a Particular Reference to the Jurisprudence of the European Court of Human Rights'. In *Religion and Human Rights: An International Journal. Vol. 7 (3)*, edited by Jeroen Temperman. Nijhoff: Brill, 2012.

Räsänen, Antti & Martin Ubani. 'Finland: The Finnish RE teacher – A Modern 'Traditionalist'. In *How Teachers in Europe Teach Religion. An International Empirical Study in 16 Countries*, edited by Hans-Georg Ziebertz & Ulrich Riegel. Berlin: Lit Verlag, 2009.

Robbers, Gerhard. 'Religionsfreiheit in Europa'. In *Festschrift für Joseph Listl*, edited by Josef Isensee, Wilhelm Rees & Wolfgang Rüfner. Berlin: Duncker & Humblot, 1999.

Rosas, Allan. 'Perus- ja ihmisoikeudet EU–oikeudessa' ('Fundamental and Human Rights in EU Law'). In *Perusoikeudet* (*Fundamental Rights*), edited by Pekka Hallberg, Heikki Karapuu, Tuomas Ojanen, Martin Scheinin, Kaarlo Tuori & Veli-Pekka Viljanen. 2nd revised edn. WSOYpro, 2011, 197–213.

Rosas, Allan & Heidi Kaila. 'Euroopan unionin tuomioistuin ja Lissabonin sopimus' ('The Court of Justice of the European Union and the Treaty of Lisbon'). In *Juhlakirja Heikki Kulla 1950 – 28/8 – 2010*, edited by Länsineva, Tuomisto, Wikström & Viljanen. Turku, 2010, 261–284.

Salomäki, Hanna. 'Herätysliikkeet suomalaisessa yhteiskunnassa' ('Revival Movements in Finnish Society'). In *Monien uskomusten ja katsomusten Suomi* (*Finland – A Country of Many Religions and Beliefs*), edited by Ruth Illman, Kimmo Ketola, Riitta Latvio & Jussi Sohlberg. Kirkon tutkimuskeskuksen verkkojulkaisuja 48, 65–75.

Schneider, Anne. *Conflicts of Jurisdiction in Criminal Matters in the European Union: Vol. I*. Baden-Baden: Nomos, 2013.

Scheinin, Martin. 'Characteristics of Human Rights Norms'. In *International Protection of Human Rights: A Textbook*, edited by Catarina Krause & Martin Scheinin. Turku: Åbo Akademi University Institute for Human Rights, 2012, 19–37.

Scheinin, Martin. 'Perusoikeuskonfliktit' (Fundamental Rights Conflicts). In *Oikeuskulttuurin eurooppalaistuminen. Ihmisoikeuksien murroksesta kansainväliseen vuorovaikutukseen*, edited by Tuuli Heinonen & Juha Lavapuro. Vantaa: Suomalainen lakimiesyhdistys, 2012, 125–141.

Scheinin, Martin. 'Uskonnon ja omantunnon vapaus PL 11§' ('Freedom of Religion and Conscience'). In *Perusoikeudet* (*Fundamental Rights*), edited by Pekka Hallberg, Heikki Karapuu, Tuomas Ojanen, Martin Scheinin, Kaarlo Tuori & Veli-Pekka Viljanen. 2nd revised edn. WSOYpro, 2011, 413–458 (Scheinin 2011b).

Scheinin, Martin. 'Secular Human Rights Perspectives: As a Challenge to Nordic Law & Religion Solutions'. In *Law & Religion in the 21st Century – Nordic Perspectives*, edited by Lisbet Christoffersen et al. København: Djøf Publishing, 2010, 125–141.

Scheinin, Martin. 'State and Church in Finland'. In *State and Church in the European Union*, edited by Gerhard Robbers. 2nd edn. Baden-Baden: Nomos, 2005, 523–528, 530, 533–534.

Sirva, Sari. 'Immigration and Religion in Finland'. In *Immigration, National and Regional Laws and Freedom of Religion*, edited by Augustin Motilla. Leuven: Peeters, 2012.

Tala, Jyrki. 'Lainlaadinnan mallit ja informaatio-ongelmat' ('Drafting Templates and Information Problems'). In *Empiirisen oikeustutkimuksen kokemukset, haasteet ja tulevaisuus*, edited by Anssi Keinänen, Mia Kilpeläinen & Ulla Väätänen. Joensuu: Itä-Suomen yliopisto, 2010.

Torfs, Rik. 'Religion et médias en Belgique'. In *The Portrayal of Religion in Europe: The Media and the Arts* (*Le portrait de religion en Europe: les médias et les arts*), edited by Norman Doe. Leuven: Peeters, 2004, 19–39.

Tuomi, Marita. 'The Subject of Peace in the Theological Discussions Between the Finnish Evangelical-Lutheran Church and the Russian Orthodox Church during Cold War'. In *The Finnish and Estonian Churches During the Cold War*, edited by Matti Kotiranta. Joensuu: Publications of the University of Eastern Finland. Reports and Studies in Education, Humanities, and Theology 15 (2016), 74–84.

Viljanen, Veli-Pekka. 'Perusoikeuksien merkitys lainsäädäntötyössä' ('Importance of Fundamental Rights in Legislative Work'). In *Perusoikeudet* (*Fundamental Rights*), edited by Pekka Hallberg, Heikki Karapuu, Tuomas Ojanen, Martin Scheinin, Kaarlo Tuori & Veli-Pekka Viljanen. 2nd revised edn. WSOYpro, 2011, 833–849 (Viljanen 2011a).

Viljanen, Veli-Pekka. 'Perusoikeuksien rajoittaminen' ('Restriction of Fundamental Rights'). In *Perusoikeudet* (*Fundamental Rights*), edited by Pekka Hallberg, Heikki Karapuu, Tuomas Ojanen, Martin Scheinin, Kaarlo Tuori &Veli-Pekka Viljanen. 2nd revised edn. WSOYpro, 2011, 139–170 (Viljanen 2011b).

Viljanen, Veli-Pekka. 'Perusoikeuksien soveltamisala' ('Scope of Fundamental Rights'). In *Perusoikeudet* (*Fundamental Rights*), edited by Pekka Hallberg, Heikki Karapuu, Tuomas Ojanen, Martin Scheinin, Kaarlo Tuori, Veli-Pekka Viljanen. 2nd revised edn. WSOYpro, 2011, 89–137. (Viljanen 2011c).

Viljanen, Veli-Pekka. 'Onko sananvapaus poliittinen perusoikeus?' ('Is Freedom of Expression a Political Right?'). In *Viestintäoikeus*, edited by Heikki Kulla & alii. Helsinki: WSOY, 2002.

Woehrling Jean-Marie. 'Laïcité, Neutralité'. In: Francis Messner (ed.), *Dictionnaire du droit des religions*. Paris: CNRS Éditions, 2nd. ed. 2022, 443–446.

Young, James. 'Regulation of the Representation of Religion in the Media in the United Kingdom'. In *The Portrayal of Religion in Europe: The Media and the Arts*, edited by *Norman Doe* (*Le portrait de religion en Europe: les médias et les arts*). Uitgeverij: Peeters, 2004.

Articles in Journals

Alaranta, Johannes. 'Rippisalaisuus' ('Seal of Confession'). *Edilex:* 12.10.2010. (www.edilex.fi/artikkelit/7328).

Dahlberg, Maija. 'Perustuslain reunaehdot lainvalmistelulle – ajankohtaisena esimerkkinä sosiaali- ja terveysuudistusta koskenut lakihanke' ('Basic Limits for Draft Legislation – A Recent Example of a Bill on Social and Health Reform'). *Oikeus* 3 (2015): 321–337.

Denman, Daniel. 'The Charter of Fundamental Rights'. *European Human Rights Review* (2010): 349–359.

Di Federico, Giancomo. 'Fundamental Rights in the EU: Legal Pluralism and Multi-Level Protection After the Lisbon Treaty'. In *The EU Charter of Fundamental Rights from Declaration to Binding Instrument*, edited by Di Federico. Dordrecht: Springer 2011: 15–54.

Halila, Leena. 'Euroopan ihmisoikeustuomioistuin ja kansallisen hallintoprosessin kehittäminen' ('European Court of Human Rights and Development of the National Administrative Process'). *Lakimies* 7–8 (2003): 1300–1305.

Selected Bibliography

Hannonen J. and Hyttinen T. 'Kiihottaminen kansanryhmää vastaan alioikeuskäytännössä' ('Incitement against a population group in the case law of the lower courts'), *Defensor Legis* (2023) 2, 307–330. https://www.edilex.fi/defensor_legis/1001130006.pdf

Hautamäki, Veli Pekka. 'Perusoikeudet ja lainvalmistelu' ('Fundamental Rights and Preparation of the Law'). *Lakimies* 2 (2014): 256–266.

Hautamäki, Veli Pekka. 'Perusoikeuden ydinalue argumenttina' ('The Core of Fundamental Rights as an Argument'). *Lakimies* 1 (2011): 82–98.

Hautamäki, Veli Pekka. 'Ydinalueen koskemattomuusvaatimus perusoikeuksien yleisenä rajoitusedellytyksenä' ('The Requirement of Integrity of the Core Area as a General Condition for the Restriction of Fundamental Rights'). *Edilex* 11.2.2016 (www.edilex.fi).

Heinilä, Aleksi. 'Kirkollisten rakennusten suojelu ja rakennussuojelua koskevien lakien keskinäiset suhteet' ('Protection of church buildings and the interrelationship of laws concerning the protection of buildings'). *Oikeustiede–Jurisprudentia-vuosikirja* (Law–Jurisprudence yearbook) Vol. 54, no LIV (2021), 65–139. Https://journal.fi/oikeustiede-jurisprudentia/issue/view/10602.

Helenius, Dan. 'Oikeushenkilön rangaistusvastuu Suomen ulkopuolella tehdyistä rikoksista' ('Liability of Legal Persons for Crimes Committed Outside Finland'). *Defensor Legis* 4 (2015): 772–790.

Helin, Markku. 'Perusoikeuksilla argumentoinnista' ('Argue with the Fundamental Rights'). *Edilex* 14.11.2012 (www.edilex.fi).

Hirvelä, Päivi. 'Ihmisoikeusvalitusten tutkiminen Euroopan ihmioikeustuomioistuimessa' ('Investigation of Human Rights Complaints in the European Court of Human Rights'). *Defensor Legis* 4 (2011): 393–411.

Jacqué, Jean Paul. 'The Accession of the European Union to the European Convention on Human Rights and Fundamental Freedoms'. *Common Market Law Review* 48 (2011): 995–1023.

Jyränki, Juulia. 'Seksuaalinen syrjimättömyys ja Euroopan unionin oikeus – näkökulmia seksuaalisten oikeuksien markkinataloudellistumiseen' ('Sexual Non-discrimination and EU Law – Perspectives on the Market Economy for Sexual Rights'). *Oikeus* 2 (2009): 99–118.

Kanninen, Heikki. 'Euroopan unionin virkamiestuomioistuin – EU:n kolmas tuomioistuin' ('European Union Civil Service Tribunal – Third EU Court'). *Defensor Legis* 6 (2005): 1325–1332.

Keinänen, Anssi & Matti Wiberg. 'Perustuslakivaliokunta lausuntovaliokuntana ja asiantuntijoiden kuulijana' ('The Constitutional Law Committee as an Opinion and Expert Hearing Committee'). *Oikeus* 1 (2012): 86–106.

Keinänen, Anssi, Maija Pitkänen & Outi Saarinen. 'Kokonaisvaltaista perustuslainmukaisuuden valvontaa' ('Comprehensive Constitutional Review'). *Oikeus* 1 (2013): 28–48.

Keinänen, Anssi, Outi Saarinen & Miika Vuorela. 'Toteutuvatko lainvalmistelun ihanteet käytännössä?' ('Do the Ideals of Law-Making Come True in Practice?'). *Lakimies* 2 (2015): 170–195.

Klatt, Matthias. 'Positive Obligations under the European Convention on Human Rights'. *Zeitschrift für ausländisches öffentliches Recht und Völkerrecht* 71 (2011): 691–718.

Korpi, Antti. 'Räsäsen vapauttava tuomio lopputulokseltaan EIT:n linjan mukainen. – Uskonnollisen puheen erityisasema Suomessa vielä tunnistamatta' ('Räsänen's acquittal is ultimately in line with the ECHR's stance. – The special status of religious speech in Finland still unrecognized'). *Defensor Legis* (2022) 4, 1117–1125. For more detail, see https://www.edilex.fi/defensor_legis/100085001 4.pdf.

Kotiranta, Matti. 'Das Verhältnis von Staat und Kirche in Finnland'. *Staatkirchenrechtliche Abhandlungen* Band 56/II (2020): 269–289.

Kotiranta, Matti. 'Kirche, Staat und Religionsfreiheit in Finnland'. *Zeitschrift für evangelisches Kirchenrecht* 45 (2000): 233–256.

Knuutila, Jyrki. 'Kirkkolainsäädäntö ja kirkon virka Suomessa kanonisesta oikeudesta vuoden 1993 kirkkolakiin ja -järjestykseen' ('Church Legislation and Church Appointments in Finland from Canonical Law to Church Law and Order 1993'). *Edilex* 15.9.2010 (www.edilex.fi/ artikkelit/7258).

Krommendijk, Jasper. 'Principled Silence or Mere Silence on Principles? The Role of the EU Charter's Principles in the Case Law of the Court of Justice'. *European Constitutional Law Review* 11(2) (2015): 321–356.

Krüger, Hans Christian & Jörg Polakiewicz. 'Proposal for Coherent Human Rights Protection in Europe. The European Convention on Human Rights and the EU Charter of Fundamental Rights'. *Human Rights Law Review* 22(1–4) (2011): 1–13.

Kumm, Mattias. 'Who Is Afraid of the Total Constitution? Constitutional Rights as Principles and the Constitutionalization of Private Law'. *German Law Journal* 4 (2006): 341–370.

Laakso, Seppo. 'Suhteellisuusperiaate yhteisöoikeudessa' ('Proportionality Principle in Community Law'). *Lakimies* 6–7 (1999): 1080–1091.

Laine, Esko M. 'Pappislupaus, pappisvala ja papin velvollisuudet reformaatiosta 1900-luvulle'. See, https://www.akiliitot.fi/liitteet/514/2/papin_rooli_ennen_ja_n yt_(nootitettu_uusin).pdf. Accessed 18 October 2019.

Leanerts, Koen. 'Exploring the Limits of the EU Charter of Fundamental Rights'. *European Constitutional Law Review* Vol. 8 (3) (2012): 375–403.

Lock, Tobias. 'The Future of the European Union's Accession to the European Convention on Human Rights after Opinion 2/2013: Is It Still Possible and Is It Still Desirable?'. *European Constitutional Law Review* 11(2) (2015): 239–273.

Lock, Tobias 'EU Accession to the ECHR: Implications for Judicial Review in Strasbourg'. *European Law Review* 6 (2010): 777–798.

Mantila, Anu. 'Saako myös tämän sanoa? Milloin puhe muuttuu rangaistavaksi vihapuheeksi?' ('Can one say this too? When does speech become punishable hate speech?'). *Oikeus* 2/2020, 154–171.

Neuvonen, Riku & Pauli Rautiainen. 'Perusoikeuskonkurrenssi Suomen perusoikeusjärjestelmässä' ('Concurrence of Fundamental Rights in the Finnish System of Fundamental Rights'). *Lakimies* 6 (2013): 1011–1031.

Neuvonen, Riku & Pauli Rautiainen. 'Perusoikeuksien tunnistaminen ja niiden sisällön määritteleminen Suomen perusoikeusjärjestelmässä' ('Identifying and Defining Fundamental Rights in the Finnish System of Fundamental Rights'). *Lakimies* 1 (2015): 28–53.

Nieminen, Kati 'Disobedient Subjects – Constructing the Subject, the State and Religion in the European Court of Human Rights'. *Social Identities* 21(4) (2015): 312–327.

Nieminen, Liisa. 'Tarvitaanko Suomessakin valtiosääntötuomioistuin?' ('Do We Need a Constitutional Court in Finland as Well?'). *Lakimies* 1 (2007): 3–24.

Nousiainen, Kevät. 'Tasa-arvon monet kasvot. Kansainvälisistä vaikutuksista Suomen tasa-arvo-oikeudessa' ('The Many Faces of Equality: International Impact on the Equality Law in Finland'). *Lakimies* 7–8 (2005): 1188–1209.

Nuotio, Kimmo. 'Holocaust Denial as Memory Criminal Law Seen Through the Nordic Lenses'. *Bergen Journal of Criminal Law and Criminal Justice*, vol. 11, no. 1 (2023): 1–29. https://doi.org/10.15845/bjclcj.v11i1.4038.

Ojanen, Tuomas. 'Constitutional Unamendability in the Nordic Countries'. *European Journal of Law Reform* (2019/3).

Ojanen, Tuomas. 'Valtiosääntöoikeus kansainvälistymisen kohteena ja välittäjänä' ('Constitutional Law as an Object of Internationalization and Mediator'). *Lakimies* 7–8 (2014): 937–952.

Ojanen, Tuomas: 'Perusoikeuspluralismi kotimaisessa tuomioistuimessa' ('Fundamental Rights Pluralism in the Domestic Court'). *Defensor Legis* 4 (2011): 442–455.

Ojanen, Tuomas. 'Perus- ja ihmisoikeudet terrorismin vastatoimissa Euroopan unionissa' ('Fundamental and Human Rights in the Fight Against Terrorism in Europe'). *Lakimies* 7–8 (2007): 1053–1074.

Ojanen, Tuomas. 'Euroopan unioni ja kotimainen perusoikeusjärjestelmä' ('The European Union and the Domestic System of Fundamental Rights'). *Lakimies* (2003): 7–8.

Ollila Riitta. 'Päivi Räsäsen syytteet hylättiin – tuomion keskeiset tulkintakysymykset' ('The Dismissal of Charges Against Päivi Räsänen – Key Interpretation Questions in the Verdict'). *Edilex* 20.4.2022 (www.edilex.fi/uutiset/75645). https://www.sananjauskonnonvapaus.fi/ajankohtaista/ott-riitta-ollila-pivi-rssen-syytteet-hylttiin-tuomion-keskeiset-tulkintakysymykset.

Pellonpää, Matti. 'Euroopan ihmisoikeustuomioistuin ja Euroopan unioni' ('European Court of Human Rights and the European Union'). *Lakimies* 7–8 (2005): 1229–1250.

Pirjatanniemi, Elina. 'Haastavatko ihmisoikeudet Suomen kriminaalipolitiikan?' ('Do Human Rights Challenge Finland's Criminal Policy?'). *Oikeus* 2011 (2): 154–174.

Pitkänen, Maija. 'Euroopan ihmisoikeussopimuksen valtion positiiviset toimintavelvoitteet ja suhteellisuus- periaatteen huomioiminen' ('Positive Operational Obligations of the European Convention on Human Rights and Respect for the Principle of Proportionality'). *Lakimies* 1 (2013): 55–73.

Saraviita, Ilkka. 'Lisänäkökohtia perustuslakivaliokunnasta lausunnonantajana ja asiantuntijoiden kuulijana' ('Further Insights Concerning the Constitutional Law Committee as an Expert Committee and Hearings from Experts'). *Oikeus* 2 (2012): 299–304.

Sabel, Charles F. & Oliver Gersterberg. 'Constitutionalising an Overlapping Consensus: The ECJ and the Emergence of a Coordinate Constitutional Order'. *European Law Journal* 5 (2010): 511–550.

Seppo, Juha. 'Church and State in Finland 1997'. *European Journal for Church and State Research. Revue eurpéenne des relations Églises – État* 5 (1988): 121–130.

Seppänen, Arto. 'Kirkko-oikeus – juridiikkaa vai teologiaa? Kirkko-oikeuden paradigmaa etsimässä' ('Church Law – Law or Theology? Looking for a Paradigm for Church Law'). *Edilex* 6.9.2010 (www.edilex.fi/ artikkelit/7251).

Stenlund, Mari & Pamela Slotte. 'Forum Internum Revisited: Considering the Absolute Core of Freedom of Belief and Opinion in Terms of Negative Liberty, Authenticity, and Capability'. *Human Rights Review* 19 (4) (2018): 425–446.

Tala, Jyrki. 'Lainsäädännön laatu Euroopassa – vertailua, ongelmia, kritiikkiä' (The quality of legislation in Europe – comparison, problems, criticism). *Lakimies* 5 (2010): 791–815.

Tala, Jyrki. 'Lainsäädäntö – oikeustieteen tutkimuksen marginaalissa' ('Legislation – At the Margins of Legal Research'). *Edilex* 31.7.2010 (www.edilex.fi).

Viljanen, Jukka. 'Euroopan ihmisoikeustuomioistuin ja yleiset opit' ('European Court of Human Rights and General Doctrine'). *Lakimies* 3 (2004): 521–525.

Viljanen, Jukka. 'The Role of the European Court of Human Rights as a Developer of International Human Rights Law'. *Cuadernos Constitucionales de la Cátedra Fadrique Furió Ceriol* no 62/63 (2011): 249–265.

Viljanen, Veli-Pekka. 'Poikkeuslakien välttämisen periaate' ('The Principle of Avoiding Emergency Laws'). *Lakimies* 6–7 (1999): 961–972.

Walkila, Sonya. 'Euroopan unionin perusoikeuskirja EU:n tuomioistuimen oikeuskäytännössä' (Charter of Fundamental Rights of the European Union in the case law of the Court of Justice). *Defensor Legis* 6 (2011): 813–819.

Weiß, Wolfgang. 'Human Rights in the EU: Rethinking the Role of the European Convention of Human Rights after Lisbon'. *European Constitutional Law Review* 7 (2011): 64–95.

Collections of Laws and Court Decisions

All laws, regulations and amendments thereto will be published in the Finnish Compendium of Legislation (Suomen säädöskokoelma, SopS) once they have been adopted. However, they are only published there as they are adjusted, not in subsequent editions.

It is difficult to estimate the exact number of laws in force in Finland. Not all of the laws in force have been aggregated in any printed work, or so far in any electronic legal information service, although this may be incorrectly claimed, for example, in advertising.

However, Talentum Media Oy's three-part Finnish Law or Edita Publishing's two-part Law Book, published annually, contains all the major laws and regulations, organized by legal field. Most of them are also in Finlex's state-of-the-art regulatory database, but there are not all the laws in force in Finland either, but the database contains selectively important acts of importance to the citizen, including subordinate acts.

Constitutions:

The Constitution of Finland (2000), https://www.finlex.fi/en/laki/kaannokset/1999/en19990731.pdf.
The four previous constitutions:
The Finnish Form of Government (AsK94/1919).
The Parliamentary Order (1928).
The Act on National Law (273/1922).
The Ministerial Responsibility Act (on the right of the Parliament to examine members of the Government and the Chancellor of Justice and the Parliamentary Ombudsman. Law on Legitimacy of Crews, 2(74/1922)).

Laws on Religious Freedom:

The Religious Freedom Act (267/1922).
The Religious Freedom Act (453/2003).

Church Laws:

Kircko-Laki Ja Ordningi 1686 (*Church Law and Order 1686*). Näköispainos ja uudelleen ladottu laitos. (Facsimile and re-loaded edition), edited by Lahja-Irene Hellemaa, Anja Jussila, Martti Parvio. Suomalaisen kirjallisuuden seuran toimituksia (The Finnish Literature Society's Publications) 444. Helsinki, SKS, 1986.
Church Act (19/2019).
Church Act (1993/1054).
The Government proposal to Parliament on the Church Act (HE 19/2019 vp).
Church Act (652/2023) (https://www.finlex.fi/fi/laki/ajantasa/2023/20230652) and other related laws:
(653/2023) (https://www.finlex.fi/fi/laki/alkup/2023/20230653).
(654/2023) (https://www.finlex.fi/fi/laki/alkup/2023/20230654).
(655/2023) (https://www.finlex.fi/fi/laki/alkup/2023/20230655).
(656/2023) (https://www.finlex.fi/fi/laki/alkup/2023/20230656).
Orthodox Church Law (985/2006).

School Laws:

Act on Early Childhood Education and Care (540/2018).
The Basic Education Act (629/1998).
Act on General Upper Secondary School Education (629/1998).
The Universities Act (558/2009). Amendments up to 644/2016 included. https://www.finlex.fi/en/laki/kaannokset/2009/en20090558_20160644.pdf.

VI. Law Periodicals and Series

Durham, W. Cole, Malcolm Evans, Silvio Ferrari, Julian Rivers & Gerhard Robbers (eds). *Oxford Journal of Law and Religion.* Oxford: Oxford University Press, since 2012.

Ferrari, Silvio, et al. (eds). *Law and Religion Studies*. Leuven: Peeters, since 2003.
Ferrari, Silvio, et al. (eds). *European Consortium for Church-State Research*. Milan: Giuffrè Editore, since 1992.
Statistical Yearbook of Finland 2012.
Statistics Finland. Available at http://www.stat.fi/tup/kirjasto_tieto/tilastolliset_vuosikirjat_en.html.
Torfs, Rik (ed.). *European Journal for Church and State Research*. Leuven: Peeters, since 1994.
Zeitschrift für evangelisches Kirchenrecht.

VII. Encyclopaedia

Heriber Hallermann, Thomas Meckel, Michael Droege and Heirich de Wall (eds.). *Lexikon für Kirchen und Religionsrecht* (in 4 volumes). Paderborn: Ferdinand Schöning, 2019. Also available in the online edition (LKRO), brill.com/lkro.
Francis Messner (ed.), *Dictionaire Droit des Religions*. Paris: CNRS editions, 2010.
Gerhard Robbers & W. Cole Durham, Jr. *Encyclopedia of Law and Religion*. Also available in Brill's Online edition 2016, https://brill.com/view/db/elro.

Selected Bibliography

Table of Statutes

Table of Statutes on the preparatory works of Finnish Law for the years 1917–2010 can be found in *Pekka Hallberg (ed.), Heikki Karapuu, Tuomas Ojanen, Martin Scheinin, Kaarlo Tuori, Veli-Pekka Viljanen, Perusoikeudet* (Fundamental rights) (2nd, revised edn. WSOYpro, 2011), pp. 1001–1024.

The Statutes are the following:

Government Bills (HE)
Reports of the Committee on the Constitution (PeVM)
Opinions of the Committee on the Constitution (PeVL)
Opinions of the Administration Committee (HaVL)
Legal Initiatives (LA)
Opinions of the Legal Affairs Committee (LaVL)
Reports of the Legal Affairs Committee (LaVM)
Reports of the Education and Culture Committee (SiVM)
Reports of the Constitutional Law Committee (KM)

The decisions of the Finnish courts are as follows:

Supreme Administrative Court (KHO), pp. 1025–1033
Supreme Court (KKO), 1033–1035
Court of Appeal (HO), 1035
Administrative Court of First Instance (HAO), 1036
Provincial Office of Justice (LO), 1036
Decisions of the Labour Court, 1036
Insurance Law Solutions, 1036

Other decisions:

Decisions of the Chancellor of Justice (OKa), 1047
Decisions of the Deputy Chancellor (AOK), 1047
Decisions of the Parliamentary Ombudsman (EOA), 1047

International court decisions include:

Decisions the European Court of Human Rights (EIT), 1036–1044
Decisions of the European Commission for Human Rights, 1044
Decisions of the European Court of Justice (the Court of Justice), 1044–1045
Decisions of the United Nations Commission on Human Rights, 1045–1046
Decisions of the UN Committee against Torture, 1047

Table of Cases

Cases (European Court of Human Rights, Articles 6, 8, 9 and 14)

X v. Denmark (1976) (Article 9 of the ECHR)
Karlsson v. Sweden (1988) (Article 9 of the ECHR)
Kokkinakis v. Greece (1993) (Article 9 of the ECHR)
Otto-Preminger-Institut v. Austria (1994) (Article 9 of the ECHR)
Kalac v. Turkey (1997) (Article 9 of the ECHR)
Bessarabian Metropolitan Church et al. v. Moldavia (2001) (Article 9 of the ECHR)
Lautsi v. Italy (2011) (Article 9 of the ECHR)
Helle v. Finland, App. No. 20772/92 (19 December 1997) (Article 6 of the ECHR)
Hokkanen v. Finland, App. No. 19823/92 (23 September 1994) (Article 8 of the ECHR)
Johansson v. Finland, App. No. 10163/02 (6 September 1997) (Article 8 of the ECHR)
Kerojärvi v. Finland, App. No. 17506/90 (19 July 1995) (Article 6 of the ECHR)
Konttinen v. Finland, App. No. 24949/94 (3 December 1996) (Article 9 of the ECHR)
Launikari v. Finland, App. No. 34120/96 (5 October 2000) (Article 6 of the ECHR)
Stjerna v. Finland, App. No. 18131/91 (25 November 1994) (Articles 8–10 and 14 of the ECHR)
Z v. Finland, 1994, App. No. 22009/93 (25 February 1997) (Article 8 of the ECHR)

Cases Affecting Freedom of Speech and Religion (Article 10 of the ECHR [on freedom of speech], and Article 11 of the ECHR [on freedom of religion])

Articles 10 & 11:

ECtHR ruling on the Case of *Jehovah's Witnesses v. Finland* (Application no. 31172/19) 9 May 2023: The Jehovah's Witnesses' religious activities in Finland and their compatibility with the data protection regulations
ECtHR's ruling in *Handyside v. United Kingdom* (5493/72, judgment on 7 December 1976)
ECtHR's ruling in *Nasirov and Others v. Azerbaijan* (58717/10, judgment on 20 February 2020)
ECtHR's ruling in *Religious Community of Jehovah's Witnesses v. Azerbaijan* (58717/10, judgment on 20 February 2020)

Table of Cases

ECtHR's ruling in *Perinçek v. Switzerland* (27510/08, judgment on 15 October 2015)
ECtHR's ruling in *Féret v. Belgia* (15615/07, judgment delivered on 16 July 2009)
ECtHR's ruling in *Manoussakis and Others v. Greece* (18748/91, judgment on 26 September 1996)

Article 10:

ECtHR's ruling in *Selistö v. Finland*, App. No. 56767/00 (16 November 2004) (Article 10 of the ECHR)
ECtHR's ruling in *Karhuvaara and Iltalehti v. Finland*, App. No. 53678/00 (16 November 2004) (Article 10 of the ECHR)
ECtHR's ruling in *Nikula v. Finland*, App. No. 31611/96 (21 March 2002) (Article 10 of the ECHR)

Other Cases

Supreme Court decision of 19 January 2001 (Appeal Court decision in its ruling no. 2792 of 13.10.1989 (KKO 1989:122))
Supreme Court decision of 19 January 2001 (no. 88/deposit no. S 99/1215)
Supreme Court decision of 13 March 2001 (deposit no. 469)
Supreme Court decision of 23 September 2001 (deposit no. 2260)
Supreme Court decision of 23 September 2002 (T 2260)
Turku Administrative Court decision of 13 June 2007 (00362/07/2302)
The Supreme Court decision in which the Central Council of Jewish Communities requested in August 2012 that the Oulu police should investigate the anti-Semitic content of a magazine called 'Magneettimedia'. The case was transferred to the national prosecutor. The Prosecutor General brought charges and the case was heard in the Ylivieska-Raahe District Court in October 2013. The District Court sentenced the editor-in-chief of the free-distribution magazine 'Magneettimedia', Kärkkäinen, to a ninety-day fine for incitement against a group. The articles in the magazine questioned such things as the actual occurrence of the Holocaust and the mass murder of Jews, describing it as a 'mythical story' and 'Holocaust brainwashing'. The articles also associated Israel with ISIS forces, Syrian gas attacks, and drug trafficking. In addition, the retail company J. Kärkkäinen Oy, which published the magazine, was fined EUR 45,000. Kärkkäinen appealed the verdict. The prosecutor also appealed and demanded a harsher sentence of conditional imprisonment. The Rovaniemi Court of Appeal upheld the original judgment, and the Supreme Court did not grant leave to appeal. Compare to two judgments by the Court of Appeal: one dated 25 May 2007 (R 07/629) and the other 18 February 2009 (R 08/607), and the recent judgment of the Helsinki District Court (30 December 2022, 5 June 2023).
Supreme Court decision (KKO 2016: 24, Male circumcision)
Supreme Court decision (KKO 2016: 25, Male circumcision)

Decisions of Insurance Court

A Muslim wanted to use the veil at work and was not offered employment. Unemployment benefits could not be withheld. The vote was 4 to 1 (*see* Insurance Law 1713:96)

A non-Lutheran refused to clean a Lutheran church. According to Insurance Law, unemployment benefits could not be withheld. The vote was 4 to 1 (*see* Insurance Law 05142/96/955)
A Jehovah's Witness refused clerical work with the Finnish Armed Forces, and unemployment benefits could not be withheld. The vote was 4 to 1 (*see* Insurance Law 12569:95)
A 'can advocate' interpretation, according to which a person can refuse to work on a Saturday without losing unemployment benefits (*see* Attorney General 420/1/99)
A pacifist who had completed service as a conscientious objector refused to work as a warehouse worker in an Armed Forces Unit, and unemployment benefits were not withheld. The vote was 3 to 2 (*see* Insurance Law 4286:99)

Court of Appeal

Mr Esa Laiho, a fake doctor. Laiho was sentenced to five years' imprisonment by the Court of Appeal. Laiho's penalty at the Helsinki District Court was lengthened by half a year. He worked as a fake doctor between 2001 and 2011 in several hospitals and clinics.
The MP Jussi Halla-Aho (Finns Party) was fined for blogging statements insulting Islam and humiliating the people. The judgment was handed down at the Helsinki District Court 2012 on the grounds of violations of religious peace and agitation against the people.
The District Court and the Court of Appeal had dismissed the charges against Halla-Aho for incitement against the people and only condemned him for violating the peace. The Supreme Court (KKO) increased the fine imposed on Halla-aho in the lower courts from thirty day-fines to fifty day-fines and added that Halla-aho was also guilty of incitement against the people. In 2008 Halla-aho was also ordered to remove parts of his blog.
The MP Sebastian Tynkkynen was fined for insulting a group of people at the Oulu District Court on 3 October 2019.
Decision of the District Court of Helsinki (14.11.2023, R22/1094) to Acquit a Christian Democrat Politician and MP, Päivi Räsänen on 30 March 2022 of Charges of Incitement (Hate Speech) Against a Population Group.

Table of Cases

Index

The numbers here refer to paragraph numbers.

Index

www.ingramcontent.com/pod-product-compliance
Ingram Content Group UK Ltd.
Pitfield, Milton Keynes, MK11 3LW, UK
UKHW020132290926
15471UKWH00003B/427